Praise for *The Paris Commune*

'In my view, *this* is the fullest account of the Paris Commune, and other Communes. This is an extremely impressive study of true significance'

John Merriman, author *Massacre: The Life and Death of the Paris Commune of 1871*

'A remarkable book – one of the most important to be published in many years on the famous Paris Commune and the other, less famous revolutionary Communes that together constituted one of the most important global events of the second half of the nineteenth century'

David Bell, author of *Men on Horseback: The Power of Charisma in the Age of Revolution*

'A remarkable example of how modern European and global history can come into engagement. His aim is as much to show how by using the comparative and connective techniques of global history we can produce a more complex kind of engagement with local historical phenomena as it is simply to understand the commune. And it is for this reason that it will become a major work of reference for historians working on other questions. There is nothing like this in English'

Richard Drayton, author of *Commonwealth History in the Twenty-First Century*

'Deluermoz's exploration of the Commune – in its Parisian core and in its national, European, and global reverberations – expands our knowledge of a history we thought we knew. Based on meticulous and widespread archival research, above all in French national and provincial archives, but also in Great Britain, Spain, and the United States, the book is both empirically rich and theoretically alert. Original in conception, generous in spirit, written with care and passion, this is an important contribution to French and transnational history'

William Sewell Jr, *Journal of Modern History*

'Quentin Deluermoz's superb new book represents the most original contribution yet to rethink the place of the Commune in the global history of the nineteenth century. His study seeks to explain how this short-lived experiment of just seventy-two days fits into broader trends and processes, both in its origins – with strong roots in the transnational activism of 1848, the remaking of urban space, the socialist dream of workers' self-government – but also its reception'

Thomas Stammers, *Nineteenth-Century French Studies*

Quentin Deluermoz is professor of contemporary history at Paris Cité University. He is the author and editor of more than fifteen books, including (with P. Singaravelou) *A Past of Possibilities: A History of What Could Have Been*; *Le Crépuscule des révolutions, 1848–1871*; and *Histoires globales des revolutions* (with L. Bantigny, L. Jeanpierre, B. Gobille and E. Palieraki). He is a co-founder of the interdisciplinary and artistic review *Sensibilités: Histoire, critique et sciences sociales.*

The Paris Commune

A Global History

Quentin Deluermoz

Translated by David Broder

VERSO
London • New York

This English-language edition first published by Verso 2026
First published as *Commune(s), 1870–1871: Une traversée des mondes au XiXe siècle*

The manufacturer's authorized representative in the EU for product safety (GPSR) is LOGOS EUROPE, 9 rue Nicolas Poussin, 17000, La Rochelle, France
contact@logoseurope.eu

1 3 5 7 9 10 8 6 4 2

Verso
UK: 6 Meard Street, London W1F 0EG
US: 207 East 32nd Street, New York, NY 10016
versobooks.com

Verso is the imprint of New Left Books

ISBN-13: 978-1-83976-818-7
ISBN-13: 978-1-83976-820-0 (US EBK)
ISBN-13: 978-1-83976-819-4 (UK EBK)

British Library Cataloguing in Publication Data
A catalogue record for this book is available from the British Library

Library of Congress Cataloging-in-Publication Data
A catalog record for this book is available from the Library of Congress

Typeset in Minion by Hewer Text UK Ltd, Edinburgh
Printed and bound by CPI Group (UK) Ltd, Croydon, CR0 4YY

Contents

Preface vii

Introduction: Returning to the Commune-as-Event 1

Part I

A GLOBAL COMMUNE (JULY 1870–APRIL 1871) 23

1. In the Name of the 'Universal Republic' 25
2. Cracks in the French Imperial Nation-State 52
3. The Commune, a Global Media Event 83
4. Strange Species of Spaces: The 'Paris Republic' and the World 111

Conclusion to Part I: Paris, France, the World, Seen from a Revolution 132

Part II

THE LIVING COMMUNE (MARCH–MAY 1871) 135

5. From Algiers to Thiers: Insurrectionary Trajectories 139
6. The Paris Commune 'from Below' 171

7. A Revolution in Time and Space: Emancipation in Action 206
8. Neither Dawn nor Twilight: An Essay on the Temporalities of the Commune 239
Conclusion to Part II: The Creation of Worlds, on Both Sides of the Ramparts 269

Part III

THE COMMUNE TRANSFORMED (1871–1880) 271

9. Putting an End to the Civil War: France 275
10. The Commune, the New Global Spectre of Revolution 304
11. A Paradox? The Strengthening of the Liberal State 330
12. 'The Body May Have Fallen, but the Idea Still Stands' 356
Conclusion to Part III: The Spectral and the Embodied 385

Conclusion: Returning to the Commune-as-Event, II 389

Afterword: The Commune, Forever Renewed 403
Index of Names 425
Index of Places 431

Preface

People are once again talking about the Paris Commune. At the end of the twentieth century – with the fall of the Soviet bloc, the demise of Communist parties, and the ebbing of the anti-authoritarian spirit of the 1970s – the Commune's relevance seemed to have faded. If it was not exactly forgotten, it had been relegated to the distant past. In France, its history had found a place in the national republican narrative, as illustrated by the Communard Louise Michel's journey through collective memory. By the end of the 1980s, this anarchist and feminist – a militant who fought against the state and capitalism and was later posthumously embraced by the West's Communist parties – had become a symbol of women's role in history and of youth rebellion against injustice. In France today, 498 streets and 190 schools bear her name.[1] The rehabilitation of the Communards by the National Assembly in November 2016 signalled that the Commune's memory had been both pacified and institutionalised.

But the 150th anniversary of the Commune in 2021 saw a surprisingly heated dispute over its political legacy.[2] Some argued publicly that France should have been commemorating the bicentenary of Napoleon's

1 Sidonie Verhaeghe, *Vive Louise Michel! Célébrité et postérité d'une figure anarchiste* (Vulaines-sur-Seine: Éditions du Croquant, 2021).

2 The first French edition of this book appeared in 2020, i.e. before the 150th anniversary of the Paris Commune. This translation updates the titles of some of the works cited as 'forthcoming', and includes additional references.

death rather than celebrating the Commune. Yet the Parisian event had never stopped being remembered through the names of civic associations, projects and artistic institutions. In recent years, the Commune has reappeared in social movements and public protests. In 2016, France's 'Nuit debout' movement, which had occupied the Place de la République, renamed the square the 'Place de la Commune-de-Paris'. In 2018, during student protests, 'free communes' sprang up on various university campuses. In May 2019, towards the end of the 'Gilets Jaunes' protests – one of the largest social movements in recent French history – a thousand demonstrators marched to Montmartre to pay tribute to the Paris Commune.[3]

Nor is it only in France that the Commune has come back to life. The 'squares movements' of the 2010s – from Spain's *indignados* to the Occupy movement in the United States – invoked the memory of the Commune. Occupy Oakland even styled itself the 'Oakland Commune', and one of its spokespersons adopted the name '*Louise Michel*'.[4] In Oaxaca, Mexico, the repression of a teachers' strike in June 2006 rekindled a multiform memory of soviets, popular councils and the Paris Commune.[5] Rojava, the Kurdish military and political experiment in north-eastern Syria, is sometimes referred to as the 'Rojava Commune', reflecting its democratic and egalitarian ambitions. And a group supporting the revolution in this region has likewise taken the name 'Internationalist Commune'.[6]

In today's globalised world, as the dominant forms of political and economic governance grow ever more standardised – and the most conservative forms of nationalism re-emerge – references to the Commune seem to express a growing desire for a 'horizontal' and 'leaderless' democracy. Many contemporary movements for justice and equality are drawn to this kind of politics.[7] The magic word 'Commune' is appearing frequently in graffiti, banners and slogans. Free 'communes'

---

3 Robert Paris, 'Les Gilets jaunes et la Commune de Paris', *Matiè et Revolution*, 1 June 2019, at matierevolution.fr.

4 'After the Crest, Part II: The Rise and Fall of Oakland Commune', *CrimethInc*, 10 September 2013, at fr.crimethinc.com.

5 Fabrizio Mejía Madrid, 'La Commune de Oaxaca', *Cités* 42: 2 (2010), pp. 53–9.

6 Stephen Bouquin et al., *La commune du Rojava: l'alternative kurde à l'État-nation* (Paris: Syllepse, 2017).

7 Yves Cohen and Marco Santana, 'Du Brésil au monde et retour: mouvements sociaux localisés et en résonance', *Brésil(s)* 7 (2015), pp. 103–22.

are springing up in certain towns and villages, albeit with a looser connection to the historical event itself.

Of course, not every reference to a Commune has a clear connection to the Parisian experience of 1871. For some – whether activists or history buffs – France's third revolution of the nineteenth century remains a key point of reference, along with once-famous personalities such as the novelist and journalist Jules Vallès and the painter Gustave Courbet. But many, in France and elsewhere, are unfamiliar with this past. For them, the meaning of the Commune can shade into the similar terms that the French use for local councils, the idea of the 'commons', or even 'community' more generally. Sometimes it is just a memory, which can carry more or less active or floating signifiers. But something of the aura of the Paris Republic of 1871 still remains in the air.

Unquestionably, the Paris Commune remains alive in the twenty-first century. It has taken on meanings of its own, on a global scale, extending beyond the ideological reinterpretations that accumulated around it during the twentieth century. Indeed, its meanings are still evolving. While the Commune remains synonymous with social struggle and the desire for equality, for instance, it is today more closely associated with the project of reappropriating democracy 'from below' than with the workers' movements with which it was long identified. One cannot help but be struck by how multi-layered the Commune's meanings are. This multiplicity reflects our contemporary moment – though not that alone. What about the events of 1871 that explains the Commune's enduring presence, and its continual metamorphoses? And what might have escaped historians' attention? This book seeks to answer these questions.

Introduction: Returning to the Commune-as-Event

Expressing a thing as it is.

Cited in Georges Didi-Huberman (2002),
citing Ludwig Binswanger (1955),
citing Gustave Flaubert (1915)

It may seem like an odd decision to publish a new study of the Paris Commune, or even of the Communes in provincial France. If few people have more than a hazy understanding of the Commune's history, it is nonetheless a terrain abundantly ploughed, scrutinised and interpreted by specialists. In 2006, Robert Le Quillec compiled a bibliography on the subject. It runs to nearly 600 pages, featuring some 5,000 entries, and includes novels, memoirs, exhibition catalogues, philosophical reflections, and of course historical studies conducted in France, the United States, the UK, Spain, Germany, and even China.[1] Reading all of them would be a life's work. At the beginning of the twenty-first century, the Commune is hardly unknown. On the contrary, there is an abundance of information and interpretations.

So, what was the Commune all about? The basic facts are not in dispute, but they bear repeating. The Commune was the third revolution in nineteenth-century France, following the revolutions of 1830

1 Robert Le Quillec, *Bibliographie critique de la Commune de Paris* (Paris: La Boutique de l'histoire, 2006).

and 1848. Unlike these earlier events, the Commune came at the end of a slow slide into revolution. This had begun with the war between the Second French Empire and Prussia in July 1870, and continued with the French military defeats, the fall of the Empire, and the establishment of a new Republic on 4 September 1870. The political transition was particularly vigorous in Paris: the capital was then an industrial centre with a high concentration of workers, as well as being one of France's most republican cities. It would be wrong to overlook the social antagonisms that existed here, and the strength of the regime's own base of support. But it is also true that, in the late 1860s, Paris had been at the centre of a powerful upswing in public meetings, reviving talk of revolution. In September 1870, when a Government of National Defence was created and Parisians were mobilised in the National Guard, some neighbourhoods experimented with forms of self-administration and attempted – without success – to seize power. The rest of the population took a more wait-and-see approach. The capital suffered a siege lasting four months, across a terrible winter. The government's capitulation in January 1871, Prussia's exorbitant demands (such as France relinquishing control of Alsace-Lorraine) and the elections in February 1871, which saw the monarchists win a majority in the National Assembly, all served to exasperate Parisians. Both the parliament and the government, led by the conservative Adolphe Thiers, were distrustful of the capital, and rolled out an array of measures its inhabitants saw as hostile. On 10 March, the National Assembly, which had earlier retreated to Bordeaux, decided to relocate to Versailles, thereby knocking Paris from its perch as the national capital. This was an almighty humiliation for the city.

It was in this already tense context that events took a turn towards revolution. Thiers, seeking to avoid any mishaps during negotiations over the peace treaty, had decided to take back control of the Paris National Guard's cannons. In the early morning of 18 March, in Montmartre, Parisians put up their first resistance to the troops sent by Versailles. The confrontation became an insurrection – a scenario that was then repeated in Belleville and at the Bastille. There now began a reconquest of the city, moving from the periphery towards the centre. This was a popular and spontaneous movement; only later did revolutionary organisations make their intervention. On the evening of 18 March, the Central Committee of the National Guard occupied the

Hôtel de Ville. The city was 'free'. But it would take another week – later known as the 'week of uncertainty' – and fresh elections, before the Commune was officially proclaimed, on 28 March.

In this same moment, other Communes emerged elsewhere in France: in Lyon, Marseille, Toulouse and Le Creusot. But the Paris Commune was the most consequential. The term 'Commune' refers here both to the period of its existence and to the group of seventy-nine elected representatives who sat in the Hôtel de Ville, soon proclaiming the 'victorious revolution'. Among them were the movement's most famous figures, including François Jourde, Jules Vallès, Eugène Varlin, Raoul Rigault, and so on. Today much is known about the make-up of this group: thirty-three of them were skilled workers (41 per cent of the total) – a first in the history of France's revolutions. They had varied political orientations, and there were constant debates between them: they included Blanquists, members of the International Workingmen's Association (IWMA – later known as the First International), Proudhonians, Jacobins, radical republicans and more. Yet these were not fixed positions, and the common point of reference – even if only as a baseline – was the idea of a 'democratic and social Republic' that had been so forcefully articulated back in 1848. During its fifty-seven meetings, the Commune took a series of measures: the remission of rents due from October to April and the abolition of conscription (29 March); the separation of church and state (2 April); secular, free and compulsory school education (also on 2 April); the abolition of night work for bakers (20 April); and the prohibition of deductions from wages in workshops and administrations (28 April). These decisions alone made the Commune a remarkable episode.

Elsewhere in the city, the memory of the French Revolution resurfaced: in the streets, people would call each other *citoyen* or *citoyenne* ('citizen'). The National Guard, whose officers were elected and subject to recall, played both a politicising and an organising role. In some workshops and municipalities, forms of self-organisation developed around the vigilance committees. Conditions differed quite significantly across the various neighbourhoods. There were many tensions among the insurgents, but also hostility towards those who were designated 'enemies' of the people: the Versaillais (the men of Versailles), the Prussians, gendarmes, policemen, the most propertied, and priests. But time was short: starting in April, the Versailles troops began to press forward, and the Commune's military troubles started to mount. Its concrete achievements also became more limited: while trade-union 'chambers' developed, only one foundry workshop, in the 15th arrondissement, was placed under collective management. The secularisation of schools similarly remained only partly complete.

In early May, in the face of growing difficulties, a split emerged at the Hôtel de Ville, pitting what were then called the 'majority', who favoured the creation of a 'committee of public safety', against a 'minority', who viewed this as a turn towards authoritarianism. The end of May brought the reconquest of the capital by government forces. This moment was marked, on the Communard side, by the torching of the city's main buildings and the murder of hostages, and, on the Versaillais side, by a vast massacre of the insurgents, which would later be dubbed 'La Semaine sanglante' – the 'Bloody Week.' The whole adventure had lasted a mere seventy-two days.

Observers soon noted that a most important event had just taken place. But most – including some of the Commune's own defenders – also pointed to the weakness of its achievements, its muddled character, and even the verbosity of its public voice. What was most striking was its apocalyptic end, and the thousands of deaths that had resulted. In short, the Commune posed tricky interpretive problems almost from the moment it ended.

Since its demise, the Commune has indeed been the subject of continual studies and interpretations – both of the events themselves and of what they signified. It is now worth recalling the main lines of interpretation, for they have helped to make it, in addition to being a major historical episode, a genuine scholarly, intellectual, and political monument of the nineteenth, twentieth and twenty-first centuries.

Histories of the Commune

The first major interpretive lens for understanding the Commune was a Marxist one. The Commune early on became a focus of left-wing, republican and socialist historical writing.[2] Then, between the world wars, it became a central subject of history written by Marxists, or otherwise

2 Jacques Rougerie, 'La Commune et la gauche', in Jean-Jacques Becker and Gilles Candar, eds, *Histoire des gauches en France, vol. 1: L'Héritage du XIXe siècle* (Paris: La Découverte, 2004), pp. 95–112.

inspired by Marxist lines of questioning – especially in the fields of economic and social history. The main academic effort dates from the period between 1950 and 1980. The question for scholars in these decades was how to place the Paris Commune within the history of the workers' movement, such as it was then conceived: the Commune seemed to represent the twilight of the revolutions of the nineteenth century, in the sequence begun by the French Revolution itself – but also, given its majority-working-class government, the dawn of the modern workers' movement. This movement was supposed to be more structured than the previous ones in terms of its organisation and ideology, and to have been fully realised in 1917. These historical works then looked for a possible revolutionary vanguard (among the members of the International Workingmen's Association), investigated the role of ideologies (which they generally found somewhat muddled), and so on.[3]

Another, strongly internationalised series of works in this tradition studied the echoes of the Commune in different lands – such as Germany, the UK, Hungary, and the countries of Latin America – in order to pin down its role in the passage from a 'romantic' age of revolt to what were identified as the more properly 'modern' struggles of the twentieth century.[4] This work was obviously marked by its Cold War

3 The chronology is an old one: Charles Talès, *La Commune de 1871* (Paris, Librairie du travail, 1924). But for these decades, see Georges Bourgin, *La Commune* (Paris: PUF, 1953); Charles Rihs, *La Commune de Paris, ses structures et ses doctrines* (Genève: Droz, 1955); Jean Bruhat, Jean Dautry and Emile Tersen, *La Commune de Paris* (Paris: Éditions sociales, 1960).

4 This list is by no means exhaustive: Eberhard Hackethal, 'Der historische Platz der Pariser Kommune im praktischen Wirken und theoretischen Denken der zeitgenossichen deutschen Arbeiterbewegung (1871–1878)', *Jahrbuch für Geschichte (DDR)* 2 (1967), pp. 75–122; Frank Strobl, 'Die Pariser Kommune und die osterreichische Arbeiterbewegung', *Weg und Ziel* 3 (March 1956); Samuel Bernstein, 'The Impact of the Paris Commune in the United States', *Massachusetts Review* 12: 3 (1971), pp. 435–46. There was also the important work of Marc Vuilleumier in Switzerland and Jan Dhondt and Daisy Devreese in Belgium. Such research often accompanied work on the First International: *La Première Internationale. L'institution, l'implantation, le rayonnement*, proceedings of the colloquium (Paris, 16–18 November 1964) (Paris, Éditions du CNRS, 1968); Julian P. W. Archer, *The First International in France (1864–1872): Its Origins, Theories and Impact* (Lanham, MD: University Press of America, 1997). Of course, this analytical work must also take into account Lenin's analysis of 'dual power', published in April 1917. The bibliography of works on the Commune compiled by Jacques Rougerie and Georges Haupt in *Mouvement social* 37 (1961), pp. 70–92, contains 430 references for the period 1940–61, many of them in Russian, Romanian, Polish or German.

context, and shaped by a specific intellectual and political orientation, though it was far from merely a reflection of it.[5] Historical objects that attract such engagement – such as the French Revolution, the First World War or Nazism – are generally taken up within what some historians and social scientists call 'configurations' or 'waves' of historiography: shared ways of posing problems and orienting inquiry.[6] Yet these configurations never unfold without debate, or without a plurality of positions. And then, new knowledge is established and interpretations are refined.

In 1971, on the centenary of the Commune, an imposing volume produced by the *International Review of Social History*, called *Jalons pour une histoire de la Commune de Paris* ('Milestones for a History of the Paris Commune') offered a kind of progress report on the existing historiography.[7] The introduction, by Jacques Rougerie, observed how far knowledge of the Commune had come over the preceding decades, while also pointing to new directions just then being developed. These included new work, some of it in the volume itself, on the Commune's reception in Latin America, the role of the First International, and discoveries about the Communes of provincial France. Like the bicentenary of the French Revolution, the centenary of the Commune shifted the way in which questions were framed, and increased our understanding of the event.

These waves in readings of history and the social sciences certainly do not follow any regular pattern. Still, in the 1960s and 1970s other readings of the Commune were advanced. They were more likely to come from the fields of sociology, philosophy and radical political

---

5 The Commune has never ceased to be the subject of debate. As early as the 1930s in *The Paris Commune* (New York: Macmillan, 1930), the liberal historian Edward Mason sought to show that it did not correspond to the Marxists' simplified vision.

6 Antoine Prost and Jay Winter, *Penser la grande guerre* (Paris: Seuil, 2004), pp. 15–50; Elizabeth Clemens, 'Afterword: Logics of History? Agency, Multiplicity, and Incoherence in the Explanation of Change', in Julia Adams, Elizabeth Clemens and Ann Shola Orloff, eds, *Remaking Modernity: Politics, History, and Sociology* (Durham, NC: Duke University Press, 2005), pp. 493–515.

7 Jacques Rougerie, Tristan Haan, Georges Haupt and Miklos Molnar, eds, 'Jalons pour une Histoire de la Commune de Paris', *International Review of Social History* XVII (1972), parts 1–2 (subsequently published by PUF in 1973, with the addition of '1871' in the title; the texts cited below refer to this work). See also 'Actes du colloque universitaire pour la commémoration du centenaire de la commune de 1871 (Paris, 21–23 mai 1971)', *Le Mouvement social* 79 (April–June 1972).

currents – libertarian readings, which were opposed to Stalinism, and inspired by the events of 1968. In 1969, the sociologist André Découflé argued for a severing of the link between the Commune and the previous revolutions, in a bid to underline its spontaneity, and its affinity with autonomy and absolute freedom. In Découflé's view, this dimension – at once essential yet undefined – had seemingly escaped even the Commune's own elected officials.[8] Without calling into question longer-term traditions of insurrection, the sociologist and philosopher Henri Lefebvre also insisted on this anarchistic dimension of the Commune, associating it more specifically with urban realities.[9] The event in Paris resonated with theories he had recently formulated about the 'right to the city' (attended by the demand for quality of life and creativity, as opposed to urbanism and the grip of commercialism) and the theory of 'moments'.[10]

Lefebvre's arguments found echoes, albeit indirectly, in a surge of interest in the Commune among scholars in the United States. This took shape amid the revival of historical sociology in the United States during the 1970s and 1980s. These scholars looked to the Paris insurrection mainly as an index of the internal crises of capitalism and urban modernity.[11] In his important book *Insurgent Identities*, based on an analysis of social networks, the historical sociologist Roger Gould proposed a way out of this debate by suggesting that the nature of insurrections can vary.[12] In his reading, the June 1848 revolution was more political, since the actors had drawn more on a class identity, whereas the Commune was more urban, its insurgents defending a certain notion of urban

8 André Découflé, *La Commune de Paris (1871): révolution populaire et pouvoir révolutionnaire* (Paris: Cujas, 1969), and *Sociologie des révolutions* (Paris: PUF, 1968).

9 Henri Lefebvre, *La Proclamation de la Commune* (Paris: Gallimard, 1965), and *La Révolution urbaine* (Paris: Gallimard, 1970).

10 Henri Lefebvre, *The Critique of Everyday Life* (London: Verso, 2014). For Lefebvre, 'moments' are intense experiences in which everyday life is suspended and possibilities for authenticity, creativity or transcendence are opened up. These moments – whether aesthetic, amorous or revolutionary – reveal the potential richness of existence, both individual and collective. This approach seeks to break with the reproduction of relations of domination.

11 Manuel Castells, *The City and the Grassroots* (Berkeley, CA: University of California Press, 1983); David Harvey, *Consciousness and the Urban Experience* (Baltimore, MD: Johns Hopkins University Press, 1985).

12 Roger Gould, *Insurgent Identities: Class, Community and Protest in Paris from 1848 to the Commune* (Chicago: University of Chicago Press, 1995).

community. Needless to say, these conclusions were themselves soon challenged.[13]

A third historiographical current, focusing on the political history of French republicanism, took shape in France from the 1980s onwards. It developed in parallel with the two other currents, while also frequently overlapping with them. The Commune had long been a major preoccupation of republican historiography: ever since the debates over amnesty for the Communards during the 1870s, republican historians had been anxious to appropriate the Commune, and at the same time troubled by its 'excesses'. A century later, this political history had been enriched and transformed. The problem was now how to situate the Commune within the establishment of 'the longest of republics' (the Third Republic of 1870–1940) – characterised by the nation-state in its 'modern' form, liberal democracy, and the republican regime. Historian François Furet took 1879 as the moment when the French Revolution had come 'back into harbour', after the Commune and the establishment of a republican-led government.[14] Meanwhile, the historian of the French Republic, Maurice Agulhon – with different intentions – began his history of the Third Republic on 4 September 1870, before the Commune. For Agulhon, the point was to emphasise the long history of which the Republic was the product.[15] This perspective, subsequently taken up in numerous works and textbooks, rested on a more or less implicit general schema of 'modernisation': the Third Republic took root because literacy was advancing, urbanisation was spreading, transportation and long-distance connections were intensifying – and so on. Of course, the authors of these works took care to distinguish between several types of modernisation – social, political, economic or cultural

13 A critical discussion can be found in Robert Tombs, 'Les Communeux dans la ville: des analyses récentes à l'étranger', *Le Mouvement social* 179 (1997), pp. 93–105, and in Jacques Rougerie, 'Autour de quelques livres étrangers', in C. Latta, ed., *La Commune de 1871, l'événement, les hommes et la mémoire: actes du colloque organisé à Précieux et à Montbrison, les 15 et 16 mars 2003* (Saint-Étienne: Publications de l'université de Saint-Étienne, 2004), pp. 215–36.

14 François Furet, *La Révolution, 1770–1880: De Turgot à Jules Ferry* (Paris: Hachette, 1989).

15 A good example is Maurice Agulhon, *La République*, vol. 1: *L'Élan fondateur et la grande blessure (1880–1932)* (Paris: Hachette, 1990), pp. 7–16.

– and to point out contradictions.[16] In this context, however, the Commune stood alone.

The scholarship of Jacques Rougerie and of British historian Robert Tombs, taken together, marked an important turning point in historical work on the Commune. In their studies, produced over the course of several decades, they renewed the questions historians had asked about the Commune. Their research brought about what they might have called a 'return to history': a renewed focus on the facts, and on the perceptions of the actors involved; the use of new sources; and a confrontation between a close knowledge of particular situations and earlier ideological, theoretical or sociological generalisations.[17] Starting with his dissertation, published as *The War Against Paris, 1871* (1981), Tombs focused on a major but largely unexamined aspect of the story of the Commune: the Versailles side.[18] He challenged the conventional image of its troops as wild and drunken rural soldiers, drawing attention to the difficult process of rebuilding this army after the defeat by Prussia, before then delving into the logic of the fighting on both sides of the French capital's ramparts. In subsequent work, Tombs reassessed the role of political and military circumstances in the outbreak of the Commune. In an overview work, published in 1999, he offered a series of responses to some of the main questions still being posed – such as how foreigners participated in the Commune, the form of government, and the role played by class.[19]

Jacques Rougerie's work was comparable in its method but distinct in its aims. Starting in the 1960s, Rougerie undertook a parallel series of reinterpretations and clarifications of the Commune's history based on

16 It is impossible to list the huge volume of works. Of particular interest are the works by Jean-François Chanet. On the post-1871 shift, see Jean-Claude Caron, *Frères de sang. La guerre civile en France au XIXe siècle* (Seyssel: Champ Vallon, 2009).

17 This position is reflected in one of the few texts co-written by the two historians: Jacques Rougerie and Robert Tombs, 'La Commune de Paris', in Michel Pigenet and Danièle Tartakosvky, eds, *Histoire des mouvements sociaux en France (de 1814 à nos jours)* (Paris: La Découverte, 2011), pp. 141–51.

18 Robert Tombs, *The War Against Paris, 1871* (Cambridge: Cambridge University Press, 1981).

19 Robert Tombs, 'Harbingers or Entrepreneurs? A Workers' Cooperative during the Paris Commune', *Historical Journal* 27: 4 (1984), pp. 969–77; '"Prudent rebels": The 2nd Arrondissement during the Paris Commune of 1871', *French History* 5: 4 (1991), pp. 393–413; *The Paris Commune* (London: Longmann, 1999), translated into French under the title *Paris, Bivouac des révolutions. La Commune de 1871* (Paris: Libertalia, 2014).

his detailed study of newspapers, inquiry reports and war council files.[20] Rougerie questioned the supposedly preponderant role in the Commune of the International Workingmen's Association.[21] Among other things, he also registered the importance of the notions of 'the people' and of 'social antagonisms' during this episode, and offered a new reading of Jacobinism.[22] Above all, his work, spanning several decades, proposed a different interpretation of the Commune as a whole. To understand the Commune, he argued, it was necessary to situate it within the rich context of nineteenth-century republicanism and socialism in France – and, in particular, in continuity with the experience of the 'democratic and social republic' expressed in 1848–51. In this latter perspective, the change of political form – in other words, the creation of a republic – cannot be detached from the transformation of social and economic relations (work and commerce) by means of Association – in the strong contemporary sense of workers' cooperation and self-organisation. Far from being just a muddle of ideas, he argued, the Commune corresponds more to a different history of the republican, socialist and working-class milieus of the 1840s–80s, richer than had been thought – a history that remains, even today, to be explored.[23]

These historiographical transformations had the paradoxical effect of rendering the Parisian revolt as an irreducible, unique event, at just the moment when communism was collapsing and great historical paradigms were breaking apart. Starting in the 1990s, research into the Commune – now less marked by urgent theoretical and political concerns – was increasingly driven by new trends in the historical field

20 Notably, *L'Enquête parlementaire sur l'insurrection du 18 mars 1871* (Paris: Librairie législative Wittersheim, 1872).

21 Jacques Rougerie, 'L'AIT et le mouvement ouvrier à Paris pendant les événements de 1870–1871', in Rougerie, ed., *1871. Jalons pour une Histoire de la Commune de Paris* (Paris: PUF, 1973), pp. 3–102; *Paris libre 1871* (Paris: Seuil, 2004 [1971]).

22 On the reappraisal of the associationist movement, see Jacques Rougerie, 'Par-delà le coup d'Etat, la continuité de l'action et de l'organisation ouvrières', in Sylvie Aprile et al., eds, *Comment meurt une République? Autour du 2 décembre 1851, actes du colloque (Lyon, 28 November–1 December 2001)* (Paris: Créaphis, 2004), pp. 267–84. See also his 'Le mouvement associatif populaire comme facteur d'acculturation politique a Paris, de la Revolution aux années 1840. Continuité, discontinuités', *Annales historiques de la Révolution française* 297 (1994), pp. 493–516.

23 See Jacques Rougerie, *La Commune de 1871* (Paris: PUF, 2009 [1988]). Other works contributed to this 'return to history'. See William Serman, *La Commune de Paris (1871)* (Paris: Fayard, 1986).

more broadly. Some areas of knowledge were enriched or deepened – for instance, regarding the Communes in provincial France, or biographies of Communards.[24] And the publication of sources and annotated memoirs continued apace.[25] But other approaches were also being brought to bear that added new dimensions to our understanding of this insurrectionary experience: the histories of cultural representations and art, the history of women and gender, the history of exile, memory, and 'sensibilities' (i.e. senses and emotions).[26] These efforts were punctuated

24 The first built on an earlier trend – Jeanne Gaillard, *Communes de province, Commune de Paris 1870–1871* (Paris: Flammarion, 1971): Ronald Aminzade, *Ballots and Barricades: Class Formation and Republican Politics in Nineteenth-Century France* (Princeton, NJ: Princeton University Press, 1993); Marc César, *La Commune révolutionnaire de Narbonne (mars 1871)* (Sète: Éd. Singulières, 2008); Jacques Girault, *Bordeaux et la Commune (1870–1871)* (Périgueux: Fanlac, 2009). For biographies, see Alain Dalotel, *André Léo (1824–1900), la Junon de la Commune* (Chauvigny: Association des Publications Chauvinoises, 2004); Michel Cordillot, *Eugène Varlin, internationaliste et communard* (Paris: Spartacus, 2016). Other fields were also covered (sociopolitical struggles in the 1860s, the webs of sociability, and so on). See Alain Dalotel, Alain Faure and Jean-Claude Freiermuth, *Aux origines de la Commune. Le mouvement des réunions publiques à Paris* (1868–1870) (Paris: Maspero, 1980); Martin Philip Johnson, *The Paradise of Association: Political Culture and Popular Organizations in the Paris Commune of 1871* (Ann Arbor, MI: University of Michigan Press, 1996); Maxime Jourdan, *'Le Cri du peuple' (22 février 1871–23 mai 1871)* (Paris: L'Harmattan, 2005); Philip Katz, *From Appomattox to Montmartre: Americans and the Paris Commune* (Cambridge, MA: Harvard University Press, 1998).

25 For instance, Jules Andrieu, *Notes pour servir à l'histoire de la Commune de Paris* (Paris: Libertalia, 2016).

26 On culture and art, see Bertrand Tillier, *La Commune de Paris, révolution sans images? Politique et représentations dans la France républicaine (1871–1914)* (Seyssel: Champ Vallon, 2004); Gonzalo J. Sanchez, *Organizing Independence: The Artists Federation of the Paris Commune and Its Legacy (1871–1889)* (Lincoln, NE: University of Nebraska Press, 1997); Hollis Clayson, *Paris in Despair: Art and Everyday Life under Siege (1870–1871)* (Chicago: University of Chicago Press, 2002). On women and gender, see Edith Thomas, *Les Pétroleuses* (Paris: Gallimard, 1963) – in English, *The Women Incendiaries* (London: Secker & Warburg, 1967); Gay L. Gulliskson, *Unruly Women of Paris: Images of the Paris Commune* (Ithaca, NY: Cornell University Press, 1996); Carolyn J. Eichner, *Surmounting the Barricades: Women in the Paris Commune* (Bloomington, IN: Indiana University Press, 2004). On the history of exile, see Paul K. Martinez, 'Communard Refugees in Great Britain', PhD dissertation, Sussex University (1981, never published); Laure Godineau, 'Retour d'exil. Les anciens communards au début de la Troisième République', PhD dissertation, Université Paris-I (2000); Thomas C. Jones and Robert Tombs, 'The French Left in Exile: Quarante-huitards and Communards in London, 1848–80', in Debra Kelly and Martyn Cornick, eds, *A History of the French in London: Liberty, Equality, Opportunity* (London: Institute of Historical Research, 2013), pp. 165–91; Michel Cordillot, *Utopistes et exilés du Nouveau monde: des Français aux*

by the publication of new conference proceedings and overview works.[27] Some have sought to revive the contemporary political relevance of the Commune. In an interpretation that aimed to shake up the typical narratives of the event, literary scholar Kristin Ross has read the Commune as containing the 'seeds' of political positions which, she argues, can address major problems in the present.[28]

In short, seemingly every interpretive schema for studying revolutions and historical processes has been deployed to study the Commune. If we add to that the many sociological, philosophical and artistic productions that have laid claim to the event, sometimes without much caution (Max Weber, Hannah Arendt, Claude Lefort, Antonio Negri, Axel Honneth, and so on), it is clear that the Commune has provided an essential site of reflection for more than a century. These reflections have covered everything from the foundations of the social order to its possible transformations within Western 'modernity' and the historical forms of emancipation. The Commune's journey is certainly an impressive one. Yet, at the same time, it seems to elude any interpretive schema. The historical problem of the Commune remains open, and, as we have seen, has even been refreshed more recently.

How can we understand the Commune? And what was its true scope? Faced with such a vast problem, many recent works have preferred to leave the answer in limbo – to defer the question. Others, even those

---

Etats-Unis, de 1848 à la Commune (Paris: Vendémiaire, 2013). On memory, see Colette Wilson, *Paris and the Commune, 1871–78: The Politics of Forgetting* (Manchester: Manchester University Press, 2007); Éric Fournier, *'La Commune n'est pas morte'. Les usages du passé de 1871 à nos jours* (Paris: Libertalia, 2013). On 'sensibilities', see Éric Fournier, *Paris en ruines. Du Paris Haussmannien au Paris communard* (Paris: Imago, 2008).

27 Laure Godineau, *La Commune de Paris par ceux qui l'ont vécu* (Paris: Parigramme, 2010). Major conferences include one in Perpignan (proceedings published in 2000) and one in Montbrison (proceedings published in 2004), as well as the most recent one, held in Narbonne in 2011: Marc César and Laure Godineau, eds, *La Commune de 1871. Une relecture, actes du colloque 'Regards sur la Commune de 1871 en France' (Narbonne, 24–26 mars 2011)*, (Paris: Créaphis, 2019). Also worth mentioning is Michele Audin's useful blog, 'La Commune de Paris', at macommunedeparis.com.

28 Kristin Ross, *Communal Luxury* (London: Verso, 2015); John Merriman, *Massacre: The Life and Death of the Paris Commune* (New York, Basic Books, 2014); Michèle Riot-Sarcey, *Le Procès de la liberté. Une histoire souterraine du XIXe siècle en France* (Paris: La Découverte, 2016).

broadly sympathetic to the Commune, in considering its short duration and meagre achievements, have concluded that what happened was maybe not so important: its exceptional character is thus owed to the simple existence of a 'Commune government' and its subsequent appropriation by Communist historiography in the twentieth century. But can our understanding really stop there? Questions remain. Some are simple: Who were these men and women? What did they do? What did they want? Some are more general: How can we explain the fact that, despite everything, these seventy-two days had such a significant political and symbolic impact in the twentieth and twenty-first centuries, and on the national, European and global scales? These questions are the threads that tie together the chapters that follow.

A Threefold Shift

This book sets itself the challenge of addressing three dimensions of the problem of the Commune's scope and meaning that have been continually reworked and reformulated over the past century and a half: its relations to time, space and political experience. The aim, therefore, is to approach each of these aspects of the Commune from a new perspective.

First, the question of space. The Commune was above all a Parisian phenomenon. But was it only that, as the 'return to history' in the scholarship of the 1980s–2000s might suggest? If that is the case, then what should we make of the Communes in provincial France, or of the Commune's numerous international echoes (examined by many previous works, though there has thus far been no overall synthesis)? Did an insurrection of this type, in the capital of the revolutions of the nineteenth century, not have other, wider repercussions? Addressing these questions requires us to take the Commune out of the national or international frames in which it has long been implicitly placed, and instead consider it within a richer matrix of various spatial scales.

To that end, this study draws on transnational and global approaches, which I understand here as research perspectives and not as objects of study in their own right. There is no need to recall the debates and redefinitions that have left their mark on what has become a vast field of study.[29] I take 'transnational' to mean an approach 'that foregrounds the fact that any historical phenomenon is inextricably linked to phenomena that are not necessarily contained within conventional political borders, even though such borders constitute the usual framework of historians' research.'[30] Such an approach demands that one study the circulations of humans, objects and ideas, the configurations that they form, and the polarities that animate them – all according to fields of force that extend beyond the usual frontiers.[31] The approach does not, therefore, stand in opposition to local analyses, or even to the national scale, since these configurations also participate in the construction of national borders. Quite the opposite is true: a transnational approach allows us to think afresh about the 'French' or 'Parisian' character of the Commune, which is often taken for granted. As for the term 'global', it does not refer to the planet as a whole; rather, it points to the examination of the vast networks of interdependencies that structure areas which are not limited to single continents.[32] Combining the two terms integrates the highly important colonial and imperial dimensions of the past and expresses the diverse array of approaches that can be mobilised to study it: the study of connections, microhistorical approaches, the situated analysis of encounters, multisite approaches, comparison, and

29 Among various surveys: in French, Philippe Minard and Caroline Douki, 'Histoire globale, histoires connectées: un changement d'échelle historiographique?', *Revue d'histoire moderne et contemporaine* 54: 4 (2007), pp. 7–21. On transnational history, among the many overviews, see 'AHR Conversation: On Transnational History', *American Historical Review* 111: 5 (2006), pp. 1441–64; Akira Iriye and Pierre-Yves Saunier, eds, *The Palgrave Dictionary of Transnational History* (Basingstoke: Palgrave Macmillan, 2009). On global history, see Kenneth Pomeranz, *The Great Divergence: China, Europe, and the Making of the Modern World Economy* (Princeton, NJ: Princeton University Press, 2001). Without taking up here the debates around terms ('world' or 'global'), see also Matthias Middell and Katja Naumann, 'Global History and the Spatial Turn: From the Impact of Area Studies to the Study of Critical Junctures of Globalization', *Journal of Global History* 5: 1 (2010), pp. 149–70; Serge Gruzinski, 'Faire de l'histoire dans un monde globalisé', *Annales. Histoire, Sciences sociales* 4 (2011), pp. 1081–91.

30 Jean-Paul Zuniga, 'Introduction', in 'Pratiques du transnational Terrains, preuves, limites' – pdf at hal.archives-ouvertes.fr, pp. 9–19.

31 Pierre-Yves Saunier, 'Circulations, connexions et espaces transnationaux', *Genèses* 57 (2004), pp. 110–26.

32 See Sebastian Conrad, *What Is Global History?* (Princeton, NJ: Princeton University Press, 2017).

so on.[33] If they have often been presented in the past as competing models, today it seems that these connected and comparative approaches, moving between situations 'on the ground' and large-scale recompositions, ought to be combined – which is what this book intends to do.[34] Unlike the method used in previous works, centred on the notion of diffusion, these approaches should allow us to secure a better grip on the forms of circulation, echoes, rejections, appropriations and redefinitions that manifested themselves in the moment of the Commune, while also integrating practices of repression. They also invite us to take into account horizons and fields of action that previously escaped attention, such as colonial spaces, and not to hesitate to make the large-scale comparisons that spontaneously spring to mind. For was not the Commune – and even the Communes – caught up in wider webs of connections? And were they not also constructed as 'events' outside Paris and France?

In this way, my approach puts this book in dialogue with the flourishing new imperial and global histories of revolutions, from the eighteenth to the twentieth centuries, and most particularly with the new history of the French Revolution.[35] Recent scholarship on the French Revolution, without denying either its importance or the role of local and national-level processes in its unfolding, has de-exceptionalised it,

33 For instance, on the microhistory of the global, see Francesca Trivellato, 'Is There a Future for Italian Microhistory in the Age of Global History?' *California Italian Studies* 2: 1 (2011), at escholarship.org; on the multi-site approach, see Michael Burawoy, *Global Ethnography, Forces, Connections, and Imaginations in a Postmodern World* (Berkeley, CA: University of California Press, 2000); and on the trans-imperial dimension, see Pierre Singaravélou, *Tianjin Cosmopolis. Une autre histoire de la mondialisation* (Paris: Seuil, 2017).

34 Some cues for reflection are offered in Bernhard Struck, Kate Ferris and Jacques Revel, 'Introduction: Space and Scale in Transnational History', *International History Review* 33: 4 (2011), pp. 573–84; Christophe Charle 'Comparative and Transnational History and the Sociology of Pierre Bourdieu', in Philip S. Gorski, ed., *Bourdieu and Historical Analysis* (Durham, NC: Duke University Press, 2013), pp. 66–84; Richard Drayton, David Motadel, 'Discussion: The Futures of Global History', *Journal of Global History* 13: 1 (2018), pp. 1–21.

35 David Armitage and Sanjay Subrahmanyam, eds, *The Age of Revolutions in Global Context (ca. 1760–1840)* (Farnham: Palgrave Macmillan, 2010). The many studies on this theme include Pierre Serna, ed., *Républiques sœurs. Le Directoire et la Révolution atlantique* (Rennes: Presses universitaires de Rennes, 2009); Manuel Covo, *Entrepôt of Revolutions: Saint-Domingue, Commercial Sovereignty, and the French-American Alliance* (Oxford: Oxford University Press, 2022).

enriched our understanding of its causes, and brought global and imperial actors, scenes and outcomes into the analysis. Similar tendencies are visible in recent scholarship on 1830 and 1848, albeit to a somewhat lesser degree.[36] Further downstream, the anarchist and revolutionary movements of the 1880s, not to mention the Russian Revolution of 1917, have also been the subject of such studies.[37] The Commune, thus far, has been an exception. It is time to rethink the Commune along similar lines, both in order to integrate it into the sequence of new revolutionary histories from 1848 to 1880 and to shed new light on what historians now call the 'global moment' of the 1860s.[38]

The second shift in perspective concerns time. This aspect of the book draws on another theoretical toolbox, taken from the social sciences of crisis and uncertainty. In the late 1990s, works providing theoretical or structural interpretations, such as the above-mentioned

36 Sylvie Aprile, Jean–Claude Caron and Emmanuel Fureix, eds, *La liberté guidant les peuples: les révolutions de 1830 en Europe* (Seyssel: Champ Vallon, 2013). The history of the People's Spring was soon considered on a European scale. See, for example, Jonathan Sperber, *The European Revolutions, 1848–1851* (Cambridge: Cambridge University Press, 1994); Sylvie Aprile, Raymond Huard, Pierre Lévêque and Jean-Yves Mollier, *La Révolution de 1848 en France et en Europe* (Paris: Éditions or Les Éditions sociales, 1998). The imperial dimension is less present, except in Miles Taylor, 'The 1848 Revolutions and the British Empire', *Past and Present* 166: 1 (2000), pp. 146–80. The publication of the proceedings of the conference 'Les Mondes de 1848', held in Paris in December 2018, filled several of these gaps. See Quentin Deluermoz, Emmanuel Fureix and Clément Thibaud, eds, *Les Mondes de 1848. Au-delà du Printemps des peoples* (Ceyzérieu: Champ Vallon, 2023). A recent account in Christopher M. Clark, *Revolutionary Spring: Europe Aflame and the Fight for a New World, 1848–1849* (London: Allen Lane, 2023).

37 Benedict Anderson, *Under Three Flags: Anarchism and the Anti-Colonial Imagination* (London: Verso, 2016); Steven Hirsch and Lucien Van der Walt, *Anarchism and Syndicalism in the Colonial and Postcolonial World (1870–1940)* (Leiden: Brill, 2010); Silvio Pons, *The Global Revolution: A History of International Communism, 1917–1991* (Oxford: Oxford University Press, 2014). On the global history of revolutions over the *longue durée*, see Ludivine Bantigny, Quentin Deluermoz, Boris Gobille, Laurent Jeanpierre and Eugenia Palieraki, eds, *Une Histoire Globale des Révolutions* (Paris: La Découverte, 2023).

38 A turn highlighted in Christopher Bayly, *The Birth of the Modern World, 1780–1914* (Oxford: Blackwell, 2003); Jürgen Osterhammel, *The Transformation of the World: A Global History of the Nineteenth Century* (Princeton, NJ: Princeton University Press, 2014); Pierre Singaravélou and Sylvain Venayre, eds, *Histoire du monde au XIXe siècle* (Paris: Fayard, 2017). See also the overview of the conference on 'the global 1860s' (Princeton, 15–17 October 2015), in Matthew Karp, 'The New World Order', *Boston Review*, 3 October 2016.

works on Parisian insurrections, were criticised for their overly rigid approach. More recent scholarship had been concerned with contingency, paying more attention to articulations between structures, actors and events.[39] This scholarship, in my view, makes three principal methodological moves. The first emphasises the multiple temporalities of social transformations. It is illustrated by the work of historian William H. Sewell Jr, who has called for close attention to the intersection of different temporal rhythms in the study of crises and revolutions.[40] A second approach emphasises the event and the crisis itself — in the sociologist Michel Dobry's definition of crises, 'fluid conjunctures'.[41] According to this view, political crises – that is, moments in which social relations and schemas of intelligibility collapse – are to be studied less in terms of their outcomes than in terms of processes. The goal is to observe the crisis as it plays out, to chart its changing landscape, the opening up of possibilities, the adjustments actors make in response, and then the struggles over how to define the situation. A third approach, slightly different from the previous one, focuses on the ruptures in meaning created by the moments of crisis.[42] Inspired by the writings of the intellectual historian Reinhart Koselleck, as well as by the philosopher Walter Benjamin, it emphasises the effects of discontinuity provoked by such events, and the way in which those ruptures – especially in revolutionary situations – affect individuals, altering their perception of history as well as the way in which they locate their own actions within it. Sensitive

39 On this (and a related bibliography), see Quentin Deluermoz and Boris Gobille, 'Protagonisme et crises politiques. Individus "ordinaires" et politisations "extraordinaires"', *Politix* 112: 4 (2015), pp. 9–29.

40 William H. Sewell Jr, *Logics of History: Social Theory and Social Transformation* (Chicago: University of Chicago Press, 2005). On these shifts, see Marc Bessin, Claire Bidart and Michel Grossetti, eds, *Bifurcations. Les sciences sociales face aux ruptures et à l'événement* (Paris: La Découverte, 2010); Adams, Clemens and Orloff, *Remaking Modernity*.

41 Michel Dobry, *Sociologie des crises politiques. La dynamique des mobilisations multisectorielles* (Paris: Presses de la Fondation nationale des sciences politiques, 2009). On the study of recent revolutionary movements, see Choukri Hmed and Laurent Jeanpierre, eds, 'Révolutions et crises politiques', *Actes de la recherche en sciences sociales* 121–2 (2016).

42 Alban Bensa and Eric Fassin, 'Les sciences sociales face à l'événement', *Terrain* 38 (2002), pp. 5–20. On the temporal and subjective experience of critical times, see Federico Tarragoni, *L'énigme révolutionnaire* (Paris: Les Prairies ordinaires, 2015), pp. 101–3; Ludivine Bantigny, *1968. De grands soirs en petits matins* (Paris: Seuil, 2018).

to the study of emotions, this approach also draws attention to revolutionary subjectivity and radicalisation, to different forms of politicisation, and to the transformative potential of visionary projects. These three methodological moves do not dovetail perfectly; there are tensions between them. But they do converge, and, taken together, are well suited to the task of grasping the Commune – a civil war and 'revolution in the making' – that was cut short while still underway.

Focusing on time and space places a third dimension centre stage: that of revolutionary experience. Thinking about experience – in particular 'from below' – can help us revisit the important question of the Commune's political nature, beyond the way in which the 'democratic and social republic' resurfaced in the maelstrom of 1871. The richness of the economic, social and political practices that spread in Paris in 1870–71, whether spontaneous or previously formulated, poses a more fundamental problem: How to describe and characterise them? Jacques Rougerie, for one, avers that they could be compared to 'direct democracy', if this expression did not carry such heavy and teleological connotations. He instead proposes that we speak of a 'first degree of politics', which he elsewhere characterises as 'true democracy'.[43] But what does this expression mean? Again, the approach taken here may help us clarify this description.

Time, space and experience go together. One of this work's aims is precisely to combine these perspectives in order to change the way we comprehend the Commune as event. Of course, these approaches are themselves part of another new 'wave' in the early twenty-first century. At the sociocultural level, they resonate with the process of globalisation, the supposed 'end of great ideologies', the recomposition of the modes of power and 'governance', upheavals in the relationship with space and time, the numerous current crises, and the return of mass revolt and revolution (such as the Arab Spring of 2010–11). At the scholarly level, while building on the methodologies of the 1990s (multi-scalar analysis, the return to the actors and to the event, the study of gender relations), this approach also reflects the recent expansion of historians' spatial horizons, new questions about temporalities, and the renewed study of 'situations of uncertainty'. We cannot escape from our moment in history. But nor is this study merely a product of the present moment, any more than the

43 Preface to new edition of Jacques Rougerie, *Paris libre 1871* (Paris: Seuil, 2002).

studies in past decades were in their time: its core goal is to provide a means to better grasp the breadth and the energy of a revolutionary event.

In that sense, the project of this book converges with an older and more personal line of research into the anthropological history of social orders. 'Orders', here, denotes not only political and administrative frameworks or actors, but all of the forces in a given society: the routines that maintain them, the conflicts that mould them, the socioeconomic hierarchies that share them, and the material spaces that organise them, as well as the imaginaries and shared assumptions that underpin it.[44] Through the upheaval that it caused, the Commune laid bare the strong foundations of these orders even as they were in the process of being reshaped. It underscored their historicity, and also raised the possibility of alternatives to them.[45] It is all the more interesting since it was situated at the end of the nineteenth century, at a decisive period in what is called economic, political and cultural 'modernity' – a word that itself dates to the 1860s. The Commune thus offers an exceptional opportunity to question the degree to which social norms had been internalised – and the possibility of shaking up or changing them. At the same time, as we have seen, the 'Paris Republic' has constantly escaped the grasp of grand narratives. The aim of this book is certainly not to impose a new one. On the contrary, my aim is to give the Commune and its resonances room to unfold, and to follow them, in order to enrich our familiar models of time, space and politics in history. What emerges are images of France, of the nineteenth century, and of their social reality that are much richer and more revealing than expected.

Commune(s) and Constellations of Worlds

One has to make choices, which are hardly self-evident, in carrying out this kind of project. Research for this book took place primarily in French libraries and archives (national, colonial, *département*-level and

44 See Quentin Deluermoz, *Policiers dans la ville. La construction d'un ordre public à Paris (1854–1914)* (Paris: Publications de la Sorbonne, 2012). The main intellectual references here are the works of Pierre Bourdieu, Cornelius Castoriadis, Arlette Farge, William H. Sewell Jr and Maurice Godelier.

45 Emmanuel Fureix and François Jarrige, *La Modernité désenchantée* (Paris: La Découverte, 2015).

Parisian archives), but also in other countries: Great Britain, Spain, the United States and Germany. Of course, given the infinite wealth of events, gaps and discrepancies in the available information, the multiplicity of local situations and the variety of rebound effects, decisions had to be made. Here the focus is certainly on the year 1870–71, which implies taking account of the upheaval that began with the Franco-Prussian War and its aftermath. Then, from there, threads are unravelled that reach both backward and forward in time.

Methodologically, I have sought to probe the abundance of connections and situations that emerged out of and around the Commune. Paris remains, despite everything, the centre of gravity, studied through familiar sources (parliamentary inquiries, the press, posters, decrees and debates of the Commune), but also other kinds of documents (on both the Commune side and the Versaillais side), some of which have been little utilised, if at all. To gain a better understanding of the wider 'Commune' phenomenon in 1870–71, this study has expanded its lens to take in four revolutionary experiences outside Paris and metropolitan France: the 1870 'Southern insurrection', in Martinique; the 'Algiers Commune' of 1871; the events in the town of Thiers (Puy-de-Dôme); and the ones in Lyon. I have also paid close attention to transnational and imperial connections by following, among others, transnational volunteers, diplomatic and economic echoes, and media coverage of the Commune. These choices, which are informed by the research questions as well as my own skills and linguistic abilities, are explained in each case.

Another characteristic of this study is certainly its reliance on a plurality of methodological approaches: cartographic and statistical treatments, the study of collective representations, ethnographic surveys, and so on. Some parts of the project draw upon serial sources, others are based on qualitative analysis of the available evidence: different kinds of evidence that produce different kinds of proof. Instead of excluding one or the other, I specify in each case the robustness of the findings at which I have arrived, and the type of relationship established between the results.[46] This foregrounding of the historian's work is

46 This points to the dilemma of researchers who, according to Carlo Ginzburg, are often torn between the impulses to 'accept a weak scientific status in order to achieve striking results, or accept a strong scientific status in order to achieve negligible results'. In this study, both kinds of investigation and results are combined. See Carlo Ginzburg, *Myths, Emblems, Clues*, transl. J. and C. Tedeschi (London: Hutchinson Radius, 1990 [1986]).

deliberate: in a period of (dis)information overload, it is necessary to remind ourselves of how history and the social sciences build their knowledge and draw the reader into participating in the work of interpretation and conclusion.

Tying together these perspectives, finally, is no easy task. To this end, I employ here a framework of analysis I have used in my earlier work: that of the sociologist Norbert Elias. I am particularly interested in his notion of configurations, centred on interdependencies, in which the elements (individuals or social formations) are modulated by these shifting relations.[47] From Elias's earliest works, such as *The Civilizing Process* (1939), this approach allowed him to tie together disciplines that had become separate (history, sociology, anthropology, psychoanalysis), to overcome certain sterile oppositions (between individual and society, or institutions and emotions), and to weave together several distinct temporal rhythms and spatial scales.[48] Such an approach should make it feasible, in my view, to pull together, without any preconceived result, the places, perspectives and levels of analysis that are set to work.

This choice may be surprising: Elias's original schema has been criticised precisely for its alleged resistance to the event, its evolutionism, and its Eurocentrism. These reservations must be taken into account. But, as he continued to revise his model, up to his death in 1990, Elias continually refined it, making it more ambitious, open to conflicts and ruptures, to the problem of state violence, and to extra-European spaces. In these pages, Elias's analytical tool is above all adjusted to the documentation, to the object of study, and to the specific needs of the investigation.[49] To quote Roger Chartier, my aim is to engage in a 'free and

47 On this notion see Roger Chartier's foreword in the French translation of Norbert Elias, *La Société des individus* (Paris: Fayard, 1991 – first German edition 1983), p. 13.

48 Norbert Elias, *Über den Prozess der Zivilisation. Soziogenetische und psychogenetische Untersuchungen* (Bale: Haus zum Falken, 1939) – in English, *The Civilizing Process* (Oxford: Blackwell, 1994).

49 On these critiques and readjustments, see Quentin Deluermoz, ed., *Norbert Elias* (Paris: Tempus, 2012) and Marc Joly, *Devenir Norbert Elias. Histoire croisée d'un processus de reconnaissance scientifique: la réception française* (Paris: Fayard, 2012). Elias's works include *The Society of Individuals* (Oxford: Blackwell, 1991), *Mozart: Portrait of a Genius* (Cambridge: Polity, 1993); and 'Freud's Concept of Society and Beyond It' (1990) in French in *Au-delà de Freud: Sociologie, Psychologie, Psychoanalyse* (Paris: Éditions la Découverte, 2010).

respectful' use of this model. While surely not free of shortcomings, this framework – which historicises all the data of the social world, and forbids any kind of naturalisation or essentialisation – turns out to be particularly important to this project.

In short, this book undertakes what could be described as a global, relational and interpretive history. The angle of approach has thus already come into focus; this study, in the final analysis, examines the connections between different regional *worlds* that developed during and after the Commune, as well as how the Commune spurred the creation of *new worlds*, be they concrete, imagined or possible.[50] I call this constellation of events, actions, hopes and ideas the 'Commune moment'. Accordingly, the pattern of this work follows a U-shape. Based on the account of the events I have just outlined, the first part explores the local, national, European, imperial and global dimensions of the Franco-Prussian War and the Commune. The second part turns to the insurrectionary Communes, their course, their experience, their results and their own temporalities, in particular in Paris. The final part, bringing together elements of the preceding two, returns to the Communes' end: the massacre, the trials, the return to order; the media and state reaction. It takes us into the reappropriations of the event by movements of social and political revolt in the long aftermath of the Commune: reconnections that are diverse, and sometimes unexpected. A new perspective on the Commune then comes into view.

50 These clarifications also account for the title of the French edition, which translates as: *Commune(s), 1870–1871: A Journey Across Worlds in the Nineteenth Century.*

PART I

A Global Commune (July 1870–April 1871)

Writing in his diary on 18 March 1871, the interpreter Zhang Deyi noted what he had seen in Paris:

> As I am copying my report, I suddenly hear cannon fire. I immediately go to the post office, which is closed and no longer accepting anything. So, I go to send a telegram, but [that office] is also closed. . . . In every street on the Right Bank, our foreign servant tells me, barricades are being built with wheels, stones, and wood, passersby are circulating with passwords, and no one should go out alone . . . I go to the station and learn that the train will not arrive until seven in the evening. . . . Perplexed, I first return home to thank the landlord and bid him farewell.[1]

This is a typical account of the early moments of the 18 March revolution, at least as experienced by certain elites and members of the middle classes, be they Parisian or passing through the capital.

1 Zhang Deyi, *Mission en France. Troisième relation des merveilles*, cited in Che Jinshan, 'Témoignage chinois de la Commune de Paris', in Béatrice Didier and Meng Hua, eds, *Miroirs croisés Chine-France (XVIIe–XXIe siècle)* (Paris: Champion, 2014), p. 132.

What is remarkable about this account is its author: the twenty-three-year-old Zhang Deyi, a graduate of the first foreign-language school in China, who was a civil servant in the Qing dynasty's Ministry of the Army. When the uprising broke out, he was in Paris, serving as an interpreter in a Chinese diplomatic delegation. Its mission was to present the Middle Kingdom's apologies to France for an incident that had taken place in Tientsin in June 1870. The neutral and factual nature of this Chinese perspective may disappoint those who might expect a ready exoticism, yet the text, interestingly, reveals some of the striking connections that existed during the Commune of 1871. These connections are only surprising at first glance, however: the Tientsin incident was closely bound to France's imperial domination of Asia. And although it had taken place in June, the diplomatic incident was also linked to the start of the Franco-Prussian War in July 1870. The outbreak of that war would itself prove decisive in the emergence of the Commune in March: indeed, these two events, however distant they may be from one another, belong to the same broader historical dynamic. The young interpreter's diary entry thus illustrates the diverse array of connections that linked the war of 1870 and the Commune to many regions of the globe.

The Paris uprising did not produce waves of revolution, as in 1830 or 1848. But there were many entanglements. This is understandable for an event that took place in a great power weakened by military defeats, an event that reverberated through a European and imperial space marked by earlier revolutions. These connections could be direct and consciously thought out. But they could also be indirect yet effective. These, too, are part of the vast configuration within which the Commune took place, and which it partly brought into existence. Part I, therefore, aims to reconstruct the urban, national, transnational, imperial and global scales within which these events unfolded – with particular attention to the last three, which are less well known. For the Commune, so powerfully rooted in the French national destiny, was also a global moment in the 1860s and 1870s – a dimension that left a marked imprint on its forms and on what followed.

1

In the Name of the 'Universal Republic'

On 28 March 1871, as the Commune was officially proclaimed, a remarkable watchword was issued. 'You will surely arrive at the next goal', announced an address from the Central Committee: 'the Universal Republic'. Was this just wishful thinking? And how far was the Commune really connected to the social, republican and national-liberation struggles of 1848–71? For anti-Communard critics, there was no doubt on this score: 'Foreigners: that is what the Paris insurgents are, for the most part.'[1] In their view, the Paris uprising was a cosmopolitan movement that had pulled together the dregs of humanity from all four corners of the earth. The judgement they passed was highly exaggerated, but it nonetheless drew on the visible presence of foreigners – including foreign fighters – in Communard ranks.

The question of the Commune's positioning remains unsettled, with regard to its place both in French history and in the global history of revolutions. In his masterful book *The Birth of the Modern World*, the historian Christopher Bayly emphasises, for instance, the synchronies between the revolutions, revolts and civil wars of the years 1848–60. He also tends to integrate the Commune into this trend, albeit mentioning it only briefly. In his more structural analysis of the nineteenth century, Jürgen Osterhammel identifies more autonomous sequences of

1 'Le chevalier d'Alix', *Dictionnaire de la Commune et des communeux* (La Rochelle: Thoreux, 1871), p. 25.

revolution or rebellion (imperial crises, revolutions). Within this framework, the Commune appears as a more isolated 'local interlude'.[2] We need, therefore, to take a closer look.

In this chapter, the focus is trained largely on transnational fighters. These protagonists demonstrate the seductive power of the insurgent French capital, and influenced both the course of events and the way these events were perceived. In this sense, transnational Communards offer insight into how the Commune tied together, or not, with the political and social struggles of previous decades.

We will begin, as has become common in the study of the Commune, with the Franco-Prussian War and the transition to the Third Republic, in order to trace the influx of foreign volunteers who came to fight in September 1870 in the name of the republican cause and the freedom of peoples.[3] From there, we will be able to address the presence of non-nationals in the Paris uprisings, and its significance.[4] Then we will consider another important connection, namely the support that various groups offered from abroad, particularly that of the International Workingmen's Association (IWMA) and its sections.

The War of 1870–71: Garibaldi's Army

On 19 July 1870, France fell into the trap set for it by Minister-President Bismarck over the disputed succession to the Spanish throne, as it declared war on Prussia. A vast military mobilisation was set underway. In the German-speaking countries, the German General Staff managed

2 Christopher Bayly, *The Birth of the Modern World, 1780–1914* (Oxford: Wiley-Blackwell, 2004); Jürgen Osterhammel, *The Transformation of the* World: *A Global History of the Nineteenth Century* (Princeton, NJ: Princeton University Press, 2014), p. 558.

3 See, for instance, Walter Bruyère-Ostells, *La Grande Armée de la liberté* (Paris: Tallandier, 2009); Gilles Pécout, 'The International Armed Volunteers: Pilgrims of a Transnational Risorgimento', *Journal of Modern Italian Studies* 14: 4 (2009), pp. 413–26; Hervé Mazurel, *Vertiges de la guerre. Byron, les philhellènes et le mirage grec* (Paris: Les Belles Lettres, 2013); Maurizio Isabella, *Risorgimento in Exile: Italian Émigrés and the Liberal International in the Post-Napoleonic Era* (Oxford: Oxford University Press, 2009); Alexandre Dupont, 'Une Internationale blanche. Les légitimistes français au secours des carlistes (1868–1883)', PhD dissertation, Université Paris-1 (2015).

4 These issues are raised in Jacques Rougerie and Sylvie Aprile, eds, *La Commune et les étrangers*, *Migrance* 35 (2010).

to bring together, in less than a month, nearly 630,000 men from Prussia, Northern Germany and the southern states on the eastern French front. Troubled by the failure of an important military reform in 1868, France faced greater difficulties. At the beginning of August 1870, it had only 244,000 men on this same front, out of a potential strength of 640,000 men. Today, the importance of this conflict for the construction or consolidation of each of these nation-states is well known. In posing as the side that had been attacked, Bismarck sought to mobilise the German nationalist feelings expressed in 1848, and thus drive forward the unification 'from above' of a German Empire under Prussian leadership. Napoleon III, for his part, hoped to put an end to the political tensions of the 'liberal' Empire of the 1860s, and to hammer home the success of the plebiscite of 8 May 1870. Tellingly, as soon as the war was declared, the French press adopted inflamed tones, and demonstrations were set in motion to cries of 'Down with Prussia!' or 'Long live the emperor!' – to the great displeasure of the republican, radical and socialist opposition. The reactions varied according to time and place. But overall, between nationalistic ardour and resigned acceptance of the conflict, the population, which was confident in its army, went along with the decision. The Franco-Prussian conflict thus appears to have been an important moment in the crystallisation of national feelings, albeit divided ones.[5] On the French side, this phenomenon became more pronounced after the fall of the regime and the proclamation of the Republic on 4 September 1870. The army was reorganised on the initiative of the new minister of the interior and war, Léon Gambetta. A more binding call-up of troops brought the French army's strength up to 579,000 men. The influx of volunteers was also on the rise. Some 30,500 of them were recorded in September – indeed, so much so that, from 11 September, the War Ministry invited the *préfets* to 'moderate the onrush' of volunteers.[6] The war rekindled French patriotic ardour.

5 Stéphane Audoin-Rouzeau, *1870. La France dans la guerre* (Paris: Armand Colin, 1989); on these divides, see Robert Tombs, *France (1814–1914)* (London: Longman, 1996).

6 François Roth, *La Guerre de 1870* (Paris: Hachette, 2004). In nineteenth-century France, a *préfet* was the state's chief administrative officer in a *département*, appointed by the central government. The *préfets* embodied the authority of the Ministry of the Interior in the provinces, supervising local administration, policing and the implementation of national decrees. On the influx of volunteers, see Service Historique de la Défense (SHD), Lx 138, 'Circulaire du ministère de la Guerre', 11 September 1870.

Still, the conflict was not limited to the Franco-German border alone. This war between two of the main European powers prompted numerous reactions and diverse expressions of support, starting in the summer of 1870. From that moment on, armed volunteers engaged alongside French troops – and nor was this transnational volunteering a specifically republican affair.[7] But this was nothing like the scale of the movement that got underway when the republican dimension of the French war effort came into view. Marseille offers a good observation post: on 13 September, the *département*'s committee of national defence received a proposal from Barcelona to create a Spanish legion, while Italian volunteers flocked to the area. On 16 September, less than two weeks after the change of regime, the *préfet* of the *département* of the Bouches-du-Rhône wrote to his colleague in Nice: 'Do not direct any more Garibaldian volunteers to Marseille: the ones we have are already an embarrassment.'[8]

Giuseppe Garibaldi had indeed very quickly offered his help to France. Such support was not insignificant: the Italian patriot and republican, aged sixty-three and now having retired to the island of Caprera, enjoyed a vast notoriety. The 'Hero of the Two Worlds' had forged his legend with his red-shirted volunteers in Brazil and Uruguay in the 1840s; his participation in all the struggles of the Italian Risorgimento in 1848; during the Expedition of the Thousand in 1859–60; and in 1867 in the attempt to capture Rome, from which he was repelled by the French. In 1864, when he came to London, 500,000 people turned out to cheer his arrival.[9] The Government of National Defence was initially unsure about his offer. His intervention posed problems to the Italian government, the consuls feared an influx of 'less than honourable' volunteers, while Garibaldi's own anticlerical positions risked alienating the men of the Church and the more Catholic populations of western France. Yet the name Garibaldi alone brought a wider dimension to the conflict, not to mention the fact that a significant proportion of the Italian population did not understand – despite the Italian government's own caution – that such an offer of aid might be

7 Simon Sarlin, *Le Légitimisme en armes. Histoire d'une mobilisation internationale contre l'unité italienne* (Rome: École française de Rome, 2013).

8 Archives départementales (AD), Bouches-du-Rhône, 1M711, Événements Politiques.

9 Lucy Riall, *Garibaldi: Invention of a Hero* (New Haven, CT: Yale University Press, 2007).

refused.[10] Ultimately, French veterans of the wars in Italy set off to seek out Garibaldi, and took him to France via Corsica. He made a triumphant entry into Marseille at the beginning of October before heading to Tours.[11] Gambetta entrusted him with an army corps mostly made up of both foreign and French *francs-tireurs*, whose field of operation covered the area from the Vosges to the border. The 'Army of the Vosges' led by the Italian general quickly rallied a significant proportion of the influx of foreign volunteers.

The archives held at the Service historique de la Défense allow us to outline the landscape of this first influx of volunteers and its impact.[12] Accurately estimating this army's real strength remains an arduous task. According to François Roth, it was composed of 6,000 men in November, and 20,000 in January. At the moment it was disbanded, in February 1871, it combined mobilised troops, thirty-six corps of *francs-tireurs* from the region, three corps of Algerian *francs-tireurs*, and seventeen corps of foreign *francs-tireurs*.[13] The composite Army of the Vosges was thus both national and transnational, but also imperial, as indicated by the presence of several Algerian *francs-tireurs* from Algiers, Oran and Constantine. Stirred by the outpouring of republicanism in the colony's cities after 4 September, most of them were French settlers. There were also 'Europeans' (such as the 'Hanoverians of Algiers'), and, according to the terminology of the time, the *indigènes* – the native population, ostensibly the 'sons and relatives of Qaids and other native leaders, loath to join the *tirailleurs*, and other Arabs attracted by the prospect of loot'.[14] As for non-nationals as such, the majority were Italians who had fought

10 Centre des Archives Diplomatiques du Ministère des Affaires Étrangères (La Courneuve, CAD), Correspondance Diplomatique (CP), Italy.

11 After the change of regime, faced with the German advance, part of the government remained in Paris, while a 'Delegation' was sent to Tours to coordinate military operations.

12 The Service Historique de la Défense (SHD) is the French Ministry of Armed Forces' archival service, which holds extensive military and administrative records.

13 SHD, LG1, Armée des Vosges.

14 In French Algeria, the term *indigènes* most often referred to the colonised Muslim population (Arabs and Berbers), who were considered subjects of France rather than citizens, and thus excluded from full political rights; colonial usage could also refer to 'Israélites indigènes' prior to (and in tension with) the Crémieux decree, which is examined later in this book. The quotation is from a dispatch from the republican committee of Bône, 15 September 1870. Archives Nationales d'Outre-Mer (ANOM), FM F80 1681, dispatches sent to the Ministry of the Interior.

alongside Garibaldi in the Italian campaigns of 1848–49, 1859–60 and 1866. For instance, Luigi Frapolli, a former military engineer and high-ranking Freemason, had taken an active part in the Italian campaigns in Modena, before heading into exile in France. There he became a colonel in the Army of the Vosges. Garibaldi's sons Menotti and Ricciotti led the 3rd and 4th brigades. Most of the fighters, whether those of the volunteer legion (800 men), Garibaldi's guides (104 people) or the legion of Garibaldian *francs-tireurs* (514 men), are surely less well known. Many Poles also added their number to these ranks. The circuits through which they arrived were plural. For instance, on 16 January the French ambassador in Vienna reported: '100 to 200 Poles want to go to Vienna at their own expense to serve under General Frapolli'.[15] We do not know if they ever arrived, but their commitment certainly fits with the Polish independence struggles of 1830, 1848 and 1863. Swiss, Belgians and, as we have seen, Spaniards were also present. By September, according to the French representative in Madrid, 'many young Spanish people' had come to the consulates in order to fight under the French flag. Republicans sought to form a Spanish legion, whose enrolment began on 1 October.[16] As Spanish republican MPs would say, this involvement echoed the struggle between republicans, liberals, conservatives and Carlists that followed the 'Glorious Revolution' of 1868. In smaller numbers, other *francs-tireurs* came from Rio (Brazil) and Montevideo (Uruguay). Most of them were French residents of these climes, but there were also Uruguayan fighters, such as Lieutenant Colonel Flores, son of the former president of the Republic.

Tracking fighters by nationality alone is not easy. Units could often include several different ones: for instance, the corps of Garibaldian *chasseurs*, presented as Italian, involved, in addition to the thirty-three Italians, ten people from Poland, three from the United States, three from Chile, and one from Algeria. And nationality does not always account for individual trajectories. Of the thirty-three Italians in question, one came from Buenos Aires.[17] One telling case is that of the Greek volunteers, according to military estimates amounting to a few dozen: one part came from Alexandria, through the intermediary of the French

15 CAD, CP, Austria-Hungary.

16 CAD, CP, Spain; SHD, 'Armée des Vosges par corps francs'.

17 SHD, Lx 138, Records from 24 February 1871.

community in the Egyptian city, alongside French volunteers and Italian republicans.[18] They bore the traces of the Mediterranean links of the early nineteenth century: former *carbonari* came to Tunisia and Egypt from the 1820s, while a number of Greeks left as a result of the economic transformation of the Ionian islands or the Greek–Turkish War of 1820–29.[19] Often, the trajectories of individuals are so varied that the question of their country of origin loses its meaning. This is especially true of those who had fought on several fronts throughout their lives, such as Garibaldi or Octavian Fariola, a democratic-republican born in Switzerland who took part in the Italian wars, fought alongside the Irish Fenians, and then in the American Civil War. Here we would more accurately speak of 'transnational' volunteering (rather than an 'international' engagement, which would imply a relation between simple, pre-given national frameworks).

That said, not all of the foreign volunteers were in the Army of the Vosges. Some could not reach it, while others were transferred elsewhere. The Irish Legion of commander Dyer Mac-Adaras, which arrived via Britain, was integrated into a 2nd foreign regiment before being directed to Bourges.[20] Veterans of the War of Secession (1861–65) were another case in point. There were Americans, but also many Frenchmen who had fought for the North.[21] For instance, Marcel Deschamp had been a *democ-soc* in 1848, fought alongside Garibaldi in Italy in 1860, and then took part in the American Civil War. In September 1870, he embarked for France, formed a free corps, and fought on the front in November.[22] Thus, there was a vast web of connections and movements. Many Romanians were also present – 900 according to the Prussian consul's count. Some came through Constantinople, and others via

---

18 CAD, CP, Egypt. These military estimates are clearly understated. Historian Xenia Marinou estimates the number of Greek volunteers actually engaged in the conflict at 1,500. See X. Marinou, 'La Grece dans la guerre franco-prussienne; les multiples facettes du mouvement de volontaires grecs', in Nicolas Bourguinat, Alexandre Dupont and Gilles Vogt, eds, *La Guerre de 1870, Conflit Europeen, Conflit Global* (Montrouge: Éditions du Bourg, 2020, pp. 169–82).

19 Julia Clancy-Smith, *Mediterraneans: North Africa and Europe in an Age of Migration (c. 1800–1900)* (Berkeley, CA: University of California Press, 2011).

20 SHD, Lx 125.

21 National Archives and Record Administration (NARA), Washington, RG 84.

22 Michel Cordillot, *Eugène Varlin, internationaliste et communard* (Paris: Spartacus, 2016).

Vienna, thanks to the intercession of an aid committee founded by a Greek priest. The call to arms – judging by the translation proposed by the ambassador – invoked the memory of 1848 and the liberal struggles for Romania's autonomy. Finally, from northern Europe, there were also a few dozen Danish volunteers. They had come through Le Havre, before being incorporated into the Army of the North.[23] They again had different motives: according to their letters, studied by Gilles Vogt, they had more to do with Francophile than republican sentiment, but also a hatred of Prussia linked to the loss of Schleswig after the Second Schleswig War of 1864. The presence of non-national volunteers from a wide range of backgrounds is clear.

Also of interest are the journeys made by these different volunteers. The position of the French authorities varied according to volunteers' country of departure. Officially, the Government of National Defence could not support people setting off to France – because of treaties, the need to respect the neutrality laws of the countries concerned, or even Prussian intervention. French representatives abroad quickly told prospective fighters that France could not give them financial encouragements. At first, they nevertheless made clear that France would be honoured to receive such support and that, if these volunteers so wished, they could come, albeit at their own expense. But from October onwards, Tours called for a halt to the sending of volunteers, both French and foreign.[24] Some flows were indeed blocked, but the general movement, having already been set underway, continued.

The financing of volunteers' transport, equipment and food was sometimes taken in hand by individuals who committed part of their fortune. More often, though, it was owed to public subscriptions, which spread both from the beginning of the conflict and again after September, sometimes with the help of newspapers or local elites. Such support was not always owed to French initiative, and there were also gestures of

23 Gilles Vogt, 'Vive la France, vive le Schleswig danois? La question du Schleswig face à la guerre franco-allemande (1870–1871)', paper given at the 'La nationalité en guerre' conference, 3–4 December 2015. See also Vogt's 'Neutres face à la guerre franco-allemande (1870–1871)? Diplomatie et dynamiques d'opinions dans les États de Suisse, de Belgique et du Danemark', PhD dissertation, Université de Strasbourg (2018).

24 In October 1870, 'the Government of Tours' referred to the delegation of the Government of National Defence sent to Tours after the siege of Paris, tasked with directing the war effort and administering the unoccupied departments of southern and western France.

solidarity to aid their travels: the rail company in northern Spain, for instance, supported volunteers heading to France.[25] Such organisation in advance of their arrival reminds us that, even if it was small in scale or sparked debate locally, this circulation of volunteers could often draw on strong social-political roots in the countries from which they arrived.

Once they had embarked, there were, then, several interconnections that helped to organise the volunteers' movements. Ports (Le Havre, Nantes, Bordeaux, Marseille) were obvious conduits. But, faced with the military authorities' growing mistrust, access routes became more diverse. In the Mediterranean, the volunteers passed through islands such as Corsica and Malta, but also through Algeria: for instance, ten fighters who came from Cartagena, a hotbed of the Spanish Republican struggle of 1868, travelled through Algeria.[26] On the ground, some republican-run city halls were used to build networks for welcoming arriving fighters, such as Toulouse for the Spanish volunteers, or Marseille: since September, that port city had been swept up in a radical movement and opposed the Tours government's decisions. Although, on 8 October, the Ministry of Foreign Affairs had informed the consul general of Egypt that it was necessary to put a stop to despatches of volunteers to France, Alphonse Esquiros – the new 'higher administrator for the Bouches-du-Rhône' – wrote to this same consul that he was touched by the dedication of the volunteers and asked for more to be sent. Marseille's city hall thus collected the 4,000 francs from the subscriptions submitted in mid-October, to be used for equipping these men.[27] A few days later, the same Esquiros asked the French representative in Constantinople whether it was possible to form an 'Eastern guerrilla'. As a result, the Ministry responded firmly to the French representative on 10 October, that he should 'take no account of what Esquiros writes or may write to you'.[28] Marseille thus served as the main point of entry for Mediterranean volunteers, and did so against the advice of the

25 CAD. It passed them off as emigrants headed towards America.

26 AD, Bouches-du-Rhône, 1 M 712, dispatch from Oran, 5 October.

27 CAD, CP, Egypt.

28 CAD, CP, Turkey, telegram. As a result of the political transition, the ranks and functions of the French diplomatic staff were disrupted. In many cases the main established representatives left their posts, and were replaced by their second-in-command. The same person could hold several titles in just a few months. This complexity explains the hesitation in the official terms I use here, even while trying to stay as close as possible to the language of the actors as it appears in the sources.

government. To understand this, we must look back to the municipal situation at the end of the Second Empire. During the 1860s, several cities had elected republican councils and defended their autonomy. With the defeat of 1870 and the political transition, these cities gained more independence, precisely in the name of the republican ideal. In favour of national unity and continuing the war, these municipal councils nonetheless thought the Republic would be better defended from below, and by 'real Republicans'. The inflow of volunteers was thus facilitated by the ongoing political fracturing of France's territory. Once these newcomers had arrived, the army had to reckon with them, despite the persistent lack of equipment.

The question remains as to who these fighters were, and what they did. It is difficult to know this, even when we focus on the Army of the Vosges, for which we have the most data. Certain generational phenomena can be identified (with reference to the past struggles of 1820, 1848 and 1860). Beyond that, we can clearly discern engagement by engineers, members of the liberal professions, people in financial difficulties, a considerable number of artisans, and factory workers (with a certain number of workers from Le Creusot, one of the largest metallurgical centres of the period). We cannot specify the age of the troops, or say if there were peasants, but – as so often in this type of collective adventure – it would seem there was a strong social diversity among their ranks. The Army of the Vosges, in particular, stands out within the French army. Composed of mobilised soldiers and *francs-tireurs*, its institutional status was uncertain. It was further distinguished by its troops' colourful clothing, which had great symbolic value (Garibaldian red shirts, Polish peaked caps, Hungarian hussar jackets), but also by its fighting techniques.[29] Imbued with the guerrilla imaginary, it fought a partisan war made up of surprise raids, like the one at Châtillon-sur-Seine on 19 November, in which Ricciotti Garibaldi took 200 German prisoners.

Self-sacrifice and death in battle were particularly valued in its ranks.[30] If zeal and heroism are familiar parts of the military

29 Maxime Du Camp, 'Souvenirs littéraires', *Revue des Deux Mondes* 51 (1882), pp. 783–816.

30 As shown by the combatants' letters, kindly forwarded to me by Mark Lause, author of *War for the Republic in the Age of Blood and Iron: A Transnational View of Giuseppe Garibaldi's Army of the Vosges and the Transformation of Republicanism, 1870–1871* (New York: Verso, 2022).

vocabulary, they took on a special meaning here. Articles, proclamations, administrative exchanges and letters were imbued with the romantic language of commitment characteristic of the early nineteenth century. The soldiers claimed to be acting in the name of the 'Universal Republic' – a term whose development had been in full flourish since the revolutions of 1848 – or even that of the older idea of 'the freedom of all peoples'. Reasons for engagement were surely more diverse: the need for money, lack of work, thirst for adventure, or any other reason. And the letters exchanged, within the army and with the outside world, are sometimes banal. Yet this discursive framework remained the common backdrop for their actions. Giuseppe Garibaldi wielded it more effectively than anyone else. On 30 January, writing of a retreat to Chalon and Chagny, he declaimed: 'Well, you saw them again, the heels of these terrible soldiers of Wilhelm, you young sons of freedom! In two days of fierce fighting, you wrote a glorious page in the annals of the Republic.'[31] This perception of the cause was reflected in the particular affective link that bound the men together and to their leader. These ties were described as friendly, filial, paternal or fraternal.[32] Garibaldi, to whom the men built up – in the words of Admiral Penhoat – 'a kind of cult', was the main figure concerned, but the phenomenon was also felt within the companies: for instance, the soldiers of the 'Nantes company' stopped fighting after the dismissal of their lieutenant, 'having engaged with him and not with others'.[33] We also find this kind of charismatic link later, in the Commune – one owed not so much to the inherent quality of the leaders themselves as to the fact that they managed to embody both these values and the shared trial of combat. Such a bond also existed in the rest of the army, yet its basic principle was that the structure and the functions should continue even if the individuals were replaced. In the case of the Army of the Vosges, this relationship was primary. This also implied a particular way of functioning: punishments for infractions were severe (those found guilty of theft could be subject to the death penalty), while both military and civilian forms of reward – which seemed in their view of little value compared to the

31 Roth, *La Guerre de 1870*, p. 370 (speech upon a retreat to Chalon and Chagny).

32 On these links in the twentieth century, see Gilles Bertrand, Catherine Brice and Gilles Montègre, eds, *Fraternité. Pour une histoire du concept* (Grenoble: CHRIPA, 2012).

33 SHD, LG1, undated petition.

determination to enter history – were rejected. Not everything worked out well: its way of functioning also led to problems managing supplies and attempts at desertion. But participation in the Army of the Vosges surely offered a singular experience in the Franco-Prussian War.

What impact did these transnational volunteers have on the conflict? Their numbers were small. Taking the most generous estimate at 50,000 men, the Vosges Army, at the height of the mobilisation, represented only 6 per cent of the total strength of the French army; as for the share of foreign volunteers among all troops, they represented less than 1 per cent of the total number of combatants.[34] These proportions correspond to the figures that can be found for other conflicts in this period: during the Italian wars of 1859, foreigners amounted to between 1.2 and 1.3 per cent of volunteers enrolled in the Sardinian army.[35] A similar proportion – though exact figures are hard to establish – can be found in Garibaldi's Expedition of the Thousand and in the American Civil War.[36] The modes of recruitment, the language mobilised and the social profiles of the volunteers are also similar. The transnational volunteer movement in the war of 1870 is thus characteristic of the time. Perhaps this was more marked by the closure of states, and more routinised than previous nineteenth-century movements of this kind.[37] Similarly, it is possible that the variety of past fighting experiences represented was greater, given France's symbolic importance.

In these circumstances, it seems that their military impact was low. There were some famous feats of arms, such as the victorious defence of Dijon by 12,000 men in January 1871. But these remained isolated cases given the scale of the defeats – not forgetting that the Army of the Vosges

34 At the end of the conflict, the authorities counted, among all troops, 36,500 French volunteers in the various *corps francs* and *corps de francs-tireurs*, and 5,530 foreign volunteers (SHD, Lx 138, *corps francs*).

35 According to Anna Maria Isastia, *Il volontariato militare nel Risorgimento. La partecipazione alla guerra del 1859* (Rome: Stato Maggiore dell'Esercito, Ufficio Storico, 1990).

36 First estimate based on the list published in *Gazzetta ufficiale del Regno d'Italia*, 12 November 1878. For the US case, see Don Doyle, ed., *Secession as an International Phenomenon: From America's Civil War to Contemporary Separatist Movements* (Athens, GA: University of Georgia Press, 2010); David T. Gleeson and Simon Lewis, eds, *The Civil War as Global Conflict: Transnational Meanings of the American Civil War* (Columbia, SC: University of South Carolina Press, 2014); Farid Ameur, *Les Français dans la guerre de Sécession (1861–1865)* (Rennes: Presses universitaires de Rennes, 2016).

37 One account of the invocation of neutrality laws is Walter Bruyère-Ostells, *Histoire des mercenaires (de 1789 à nos jours)* (Paris: Tallandier, 2011), Chapter 3.

consisted not only of foreigners. But their symbolic impact was considerable. Garibaldi's aura was fully apparent in 1871: he was elected in five *départements* in the February 1871 elections, while the epithet 'Garibaldian' was used by the French volunteers from several large cities.[38] The battles waged by the Army of the Vosges clearly gave an international scope to the French republican cause, in France and abroad, and this dimension would endure even afterwards. This did not come without a degree of reluctance on the part of French authorities, as evidenced by the mistrust shown by the army, the Government of National Defence and the National Assembly when Garibaldi came to Bordeaux on 13 February 1871. These reactions illustrate the play of tensions between this transnational dynamics of the conflict and the greater structuring of the national territory that was now underway.[39]

The Commune's Cosmopolitan Fighters

This movement would also have its effects on the Commune. Since the territory in which the Army of the Vosges operated was not covered by the armistice treaty, for a time it continued fighting even when the other fronts had come to a halt. In February, after Garibaldi's resignation, the Minister of War entrusted its command to Admiral Penhoat, who declared himself 'Breton and Catholic'. When the armistice expired, the admiral received the order to dismiss the army. The operation lasted several weeks, and on 16 March the Army of the Vosges was disbanded.[40] Most volunteers returned home. Yet many stopped along the way, to the point that the army expressed concern about the acts of brigandage being committed in the centre of France. Some left to fight in the cities that had launched insurrections (sometimes called 'Communes'), from Lyon to Marseille and Le Creusot. Still others joined the Paris Commune. Such was the case of Maximilien Rogowski, a veteran of the Polish uprising who had become a costermonger in Marseille.

38 Riall, *Garibaldi*.

39 To this could be added the post-war trials aimed at discrediting this army. According to Lause, this convergence of interests explains the relative fading of this mobilisation subsequently.

40 LG1, Admiral Penhoat, 'Rapport sur le licenciement de l'armée des Vosges', March 1871 (undated but after 18 March).

Commander of the Polish cavalry in Garibaldi's army, he put himself at the disposal of the Commune at the end of March: we later find him in command at the redoubt at Hautes-Bruyères, and then at Fort Ivry.[41]

Yet the paths of the Commune's transnational fighters were more varied, as evidenced by the case of General Cluseret.[42] The son of an infantry colonel, he graduated from Saint-Cyr military academy in 1843, and participated in the repression of the Parisian workers in June 1848. After a spell in the Bureaux Arabes in Algeria, he joined Garibaldi's side in the Italian company, before fighting in the American Civil War where he earned his general's stars, and then in the Irish Fenian Rebellion (1867).[43] Back in France, he befriended the bookbinder Eugène Varlin, joined the First International, and frequented revolutionary journalistic circles. Condemned by the liberal Empire, he returned to the United States, and then came back to France in response to the events of 4 September 1870. He took part in the Communes of Lyon, Marseille and finally Paris.[44]

The example of this general, both French and American, reminds us of the difficulty of identifying 'foreign' fighters, especially at a time when the legal and social definitions of the foreigner remained blurred.[45] Let us remember that we are using this term here to refer specifically to individuals who fought on other battlefields. In other words, this includes French exiles from after 1848 or 1851, who fought on other fronts and were now returning; people who arrived in France after the failure of an insurrectionary movement in their home country, and who mobilised again in 1870; and foreign volunteers from other countries to fight in France in the name of the Republic. This is a delicate matter to unpick insofar as it is necessary to be able to trace individual trajectories,

41 Entry in the *Dictionnaire biographique du mouvement ouvrier*, founded under the direction of Jean Maitron, at maitron-en-ligne.univ-paris1.fr – henceforth *Maitron*.

42 On Cluseret, see Florence Braka, *L'Honneur perdu du Général Cluseret. De l'Internationale au nationalisme* (Paris: Hémisphères Éditions et Maisonneuve & Larose, 2018).

43 The Bureaux Arabes were administrative structures in Algeria set up by General Bugeaud in 1844 and run by French military officers, exercising broad discretionary powers.

44 Archives de la Préfecture de police de Paris (APP), BA 1015, 'Gustave Cluseret'. See also his correspondence in Archives Nationales (AN), 441 AP, fonds Cluseret.

45 Gérard Noiriel, *État, nation et immigration. Vers une histoire du pouvoir* (Paris: Belin, 2001).

especially given that the Paris Commune represents a particular situation. The 'second siege' made it harder for people to move around, and the Commune's more revolutionary and social character also put some of them off.[46] Moreover, the capital in any case had a sizeable contingent of foreigners, at a time when France was one of the few lands of immigration: the Paris census for 1866 counts 104,074 foreigners, or 5.8 per cent of the population (compared to 1.7 per cent of the overall French population). These were mainly Germans, Belgians, and to a lesser extent Swiss, Italians, Poles and Luxembourgers. Among them were several hundred refugees from previous European political struggles (the Polish insurrections, the Italian wars of liberation, and so on).[47] Many mobilised, at least in part, on behalf of these causes, sometimes even with a generational leap: a son of a Polish refugee from 1831, and himself born in Vierzon, Auguste Okolowicz had been a soldier during the Crimean War (1854), then singer and director of the Casino Cadet in Paris, before becoming captain of the French volunteer legion during the first siege. During the Commune he was elected commander of the 90th Battalion, before being incorporated into Dombrowski's staff.[48] Lastly, from September, fighters from abroad arrived in the north of France or in Paris. From London, the Italian Amilcare Cipriani reached the French capital on 4 September, together with other compatriots in a 'Cibaldi legion'. Born in Rimini, this 'travelling clerk' had fought in Crete in 1865, where he befriended Gustave Flourens – so it is not too surprising that we find him as a guard in Flourens's battalion, and in combat at the end of November 1870 at Maisons-Alfort. After a brief stay in Lyon, he returned to Paris on 22 March to submit himself to Flourens's command: he became lieutenant colonel of his battalion.[49] These other trajectories do not mean that there was no connection with the Garibaldian army of winter 1870: even apart from the soldiers who came over to its side, the Paris Commune soon proposed to Garibaldi that he should become commander-in-chief of the

46 Masaï Mejiaz, 'Les Frontières du Paris insurrectionnel (1870–1871)', master 1 dissertation, Université Paris-13 (2011).

47 Delphine Diaz, *Un asile pour tous les peuples? Exilés et réfugiés étrangers en France au cours du premier XIXe siècle* (Paris: Armand Colin, 2014).

48 Entry from the *Maitron.*

49 SHD, 8J, 19e conseil, dos 81, interrogatoire A. Cipriani, 29 June 1871. Gustave Flourens (1838–1871) was a French revolutionary leader and writer, and a leading military figure in the Paris Commune.

National Guard, and many of the Parisian insurgents cast themselves as 'Garibaldians'. So, connections did exist, but such gaps between them made the Paris Commune more of a second surge within the broader volunteer movement.

Can we venture to estimate how many of these fighters there were? Official figures, such as the estimate of 'around 1,725 foreigners' arrested, given by General Appert, are of little use, as are the lists of foreigners who participated in the Commune established after the fact.[50] The definition of 'foreigner' therein is flexible, being based both on combatants' names and on the Versaillais assumption regarding the 'cosmopolitan' character of the Commune.[51] In contrast, many who were 'foreigners' in terms of their civil status were perfectly well integrated into Parisian society and were rarely identified as foreign: the few Germans in Paris who took part in the Commune, despite the expulsion order of 28 August, were clearly not considered Prussian in their local neighbourhoods. They often found themselves behind the barricades, like many others, through networks of neighbours, political affinities, friendships or intimidation, and are thus not really part of our corpus.[52] Conversely, legions of foreigners were formed to take part in the Commune as 'national' units: such was the case of the Belgian federal legion, commanded by Colonel Melotte, a railway worker from Belgium who had moved to Paris in 1867.[53] A thirteen-strong battalion of Polish chasseurs was also formed, led by a violinist who had become a refugee

50 Rougerie and Aprile, 'Introduction', pp. 4–13. There are generalised clarifications on 'foreigners' in the above-mentioned overviews, in which we often find the same figures (Frankel, Dombrowski, Wroblewski, and so on). Some more targeted studies appear in Marianne Guichaoua, 'Les Étrangers dans la Commune de Paris : entre mythe et réalité', master's dissertation, Université Paris-1 (1983); Philippe Chollier and Natacha Lillo, 'Les étrangers durant la Commune de Paris', in Natacha Lillo, ed., *Histoire des immigrations en Île-de-France, de 1830 à nos jours* (Paris: Publibook, 2012), pp. 43–8. The lists compiled after the fact are to be found in the Archives Nationales or in the archives of the Préfecture de Police.

51 Robert Tombs, 'Les Versaillais et les étrangers', in Rougerie and Aprile, *La Commune et les étrangers*, pp. 34–42. On the caution that needs to be adopted towards onomastics – in a completely different context – see Claire Zalc, *Dénaturalisés. Les retraits de nationalité sous Vichy* (Paris: Seuil, 2016).

52 Mareike König, 'Les immigrés allemands à Paris (1870–1871)', in Rougerie and Aprile, *La Commune et les étrangers*, pp. 60–70. This is probably also the case for the Luxembourgers. See Henri Wehenkel, 'Les communards luxembourgeois', in ibid., pp. 73–81.

53 SHD, Ly94, corps francs de la Commune.

in Paris after the 1863 insurrection. Some units had a largely symbolic value, while others were far from idle: an Italian legion formed in mid-April at the Prince-Eugène barracks fought in Vanves in May. Naturally there was no immediate link between one's position as a refugee and one's Communard commitment. The Polish case illustrates this.[54] The 'colony', as it was then called, boasted around 2,000 people, bringing together – to put it schematically – both the more conservative exiles of the insurrection of 1830–31 and the more liberal or radical ones from that of 1863–64. Having more or less blended together by the time the Empire had come to an end, this grouping split again at the moment of the Commune. Some of them joined Versailles – out of political affinity (for instance, Prince Poniatowski) or as a repayment for their refugee status (such as Count Zamoyski, who supported the Republic founded on 4 September). Others joined the Parisian uprising in the name of France: as champion of Poland, emancipation or nationhood, in the broader quest for the liberation of peoples. Among these we find famous personalities such as Jaroslaw Dombrowski, and other less-well-known ones like Alexis Plaskowski, a staff lieutenant in the 17th legion.

This last example is of interest, as it suggests that there were also transnational volunteers in the Paris National Guard. For the sake of convenience, my focus here will be on non-nationals. From September 1870, enlistment for the Guard – extended to able-bodied men between twenty and forty years of age – in principle concerned only French citizens. Under the siege and then during the Commune, however, involvement owed much to interpersonal ties (whether among neighbours, family members or those linked by their jobs) and reputation, especially if they had military experience. It is thus unsurprising that non-nationals were present, whether because they were well established in their neighbourhoods, because they had participated in military organisations in early 1870, or because they had known military records. This, however, does not allow us to put a figure on their total number, either. To get an idea, I conducted a study into three battalions: the 184th (13th legion), the

54 For details on this, I refer the reader to my article, 'Être étranger sous la Commune, les soubresauts du rêve nationalitaire au xixe siècle', in Rougerie and Aprile, *La Commune et les étrangers*, pp. 23–33. As for the Poles, there is an old and abundant Polish bibliography which unfortunately I am unable to consult: Krystyna Wyczańska, *Polacy w Komunie Paryskiej* (Warsaw: Wyd. MON, 1957 [expanded edn 1971]); and Jerzy W. Borejsza, *W kręgu wielkich wygnańców (1848–1895)* (Warsaw: KiW, 1963).

128th (11th legion) and the 3rd (8th legion). Unfortunately, their rolls of names almost never indicate their place of birth or how they had arrived at this point. Judging by their names – which is a poor indicator – we get the impression that foreigners had a weak presence among the mass of *fédérés*. The observation at least invites a correction of a certain optical illusion, by recalling that the vast majority of fighters were indeed Parisians (born in Paris or arriving as a result of interregional migration), well established in their local neighbourhoods. However, some transnational volunteers did crop up in general archival research, such as Malato Di Cornetto, a trader born in Trapani (Italy), involved in the Italian struggle in Sicily in 1848. Present in Rome with Garibaldi and commander of the barricade on the faubourg Saint-Martin in December 1851, Di Cornetto participated in the battles for Italian unification in 1859 before again settling in Paris. A National Guardsman during the siege, he was elected captain of his battalion (the 160th) under the Commune.[55] These examples moreover suggest that a number of these fighters were part of the National Guard's hierarchy. Using information from the *Maitron* biographical dictionary, Jean-Louis Robert notes that, out of 481 foreign Communards listed whose military record is mentioned, about half have a rank (senior officer, officer or non-commissioned officer).[56] It is difficult to draw firm conclusions, given the aforementioned challenges in defining a 'foreigner'. But more targeted studies confirm this impression. The Île-de-France guerrilla movement, studied by Rémy Valat, included six 'Polish ex-officers', designated as such, out of the 300 people involved. Nor was the imperial dimension absent: of the three officers, one was Polish and another a former Zouave; of the seventeen NCOs, two were Polish and three came from the Algerian troops.[57] Such overrepresentation is, again, understandable: in their elections, National Guardsmen tended to choose people they knew and trusted – whether well-known

55 APP, BA 1170.

56 Jean-Louis Robert, 'Les étrangers communards dans le Maitron', in Rougerie and Aprile, *La Commune et les étrangers*, pp. 47–59.

57 The Zouaves were colonial light infantry regiments of the French army, first raised in Algeria in the 1830s. Though initially recruited among local populations, they soon came to be composed mainly of European settlers. Rémy Valat, 'La Garde nationale sédentaire de Paris pendant le premier siège et la Commune. Un essai d'armée populaire révolutionnaire? (12 août 1870–29 août 1871)', PhD dissertion, Université Paris-1. This work is unfortunately unfinished: I thank the author for generously supplying me with the data collected.

militants, former soldiers with experience in France's armed forces (in Crimea, Italy, Algeria or Mexico), or foreign fighters who, in principle, combined combat knowhow with the symbolic significance of previous struggles. These conditions, of course, could overlap.

This phenomenon appears more clearly in the upper ranks, such as among legion colonels (each arrondissement had one legion). Taking replacements into account, we can establish a list of twenty-two names covering the whole period.[58] The paths of these individuals are easier to follow, and not surprising: those elected as colonels included workers or employees who fought during the siege and who were elected legion leaders (such as Charles Grill, 2nd legion); political militants, sometimes Freemasons, members of the International or of some other organisation (Nicolas Thévenot, 4th legion); and those who had fought several campaigns in the French army (Maxime Lisbon, 10th legion). Finally, three correspond to the proposed definition of transnational combatants. Adolphe Spinoy, colonel of the 3rd legion, was a former captain among the Belgian army. Ludomir Matuszewicz was the son of a refugee from the Polish uprising of 1831. He pursued a long career in the French army on various fronts (he was awarded the Légion d'honneur in 1864), and, at the end of the Empire, he was close to the republicans and revolutionaries. As for Joseph Lucien Combatz, he was the very image of the transnational volunteer in the second half of the nineteenth century. Born in Savoy before its annexation to France, this telegraph officer participated in the Italian wars in the late 1850s. In 1866, he was commander of the Garibaldian legion in the Tyrol, then, the following year, of the Garibaldian Corps in Crete. Later, in September–October 1869, he led the Aragonese volunteers in the Sierra de Ronda. Present in Paris during the Franco-Prussian War, Combatz became delegate of the twenty arrondissements. Under the Commune, he was appointed director of telegraphs on 19 March. After he expressed his wish – citing his previous experiences – to take part in the fighting, Rossel named him head of the 6th legion on 12 April.[59] Like several other officers, he was thus not elected, but appointed by the general staff of the War Ministry.

58 I have drawn on the lists available at the SHD and the one prepared by Robert Tombs.

59 All information from *Maitron*. On Combatz, see SHD, 8J, 6e conseil de guerre, dos 679.

These men's place is even more visible at the level of the high command. There were four successive War Delegations: Brunel, Eudes, Duval, and then the last one, successively held by Cluseret, Rossel, and briefly Delescluze. Of these four, the longest tenure – from 3 to 30 April – went precisely to Cluseret, as we have seen. A similar observation can be made for military commands. Taking into account the 5 May reorganisation, which clarified the previous arrangements, the Blanquists Eudes and Bergeret were in charge of the 1st and 2nd reserve brigades. La Cecilia was in 'command of the centre', Wroblewski the left flank, and Dombrowski the right. The latter was a prominent figure in insurgent Paris. Born in 1837, Jaroslaw Dombrowski was the son of a wealthy Polish landowner, and educated at the military academy in St Petersburg. While stationed in Poland, he took up the cause of the 1863 insurrection. He fled after his arrest, drew close to the German socialists, and then went to Paris. He was elected once to the Representative Committee of Polish Emigrants; his second bid for election failed because of his overly 'advanced' ideals. In 1870 he became close to the IWMA. During the siege, he tried to set up a cavalry detachment, which the French general staff rebuffed. After a spell in Lyon, Dombrowski returned to Paris, and to the Commune, to offer his services. He was proposed and then elected head of the 11th legion. After the defeats of 2–5 April, he was appointed commander-in-chief of fortified Paris by the Central Committee. These commanders, moreover, appointed their staffs, within which other such foreign fighters are also visible. For instance, Wroblewski surrounded himself with Roman Czarnowski, a refugee from the 1830 insurrection, and Alexander Wernicki and Stanislas Roczinski, both players in the 1864 Polish uprising. Dombrowski's staff is better known, as it was the subject of a thorough dossier produced by the Versaillais.[60] This document allows us to identify several logics of composition. The first is that of the dynamics of the war.[61] This is demonstrated by the presence of Georges Benoît, a man from Lyon who took part in the Army of the Vosges and was introduced to Dombrowski by Garibaldian soldiers. Other members, met in the 11th

60 APP, BA 1039. Dossier produced between 1871 and 1875.

61 SHD, Ly 2, on Dombrowski's staff: the list varies during these events, but in May it included: Favy, Lavigne, Jammet, Barilier, Weyl, Hutzinger, Laurier, Coussin, Tilliard, Huet, Rozalowski, Hefter, Vincent, Heinsze, Dufaud, Carlo, Potapenko, Borneiwski, Segoillot, Bercot, Mangnan, Favre, Bailla, Monchau, Lesnuer, Mayet, Grazidou, De Givry and Devillier.

legion, include his colonel, Étienne Favy, who worked at a tailor's, and Antoine Lavigne, 'man of letters and metallurgist', a former army sergeant. Others, by contrast, were more related to the Polish experience of 1863. Vladimir Rozalowski, a refugee after this insurrection, was a member of the steering committee of the Union of Polish Emigrants before the war; Auguste Okolowicz, whom we have already met, opened the Casino Cadet hall to meetings of Poles during the siege; Alexis Plaskowski, another refugee from 1863, was a staff lieutenant in the 17th legion, before going on to join Dombrowski.[62] No doubt, the participation of these transnational fighters and their relationship with earlier struggles is more visible at this command level. These men were, moreover, highly skilled in wielding the romantic language of commitment, and elicited the same types of bonds as those I noted earlier when discussing the Army of the Vosges. '[Dombrowski] is truly loved by his men', testified citizen Johannard during one session at the Hôtel de Ville, after having underlined 'the admiration that the National Guard feels for this general'.[63] These foreign soldiers were certainly not the only ones who embodied democratic or republican struggles of that time: one often mentioned at the time was Léo Frankel, a Hungarian goldsmith who had travelled through France and the German-speaking countries. A former Lassallean, he had joined the International. During the Commune, he was a member of the Labour and Trade Commission. Together, these men thus ensured the link between the Commune and the 'Universal Republic' – an association certainly reinforced by the presence of the other, harder-to-identify transnational fighters who took part in the people's army of Paris.

Arising with Starvelings from Their Slumber: The International Workingmen's Association

These long-distance connections also relied on more organised channels – starting, of course, with the International Workingmen's Association (IWMA). This is not unrelated to what we have seen thus far: many transnational combatants were Internationalists (like Gustave Cluseret and Jaroslaw Dombrowski), while others simply declared themselves as

62 Information completed with the aid of the *Maitron* records.

63 *Journal officiel de la Commune (JOC)*, 25 April 1871.

such: the label 'Internationalist' was in wide circulation during and after these events.[64] The question of the role that this Workingmen's Association played in the unfolding of the Commune has given rise to an abundance of analysis and interpretation. Founded in London in 1864, the IWMA had several predecessors, from the Fraternal Democrats (1845–48) to the International Association (1856–59).[65] Its creation also derived from the by-products of British Chartism, the growth of the British trade unions, the presence of political refugees in London, and the acceleration of industrialisation and worker-migration in the 1850s. Significantly, it was born of the meeting in 1862 between French workers, delegates to the International Exhibition in London (their trip was financed by the Second Empire), and British trade unionists – and then, a year later, members of the committee for aid to Poland. From an institutional point of view – in a sense, seen 'from above' – the IWMA consisted of a general council, located in London, which included personalities such as the former Thuringian tailor and '48er refugee Johann Georg Eccarius, the former Chartist Alfred Walton, the French mutualist chiseller Tolain and the communist economist and philosopher Karl Marx. The Association grew through sections that developed throughout Europe, mainly in Great Britain, France, Belgium and Switzerland, and, to a lesser extent at first, in Prussia, Italy, Spain, the Netherlands and the United States.[66] The International, as it began to be called in 1870, was simultaneously a trade-union organisation, an international political association and a site of reflection and exchange. Its aims encompassed the project of a union of nations, the promotion of the freedom of peoples, and the defence of proletarians – who 'have no country' – against speculation and their common oppressors.[67] The themes and debates that existed within it

64 This explains the palpable hesitations in many of the *Maitron* entries.

65 Arthur Lehning, *De Buonarroti à Bakounine. Études sur le socialisme international* (Paris: Champ libre, 1977); Fabrice Bensimon, 'L'Internationale des travailleurs', *Romantisme* 163 (2014), pp. 53–62.

66 Marcello Musto, *Workers Unite! The International 150 Years Later* (New York: Bloomsbury, 2014), p. 68. See also the altered chronology proposed in Fabrice Bensimon, Quentin Deluermoz and Jeanne Moisand, eds, '*Arise Ye Wretched of the Earth!*': *The First International in Global Perspective* (Leiden: Brill, 2018), p. 387. A more general overview appears in Mathieu Léonard, *L'Émancipation des travailleurs. Une histoire de la Première Internationale* (Paris: La Fabrique, 2011).

67 This was in contrast to the later period, marked by the 'national phase' of the international labour movement'. See Marcel Van der Linden, 'The Rise and Fall of the

cannot, therefore, be reduced to the famous and singular opposition between Karl Marx, who promoted a unification of the workers' movement, and Mikhail Bakunin, who favoured a more anarchist position emphasising the autonomy of its sections. Several points of view were exchanged during large congresses of delegates from various countries, such as the one in Geneva, the one in Lausanne, and the famous Basel Congress in 1869, which asserted support for the collectivisation of the means of production.

Seen from below – from the IWMA's sections, from working-class environments, and from republican or socialist circles – the picture is rather different. Its sections were often just one among many formal or informal organisations – to which they had to adapt through hybridisations, splits and exclusions.[68] The mobilisation of the International's cause could here be used to support local or workplace issues, such as the fight against haggling or against employers' use of less-well-paid foreign workers. From this point of view, the IWMA represented a moral ideal and a form of transnational working-class solidarity. For example, the IWMA enabled a free loan system for supporting strike actions: the financial support provided during the strikes of the Parisian bronze workers (1867) and the building workers of Geneva (1868) quickly became landmarks which attracted a large number of members towards it. Given the diversity of its categories of thinking, as well as the plurality of workplace experiences, a vast mosaic unfolds here: the IWMA was constantly in the process of creation. A kind of Internationalist discourse took hold through the newspapers, via both internal and external debates, and by way of these 'high points' of action. But its overall coherence rested largely on the authorities' fears, and on the mass-media logics that exaggerated its strength. By the end of the 1860s, they had already made it into a myth, enveloped in legends like that of the extraordinary riches said to be in its coffers, even as the IWMA struggled to balance its finances.[69]

First International: An Interpretation', in Fritz Van Holthoon and Marcel Van der Linden, eds, *Internationalism in the Labour Movement, 1830–1940* (Leiden: Brill, 1988), p. 325.

68 No one has shown these slow processes and recompositional movements better than Marc Vuilleumier in his work on the Swiss case: *Histoire et combats. Mouvement ouvrier et socialisme en Suisse (1864–1960)* (Lausanne: Éditions d'En Bas, 2012 [2004]).

69 On these financial flows, legends and transnational connections, see Nicolas Delalande, *La Lutte et l'Entraide. L'âge des solidarités ouvrières* (Paris: Seuil, 2019).

The French case is typical of this history. The first French branch of the IWMA was established in Paris's rue des Gravilliers, in March 1865. It soon met with success, after the great strikes of the bronze workers and tailors of Paris in 1867. In 1870, it had several tens of thousands of members in France, divided into different centres (Paris, Rouen, Lyon . . .), to which must be added its sympathisers who were not members.[70] This momentum was undermined by a vigorous response from the Empire, and even more so by the declaration of war – though we should not exaggerate the effects that this had on its grassroots organisation in Paris. The IWMA's Paris sections were active during the siege, alongside other organisations with which they at least somewhat overlapped (the vigilance committees and the Central Committee of the twenty districts, the National Guard, and even municipalities such as that of the 17th arrondissement). The passing of the months from November 1870 to May 1871, says Jacques Rougerie, was marked by complex ebbs and flows, while these sections adopted various tones: sometimes Blanquist, sometimes republican, sometimes associationist.[71] As we know, the IWMA did not play any role in the events of 18 March: on the other hand, its members, mostly skilled workers from the capital (shoemakers, bronzeworkers, clerks), were present among the cadres of insurgent Paris: they numbered some thirty-two of the Commune Council's ninety-two members (with Varlin in charge of supplies, and Vaillant of education). Many counted among the officers of the National Guard.[72] Clearly, these affiliations may have played a role in the idea of the Parisian revolution establishing wider connections. But this was not unique to the Internationalists, and nor was this reflex automatically shared among their ranks. The historiography has shown that it is difficult to describe these men's role by focusing on this attachment alone: during the Commune, these 'Internationalists' were just as much tradesmen, militants within their own workers' clubs, insurgent Parisians, Frenchmen at war, inhabitants of their neighbourhoods . . .

70 Jacques Rougerie, 'Les sections parisiennes de l'AIT' and Jean Maitron, 'Les effectifs de l'AIT', in *La Première Internationale. L'institution, l'implantation, le rayonnement*, proceedings of the colloquium (Paris, 16–18 November 1964) (Paris, Éditions du CNRS, 1968).

71 Jacques Rougerie, 'L'AIT et le mouvement ouvrier à Paris pendant les événements de 1870–1871', in Rougerie, *1871. Jalons pour une Histoire de la Commune de Paris* (Paris: PUF, 1973), pp. 3–102.

72 Léonard, *L'Émancipation des travailleurs*.

The IWMA nevertheless did play a role as a transmission belt for the Parisian adventure. This was not initially owed to the General Council. At first hesitating in the face of military events, the Council soon came out in opposition to a German war of 'conquest' after the proclamation of the French Republic on 4 September, and then the announcement of the Prussian plan to annex Alsace-Lorraine. The General Council welcomed the advent of the Republic on 9 September (though declaring that it would not launch any action until after peace was achieved), while in Prussia the Brunswick Committee opposed the war starting from 5 September, before it was repressed by the Prussian authorities. After 18 March, it followed the events closely, but also with a certain circumspection. The elections on 26 March – and above all Paris's patriotism, which appeared as a replay of 1789–94 – were particularly surprising to Karl Marx. It is not that the General Council was uninterested: on 23 May, Marx commented: 'The principles of the Commune are eternal . . . they will present themselves again and again until the working class is liberated.' But it remained cautious. It followed in train with the mistrust shown by the London trade unions, also citing the difficulty of obtaining any reliable information. Moreover, even once the decision to support it had been made, the IWMA's address was slow in coming, due to Karl Marx's ill health.[73]

The International's support was most evident at the level of its sections, but also that of other associations to which they were more or less linked. In London, republican meetings were held from September onwards, notably by the Universal Republican League and the International Democratic Association.[74] On 16 April, the latter organised the large rally in support of the Commune in Hyde Park, with fanfare, flags and slogans ('Long live the Commune!' and 'Long Live the Universal Republic!'). The text of the congratulatory address is eloquent:

> We salute you in the name of the Universal Republic, and we thank you from the bottom of our hearts for the great work you are

73 *Le Conseil général de la Première Internationale (1870–1871)* (Moscow: Progress/ Paris: [23 rue Royale, 75008], 1975). Sessions from 11 April to 30 May.

74 Meetings and petitions combined the defence of the republican ideal with a call for the recognition of the new French regime. Among the main supporters were Richard Congreve and Charles Bradlaugh, who organised several meetings in September–October in Liverpool, Manchester, Leeds, Sheffield, Newcastle and in Scotland (Edinburgh, Aberdeen) (CAD, CP, England).

> accomplishing at this moment. . . . We, the people of London, assured that you are fighting for the freedom and emancipation of the whole of humankind, extend to you the hand of friendship and fraternity.

Addresses were issued and support meetings held in Geneva and Brussels, but also in Florence, Barcelona and German cities such as Berlin, Elberfeld, Hanover, Hamburg, Leipzig and Dresden.[75] August Bebel, a member of the newly formed SDAP, just elected to the Reichstag, cautiously defended the Commune on 11 April by making the link with the German situation and what he called the problem of 'big finance'.[76] The tone varied: it was more democratic in the democratic society of Florence, more socialist and working-class when sections of the International were involved. Some groups really did support it while others did not, often based on very local issues: here the Paris Revolution found itself wrapped up in the vast patchwork of workers', republican, radical and socialist associations, who came from diverse sources and had complex interactions among themselves. The Commune was also sometimes associated with ongoing struggles,[77] such as that with the English-language section of the IWMA in New York City, which combined in a single 'sympathy meeting' the Paris Commune and the locked-out miners of Pennsylvania.[78]

These resonances call for a final comment. The Commune, as we have seen, stands largely in continuity with the 'democratic and social' Republic that emerged in 1848 and 1850–51, particularly in Paris. Yet this perspective – with the theme of the union of classes, the associationist project, and the organisation of labour and rejection of industrial servitude – was not only 'French'. Historians have recently re-evaluated the importance and role of the radical cultures of the first two-thirds of

75 The Geneva meeting brought the revival of the IWMA in Switzerland. Marc Vuilleumier, 'La Première Internationale en Suisse', *Revue syndicale Suisse* 9 (September 1964), pp. 3–15.

76 Roger Morgan, *The German Social Democrats and the First International (1864–1872)* (Cambridge: Cambridge University Press, 1965), p. 215; and August Bebel, *Aus meinem Leben*, vol. II, 'Die erste Session des Deutschen Reichstags', zeno.org

77 The years 1870–1871 indeed saw a surge in the number of strikes; see *Marx-Engels-Gesamtausgabe* (MEGA), *Erste Abt. BD 21, Apparat, Einführung*, 1131, pp. 10–11.

78 Procès-verbaux de la Commune de Paris, 23 May 1871.

the nineteenth century. Thus, in Britain, the Chartist movement took root in various professional and spatial universes, and was enriched by a social dimension – did they not call, in 1850, for 'the Charter, the Land and the organisation of labour'?[79] Similarly, in the German-speaking countries, the post-1848 associationist movement, with its radical tendencies, was very powerful (*Radikaldemokratie*). While it was partly influenced by the Lassallean movement, the diversity of its political and social situations and proposals cannot be reduced to the latter.[80] However, neither were these experiences wholly unknown to each other. Though intermittent, connections did exist: intellectual ones, through the press and full or partial translations of books; physical ones, through the migration of refugees and the highest-skilled workers; and historical ones, according to shared experiences (around 1789–93, 1830–31, 1848–50, and so on).[81] No doubt the transnational dimension is less apparent, as these currents were rooted in the daily experience of work. But these intersections help explain both the existence of a certain similarity between these movements and the fact that, although it appeared unique, the Commune was able to resonate among them.

It cannot be said that the Commune was part of a vast and coherent movement of social and political resistance. But it is equally difficult to argue that it was just a 'hapax' (a one-off event), far removed from the republican, socialist or social currents of the post-1848 years. On the contrary, it had been closely linked to them: to the Italian wars from 1848 to 1866, the Polish insurrections of 1848 and 1863, the American Civil War of 1861–65, the rise of social conflicts and strike movements in the late 1860s . . . The Commune therefore spotlights this vast space of republican and socialist dissent in the years from 1848 to 1870 – though clearly crystallising it in its own distinctive way.

79 Malcolm Chase, *Chartism: A New History* (Manchester: Manchester University Press, 2007).

80 Thomas Welskopp, *Das Banner der Brüderlichkeit. Die deutsche Sozialdemokratie vom Vormärz bis zum Sozialistengesetz* (Bonn: Dietz Nachfolger, 2000).

81 F. Bensimon, 'L'Internationale des travailleurs'; Friedrich Lenger, 'Beyond Exceptionalism: Notes on the Artisanal Phase of the Labour Movement in France, England, Germany and the United States', *International Review of Social History*, 36: 1 (1991), pp. 1–23.

2
Cracks in the French Imperial Nation-State

This transnational horizon is not the only one in play. The movements of these volunteers – and the growth of international working-class organisation – were clearly aided by the conditions of exchange characteristic of the 1860s. Indeed, both were also a reaction against some of the economic, political and military forms that were now becoming established. But the series of events that was later termed the 'Terrible Year' also sprang from other – perhaps more unexpected – networks of long-distance relations. This time, these connections concerned the strengthening of nation-states in the era of what is inaccurately called history's 'first' wave of globalisation.

As with other countries, historians have begun to show how France – long presented as the nation-state par excellence – was above all a complex tangle of both internal and external dynamics. The 1850s and 1860s marked a key moment in this process. The nation-state was then crystallising, with strengthened means of surveillance, the practice of universal male suffrage, the development of national identity, the increased interconnection of the national territory by railways and – at a more anthropological level – a slow shift in the thresholds of sensitivity to violence. But these were also the years of technological advances in transport (ships, trains), armaments, and communications (the telegraph), and this brought an increase in trade and an acceleration of migration and the international circulation of capital. These latter processes were accompanied by the development of free trade, as well as the renewal of imperial endeavours – whether through conquest or informal empire.[1] These two phenomena, the consolidation of the nation-state and globalisation, went hand in hand – albeit not without discrepancies between them.[2] Through their shock effect, the events of 1870–71, and in particular the Commune, put to the test these multifaceted interactions, which they also brought more clearly into view. Conversely, these interactions explain the diversity of the echoes produced by these events, and why they had the potential to affect so many countries and regions.

War, the Commune and International Law

In autumn 1870, as defeats mounted, the territory of metropolitan France was thrown into tumult. The Republic found itself in a situation of dual power, divided between Paris and Tours, which weakened decision-making. The north-east of its territory was under German military occupation, which would eventually turn into administrative control. In the south, republican cities organised themselves into leagues like the 'Ligue du Midi', which were intent on defending the nation regardless of what Paris, Tours or Bordeaux might think.[3] Contrary to Gambetta's fears, these leagues did not express secessionist yearnings inspired by revolutionary federalism. Rather, they brought together several cities in

1 There is now an abundant bibliography on this theme. See Emily Rosenberg, ed., *A World Connecting (1870–1945)* (Cambridge, MA: Harvard University Press, 2012); Kevin H. O'Rourke and Jeffrey G. Williamson, *Globalization and History: The Evolution of a Nineteenth-Century Atlantic Economy* (Cambridge, MA: MIT Press, 2001); Pierre Singaravélou, ed., *Les Empires coloniaux (XIXe–XXe siècle)* (Paris: Points, 2013); Martin Geyer and Johannes Paulmann, eds, *The Mechanics of Internationalism: Culture, Society, and Politics from the 1840s to the First World War* (Oxford: Oxford University Press, 2001).

2 On this dual process, I would refer the reader to my own work: Quentin Deluermoz, 'La 'France' dans la décennie 1860: une perspective globale', in Deluermoz, *Le Crépuscule des révolutions (1848–1871)* (Paris: Seuil, 2012). For a broader perspective, see Quentin Deluermoz, ed., *D'ici et d'ailleurs. Histoires globales de la France contemporaine* (Paris: La Découverte, 2021); Christophe Charle, *La Crise des sociétés impériales (1900–1940): Allemagne, France, Grande-Bretagne. Essai d'histoire sociale comparée* (Paris: Seuil, 2001).

3 Sudhir Hazareesingh, 'Republicanism, War and Democracy: The Ligue du Midi in France's War against Prussia (1870–1871)', *French History* 17: 1 (2003), pp. 48–78.

the name of municipal autonomy and republican defence, seeking to uphold the integrity of part of the nation. However, their existence heightened tensions with more conservative groups and certain rural areas, further undermining the much-hoped-for 'national unity'. The Gambetta and then Thiers governments dug in their heels in order to hold back these emerging cracks. The threat, however, played out both inside and beyond France. Revealingly, the diplomatic activity of Thiers, and that of Jules Favre, underscored the importance of pre-existing networks of relations, which both extended and sustained the French state. The famous lawyer, an eloquent Republican opponent of the Second Empire and aligned with the Liberal ranks, had served as minister of foreign affairs since the Government of National Defence.

The case of international law is exemplary in this respect, all the more so as it is emblematic of the shifts in the 1850s–60s evoked in this chapter's introduction. Many of the prevalent practices and principles in the eighteenth century, informed among other things by the works of Emmerich de Vattel and Hugo Grotius, remained operative: the theme of civilisation and barbarism, the law of nations, restraint in the use of violence . . . But many shifts had also taken place. For example, the revolutionary and Napoleonic wars of the beginning of the nineteenth century had shattered the theme of the 'just war', according to which states should not use more force than necessary.[4] This was followed after 1850 by a broad restructuring of this terrain, as evidenced by several indicators. The rise of interdependencies brought a proliferation of multilateral and international conventions. Moreover, during the American Civil War the 'Lieber Code' (1863) was established: it formalised for the first time, albeit not without ambiguity, a set of customary rules of war. It was soon adopted in several other cases: notably by Prussia, which took it up at the moment of war in 1870.[5] New institutions and treaties also came into effect, with the foundation of the Red Cross in 1863, and later the Geneva Convention, signed in 1864 by twelve nations including Prussia and France. More universal in its application, it provided for the first time an a priori guarantee of protection for wounded

4 David A. Bell, *The First Total War: Napoleon's Europe and the Birth of Warfare as We Know It* (Boston: Houghton Mifflin, 2007).

5 John Fabian Witt, *Lincoln's Code: The Laws of War in American History* (New York: Free Press, 2012).

soldiers in all wars.[6] Lastly, jurists were developing new conceptions of international law, in what was then thought to be a context of peace and lasting economic development. Seeking to articulate nationalism and internationalism – with a view to liberal reforms in the economic sphere – their ideas, published in the new *Revue de droit international et de législation comparée*, sought to combine peace, economic development, humanitarianism and the justification offered by 'civilisation'. This more formalised concept was beginning to be used by the European powers – at least rhetorically, and where it suited their own needs. It also updated the terms of the pre-existing division between 'civilised countries', for which international law was intended, and the others, which could therefore be colonised. For the former, the official objective remained that of limiting the violence of war between civilised societies in the long run.[7]

This emerging body of law and the language that accompanied it were present in the Franco-Prussian conflict. The Geneva Convention was often invoked. The Red Cross worked on the ground, and with it many international ambulances and hospitals considered neutral.[8] It is thus unsurprising that the belligerents used these tools to influence international relations. Denunciations and counter-denunciations fed intense diplomatic activity throughout the whole conflict. On 31 August 1870, the French minister of foreign affairs communicated to his counterpart in Washington his rebuttal of the 'Prussian government's allegations regarding the non-compliance with international law by the French who allegedly shot at parliamentarians and ambulances'. He cited, in contrast to these allegations, cases of Prussian abuses: he claimed that these were characteristic of general Prussian conduct which should see it 'banished from the ranks of civilised people'.[9] The rival

6 This protection existed in the eighteenth century but relied on prior agreements between military leaders ahead of specific wars. I thank Renaud Morieux for these clarifications.

7 Martti Koskenniemi, *The Gentle Civilizer of Nations: The Rise and Fall of International Law (1870–1960)* (Cambridge: Cambridge University Press, 2004).

8 Bertrand Taithe, 'The Red Cross Flag in the Franco-Prussian War: Civilians, Humanitarianism and War in the "Modern" Age', in Roger Cooter, Steve Sturdy and Mark Harrison, eds, *War, Medicine and Modernity* (Stroud: Sutton, 1998), pp. 22–47; Rachel Chrastil, *The Siege of Strasbourg* (Cambridge, MA: Harvard University Press, 2014).

9 NARA, Washington, M53. The Americans' position was rather particular, since the German states entrusted them with the protection of their interests in France during the conflict.

evidence and arguments were the lifeblood of the press, as well as of diplomatic cabinets. Prussia criticised attempts to violate laws of neutrality when, given its accumulation of defeats, France increasingly denounced 'Prussian atrocities'.[10] 'Prussia is wilfully deaf to world opinion', Jules Favre sententiously noted in an 8 November 1870 circular intended to provoke the intervention of the great powers. Referring to civilisation, humanity, or to the world's gaze was certainly nothing new, but at that moment these terms acquired a specific meaning: they were based on the idea of an international public opinion (with the development of the press), a sensitivity to humanitarian concerns (heightened after the Crimean War), and a conception of law less moral than positive.[11] This so-called 'modern' legal order was supposed – at least as far as Jules Favre hoped – to be more effective.[12]

This same reference was in fact deployed as early as September 1870, after the advent of the Republic, in order to support the requests for official recognition of the new regime. Admittedly, the continuity of the state as a legal person is guaranteed independently of its regime. But this validation nevertheless remained necessary to maintain the country's juridical identity. The United States was the first to recognise the French Republic, on 6 September.[13] Then came Italy, Greece, Portugal, Spain and several Latin American republics, including Chile, Peru and Argentina. Russia and Austria-Hungary took a more wait-and-see approach, as did Britain, which took the lead in a 'league of neutrals'.[14] The diplomatic

10 On the occupation, see Guillaume Parisot, 'L'Invasion et l'Occupation allemandes dans le département de l'Aisne (septembre 1870–octobre 1871)', master 2 dissertation, Université Lille 3 (2009); Claude Farenc, 'Problèmes de l'occupation allemande en Champagne (1870–1873)', PhD dissertation, Université Paris-1 (1976); Olivier Berger, 'Les "Crimes de guerre" et exactions de l'armée prusso-allemande dans les départements de l'Essonne, des Hauts-de-Seine et du Val-de-Marne (1870–1871)', master 2 dissertation, Université Paris-4 (2006).

11 On the French Revolution, see Suzanne Desan, 'Foreigners, Cosmopolitanism, and French Revolutionary Universalism', in Suzanne Desan, Lynn Hunt and William Max Nelson, eds, *The French Revolution in Global Perspective* (Ithaca, NY: Cornell University Press, 2013), pp. 86–100.

12 It was designated using this term. See 'Note sur les sujets de la confédération qui veulent des passeports pour retourner en Allemagne', 21 July 1870 (CAD, 2QO 58).

13 M. Wahburne to J. Favre, 7 September 1870, Foreign Relations of the US (FRUS), p. 116.

14 On these balances, see the classic Pierre Renouvin, *Histoire des relations internationales, Vol. II: De 1789 à 1871* (Paris: Hachette, 1954).

exchanges with the main power of the day after October 1870 were strained: they were divided between the requirement for compliance with the laws of neutrality, over which Prussia kept a watchful eye, and the call for a reaction deemed necessary in the name of these principles of civilised war, supported by France. 'This position', the French minister of foreign affairs insisted, 'cannot continue without seriously undermining the feelings of humanity for which England has always been renowned.'[15] The appeal to what was called a 'civilised' justice became more insistent after the announcement of the Prussian plans for the annexation of Alsace-Moselle. States other than France also referred to it: on 8 September, the sultan of the Ottoman Empire offered to intervene 'as a member of the Concert of Europe' to help preserve the integrity of French soil, 'in the name of humanity and civilisation'.[16] The proposal was not wholly unselfish (there was already talk of revising the 1856 Treaty on the Black Sea), and the offer was politely rebuffed.

The recurrent invocation of international law did not stop the German states from going ahead with their military project and annexing the north-eastern part of France's territory. We know why. The logics of this body of law (with its eighteenth-century, post-Napoleonic and other variants) do not succeed one another in a neat sequence, but rather overlap. Moreover, it rarely prevents conflicts and military violence, especially when two of the main powers of the day oppose each other (remember that in six months the conflict claimed twice as many dead as the American Civil War over the same period). This does not mean it was absent from the conduct of the war. As Martti Koskenniemi notes, in reality international law and international powers neither align with nor submit to each other. On the one hand, this common legal vocabulary, which lacked the robustness of what would later be meant by 'international law', was active in the 1870–71 conflict; on the other hand, the protagonists, especially the winning side, could either not follow it or else use it to their own advantage – all the more so since this international law had no fixed orientation and was already the subject of debate before the conflict.[17] In this context, the French authorities' diplomatic

15 CAD, CP, England.

16 CAD, CP, Turkey, 8 September 1870.

17 Andrew Fitzmaurice, *Sovereignty, Property and Empire (1500–2000)* (Cambridge: Cambridge University Press, 2014).

activity can be read as a work of 'legal imagination' faced with a situation not seen since the 1850s (the occupation of one 'civilised' European power by another). It was then confronted by other points of view, such as that of the German jurists who sought to justify the annexation of Alsace-Lorraine in the name of history and these same international references.[18] This legal framework, and these principles, were just as ineffective at the London Conference of January–March 1871, which remained focused on the revision of the 1856 treaty demanded by Russia. Britain did eventually secure mention of the French case – but 'out of session', and after the capitulation of Paris. The imperial agenda here clearly won out over the continental one.[19]

A few weeks later, when the Commune erupted, Jules Favre could nevertheless use this same framework to his advantage. Faced with the events in the capital, the French foreign minister first downplayed them: according to a circular of 21 March, after these 'deplorable events', deemed the workings of 'seditionists', 'the population of Paris is beginning to feel the magnitude of the mistake it has made . . . The outcome is not in doubt.' Caution was probably called for, seeing as France was still negotiating the conditions for the application of the peace treaty, which had only recently been ratified by the National Assembly: the events in Paris risked weakening the credibility of the newly elected Chamber, and the government had to appear solid. The following month, the tone changed. At the end of April 1871, Favre emphasised the threat that the Commune – a 'formidable insurrection' – posed to the civilised world. Representatives and consuls relayed this language, which was soon echoed by that of other powers: according to the French ambassador in Vienna, all Austro-Hungarian minds were focused on France, and wished for the victory of 'a cause which is that of Order and civilisation in the world'. In depicting the Commune as a threat to the social order and civilisation, the French minister thus managed to make it into a common enemy of the established states. Perhaps his move was even more astute. In the 1860s,

18 These arguments are developed in 'Notes for Peace Negotiations' (CAD, 2QO 77). On 'legal imagination', see Martti Koskenniemi, 'What Should International Legal History Become?' in Stefan Kadelbach, Thomas Kleinlein and David Roth-Isigkeit, eds, *System, Order, and International Law: The Early History of International Legal Thought from Machiavelli to Hegel* (Oxford: Oxford University Press, 2017).

19 Prussia had threatened to support Russia against Great Britain if the question was raised. See Renouvin, *Histoire des relations internationals, Vol. II.*

Favre participated in the great debates of this period on Algeria and on the Mexican expedition.[20] He was familiar with the issues at stake in the international law of the time. One of the primary and growing problems the latter had had to confront was that of the relationship between national sovereignties, municipal law and imperial realities.[21] The proposals then envisaged took different forms depending on the country (the United States, France or Germany). Over time, a solution gradually took shape: it was agreed that these various sovereignties could be enshrined through a redistribution of international–domestic relations, and by asserting that only the national sovereignty, proper to the modern state, could not be submitted to another. By ostracising the Paris secessionists, with their municipal government, from international society, Jules Favre's reaction can thus be read as a way of reaffirming, before all parties, the foundation of French national sovereignty at a moment of acute challenge. In the heat of the event, the terms in which the question was posed were surely less precise; but this background ought not be neglected. In any case, his stance allowed him to present France as being at the forefront of civilisation's struggle against emerging threats, thereby symbolically and practically reintegrating the country into the Concert of great powers. Shaken by the war, international law thus became an important element in turning the screws on the Paris Commune, even though it defended its own existence in the name of justice – and partly, as we shall see, of that same law.

The Republic, a French 'Chapking'

The legal sphere was not the only one affected. As in the previous case, it is worth starting here from the dynamics opened up by the Franco-Prussian War. In 1860, France and Britain accounted for 90 per cent of worldwide foreign investment.[22] Paris was the world's second-largest

20 Miquel de la Rosa Lorente, 'Liberals and the Empire: Responses to French Expansionism under Napoleon III in Algeria, Cochinchina and Mexico (ca. 1858–1870)', PhD dissertation, European University Institute (2017).

21 See Stephen Sawyer, 'An American Model for French Liberalism: The State of Exception in Édouard Laboulaye's Constitutional Thought', *Journal of Modern History* 85: 4 (2013), pp. 739–71.

22 O'Rourke and Williamson, *Globalization and History*, pp. 208–9.

banking centre, and France was fully engaged in informal imperial domination: the combination of private institutions, local networks, its diplomatic role, and international banks enabled it to play a role in many non-European economies. In this context, the events of 1870–71 were indeed among those nineteenth-century European crises that had global repercussions.[23] This economic dimension also played a part in the pressure from British civil society in favour of intervention, in addition to a certain humanitarian sensibility, particularly on the part of the City. While the suspension of French trade initially benefited London's financial interests, it gradually became more of a threat. In March, according to France's representative there, the British press had become unanimous in saying that 'the Prussian government is . . . regarded as a troublemaker who does not want to leave [space] for trade, for industry, for the peaceful course of civilisation'.[24] Of course, such statements must be treated with caution. But there is no doubt that commercial and financial activity was disrupted, especially in areas where French investments were significant – the Mediterranean, Latin America and Asia. In Argentina, for example, the 'news of warfare on the continent and at sea had thrown business into disarray', and paralysed trading from August onwards. After the news of Paris's capitulation, the 'stock exchange and trading houses [were] closed, all transactions [were] suspended'.[25] The same was true in Peru, where 'business [took] a wholly expectant attitude, following the news from Europe'.[26] As in Turkey, which considered that 'its most important interests were engaged in the Franco-Prussian conflict.'

In such a context, it is understandable that several of the elements of French imperial power should have been affected – not least the diplomatic balance of power. In Mexico, where the memory of the Bonapartist expedition of 1861–67 remained strong, the government welcomed the advent of the Republic. But it put two conditions on reconciliation: the abandonment of all monetary claims and the signing of a treaty which would put France on an equal footing with

---

23 Niall Ferguson, 'Political Risk and the International Bond Market Between the 1848 Revolution and the Outbreak of the First World War', *Economic History Review* 59: 1 (2006), pp. 70–112.

24 CAD, CP, England.

25 CAD, CP, Argentina, 28 February 1871.

26 CAD, CP, Peru, 13 September 1870.

northern Germany.[27] Jules Favre refused. On the other side of the world, Siam's reaction was even clearer, and more confrontational. This kingdom, one of the most modernised Asian states of the period, had seen its influence eroded by France's expansion into the Indochinese peninsula – in particular in neighbouring Cambodia, which had become a French protectorate in 1863.[28] Early in the Franco-Prussian War, Siamese authorities let it be known that they would be willing to accept a British protectorate, with the explicit aim of weakening France's position in Cochinchina. By October, they even ostentatiously displayed their 'most exaggerated sympathies' for Napoleon III. According to the French consul, writing in March 1871, 'since our disasters, a kind of spirit of hostility against France' had taken hold – which he took as proof of 'Siamese deceitfulness'. His concern at the time was heightened by the visit of a Cambodian embassy to Siam, sent by King Norodom. Upon its return, the embassy reported that Siamese ministers had received them with hauteur, and had told them 'that France had truly fallen and that they did not fear her'. As a concrete sign of this contempt, and in open violation of the 1869 treaty regulating fishing in the Great Lake of Cambodia, the Siamese government even imposed a heavy tax on a French 'Annamite' barque – a vessel from Annam (present-day central Vietnam) under the French flag – used by the Cambodian delegation.[29] These humiliations, at least as felt by France's consuls and representatives, were also felt in the Ottoman Empire.[30] At the Sultan's court, reported the chargé d'affaires, the French Republic was mocked with the degrading sobriquet of 'Chapking' – a mocking epithet (literally 'mischief' or 'naughtiness').

More directly, many of France's debtors took advantage of the situation to suspend loan-repayment instalments, or to declare openly that they would not pay them. In Haiti, on 6 June 1871 (on this date, news of the Commune's defeat was yet not known), an annoyed consul noted:

> one cannot hide from the fact . . . that the disasters and setbacks that have beset our unfortunate country have, little by little, exercised a

27 CAD, CP, Mexico.

28 Norman Owen, ed., *The Emergence of Modern Southeast Asia: A New History* (Singapore: Singapore University Press, 2005).

29 CAD, CP, Siam.

30 CAD, CP, Turkey, letter dated 14 September.

> disagreeable influence, I would not say on the Haitian people, but on its government. . . . If it wanted to, this government could easily find the means to pay the arrears of its double debt.[31]

In general, French representatives requested the sending of a frigate in such cases, in order to practise 'gunboat diplomacy'; but at that moment such vessels were barely available. In Venezuela, while the people of Caracas expressed sympathy for the French Republic, payment of the French indemnity was also suspended. In the Ottoman Empire, the permission of the Prussian high command was even required – via London and Paris – to lift the obligations arising from the 1869 loan.[32]

The tribulations of the Japanese official Samejima Taka Nabou indicate another important area then affected: that of military technology and knowhow transfer. On 26 November 1870, the Japanese government sent France this fifth-rank official to exercise the functions of *ben-mu-chi*, 'envoy handling affairs' – a title the legate considered rather vague. He was accompanied by twelve young people who were meant to study the art of warfare there. Arriving in France in February 1871, the group were quickly moved to a new location in England 'safe from the turmoil of the war'. In the meantime, the envoy's official title changed several times, to the point that the real status of his mission was uncertain. A few months later, the mystery became clearer: two years earlier, a higher council chaired by the Mikado had decided to adopt France's programme of military instruction for the land troops, and Britain's for the navy. This mission had been interrupted following France's defeats. The Japanese foreign minister reassuringly insisted: 'this does not change anything about our opinion on the merits of the French army which has shown so much bravery against numerically superior troops' – though this had not prevented the government from attempting to amend the French–Japanese conventions in August. But the government's hesitation, at that moment, mostly played out at a different level:

31 Since 1825, France has unfairly imposed a huge debt on Haiti, after Haitians gained their independence and freed themselves from slavery. The French monarchy demanded that Haitians pay reparations to their former enslavers in compensation for the loss of their property rights. As they did not have the funds to pay, the Haitians had to take out a loan from French banks. This is why it is referred to in the note cited here as a 'double debt'. CAD, CP, Haiti.

32 CAD, CP, Turkey.

it above all intended to avoid French interference in the development of the training programme. Once the French diplomatic agent on the spot understood this reluctance, he secured final approval for the project, accepting the condition that the organisation of the training corps would not fall under the authority of the French government. He soon realised that Samejima's trip had another purpose: to recruit instructors if the opportunity arose. The changes in the envoy's official title were crucial here, as they could either permit or prevent such recruitment. With this clarified, the Japanese envoy was then able to request officers from the French War Ministry.[33] Thus, in this case, the Japanese government clearly took advantage of France's weakness to secure a transfer of knowhow that corresponded to its mode of borrowing: here, the war facilitated the process of 'modernisation without Westernisation' characteristic of the Meiji era.[34]

The Egyptian situation was even more worrying for France. A few years earlier, the khedive had established a commission of investigation, with the view to an Egyptian judicial reform in which France had played a leading role. However, in January 1871 it was abandoned. At the same time, British agents suggested to the khedive that the time had come for a British company to take over the Suez Canal: the loss of French influence was manifest. But the situation was even more serious. In the latter half of 1870, the Egyptian government had taken out two loans to repay a debt of £38 million (largely related to the funding of new infrastructure): one, for £7 million, from the Société franco-égyptienne, and the other, for £31 million, from Émile de Girardin's Société générale. Yet, following the events of summer and autumn 1870, these two firms had to defer their commitments for the months of July, September and October. They promised to honour them after the war, but this did not ameliorate Egyptian difficulties: the government was forced to issue new treasury bills and take out another loan, this time from the Ottoman imperial bank and the Oppenheim Bank. Located in Cologne, the latter was one of the major players in the industrialisation of the German Ruhr at the beginning of the century, and its leaders were close to Wilhelm I. The terms of the loan were extremely harsh (20 per cent

33 CAD, CP, Japan, 26 November, 16 February, 4 June 1870–1871.

34 Pierre-François Souyri, *Moderne sans être occidental. Aux origines du Japon aujourd'hui* (Paris: Gallimard, 2016).

interest), with revenues from the railways serving as a guarantee. The Franco-Prussian War thus proved a disaster for an Egypt already hit hard by the economic crises of 1864 and 1866 – and for France, which lost solid positions.

In this context, the outbreak of the Commune in March often appears the latest blow in a long line of setbacks. The Paris uprising threatened the republican state at a time when it was trying to stabilise itself after the February elections, an event that had been rather well received by foreign countries. So, when diplomatic correspondence did mention the Commune, it underscored how much this new upheaval further undermined the fragile confidence of the moment. In Constantinople, France's representative reported with concern on 31 March, 'The Sublime Porte could not be more upset about the persistence of the events in Paris, in that these events delay the conclusion of the loan.' Restoring the French position, he continued, would be difficult. The revolutionary events, moreover, called into question another equally essential dimension of French imperial power: religion. In Jerusalem, on 14 June, the Commander-in-Chief of the Levant reported religious tensions in the Holy City. The 'situation of France, always delicate in Jerusalem', he observed, had 'become even more difficult since the war'. It was threatened by both local dissidents, who challenged its authority, and by the Catholic nations, which sought the protection of Latin states. Now, according to these opponents, 'the protection of holy places must cease to be a prerogative of a nation that no longer respects the principle of religion and authority'. It is not known to which exact events this was referring: the Paris Commune, or the Communes in Marseille or Algiers, the latter two being better known around the Mediterranean. In any case, news of the occupations and degradations of churches by republican revolutionaries had got around – and practices considered emancipatory in France itself, as they were meant to combat religious ignorance, might in turn become a threat to French imperial power. In some regions, these attacks on religion were even interpreted as evidence of the new weakness of the metropolitan social order. In January 1871, the French chargé d'affaires in China, Julien de Rochechouart, reported that a Shanghai socialist newspaper 'took the liberty of reporting the decrees of Mr Esquiros on the banishment of religious corporations and the sequestration of their property'. He immediately had the publication banned: 'All that is published in Shanghai is more or less translated into

Chinese and knowledge of such a document could get us all massacred.' In China, too, the effects of the Paris Commune were a sensitive matter: on 19 April, the same Rochechouart noted in this regard: 'Despite their loathing of everything foreign, the Chinese nevertheless take great care to keep abreast of events in Europe and no one is as well or as quickly informed as they are.'[35] A month later, when news of the Commune's defeat had not yet arrived, he specified: 'The atrocities committed in Paris by the members of the Commune have done us more wrong than all the victories of the Prussians. Everyone anxiously awaits the result that the use of tough means will surely bring.'[36]

The French events of 1870–71 thus had global repercussions. Better than any other indicator, they concretely show – at the legal, military, economic and symbolic levels – this imperial dimension of the French nation-state. They also reveal how closely these dimensions were connected: for if the cohesion of the metropolitan territory was necessary to maintain France's power and presence on a global scale, the latter clearly in turn played a key role in the country's ability to maintain its influence and its internal cohesion.

Both Sides of the Imperial Mirror: The Tientsin Enquiry and the Kabyle Insurrection

But what was happening on the ground, especially where French imperial and colonial influence most made itself felt? Perhaps it is necessary to adopt an even more imperial viewpoint, one focused on these hierarchically organised, more polycentric agglomerations of territories. This already allows us to note the silences and the reactions that did not take place: in Senegal, the Empire was replaced by the Republic without special difficulty. In France's Indian trading posts, the announcement of the Republic frightened the British, who feared revolutionary unrest, as well as Indians concerned about their customs being put into question. But after the elections, continuity prevailed.[37] Further south, on Réunion

35 CAD, CP, China, 19 April 1871.

36 CAD, CP, China, 30 May 1871.

37 Jacques Weber, *Les Établissements français en Inde au XIXe siècle (1816–1914)* (Paris: Librairie de l'Inde, 1988), p. 1335.

Island, apart from a few proclamations published in newspapers, the echoes of these events were soon stifled.[38] A similar picture emerged in Cochinchina. The relations between Empires and metropoles, asymmetric by definition, could sometimes be rather loose. Yet in some places, the control of territories and populations was then undermined. Here I will discuss the cases of China and Algeria, as they were more visible in the archives I consulted. This time, I will try to reconstruct the vernacular perspective and the non-European historical dynamics, in order to achieve a better understanding of how these events played out on both sides of imperial domination. Far from seeking to align these regions with a metropolitan chronology, my aim is to see how these events – the war, and then the Commune – were also caught up in other power relations, retranslated into these spaces, and became part of other regional histories.

Tientsin, June 1870–June 1871: the other popular sovereignty

Let us start with the 'affair' of the Tientsin massacres, mentioned at the beginning of Part I. Tientsin is an imperial prefecture and port located at the mouth of the Hai He. About 100 kilometres south of Beijing, it was opened to foreign trade after the Second Opium War. The Treaty of Tientsin (1860) had granted concessions to Britain, France and the United States. In the context of Napoleon III's policy on religion, France was specifically responsible for the protection of Catholic missions.[39] However, on 21 June 1870, an angry crowd destroyed the church of Notre-Dame-des-Victoires, other British and American churches, and various Catholic schools and hospitals. Many Chinese converts and foreigners were massacred. The wave of anger was owed particularly to a series of rumours: for several years, writings had been circulating depicting atrocious scenes in which Europeans cut out the eyes of the

38 Jérome Quaretti, 'Échos de la Commune à l'île de la Réunion', in Jérôme Quaretti and Gilbert Larguier, eds, *La Commune de 1871. Utopie ou modernité*, conference proceedings (Perpignan, 28–30 March 1996) (Perpignan: Presses universitaires de Perpignan, 2000).

39 Pierre Singaravélou, 'Dix Empires dans un mouchoir de poche. Le territoire de Tientsin à l'épreuve du phénomène concessionnaire (années 1860–1920)', in Hélène Blais, Florence Deprest and Pierre Singaravélou, eds, *Territoires impériaux. Une histoire spatiale du fait colonial* (Paris, Publications de la Sorbonne, 2011), pp. 271–96.

dead, ate children, and tore open the wombs of pregnant women.[40] In this case, there were suspicions of abduction of children for the benefit of the orphanage. This imaginary was not unique to the region, since such cases were found in Paris in the eighteenth century.[41] But here it was adapted to the situation of European domination (Western medicine and religious rites being called into question) as well as the Chinese context (denouncing practices of witchcraft that obliterated all consciousness). Relayed by the media, this event became a 'global affair', thereby confirming for Westerners the latent savagery of the Chinese. The French consul, who was most directly concerned, lobbied after the fact for exemplary punishment. But the previously effective 'gunboat diplomacy' here again proved impossible. The emperor's reaction was slow in coming. An emissary, Tseng-Kuo-Fan, arrived on Beijing's orders to take up the case, but the investigation ground along in slow-motion. It would be over two months before some of the suspects were arrested and local mandarins were threatened with exile. Meanwhile, hostility towards Christians had not ceased, as letters from missionaries to the chargé d'affaires indicate.

The attitude of the Chinese regional and central authorities moved back and forth like the swing of a pendulum, one seemingly calibrated to the arrival of news from Europe. The French military setbacks, known at the beginning of September, slowed any decision on what sanctions should be implemented. The risk of the response becoming bogged down became a reality: the news from Europe was unclear, and came with almost a month of delay; and with winter, the ice threatened to cut off all communication with Beijing for six months. At that time, the Chinese emperor refused to proceed with the additional prosecutions requested by the Europeans. Two reasons were given: firstly, even if the whole people of Tientsin participated, it was deemed ignorant and therefore excusable; secondly, while the mandarins involved had been

40 CAD, CP, China. The account is supplemented by the documents collected in 'The Tientsin Massacre, and Documents Being Published in the *Shanghai Evening Courier*, 16 June–10 September 1870' (British Library, 9004 L2), and by the analysis provided in John Fairbank, 'Patterns Behind the Tientsin Massacre', *Harvard Journal of Asiatic Studies* 20: 3–4 (1957), pp. 480–511 (data and translations from Chinese taken from this article).

41 Arlette Farge and Jacques Revel, *Logiques de la foule. L'affaire des enlèvements d'enfants (Paris, 1750)* (Paris: Hachette, 1988).

exiled, this was primarily because they had tried to escape the wrath of their sovereign. Much to the chagrin of Western representatives (French, British, Prussian, Russian, American), the imperial decree conveying the final decision thus spoke of a domestic affair, and made no reference to France. An ambassador named Chong-Ho was nevertheless sent to Paris at the end of October, bearing a letter from the emperor. He was the man accompanied by the interpreter Zhang Deyi, whom we met in Paris at the beginning of the Commune. He arrived on 25 January in Marseille, on 3 February in Bordeaux, in Paris on 18 March, and in Versailles on 29 March.

By December the situation had calmed down: the designated culprits were punished, and the legation received 5,500 taels (45,000 francs) in compensation. But tensions returned in March. As news of the French surrender became known, added to the British difficulties in the negotiations over the Black Sea, the Chinese government published a 'note on religious missions' which directly threatened the Catholic missions in the Chinese countryside. The chargé d'affaires was wounded by the sense of distance that had developed: 'We are experiencing the most humiliating situation for our dignity', he bitterly observed; 'I am referring to the court's refusal to recognise our official existence and to grant us the customary immunities.'[42] He added that this attitude could be explained by the excesses of the Chinese character and the struggles for influence in the court, but also by 'the fading of our prestige as a result of the complications and events in Europe'. The problem was all the more serious in that the case had created ripples elsewhere. The Tientsin massacre, and then the news of the French defeats, had also had repercussions in Japan – though this was truer among the population, which was also hostile to Christianity, than in the government. The situation was so worrying that – in line with a remarkable trans-imperial solidarity and despite the ongoing Franco-Prussian War in Europe – the Prussian minister in Japan suggested to his French counterpart they should avoid possible naval clashes in the region, and instead join forces to resolve the breach opened by the Tientsin massacre: a proposal accepted by most other powers represented.[43] In such a regional and political context, the

42 CAD, China, 3 March 1871.

43 CAD, CP, England, 25 October 1870.

news of the Paris insurrection, when it was circulated in China, could only appear terribly gloomy.

For all these reasons, it is understandable that the French authorities and European governments opted for caution in the spring of 1871, when the Paris Commune was clearly in place. In April, Jules Favre maintained the French military force in Japan.[44] Then, aware of the weakness of its position, especially in matters of religion, he suggested to Rochechouart that he should compromise with the Chinese government. 'What would we say if Chong Heu [*sic*] pulled out of his hat a battalion of Chinese missionaries, roaming through our countryside and extolling the merits of Confucius?'[45] He instructed the chargé d'affaires to persuade the Chinese, through his words and his policies, that 'France comes as a friend who respects their traditions'. The French – representatives, traders and missionaries – thus expressed deep worries throughout the course of the year. They were heightened by a sense of the inscrutability of the administrative attitudes and practices of the Chinese – a perception further fuelled by the racial stereotypes of the 1860s that portrayed the Chinese as deceitful, capable of shifting in an instant from the most distant reserve to the most extreme behaviour. The cultural distance seemed considerable.

What about the Chinese side? Here the story takes a different turn. Its starting point, instead of being placed – as in a certain Western historiographical tradition – at the time of the two Opium Wars (1839–42 and 1856–60), might be set much earlier. The administrative layers that emerge from diplomatic and consular exchanges – mandarins, governors and other local officials – point more directly back to the establishment of the Qing Empire on Chinese territory in the seventeenth century.[46] Located in Beijing, the central administration consisted of the Grand Secretariat and the 'Six Councils'. Its reach was extended through multiple secondary structures: each province also had a governor, and each prefecture a prefect, both offices enjoying a certain degree of autonomy. These different levels could come into conflict with each other, and they were not divided according to Western criteria. This explains the diversity of – and

44 CAD, CP, Japan, 11 April 1871.

45 CAD, CP, China, 31 May 1871.

46 Most of the information on the Chinese Empire is taken from William T. Rowe, *China's Last Empire: The Great Qing*, vol. 6 of the *History of Imperial China* series (Cambridge, MA: Harvard University Press, 2012).

competition between – the actors supposed to take charge of the Tientsin affair. This perspective helps to make better sense of certain aspects of the case. The slowdown in the judicial process in August, for example, was also owed to the fact that the emperor's external representative, Tseng Kuo-Fan, was pitted against one of his enemies, an administrative officer involved in the massacre called Cheng Kuo-Jui. Recruited through examinations, these administrators typically served outside their native region, and often found themselves confronted with other local power structures (village chiefs, merchant guilds, local mandarins, or the famous 'literate class'). This array of authorities on the ground made up a mosaic, with an unstable interplay of different dependencies. In this context, the justification of the imperial decree, which so annoyed the representatives and consuls, should be taken seriously: the real problem for the emperor was not to punish the mandarins in response to the European demands, which would have weakened him, but indeed for having tried to escape his wrath – a motive that better fits the type of hierarchical link that could be deployed at that time between these local and imperial levels.

This decision, and the following decree on religious missions, can also be understood in a different way if we take into account other tensions within the Chinese social-political space. Even if the Chinese Empire was not experiencing the irresistible decline that has long been attributed to it, it surely was in crisis from the beginning of the nineteenth century. This was expressed in rebellions like the one in Tienstin. A Muslim revolt had broken out in the north in December, before the situation was put back under control in January. Also in December, the French consul reported a further uprising in a neighbouring province, mentioning that the leader was the 'famous' Chen No Zowai, who 'owe[d] his popularity among the Chinese bourgeoisie to his role in the Tientsin massacres'. Perhaps in this we also see the phenomenon defined by Eric Hobsbawm in terms of 'social banditry'. In any case, the reference to this leader also underlines the local roots of many of the actors involved in the Tientsin massacre, as well as the latent challenge to imperial authority from within Chinese society.

Yet the Empire's fragility was also heightened by the nineteenth-century intrusion of the Western powers, which were especially distrusted. In this context, the rejection of foreigners, and in particular of Christianity, could also be useful for the authorities. Indeed, the Christian problem had its own specific aspects. In the mid-nineteenth century the establishment of Catholic and Protestant missions, which had a long history in China, took on a more proselytising form. While China had a great diversity of religious groups, the integration of Christianity posed specific difficulties, whether the reasons were cultural (the clash between its monotheism and the Chinese gods), political (carrying with it the shadow of foreign power), or social (converts had to cut themselves off from the rest of society).[47] This helps explain these rumours in the cities and the countryside, where popular sources met with interventions by the literate classes.

Here we reach the last point: the authorities were surely not insensitive to such popular reactions, especially as they still had bad memories of the Taiping episode (1851–64), which had led to widespread secessionism in the south of the Empire in the name of Christian values.[48] The manifest sympathy towards this popular mobilisation may, moreover, have corresponded to a Confucian approach emphasising the search for balance and stability. The passage of the decree stating that 'if the whole people participated, it is ignorant and can thus be excused' is therefore not without its own significance. This attitude, the historian John Fairbank tells us, is indeed part of the 'Confucian equivalent of popular sovereignty – the doctrine that the regime not only could not ignore popular sentiment but in fact could rely upon it as a decisive source of strength'.[49] In this sense, this position was also a way for the government to draw on this source of legitimacy, albeit without endorsing the use of violence, at a moment when it was itself under strain. The threat to the missions then appears as a further possible means of restoring legitimacy while weakening the Europeans. In other words, from the Chinese perspective, each piece of news from Europe – and notably the Paris Commune – provided an opportunity for these various actors to intervene in this field of interacting forces. Clearly, Favre and Rochechouart perceived the gulf between these two worlds and, even without fully grasping it, could henceforth see the fragility of their

47 Fairbank, 'Patterns Behind the Tientsin Massacre'; Robert Bickers, *The Scramble for China: Foreign Devils in the Qing Empire (1832–1914)* (London: Allen Lane, 2011).

48 This secession led to the most terrible massacre of the nineteenth century. On the long aftermath of this conflict, see Tobie Meyer-Fong, *What Remains: Coming to Terms with Civil War in Nineteenth-Century China* (Stanford, CA: Stanford University Press, 2013).

49 Fairbank, 'Patterns Behind the Tientsin Massacre', p. 510.

position in China. The events of the war, and then in Paris, thus appear rather remote – and reinvested with the interplay of wholly different tensions.

Algeria, 1871 or 1288 AH: 'The Lord of the Worlds will demand an account'

The situation in Algeria was somewhat similar, although it was a colony and indeed the 'jewel' of the French Empire. Conquered between 1830 and the 1850s, Algeria had been French territory since 1848, in the form of three *départements* (Algiers, Oran, Constantine), each divided between civilian and military territories. The Algerian sociopolitical space was then deeply transformed by the Bonapartist policy of the 'Arab kingdom', known as the 'indigenophile' approach – though this was interrupted by the series of disasters called the 'great famine'.[50]

The events of 1870–71 brought a far-reaching upheaval in this framework. From the French point of view, they had three aspects. There was the war itself: confident in the value of troops tried and tested in Crimea, Italy or Mexico, Napoleon III sent a major share of the soldiers stationed in Algeria to the army of the Rhine. This explains the exploits of the 'Turcos' in the battles of Reichshoffen, Wissembourg and Woerth.[51] As a result, troop numbers in Algeria fell from 60,000 in July to 44,000 in August, and then to 32,000 – the greatest decline at any point in the Second Empire.[52] Algeria, moreover, served as a training ground for the least battle-hardened of the mobilised National Guards. It also received French soldiers or officers who had been taken prisoner by Prussian troops and then freed on parole (they promised not to take up arms against the enemy), though this prompted strong reactions in the colony. The Franco-Prussian War was also an imperial war.

50 Among many other works, see Kamel Kateb, *Européens, 'indigènes' et juifs en Algérie (1830–1962)* (Paris: PUF, 2001); Abderrahmane Bouchène, Jean-Pierre Peyroulou, Ouanassa Siari-Tengour and Sylvie Thénault, eds, *Histoire de l'Algérie à la période coloniale (1830–1962)* (Paris: La Découverte/Algiers: Barzakh, 2012).

51 Bertrand Taithe, *Citizenship and Wars: France in the Turmoil (1870–1871)* (London: Routledge, 2001).

52 ANOM, FM F80 1681, dépêches télégraphiques; André Corvisier, *Histoire militaire de la France*, vol. I (Paris: PUF, 1997); SHD, 1H191, 'Analyse des opérations militaires et maritimes pendant l'insurrection de 1871', report by Admiral de Gueydon to Thiers, February 1872.

The second aspect of the 1870–71 events concerned the change of regime in metropolitan France. At the end of the Second Empire, Algeria had become a major political focus of the struggles between Bonapartists, Liberals and Republicans. The latter, opposed to the 'sabre regime', favoured the complete assimilation of the colony. After September, under pressure from the Algerian defence committees who came to Tours, the minister of justice, Adolphe Crémieux, took a series of measures. The best known is the 24 October 1870 decree on the naturalisation of the indigenous Israelites of Algeria. It made the latter into full citizens who could vote or participate in the National Guard. Yet it also created a legal split within the indigenous population, making the Jews appear to be on the side of the colonisers, even while locally they continued to be considered as part of the indigenous population.[53] The second set of measures established, as had long been awaited, a civilian government in Algeria. But the status of the colony continued to evolve.[54] A more consensual division of tasks between military and civilian authorities was quickly established, and then various formulas were tried out, until the arrival in February 1871 of Louis-Henri de Gueydon, a monarchist and Catholic naval admiral, officially announced as 'CIVILIAN governor-general'.[55]

Finally, there were the reactions of the colonists in Algeria. The proclamation of the Republic had a significant impact on the community of Republican deportees of June 1848, December 1851 and 1858 (after the Orsini attack).[56] I will discuss this republican and revolutionary

---

53 Valérie Assan, 'Une minorité 'indigène' entre citoyenneté et exclusion: les Juifs en Algérie colonial', in Anne-Claire de Gayffier-Bonneville, Samia el-Mechat and Éric Gojosso, eds, *Les Minorités ethniques, linguistiques et/ou culturelles en situations coloniale et postcoloniale (XVIIIe–XIXe siècle)* (Paris: Libraire générale de droit et de jurisprudence, 2015), pp. 33–42; Laure Blévis, 'En marge du décret Crémieux. Les Juifs naturalisés français en Algérie (1865–1919)', *Archives juives* 45: 2 (2012), pp. 47–67.

54 For details, see Jean Meyer, Jean Tarrade and Annie Rey-Goldzeiguer, *Histoire de la France coloniale*, vol. I (Paris: Armand Colin, 1991), Chapter 18; Charles-André Julien, *Histoire de l'Algérie contemporaine, Vol I: La Conquête et les Débuts de la colonisation (1827–1871)* (Paris: PUF, 1964) – esp. Chapter 9, pp. 453–500); and Charles-Robert Ageron, *Les Algériens musulmans et la France (1871–1919)* (Saint-Denis: Bouchène, 2005 [1968]).

55 ANOM, FM, F80 1682, Poster (and press), Algiers, 9 April 1871 (the capital letters appear in the signature).

56 On 14 January 1858, Felice Orsini, an Italian republican and patriot, carried out a bomb attack against Napoleon III in front of the opera house in Paris.

movement later on. For now it will suffice to note that, in the large urban centres (Algiers, Constantine, Oran) and in several other localities, counter-powers were taking shape that opposed the new governmental arrangements. The actions of republican colonists or the angry mob caused the departures of the Bonapartist General Durrieu, General Esterhazy, and then the Prefect Warnier, who had been present in Algeria since 1834.[57] Next came General Lichtilin and the provisional extraordinary *commissaire* Charles Du Bouzet, until the arrival of Gueydon. With regularity and firmness, these republican colonists demanded greater municipal autonomy and a policy of immediate assimilation. Thus for several months the administration of the colony and its political legitimacy were shaken.

These upheavals were obviously not a matter of indifference for the Algerian people, the so-called *indigènes*. Noting that the choice of terms is far from neutral, we will follow Sylvie Thénault's suggestion and call the colonised populations of Algeria 'Algerians', and the others 'colonists'.[58] This choice is all the more justified in this case as the term is still mostly used in this sense. The news of French defeats had quickly become known, and was also carried by the Algerian fighters who returned to the colony, as well as by the tribal chiefs who had come to Algiers such as the bachagha, Mohammed al-Hadj al-Muqrani (henceforth Mohammed al-Muqrani).[59] Tensions could already be felt in the late imperial period, and they came out into the open in autumn 1870. They also took on a regional dimension, with movements occurring across the Tunisian border and in the Moroccan Rif.[60] Algerians' reading of what was happening – or at least, that among the Algerians who were preparing to rise up – is relatively well known, and can be specified with the help of al-Muqrani's appeals for revolt, intercepted and translated by the army. The military translations are not the most faithful, but they do allow us some sense of the insurgents' language.[61] The

57 ANOM, 12X-291, Auguste Hubert Warnier file (1810–1875).

58 Sylvie Thénault, *Violence ordinaire dans l'Algérie colonial. Camps, internements, assignations à résidence* (Paris: Odile Jacob, 2012), pp. 16–17.

59 SHD 1H 375, letter from the general commanding the south of Dellys, 6 March 1871.

60 CAD, CP, Tunisia; same in Morocco (CAD, CP, 24 October 1870).

61 SHD, 1H375, 'division d'Aumale' file. The translated letters I have used come from this file. The comparison between the originals and the translations was made possible through the kind help of historian M'hamed Oualdi.

first point, as mainly related by French military personnel, was connected to the fall of the emperor. The loss of a unique leader – whose position endowed him with a charismatic aura, and who was able to draw on the submission of the tribes – would seem to have come at great cost to the cohesion of the colony. The other elements are more present in the calls for revolt. The military defeats indicated the weakness of the occupier: 'there's not even a trace of these infidels left; they've all gone home to fight the war against the Prussians'.[62] The Crémieux decree was also ill-received. It seems to have confirmed certain Arab populations, who were contemptuous of the Algerian Jews, in their view that the new regime was weak.[63] Above all, naturalisation, correlated with the abandonment of the religious code, appeared as a possible direct threat to Islam. Finally, questions of government policy and Algiers's demands were well understood: with the end of the military regime, the policy of occupation and the ring-fencing of land would resume. 'The civilian will arrive' is a leitmotif of these letters: 'The civilian wants to take command and take revenge on Muslims', one of them insisted at the end of March 1871.[64]

The first serious incident occurred in mid-January, with the revolt of the Spahis of Ain-Guettar (Souk-Ahras circle).[65] Ready to fight in Algeria, they refused to leave their homes to head to metropolitan France. Soon subdued, their opposition cost them the destruction of their farms and the death of the inhabitants. Further unrest followed. In mid-March, the bachaga, Mohammed al-Muqrani, a descendant of an important Medjana family, sent his *mandat de traitement* and a declaration of war. On 16 March, with the support of several tribes, he attacked the town of Bordj Bou Arreridj, in eastern Algeria. The situation changed with the declaration of a holy war, on 27 March, by the son of Sheikh

62 SHD, 1H375, Letter from al-Muqrani, 27 September 1870.

63 The term 'Arab' is used here for the sake of simplicity, though it should be understood broadly, as many Berber and Kabyle groups were generally also concerned. Moreover, the term 'Arab' was often employed in contemporary sources as a generic designation. The same precision applies to the Kabyle uprising discussed later; despite its name, Arab populations were also involved.

64 SHD, 1H375, Letter from Bou Mezrag, 31 March 1871.

65 The provinces were divided into several administrative levels, military subdivisions, and circles. The Spahis were light cavalry units in the French colonial army, recruited locally in Algeria (often of Arab or Berber origin) and serving under French officers.

El-Haddad, and then by the sheikh himself. The leader of the powerful Rahmaniyya brotherhood, then in holy isolation in the valley, he enjoyed great popularity, especially in rural Algeria. His efforts were concentrated on Bougie and Sétif. In the Mitidja plain, the insurgents occupied several villages, setting fire to houses and killing inhabitants. The most famous massacre took place in Palestro, south-east of Algiers: forty-six French settlers were killed, burned and mutilated.[66] The revolt gradually took on a rural character, relayed by marabouts or local chiefs, and opposed any further colonial presence. In mid-April, concern among the colonists turned into panic. According to Admiral de Gueydon, nearly 800,000 people were joining the uprising. After the death of al-Muqrani, shot dead on 5 May, his brother Bou Mezrag took over the leadership of the insurrection, keeping alive the call for holy war. Fighting raged in May and June in the provinces of Algiers, Constantine and the Sahara, under the impetus of a sharif called Ben Choucha, who was also an enemy of al-Muqrani's. The French troops only regained the advantage in June and July.[67]

These events had an evident connection with the metropolitan situation: the transition, the war, but also, in particular, the Communes movement. In one sense this was a direct link. The proclamation of the Commune in March 1871 revived the insurrectionary movement in Algiers, which saw the event in Paris as confirmation of the validity of its struggles. This renewed offensive severely hampered Governor Gueydon's ability to act. At the same time, the Algerian insurgents took it as further proof of French weakness. The second type of link was more indirect: mobilised for the second siege of Paris, French troops could not come to Algeria as reinforcement, despite the appeals for help coming from the generals on the ground. The telegraphic dispatches show the War Ministry's difficulties in responding to this situation: on the one hand, it pieced together parts of the army in the urban centres (Toulouse, Moulins) in order to send them to Versailles. On the other hand, it sent to Algeria some battalions that were stationed in eastern and south-eastern France. One contingent did arrive in April, but

66 On this event, see Raphaëlle Branche, *L'Embuscade de Palestro (Algérie, 1956)* (Paris: Armand Colin, 2010), pp. 93–101.

67 Sources: James McDougall, *A History of Algeria* (Cambridge: Cambridge University Press, 2017); Mohammed Brahmi Salhi, 'L'insurrection de 1871', in Bouchène et al., *Histoire de l'Algérie à la période coloniale*, pp. 103–9.

municipal authorities in Dijon, Lyon and Marseille put the brakes on the troops' movements: they did not want to lose the soldiers based locally, and pointed out that urban revolutionary uprisings had been repressed just recently.[68] Some soldiers also arrived from Paris, since, in the Versailles army, Marshal De Mac-Mahon punished both hotheads and the recalcitrant by sending them into the battalions of the African light infantry: the 'war against Paris' itself had an imperial element.[69] Yet troops available for Algeria remained scarce. Here, the Commune – or rather the Communes – served both as a pretext (reinterpreted by colonists and colonised alike) and as a catalyst, even if it was, of course, only one factor among others.

As Gueydon summarised the situation: 'The fall of the revolutionary commune of Paris finally allowed the government to send major reinforcements and these operations could take on the character of unity and decisiveness which it had hitherto fatally lacked.'[70] Reinforcements arrived at the end of May, and the number of men rose to 85,000.[71] On 5 August the so-called 'pacification' operation in Little Kabylie began, carried out by General de La Croix. Five French military columns in parallel encircled the mountainous Bou Taleb area. On 12 October, the insurrection was considered crushed. The French colonial authorities, whether military or civilian, republican or conservative, were unanimous in seeing the Kabyle revolt as 'treason' against France, which the colonised populations had perpetrated against their 'civilisers' at the worst possible moment.

Of course, the perspective of the Algerian insurgents, at least insofar as it can be captured, tells a quite different story. Here, the Kabyle insurrection discloses its own sites, such as the markets where information was disseminated, and its dates, such as Eid-el-Kebir, chosen for the outbreak of the revolt. It reveals its modes of mobilisation (letters or rosaries distributed in the insurgent regions) and its warfare practices, such as the *nefra* – a feigned panic staged to disorganise the enemy.

The various calls to arms also bring to light the complex web of both hierarchical and horizontal relationships that characterised this space

68 SHD, Lu3, movements of armed troops from Versailles.

69 Tombs, *The War Against Paris*.

70 Gueydon, 'Analyse des opérations militaires et maritimes pendant l'insurrection de 1871', February 1872.

71 Corvisier, *Histoire militaire de la France*, vol. I.

– one which the French authorities' preferred term 'tribe' offers little help in understanding. Some show a relationship between equals. In these cases, Mohammed or Bou Mezrag al-Muqrani would remind their interlocutor of the situation, refer to the duty of holy war, or appeal to the honour of their interlocutor. The insurgent leader could also impose this decision on a given group or its head, making them join the fight in the name of alliance agreements that, this time, left little room for choice: 'You give thanks to God for your coming and you declare that you are in obedience.'[72] In other cases, by contrast, he had to prompt or wait for a collective decision to be taken by the group. The discussion among male peers, which gave rise to the myth of 'Kabyle democracy', was present in the conflict, even while sitting alongside more vertical relationships. Still other requests may have been addressed to the famous *chertyas*, which historians have compared to insurrectionary committees. These assemblies of a dozen or so individuals effectively provided oversight over the *qaids*, gathered arms or organised the fighting.[73] A group's commitment to the cause was not always unanimous: some might join the struggle, while others even joined the colonists' side.[74] Far from the representations implicit in colonial sources that present the Arab insurgents as a coherent 'whole', this insurrection thus mobilised a vast array of power relations.

The revolt also had its roots in well-established social and cultural realities, and thus in richer historical dynamics. In the sociopolitical sphere, as Idir Hachi reminds us, in addition to the war and rebellions by the colonists, it stemmed from the disasters of 1867–69. The effects of colonisation – visible in the precarity of rural Algeria and in the fact that insurgent areas were those most recently conquered – were therefore an important factor.[75] Yet the temporalities at play, as in the

72 SHD, 1H375, Bou Mezrag to Oulad Si Amer, 27 March 1871.

73 *Qaid*: tribal leader. On this comparison regarding the chertyas, see Salhi, 'L'insurrection de 1871'; on the 'Kabyle myth', see Patricia M. E. Lorcin, *Imperial Identities: Stereotyping, Prejudice and Race in Colonial Algeria* (London: I. B. Tauris Publishers, 1995).

74 SHD, 1H375, 28 April 1871, Si Abd el-Rahman ben Mohammed, qaid of the Oula Si Salem.

75 Idir Hachi, *Histoire sociale de l'insurrection de 1871 et du procès de ses chefs* (Constantine, 1873), PhD dissertation, Aix-Marseille University (2017). The nibbling away of land continued despite the *sénatus-consulte* of 1863: Didier Guignard, 'Conservatoire ou révolutionnaire? Le sénatus-consulte de 1863 appliqué au régime foncier d'Algérie', *Revue d'histoire du XIXe siècle* 41 (2010), pp. 81–95.

Chinese example, reached further back. The persistent influence of Ottoman frameworks, either altered or updated, is telling in this regard. El-Mokrani's gesture testifies to this: his family had pledged allegiance first to the Ottoman Empire, then to Abd el-Kader, and finally to the French occupier, in exchange for authority over the Medjana. His initial opposition, before events took a different turn, was above all driven by the desire to restore an established system of social relations. At the outset, his rebellion concerned less the French presence itself than a regime that had betrayed him (the Second Empire), another that heightened colonists' appetites for Algerian land (the Republic), and, beyond those, the concern to restore his dignity.[76] The revolt of the Spahis, who had first appeared in the Ottoman period, offers another example of this influence: according to an age-old principle, their service was indeed supposed to be carried out only within certain geographical limits. Finally, in a different domain, religion played a very important role, as shown by the involvement of religious organisations, and especially the powerful Rahmaniyya brotherhood. To understand its force, we must now consider other historical movements that extended beyond the Algerian context. At the turn of the eighteenth and nineteenth centuries, Sufism was experiencing a revival. This was based in particular on a rereading of the hadith, a critique of 'traditional Sufis', and the creation of more structured organisations. Facilitated by the acceleration of exchanges within the framework of the 'Ottoman peace', the movement was organised around major religious centres – Medina, Mecca, Cairo and others – and extended from the Maghreb and the Middle East to India and China.[77] The extent of this rupture has been debated by researchers, but they agree that *something* was indeed happening in the eighteenth century. The appearance of new or renewed *tariqas* (a term poorly translated as 'brotherhoods') is one trace of it.[78] The

76 Mouloud Haddad, 'Les maîtres de l'Heure. Soufisme et eschato-logie en Algérie coloniale (1845–1901)', *Revue d'histoire du XIXe siècle* 41 (2010), pp. 49–62.

77 Marc Gaborieau and Nicole Grandin, 'Le renouveau confrérique (fin XVIIIe–XIXe siècle)', in Alexandre Popovic and Gilles Veinstein, eds, *Les Voies d'Allah* (Paris: Fayard, 1996); Kamel Chachoua, *L'Islam kabyle. Religion, État et société en Algérie* (Paris: Maisonneuve & Larose, 2002).

78 On this discussion, see Rachida Chih and Catherine Mayeur-Jaouen, 'Introduction: le soufisme ottoman vu d'Égypte (XVIe–XVIIIe siècle)', in *Le Soufisme à l'époque ottoman* (Cairo: IFAO, 2010), pp. 1–55.

Rahmaniyya was itself founded in the early nineteenth century by the father of Sheikh El-Haddad, who had made the pilgrimage to Mecca and studied at the celebrated Al-Azhar Mosque in Cairo.[79] Another indication of this dynamic was the intensification of missionary practices and the multiplication of jihads over the course of the nineteenth century, such as the Fulani jihad, whether directed against other Muslim populations or European settlers. The Muslim revolts seen in China are one example; and the Kabyle insurrection of 1871 is another. In this sense, the latter is also one of the forms – both anticolonial and with its own specific features – of this non-European, global history of the Muslim worlds.[80]

Taken together, these dynamics intersected. They enable a better understanding of the modalities of the revolt and the way it was perceived. Here, the frame of reference was not 1871 AD, but 1288 AH. With these elements in mind, certain features come into sharper focus. For instance, it has an obvious messianic framework, as illustrated by expressions such as 'The reign of the French is over', 'The Lords of the Worlds will demand account of it'.[81] Characteristic of many insurrectionary movements, such messianism corresponded well to a Sufi world in which mystical experience is decisive. Not that every fighter believes in it: but the irruption of this sacred temporality of jihad, supported by institutions and practices, unquestionably leads to a rupture in the sense of the world's order. For the insurgents, it rendered plausible not only a French defeat, but a change in the course of history. Our own expertise can only take us so far.[82] At the very least, it appears that the Arab revolt

79 Alain Mahé, *Histoire de la Grande Kabylie (XIXe–XXe siècle). Anthropologie historique du lien social dans les communautés villageoises* (Saint-Denis: Bouchène, 2001), p. 195.

80 Hélène Blais, Claire Fredj and Sylvie Thénault, 'Désenclaver l'histoire de l'Algérie à la période coloniale', *Revue d'histoire moderne et contemporaine* 63: 2 (2016) – esp. the introduction, pp. 7–13. On the 'global history of the Muslim worlds', see Nile Green, *Sufism: A Global History* (Chichester: Wiley-Blackwell, 2012).

81 SHD, 1H375, From Bou Mezrag to the Oulas el-Ajez, April 1871.

82 For instance, the vague term 'jihad' does not, it seems, help to grasp the nature of the religious, social and political aspects that this reference supposes. On the uncertainty of the words used on this score ('fundamentalism', 'mysticism'), see Rudolph Peters, 'Erneuerungsbewegungen im Islam vom 18. zum 20. Jahrhundert und die Rolle des Islams in der neueren Geschichte: Antilkolonialismus und Nationalismus', in Werner Ende and Udo Steinbach, eds, *Der Islam in der Gegenwart* (Munich: Beck, 2005 [1984]), pp. 90–128.

of 1871 was not part of some archaic, timeless cultural structure, as some colonists suggested, but rather belonged to another history, or part of history.

Unlike the Chinese case, however, this Algerian story is clearly more bound up in European history, particularly as a result of colonisation. This would explain why many 'tribes' remained loyal to the colonial power. If this is sometimes forgotten, the Kabyle insurrection was also a war between colonised populations. In any case, multiple histories – both interconnected and out of sync – emerged into view and collided during the various events of 1870–71, articulated in this last case in a different web of relations.

There are undoubtedly many ways to account for the cracks that thus opened up. From my point of view, one of the most interesting suggests that both metropolitan and colonial French authorities were, at that moment, experiencing the effects of what American historian Lauren Benton has called 'legal anomalies'.[83] Benton tells us that, on account of inter-imperial competition going back to the fifteenth century, as well as the initial conditions of conquest and the geographically fragmented conceptions that legitimised it, legal spaces under various forms of sovereignty took shape in the imperial worlds, which the strengthening of European territorial control in the nineteenth century did not eliminate. The events of 1870–71 also reveal this reality, which the colonised or dominated populations drew upon to oppose or challenge the legitimacy of the French presence. These anomalies are visible here in the confrontation between the Western definition of revolt and the Chinese Empire's judicial approach. And they are even more visible in Algeria, with the contrasting legal-administrative effects of the change of regime on the French and Algerian sides, respectively.

Yet, considered on a global scale, given their number and duration, these 'anomalies' are not exceptions: rather, they are variations in forms of order that in turn question the legal basis upon which the nation-state was being built at the same time. What Benton calls the 'modular conditions of empire' thus contributed greatly to the construction of the global order in the nineteenth century, and, the historian argues, must now be

83 Lauren Benton, *A Search for Sovereignty: Law and Geography in European Empires (1400–1900)* (Cambridge: Cambridge University Press, 2010).

moved to the centre of our analysis.[84] From this point of view, the war, the political transition and the Paris Commune are revealing of this situation and its potentialities. They appear as an opportunity for an assault – even if a temporary one – against this global order, in a history that does not simply centre on Europe. Interestingly, if the Communes of Paris, Marseille or Algiers play a role in this perspective, they do so not by virtue of their shared status as emancipation movements. Rather, in these other lands, they appear as events coming from an authoritarian, dominating and colonial system, which could then be used against it.

Here emerge other lesser-known faces of the Commune, which were nonetheless active at this scale. These other faces can in turn help us to examine the event in Paris differently: from this point of view, it may very well appear as a 'legal anomaly' that shook the metropolitan order, and thereby helped open up the breaches created by the anomalies that already made up the imperial space. This may fortuitously provide another element in explaining why other imperial powers had an interest in ensuring the failure of this Parisian experiment: in some respects, the Commune also weakened certain parts of the inter-imperial order.

84 Ibid., p. 299.

3

The Commune, a Global Media Event

Meanwhile in France, but also in Britain, the United States and beyond, attention-grabbing headlines – 'Revolution in Paris', 'The Reign of Terror in Paris', and so on – were emblazoned across the leading newspapers of the day. Clearly, one reason why these events had such an impact was that they were so widely known: the war, the proclamation of the Republic and the Communes were media events: and, in the Paris Commune's case, perhaps one of the most important of the nineteenth century.

Too little attention has been paid to this phenomenon, and to the plurality of readings to which the events in Paris immediately gave rise. Yet, in truth, such a line of inquiry is no simple matter. Even when dealing with a single country, debates on the analysis of media discourse tell us, it is necessary to study not only the conditions of production and reception but also the modalities of writing and the webs of meaning that they mobilise.[1] Such an inquiry becomes more complicated still at the transnational level, where it must also integrate the uneven rate of dissemination, the multiplicity of perspectives and reference points, and the rich variety of interpretive frameworks that may be involved.[2]

1 For France, see Pierre Laborie, 'De l'opinion publique à l'imaginaire social', *Vingtième siècle. Revue d'histoire* 18 (1988), pp. 101–17; Brigitte Gaïti, 'L'opinion publique dans l'histoire politique: impasses et bifurcations', *Le Mouvement social* 221 (2007), pp. 95–104.

2 On these approaches and methods, see Dominique Kalifa, Philippe Régnier, Marie-Ève Thérenty and Alain Vaillant, eds, *La Civilisation du journal. Histoire culturelle et littéraire de la presse française au xixe siècle* (Paris: Nouveau Monde Éditions, 2011);

In seeking to address this methodological difficulty, I have combined qualitative and quantitative approaches based on samples of the press coverage. This chapter makes no claim to exhaustiveness, but by proceeding in this way, it aims to bring to light this densely woven fabric of words, giving a sense of its main lines. Indeed, a stereotyped discourse hitches itself onto the mesh of links, hiatuses and nodes discussed in the previous chapters, while not entirely corresponding to them: and this, too, adds fresh material to this already rich 'global commune'.

The Transformations of the Information Sphere under the Test of 1870–71

We can easily understand why the events of 1870–71 attracted such great media attention. After all, in less than a year, there followed in rapid succession a war between states, the advent of a new republic, the creation of an Empire (Germany), and a social revolution on European soil – events which everyone understood were sure to have major geopolitical consequences. But there is more to this issue: in a sense, these events also came at the right moment, in media terms. The means by which information was disseminated had indeed changed profoundly since the 1850s. In France, with rising literacy and improved technical capabilities, the number of titles was booming – as were their print runs. One emblematic case was *Le Petit Journal*, founded in 1863 by Polydore Millaud; its daily circulation had soared from 38,000 copies upon its creation to 469,000 in 1869.[3] The press continued to be marked by a great diversity of opinions, especially after the partial liberalisation in the late 1860s; but with the arrival of these newcomers, it reached a wider audience.

Marie-Ève Thérenty, 'Pour une histoire littéraire de la presse au xixe siècle', *Revue d'histoire littéraire de la France* 103: 3 (2003), pp. 625–35; Christophe Charle, 'Peut-on écrire une histoire de la culture européenne à l'époque contemporaine ?', *Annales. Histoire, Sciences sociales* 65: 5 (2010), pp. 1207–21.

3 Dominique Kalifa, *La Culture de masse en France, Vol. I: 1860–1930* (Paris, La Découverte, 2001); Claude Bellanger, Jacques Godechot, Pierre Guiral and Fernand Terrou, eds, *Histoire générale de la presse française, Vol. II: De 1815 à 1871* (Paris: PUF, 1969).

Such developments in the media had come earlier in Britain: already in the 1830s, a weekly like the *Penny Magazine* reached just under a million readers, and in the Victorian era we can count about 2,500 different titles.[4] There was a comparable situation in the United States, although there the shift was less marked given the country's greater size. Newspapers had enjoyed spectacular growth during the Civil War, and the number of titles (dailies and magazines) increased from 2,526 in 1850 to 5,800 in 1870.[5] The telegraph, the railway and the development of the postal service allowed some titles, such as the *New York Tribune*, to become national press organs. Yet this expansion remained geographically circumscribed: in the German-speaking world, given the weight of censorship and a late industrialisation process, the press remained confined to a more bourgeois readership and a regional audience; the biggest newspaper of this moment in Italy, *Il Secolo*, also reached a readership of this type (with a circulation of 30,000); further afield, in China, most newspapers were the creations of foreigners.[6] The situations varied, but the press was clearly on an upward trend.

Its ascent was boosted, moreover, by unprecedented transnational dynamics, such as the development of press agencies.[7] Havas was created in France in 1831, followed in 1851 by the German agency Wolff and Britain's Reuters. These increasingly powerful organisations ended up signing information-sharing contracts, to the point of reaching, in January 1870, an outright division of the world into spheres of news circulation. Their importance made itself felt during the Franco-Prussian conflict, as illustrated by disputes over equal treatment in reporting. On 3 August 1870, Reuters sent a letter to the French ambassador in London saying it had 'received the Paris dispatches with some

4 Stéphane Lebecq, Fabrice Bensimon, Frédérique Lachaud and François-Joseph Ruggiu, *Histoire des îles Britanniques* (Paris: PUF, 2007).

5 Michael Emery and Edwin Emery, *The Press and America: An Interpretive History of the Mass Media*, 7th edn (Englewood Cliffs, NJ: Prentice Hall, 1992); Frank L. Mott, *American Journalism: A History (1690–1960)*, 3rd edn (New York: Macmillan, 1962).

6 On these contrasting European situations, see Christophe Charle, *La Dérégulation culturelle. Essai d'histoire des cultures en Europe au xixe siècle* (Paris: PUF, 2015); and, on a global scale, Jürgen Osterhammel, The *Transformation of the* World: *A Global History of the Nineteenth Century* (Princeton, NJ: Princeton University Press, 2014), p. 29.

7 Donald Read, *The Power of News: The History of Reuters (1849–1989)* (Oxford: Oxford University Press, 1992); Michael B. Palmer, *Des petits journaux aux grandes agences. Naissance du journalisme moderne (1863–1914)* (Paris: Aubier, 1983).

delay'. Indeed, it was 'the impression produced by the first dispatch that influences the press and the public'. The Prussian administration was more alert, and – the Reuters representative continued – 'To avoid any claims of bias, which I am committed to avoid, it is important that I receive the French version [of the military events] more quickly.'[8] The ambassador reacted immediately: 'We have a real interest', he wrote to the minister, 'that not only the reports coming from Berlin should reach the Reuters agency . . . Your excellency is not unaware of the vast publicity that it would give to all these communications.' Subsequently, official war bulletins were sent directly from the French army's headquarters to the British press agency. The war of 1870 was also an information war.

Improved means of communication – steamboats and telegraph lines – constituted another decisive factor. The most important development was the laying of undersea cables, and especially the transatlantic cable completed in 1866: while, during the US Civil War, information took ten days to reach Europe (by ship), it could now get from one continent to another in a few hours, before being duplicated on domestic telegraph lines. This network complemented older ones, such as that of *The Times*, whose articles had long been translated on a large scale, although they were transmitted via slower routes. Thus, by the end of the 1860s, veritable information routes had taken shape. Again, the speed of access to information varied according to the region in question. The French defeats were known within a few hours in Madrid, St Petersburg and New York. But this information took sixteen days to reach Brazil, more than a month to arrive in Argentina, and between one and two months to get to Japan.[9] In these latter cases, sources and dates were often mixed up: on 29 September, the Chilean legate received official dispatches from 4 August, political correspondence from Europe dating up to 10 August, and further material that had arrived via the United States by 20 August. Added to this were a series of 'contradictory' news items arriving via Havana and Jamaica, which, he specifies, 'it is said, go up to 5 September, but whose authenticity is difficult to verify'.[10] In such conditions, the announcement of the proclamation of the French Republic surely

8 CAD, CP, England, 3 August 1870.

9 CAD, CP, Brazil, Argentina, Japan (for instance, the 6 September 1870 circular reached Buenos Aires on 15 October).

10 CAD, CP, Chile, 29 September.

appeared as rather uncertain information. Different countries did not experience the war and these political events at the same pace. But most of them would eventually become informed – and, most importantly, all of them were tense with the feeling that a real 'news event' was taking place over in Europe.

Added to this picture is the role of the 'correspondents' present on the ground, hired by the various press organs. War reporting had taken concrete form during the Crimean War of 1854–56, which made the siege of Sebastopol one of the 'big stories' of the 1850s.[11] This practice was given systematic and professionalised form during the American Civil War, as the major US dailies invested heavily in providing the latest news – and making their reporting reliable. Hence, by the time of the Franco-Prussian War, there were already journalists with frontline experience. For instance, the famous Irish news correspondent William Howard Russell, at *The Times*, had already covered the twenty-two months of the Crimean War, the Sepoy Mutiny of 1857, the US Civil War, and the Austro-Prussian War of 1866 before making his way to France in 1870.[12] Press access had itself become a real international issue. On 27 September, a deputation from the British and US press (consisting of representatives of *The Times*, the *Pall Mall Gazette*, the *Morning Post*, the *Observer*, the *Daily News* and the *Daily Telegraph*) addressed itself to the French embassy in London. It called for easy access for correspondents, to 'make known to the two hemispheres the great deeds of the defence of Paris, which is happening before their eyes and whose importance they fully appreciate'. To reassure French authorities, in a context of heightened fears of espionage, the British and US embassies guaranteed that they would check the identity of those who did come to France.

Many of these reporters were thus present in France between autumn 1870 and spring 1871. Such was the case for the young Reuters correspondent, George D. Williams, whose love letters to his fiancée have been preserved in the Reuters company archives. Exchanged between two impassioned souls, they testify to the working conditions on the

11 On the British case, see Stefanie Markovits, *The Crimean War in the British Imagination* (Cambridge: Cambridge University Press, 2009).

12 Caroline Chapman, *Russell of 'The Times': War Despatches and Diaries* (London: Bell & Hyman, 1984).

ground. On 7 November 1870, Williams wrote: 'They want me to tell them about the war and what I think and to take sides. But I am weary of the war.'[13] They also shed light on the competition between the main titles to get the freshest news. 'I look forward dear to making a much better thing with journalism than Reuter', he reported, when he learned that the *Pall Mall Gazette* had asked him for examples of his letters to use in an article.[14] These reporters of various nationalities (including French journalists and foreigners long settled in the country) were still present at the time of the Commune, in March 1871. But while some of them were in Paris, the majority were based in Versailles, along with their French counterparts.

These factors explain this event's resonance. A final one must be added: the social imaginaries, crossing national borders, that acted as echo chambers. The case of France is particularly relevant here: after 1789, 1830 and 1848, and the large-scale echoes or oppositions that they aroused, the country appeared to be the home of revolutions par excellence. Upon the declaration of the Republic, *The Times* wryly commented, 'History, after all, repeats itself. Even France, the exception of all rules, is found to have her orbit and her cycles.'[15] Different layers of representation intertwined: France was seen as an industrial and imperial power as well as the land of a great and ancient culture, both intellectually and artistically. Paris, moreover, occupied a significant place in this picture, since the capital of revolutions was also what Walter Benjamin called the 'capital of the nineteenth century'. It illustrated a certain political and cultural modernity, recently embodied in Haussmann's transformations of the city. Paris was also the 'capital of signs', the troubled site where the progress of the age was deciphered, and the object of the very 'myth of Paris'.[16] Crystallising older currents (such as the image of Paris as the 'New Jerusalem' of medieval times), this myth had established itself in European Romanticism of the 1830s, and its audience extended far beyond French or even European

13 Letter from Tours, 7 November 1870. The letters are held in the Reuters archive. My thanks to Mr John Entwistle, responsible for these archives, for making me aware of the letters.

14 10 January 1870 letter, Letters from the correspondence of George D. Williams, Reuters archives.

15 *The Times*, 5 September 1870.

16 Walter Benjamin, *Paris, capitale du xixe siècle. Le livre des passages* (Paris: Cerf, 2000 [1939]); Karlheinz Stierle, *La Capitale des signes. Paris et son discours* (Paris: Éditions de la MSH, 2001).

borders. Both its bright side (Paris, capital of culture and the mind) as well as its darker side (Paris, city of the underworld) were themes taken up or imitated elsewhere, from Russia to the states of Latin America.[17] This particular position can be expressed in statistical terms: France, together with Great Britain, was the pre-eminent power in producing and exporting novels, and Paris remained the backdrop or inspiration for many novels, whether French or otherwise.[18] Hence the events that affected this country and this city were not to be ignored, and seemed to carry a great deal of meaning. This distinctive feature of Paris was for instance felt during the bombing of the city in early January 1871, which sparked strong disapproval. The French consul in Uruguay echoed this on 1 March, not without a certain bias: 'The sympathies of all will remain with us amidst our ruin, because Paris will never cease to be the intellectual centre where all foreigners will always want to make a pilgrimage to pay homage to this capital of the civilised world.'[19]

'Revolution in Paris': The Commune on the Front Page

How should we evaluate this media presence? Many indicators testify to the European, transatlantic and global audience of the conflicts of 1871. Some works have illustrated the British and German reception of these events.[20] Others, less often mentioned, have documented the US case. 'No political or economic issue in the United States, save governmental corruption, received more headlines in the American Press of the 1870's than did the Paris Commune', the historian Samuel Bernstein concluded in 1971.[21] Moncure D. Conway's reports for the

17 Dominique Kalifa, *Les Bas-Fonds. Histoire d'un imaginaire* (Paris: Seuil, 2013).

18 Franco Moretti, *Atlas of the European Novel (1800–1900)* (London: Verso, 1999); Donald Sassoon, *The Culture of the Europeans* (London: Harper, 2006).

19 CAD, CP, Uruguay.

20 On the British case, see Katie Watt, *Contemporary British Perceptions of the Paris Commune*, PhD dissertation, University of Cambridge (1999); for Germany, see Alexander Abusch, 'Le retentissement de la Commune de Paris en Allemagne', *Europe* 64–65 (1951).

21 Samuel Bernstein, 'The Impact of the Paris Commune in the United States', *Massachusetts Review* 12: 3 (1971), p. 436. See also his 'The American Press Views the Commune', in Bernstein, *Essays in Political and Intellectual History* (New York: Paine-Whitman, 1995).

New York World reached New York, the country's information hub, from France within only a few hours. They were then relayed by the domestic telegraph or the Associated Press, which distributed excerpts of articles to the 200 newspapers signed up to its service. This circulation gave rise to a gigantic wave of words that swept across the United States in various forms, making a striking impression on the mind. Traces of it can even be found in private diaries, such as that of the Massachusetts farmer Caroline Barrett White, who noted in March: 'the papers are full of acts of violence and bloodshed among the French people in Paris.'[22]

The echoes were not always favourable to France during the Franco-Prussian conflict: in Mexico, Turkey and Siam, judging by the consular reports, the local press was rather pro-Prussian. At least the events themselves became widely known. Elsewhere, support for the French was clearer, especially after the proclamation of the Republic or the news of French defeats. On 8 March 1871, when the announcement of Paris's capitulation reached Bogotá (Colombia), the local population attacked the Germans who went to celebrate this event, with musicians, in the street. The consul reported that the crowd noisily flocked to the consulate building with shouts of 'Viva la Francia' and 'Abajo los Prusianos'. Other demonstrations of support took place in Peru. If many motives may have prompted such actions, these examples show that the events of 1871 could have a profound effect even in the most distant climes. On the other side of the world, in addition to the Chinese case already mentioned, the *Times of India* informed British-Indian elites about the European events: my study shows more than a hundred occurrences of the words 'Paris' or 'Commune' in articles spanning the period from March to July 1871. These were most often dispatches or articles from British newspapers. But they may then have circulated among the Indian elites, in English or even in translation – although I have not been able to verify this.[23] So, the war, the Republic and the Commune were widely

22 Caroline Barrett White, *White Diaries*, 20 March 1871. The whole exposition is drawn from Philip Katz, *From Appomattox to Montmartre: Americans and the Paris Commune* (Cambridge, MA: Harvard University Press, 1998), p. 70.

23 On the dissemination of news in Indian cities, see Christopher Bayly, *Recovering Liberties: Indian Thought in the Age of Liberalism and Empire* (Cambridge: Cambridge University Press, 2012); and Chandrika Kaul, ed., *Explorations in Modern Indian History and the Media*, special issue of *Media History* 15: 4 (November 2009).

followed around the world, giving the sense that the Parisian revolt drew particular interest.

Still, we should avoid settling for an impressionistic collection of indicators. We can get a more precise measure by taking inspiration from historian Gordon Winder's research assessing the global dimension of the City of London – that is, by drawing on the evidence offered by Reuters wires. His method can be taken up here, albeit adapted to the purposes of the present study.[24] The procedure consists in identifying all the telegrams sent by the British agency for one week after an event, counting how many words were devoted to it, and comparing that with the number related to other happenings (classified by type as political, commercial, military or diplomatic news). This allows us to document the discursive presence of an event in relation to the whole volume of information circulating on Reuters during this same moment. The agency's network included Great Britain, the United States, Canada, South Africa, India, Australia, parts of Latin America and southeast Asia. This coverage certainly did not encompass all available information, and the mass of data sent from London reached these spaces unevenly, depending on the mode of communication (ship or telegraph), or the type of contract signed with the agency.[25] Still, the measure remains a relevant one: of the three agencies, Reuters was the least implicated in the conflict, it covered the largest area, and the news it carried followed parallel circuits, in particular on the competing networks. These telegrams thus represent an appropriate observation point on the global circulation of news. I have chosen to focus on three dates: the bombing of Paris in early January (2–8 January 1871); the 18 March uprising (18 March–24 March 1871); and the Bloody Week (21–8 May 1871). The first was selected because the bombing appears in the diplomatic archives as an especially intense moment of international uproar, and because its temporal and spatial concentration facilitates comparison with the event beginning on 18 March. The results are summarised in the two maps that follow (the third event is addressed in Part III).

24 Gordon M. Winder, 'London's Global Reach? Reuters News and Network, 1865, 1881 and 1914', *Journal of World History* 21: 2 (2010), pp. 271–96.

25 Simon Potter, *News and the British World: The Emergence of an Imperial Press System* (Oxford: Clarendon, 2003); Terhi Rantanen, *The Media and Globalization* (London: SAGE, 2005).

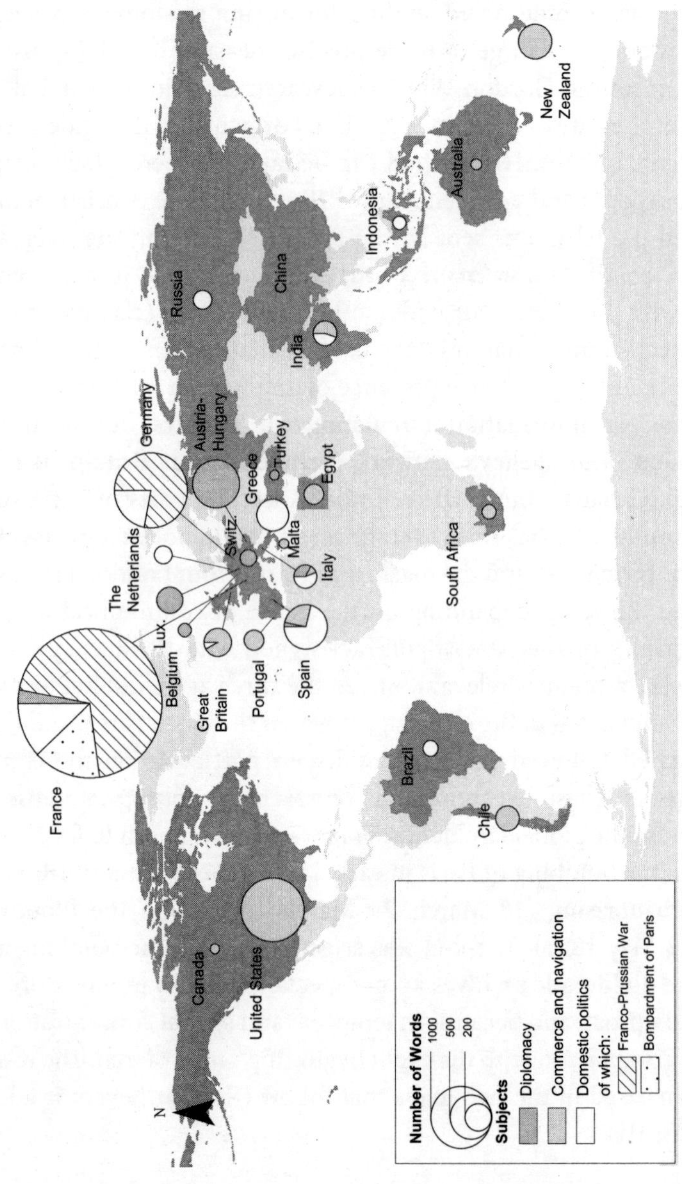

Source: Telegraph Books, Reuters Group Archives, 1871. Conceived by Quentin Deluermoz. Drawn by Anaïs Marshall, 2018.

Map 1. The week of the Paris bombings (2–8 January 1871) as covered by the Reuters network

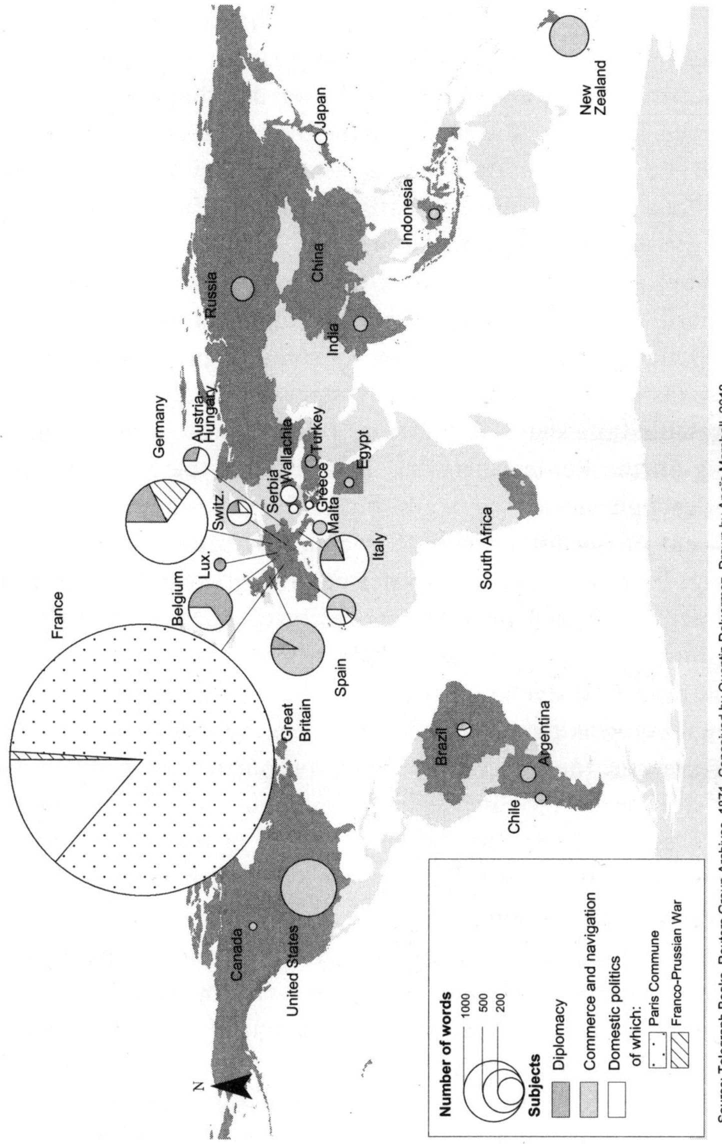

Map 2. The week of the March 18 uprising on the Reuters network

These documents show the strong media presence for the events of 1870–71, together with the importance of the Commune relative to the bombing of Paris. It would be worth extending this line of inquiry to other dates, like 4 September 1870. But what was previously only an impression now finds statistical confirmation: in media terms, the Commune clearly stands out above the war and the proclamation of the Republic. Judging by the third map (p. 310), 18 March was even more of an event than the Bloody Week. Its resonance is surely explained by the shock of a fresh revolution in Paris, after the defeats, the political overhaul, the siege and the capitulation.

Above all, it was very closely followed: the key point here is the extraordinary scale of this media coverage. During the bombing of the French capital, the war took up some 46 per cent of reporting. This was already a high figure – since, it should be recalled, this represented the share of that story relative to all information circulating on the Reuters network. Paris itself – the bombing and the political episodes at the beginning of the year – represented only 2 per cent of the total. With 18 March, the proportions completely changed: France occupied 75 per cent of all coverage, far ahead of Germany, with the United States even further behind. And the insurrection that led to the Paris Commune alone represented 64 per cent of all reporting, even at a moment when other important developments were taking place, such as the coronation of the German emperor and the peace treaty. This proportion dropped to 54 per cent during the Bloody Week; but even this was still a remarkable figure, especially at a time when the Treaty of Washington was being signed (settling the dispute between Great Britain and the United States over the Alabama Claims).

The structure of the Reuters network's reporting surely contributed to the overrepresentation of Paris (the agency was largely focused on European capitals). But the scale of the figures makes the conclusion inescapable: between March and May 1871, Paris was the central focus of the media world. Even if we bear in mind the effects of the counting method, comparison with the data from Gordon Winder confirms its quite exceptional character.[26] In the week of the Lincoln assassination

26 The difference in numbers between my data and Gordon Winder's suggests that the word-counting methods were not the same, but that the overall sizes are comparable.

in 1865 – a 'normal' week, since the news only reached London later – the news arriving from continental Europe had represented 56 per cent of the total, and that from Paris 14 per cent. In the week following the assassination of Tsar Alexander II in 1881, the fifteen leading European cities together accounted for 62 per cent of the total, with St Petersburg alone making up 37.7 per cent. After the assassination of Archduke Franz Ferdinand in 1914, the data is less reliable: newspapers drew on other sources, and although the range of countries covered by the agency had grown since 1871, the concentration of news sources had diminished. At no other moment, however, does the share for a single location appear to have reached such a level. The conclusions, of course, depend on what is being analysed: considering its overall duration, the US Civil War was certainly a more important media event, especially as the changes in news production prepared the ground for the reception of events in subsequent years. That said, it can clearly be argued that the Paris Commune was one of the world's biggest media events in the second half of the nineteenth century. The fact that it was concentrated in time and space undoubtedly contributed to its visibility.

The Paris Commune was thus an event in itself. It stood out from the Franco-Prussian conflict, as we have seen, as well as from other revolutions in the provinces. Neither Marseille, nor Lyon, nor even the Algiers Commune or the Kabyle insurrection, were ignored.[27] But mentions of them were drowned out by the mass of words devoted to the Parisian event. The capital acted as a screen, concentrating all attention upon itself. But could anyone really know what was happening? Both journalists and readers soon concluded, with some disappointment, that media coverage did not deliver reliable understanding of the facts. In May, the *New York World* complained:

> It is not yet possible to know with accuracy what ha[s] actually happened in Paris . . .[T]he story of this tremendous conflict comes [to us] in the short, sharp, fragmentary, and unqualified accents of the telegraph, reflecting from day to day and from hour to hour the excited and necessarily incomplete impressions of observers who are

27 Notably in Reuters despatches, *The Times*, US dailies and indeed the Mexican press.

> near enough to the terrific drama to be shaken by its terrors without being near enough to analyze its action.[28]

The nature of reporting depended on the conditions in which news was gathered. The telegraphic style demanded a particular, concise way of writing, focused on the search for the 'scoop' and the 'remarkable' facts that readers now expected. This was particularly true of the US press – so much so that it came to be called the 'American way'. But in 1870–71 the phenomenon also affected the publication of telegraphic dispatches in more traditional newspapers, where they appeared in specific columns. Field conditions did little to improve matters, whether during the Franco-Prussian conflict or the Commune: indeed, the telegraph lines were cut off, except intermittently, and travel was all but prohibited. There surely were journalists in the city, whether working for French or foreign newspapers – all of them pompously titled 'our local correspondent'; but they usually remained near the embassies. Most of them, above all, observed events from Versailles; and even when they tried to take a professional distance, they were still influenced by official news or by the virulence of the French press. When, at more infrequent intervals, they produced feature articles, many reporters and columnists focused more on the historical significance or the consequences of the event than on what the political or ideological project of the Communards might be. The Commune thus continued to be viewed from afar.

As a result, the information circulating on Reuters's network and in the newspapers was focused primarily on particular events, seen in raw and fragmentary form. Readers knew the main actors in this story, whether individuals (Courbet, Cluseret, Assi, Varlin, and so on) or collective ones (the National Guard, the Commune, the vigilance committees), as well as their main deeds (the proclamation of the Commune, the calm in the streets, attacks on churches, the Committee of Public Safety). They also had knowledge of most dispatches and statements, from Adolphe Thiers, the General Staff and the Commune. Some of the Commune's manifestos were even translated, at least into English, German and Spanish, and widely circulated. Interpretation, however – whether in the form of reasoned reflection or hasty judgement – remained marked, at this distance, by the aforementioned stereotypes

28 Cited in Katz, *From Appomattox to Montmartre*, p. 66.

about France, Paris and revolution. The war, the Republic and the Communes were the object of a vast discursive fabric, which was produced hour by hour, but remained blurred. The Paris Commune thus appears to have been both omnipresent and ever-uncertain.

European and Transatlantic Appropriations of the Commune: Four National Examples

This intense attention was also owed to the fact that these developments, in many countries, were almost becoming domestic political events. This both precise and almost abstract information about a war, a revolution, and France echoed through many local and national debates. In some places, it exposed latent axes of dispute – or even displaced them. Four case studies, centred on policy debates, will allow us to appreciate this phenomenon and to get a better sense of the variety of perspectives in play. Northern European countries apart, the selection includes spaces central to the circulation of information, as well as others that, though apparently more marginal, also point to the richness of the possible appropriations of the Commune. This choice was also based on the availability of existing studies or documentation. I will therefore examine the United States, Spain, Romania and Mexico. These case studies will help to move away from a too easily adopted 'diffusionist' model.

Reconstruction versus Civil War: the United States

The events of 1870–71, and above all the Commune, became a real 'national event' in the United States – the first of this scale, according to historian Philip Katz.[29] Even before it ended, the Paris Commune appeared in the form of etchings in the largest illustrated weeklies of the day, such as *Frank Leslie's Illustrated Newspaper* and *Every Saturday*. Quickly integrated into US commercial culture, it was even the subject of a 'relief view of Paris' at San Francisco Hall in spring 1871. But the event was more immediately an issue of political debate in the Reconstruction-era United States: the 'Civil War in Paris' could hardly

29 Ibid., pp. 61–117.

escape comparison with America's own Civil War (1861–65). The Commune thus inserted itself into the fault-lines of the US political debate. According to Philip Katz's analysis, which I will follow here, these ran between supporters or members of the Republican Party and the Democratic Party, as well as between North and South.

The debates began with the Franco-Prussian War. In July–August 1870, France had the support of the former Confederates (Napoleon III had supported the South), many Irish Americans, and the Democrats in reaction against Prussian militarism. The Republican Party and most Northerners favoured Prussia. The proclamation of the Republic on 4 September 1870 changed these dividing lines. President Ulysses S. Grant saw this as a sign of the worldwide development of republicanism and was one of the first to recognise the French government. Some Republicans who had opposed Napoleon III's Empire began to support France. However, convergence with the Democrats was far from automatic. Within the Republican Party itself, another faction remained opposed to the young French Republic. And many Northern elites now preferred the 'Best Men' system, distrusting the idea of popular government as well as the principle of local autonomy.

When the Commune burst onto the stage, this further disrupted previous dividing lines. Northern Republicans were confirmed in their opposition: for both conservatives and radicals, the Commune demonstrated that France was decidedly incapable of having a republican government. Worse, the popular government in Paris threatened to sully Americans' high ideals about the Republic. On 4 April the *New York Times* bitterly concluded: 'For many years to come the crimes of the Parisian socialistic Democracy will be charged upon liberty, and the first demands of [the people] will be confused with the wild ideas and savage crimes of the French Communists.'[30] The 'horrors' of the Commune fuelled the Republican Party's internal debates: did these ignorant and immoral Parisians not show the danger of allowing too many people – immigrants, women, formerly enslaved people – the vote? These events were also used to discredit their Democratic or Southern opponents: both were associated with the rejection of a central state authority that Republicans presented as legitimate. Henry Bowen of the *Independent* crassly described the Commune as a 'French Ku Klux Klan', uniting the

30 Ibid., p. 95.

Paris revolt and the racist organisation under the same banner of anarchy and arrogance.

Of course, the Democrats took a different view. They presented the Commune as an example of the illegitimate use of force. This time, however, the French example served above all to discredit home-grown Reconstruction. For instance, Northern Democrat Manton Marble, a journalist and owner of the *New York World*, cited the tyranny in Paris in order to denounce the excessive use of a centralising and partisan-controlled authority. However, he made clear, the Northern Republicans were even worse than the Communards, who at least were ignorant, while Americans had been 'educated in the principles and invited to the practice of liberal thought and of political freedom for many generations'.[31] Marble also drew on the events in Paris to highlight the failure of the Southern secessionists: both were accused of having sullied the lofty ideal of states' rights. Criticism of the Commune remained a constant among Southern Democrats, though once again their own target lay elsewhere. But, even in their opposition to it, the French event remained an opportunity to suggest the value of a collective revolt against a centralising and oppressive power. The racist reading that likened the Communards to Black people as 'savages' would only come later, after the events.

Naturally, not all of the press made such comparisons. But for a few weeks the Commune served as the prompt for an intense debate on the nature of the American political situation. In this context, support for the Commune was surely in the minority. The few members of the US sections of the International Workingmen's Association (IWMA) did defend the Commune.[32] The famous radical feminist Victoria Woodhull hailed the Parisian events as the onset of the 'universal Republic'. Wendell Philipps, a leading figure in the abolitionist movement, saw in the Commune an extension of the principles of American republicanism, as well as a fight for the right to local self-government. On the other hand, the labour question was not posed in clear terms (indeed, such a focus would have to wait for Karl Marx's defence of the Commune after the end of May 1871). But, above all, these supports remained scant. The Commune was thus

31 18 May 1871, cited in ibid., p. 103.

32 Michel Cordillot, *Utopistes et exilés du Nouveau monde: des Français aux Etats-Unis, de 1848 à la Commune* (Paris: Vendémiaire, 2013).

appropriated by partisan conflicts, along dividing lines that may today seem confusing. Yet they reveal how the Parisian 'secession' exposed and fuelled the latent debates of an America barely having emerged from the Civil War: between centralism and federalism, popular sovereignty and delegated power, the workers' movement and industrial capitalism.

Republican federalism and the international cause: Spain

The reception of the Paris Commune in Spain was just as important, though perspectives were rather different. This will be all the more visible here, as I will focus in particular on republican readings of the Commune. Apart from the island of industrial development in Barcelona, Spain was less industrialised than the United States, and its rich variety of political press outlets did not achieve the same print runs as its US or French counterparts. Most importantly, Spain had for two years already been immersed in the period known as the 'Sexenio Democrático' (1868–74): in 1868 the 'glorious revolution' (a military coup followed by a civilian revolution) had brought Bourbon rule to an end. A constitutional monarchy was established, with legislators elected by universal male suffrage. Two strong sociopolitical forces stood in opposition to this: the monarchist Carlists, and republicans, who favoured popular sovereignty. In the meantime, a republican and abolitionist movement in the Cuban colony had entered into struggle, provoking a conflict with the Spanish army. This provided the backdrop to interpretations of the French events, and especially the outbreak of the Commune.

Monarchists, Carlists, conservatives, and the ruling liberals such as the security minister, Práxedes Sagasta, cited the Commune as a symbol of anarchy. For them, it showed the threat posed by republicans and internationalists, worldwide but especially in Spain. 'Progressives' – liberals concerned to improve the lot of the population through reforms 'from above' – were also suspicious of this democratic and popular revolution. However, federalist republicans, especially those gathered in the main opposition force, the Republican Democratic Party (Partido Republicano Democrático Federal), looked kindly on the Commune.[33]

33 These distinctions are inspired by the analyses offered in Jesús Millán and María C. Romeo, 'Was the Liberal Revolution Important to Modern Spain? Political Cultures and Citizenship in Spanish History', *Social History* 29: 3 (August 2004), pp. 284–300.

They had already supported the republican revolution of 4 September. They rapidly came to see the Commune, whose legitimacy seemed to be based on a popular, federalist approach, as an encouragement to their own struggles.[34] The newspaper *La Igualdad* enthused on 23 March, and then again on 26 April: 'No more of the militarism or obstructions to individual initiative, to which the proletariat owes its servitude . . . Honour and eternal gratitude to our brothers in Paris, who are fighting for the triumph of the Federal Republic.'[35] Some republican leaders also defended Paris publicly – notably Baldomero Lostau, an MP for Barcelona, in a famous parliamentary debate.

Lostau here also introduced another dimension, declaring in that same speech that he belonged to the young International. The IWMA was indeed the other hub of positive receptions of the Commune. Established in Spain in the late 1860s, in the Federación Regional Española (FRE), its links with the Alliance for Socialist Democracy had intensified after the visit of the 'Bakuninist' Giuseppe Fanelli, and the anarchist tendency was now becoming dominant. For these militants, the Commune appeared as the promise of a possible working-class order created 'from below', which would cast aside both the state and industrial capitalism.[36] The Communard moment, as the Spanish historiography of the workers' movement has shown, was a time when struggles became more internationalised, and this anti-authoritarian vision of the International gained ground.

Two clarifications are in order, however. In 1870, while the FRE's membership, at 2,000, was considerable, they remained in the minority compared to the federalist republicans. Secondly, the process of reception of the Commune was more complex. This has recently been suggested by the historian Albert Garcia-Balañà in a study of skilled workers in the Barcelona region.[37] He points in particular to the cotton

34 Interpretation offered in José Álvarez Junco, *La Comuna en España* (Madrid: Siglo XXI, 1971). See also Carlos Serrano, 'L'Espagne, la Commune et l'Internationale', in Jacques Rougerie, ed., *1871*. Jalons pour une *Histoire* de la Commune de Paris (Paris: PUF, 1973), pp. 222–39.

35 Cited in Serrano, 'L'Espagne, la Commune et l'Internationale', p. 227.

36 Clara E. Lida, 'La Comuna de París y sus repercusiones: el caso español', in Guillermo Palacios and Erika Pani, eds, *El poder y la sangre. Guerra, estado y nación en la década de 1860* (Mexico City: Colegio de México, 2014), pp. 183–95.

37 Albert Garcia-Balañà, '1871 in Spain: Transnational and Local History in the Formation of the FRE-IWMA', in Fabrice Bensimon, Quentin Deluermoz and Jeanne

sector, which was especially combative: it brought together groups of workers who were both hierarchically organised (between those who operated the looms and those supporting their operation), and autonomous, organised around unions such as the 'Tres Clases de Vapor', which brought together almost 9,000 men. They had been involved in the republican and social struggles of the period, including strikes; and a few years earlier, during the 1868 revolution, they had fought on the side of republican federalism. They were especially numerous in the ranks of the citizens' militia, the 'Volunteers of Freedom' (Voluntarios de la Libertad), close in principle to the National Guards, and an important site of working-class politicisation. Thus the proximity to the experience of the Commune took a specific form here: it corresponded more to the patchwork of working-class, republican and radical receptions already noted.

It is important to recognise that in Spain, too, the Commune was quickly caught up in the dynamics of partisan debates. The government and the liberal and conservative press would soon wield it as an emblem of disorder and savagery, in order to collectively discredit the opposition coming from Internationalists, from republicans, and from the street itself. Referring to the Spanish Republicans, Sagasta denounced 'the only [party] in the world that associates itself with the Commune and sends ambassadors to congratulate them even though the facts are already clear'.[38] In response, the Republicans clarified their position: through the press, their leader, Francesc Pí y Margall, celebrated the 'beautiful spectacle of a city which for centuries was the queen and lady of France, defending and fighting for the autonomy of all the countries and peoples of the Republic'. The FRE, for its part, was expanding, while maintaining strong ties with the local experiences just mentioned. Unionised workers and 'plebeian' republicans also identified at that time with the Communards, and with what they considered demands relevant to 'all the peoples of the Earth'.[39] These local dynamics gave Spanish internationalism some of its particular tone: here, the Commune 'took

---

Moisand, eds, *'Arise Ye Wretched of the Earth!': The First International in Global Perspective* (Leiden: Brill, 2018), pp. 221–37.

38 The Federal Republican Party had indeed sent a delegation to Paris to inform itself of events considered overly distorted by the Versaillais press.

39 These two latter citations are from Serrano, 'L'Espagne, la Commune et l'Internationale'.

hold' in an entirely distinctive way. By contrast, no link seems to have been made with the Cuban struggle, whether due to geographical distance or to the discomfort of Spanish republicans still attached to the Empire.[40] Connections between struggles, it might be remembered, never emerge immediately or automatically.

Paris, symbol of the freedom of peoples: the Romanian example

Let us now turn east, to Romania. The Balkan world of the nineteenth century presented a quite different reality. Romania was a barely industrialised or urbanised country: Bucharest had only 150,000 inhabitants, and the peasantry, just freed from serfdom (1864), represented some four-fifths of the population.[41] The press had a rather limited circulation, and news from Europe was taken from British, French or German publications: hence, while the French events were geographically less remote than in the American case, their echoes in Romania were muffled, and concerned only a minority of individuals, limited to the urban petty bourgeoisie.

Yet their reading of French events was driven by keen interest, and deserves attention.[42] Indeed, these enlightened elites had long been imbued with French culture, and many spoke the language. The revolutions of the nineteenth century had also been strongly influential. The liberal ideals of the 1820s, developed in Poland and on the Italian peninsula during the Napoleonic occupation, and even during the Greek war of independence, had a real echo in Romania. Meanwhile, the Springtime of Peoples in 1848 played an even more decisive role. After the uprising, a very liberal constitution was drafted. A national feeling developed among these elites, in its contemporary form, meaning one concerned

40 See Jeanne Moisand, 'L'internationale des Communes. Républiques radicales et internationalisme ouvrier, France, Espagne et leurs colonies (1868–1878)', paper delivered at the 'D'une révolution à l'autre. Histoire des circulations révolutionnaires (XVIIIe–XXe siècle)', conference, Université Paris-Est Marne-la-Vallée and Université Paris-Diderot, 12–14 June 2013.

41 Dan Berindei, 'The Nineteenth Century', in Dinu C. Giurescu and Stephen A. Fischer-Galaţi, eds, *Romania: A Historic Perspective* (New York: Columbia University Press, 1998), pp. 222–7.

42 Andrew Wachtel, *The Balkans in World History* (Oxford: Oxford University Press, 2008).

with the recognition of peoples and of self-determination.[43] The revolutionary surge was quickly suppressed by Turkish and Russian troops, but the ideals and the memory remained.

They also took on a particular tone in this region. It had long been split between three spheres of influence – the Ottoman, the Hungarian, and the Russian. For instance, the political organisation of the two Romanian provinces, Moldavia and Wallachia, was marked by the legacy of the Ottoman Empire. While the 1848 movement had been brought to heel, autonomy (though not independence) was achieved during the Crimean War. Then, in 1857, the two regions were unified under the name of 'Romania'. Romania became a constitutional monarchy under Ottoman suzerainty and European protection. Elected in 1859, Prince Alexander Cuza was overthrown by a military coup in 1866, and then replaced by Karl of Hohenzollern, cousin of the king of Prussia, under the name Carol I. A new constitution was set out, and the sitting government became more conservative. There followed a period of instability, which could still be felt in 1870.

Given the existence of residual Ottoman imperial domination, a king of Prussian descent, the memory of 1848, and interest in France, it is understandable that the Franco-Prussian War, the Republic, and then the Commune had a real impact here. From the first outbreak of hostilities, a vast Francophile movement mobilised in the main cities. The French imperial authorities were initially wary of this, considering it to be a subversive force.[44] As we have seen, about 900 Romanians joined the Franco-Prussian War 'in the cause of liberty'. The proclamation of the Republic then prompted a movement which temporarily brought together very diverse groups: conservative-leaning Moldovan separatists, supporters of Cuza, liberals, radicals like Constantin Alexandru Rosetti and his newspaper *Românul*, republicans, and a smattering of socialists. All were united in their opposition to the king, who was identified with Prussia. Regional tensions sharpened in the shadow of the French events: in March, upon the German victory, a large anti-German

---

43 Steven Soward, 'Twenty-Five Lectures on Modern Balkan History' (1996), online at staff.lib.msu.edu; Anne-Marie Thiesse, *La Création des identités nationales. Europe (XVIIIe–XXe siècle)* (Paris: Seuil, 1999).

44 On what followed, see Georges Haupt, 'La Roumanie', in Rougerie, *1871. Jalons pour une histoire de la Commune de Paris*, pp. 477–89. The newspaper excerpts in the following paragraph are also taken from this article.

demonstration attacked the country's embassy in Bucharest, prompting the ministry to resign.[45]

The outbreak of the Commune after 18 March 1871 continued to be read through this prism. This reading was even stronger because the symbolic presence of Romanians in the Paris National Guard – often students who had remained in the city – quickly became widely known. Among these Romanian liberals and radicals, the Commune somehow seemed to herald a liberal prospect, in the early-nineteenth-century sense of the term: the force of national sovereignty, the recognition of civil liberties, and the promise of emancipation. It was here understood as a communal republic that had emerged from a popular revolt against the invader and against tyranny. 'In Paris', one of these newspapers reported, 'the fate of the liberal world is being decided and thus Romanians must take an interest in these events.' For them, the Commune justified the principle of their own struggle against the established authorities and against Ottoman tutelage. Its socialist or social dimension was not widely perceived in Romania, a land of few industrial workers. By mid-April, however, this had begun to be noticed, seized upon by conservatives warning of the 'communist' danger. Republican agitation nonetheless reached its peak at this point, fuelled by solidarity rallies in Germany, especially the one in Hamburg on 13 April. The movement then began to run out of steam. It suffered a sharp setback with the municipal elections in Bucharest, which turned out to the conservatives' advantage. The latter quickly claimed that the liberals' support for the Commune explained their defeat. By mid-May, the debate that had stirred such controversy in the preceding months had fallen silent. The Commune, seen as the promise of the liberation of peoples – an idea found in other newspapers around the world at the beginning of the Paris events – had here become inaudible, and would remain so for a long time.

The Commune, a revolution in the 'Old World': the Mexican perspective

Mexico closes the circle by bringing us back to the American continent. At first sight, turning to this country may seem an incongruous choice, for

45 CAD, CP, Bucharest, 24 March 1871.

both it and the region as a whole are usually considered more in light of what followed after the Commune, through the establishment of IWMA sections.[46] Yet one should not forget the intense democratic and associational life that stirred countries like Chile, Colombia, and indeed Mexico, from the 1840s to the 1870s.[47] This associational movement, already vigorous in the early nineteenth century, took on new force after the Ayutla Constitution of 1857, which introduced universal male suffrage, and above all after the Reform Wars of the 1860s. It accompanied the development of political clubs and newspapers, while for much of the population it also drew on a strong current of civic Catholicism. The citizens' militias set up in rural communities during the French expedition to Mexico fostered a process of peasant politicisation. Finally, in the 1860s–70s, mutual societies and associations defending workers' rights proliferated, sometimes founded on highly egalitarian principles.[48]

These forms of politicisation outside the central state did not map neatly onto the political opposition between conservatives and liberals, which were more present in the cities. Moreover, the terms themselves bore little resemblance to their European counterparts at the time: each could identify with a form of republicanism. Thus, in this essentially rural region – split between the subsistence economy and export agriculture, and peppered with a handful of industrial centres – a particularly rich and dynamic democratic life developed. Those directly involved were well aware of this; as one Guadalajara newspaper explained in 1862 during the war against France, Mexico represented 'the interests of the New World, a land of democracy, combating the interests of the Old World, a land of tyranny and human degradation.'[49] Attention

46 Marcelo Segall, 'En Amérique latine. Développement du mouvement ouvrier et proscription', in Rougerie, *1871. Jalons pour une histoire de la Commune de Paris*, pp. 325–69.

47 See Cristiàn Gazmuri, *El '1848' chileno. Igualitarios, reformistas radicales, masones y bomberos* (Santiago: Universitaria, 1999); Sergio Grez Toso, 'Les Mouvements d'ouvriers et d'artisans en milieu urbain au Chili au XIXe siècle (1818–1890)', PhD dissertation, EHESS, Paris (1990); James Sanders, *Contentious Republicans: Popular Politics, Race, and Class in 19th Century Colombia* (Durham: Duke University Press, 2004); and Carlos Forment, *Democracy in Latin America (1760–1900)* (Chicago: University of Chicago Press, 2003).

48 On all of this, see Forment, *Democracy in Latin America*.

49 'El Voto del Pueblo (Guadalajara), 29 June 1862', in James Sanders, 'The Vanguard of the Atlantic World: Contesting Modernity in Nineteenth-Century Latin America', *Latin American Research Review* 46: 2 (2011), pp. 104–27, in particular p. 112.

among the elites to the 'European model' remained strong, yet from the 1840s onwards the idea took hold that the 'true Republic', the modern Republic, had found its most favourable terrain on the Western side of the Atlantic.

In these conditions, the events of 1870–71 could hardly fail to arouse great interest. Indeed, they were closely followed in the papers that have been consulted (*La Voz del Pueblo*, *La Brújula*, *La Voz de México*, *El Monitor Republicano*, *El Federalista*, *El Socialista*, *El Siglo XIX*).[50] Their echoes could stay at the level of factual reporting, as in the case of *La Voz del Pueblo* (in the Sinaloa region), or else be more developed, as in the liberal *El Siglo XIX*, one of the country's leading newspapers. Each week, this paper devoted its first five columns to the 'Parisian letters' of a correspondent on the ground. Also in its pages, the main dispatches and statements were translated into Spanish, such as the famous manifesto of the Commune of 19 April 1871, here published on 29 May. To counteract both the geographical and technical distance, the dailies built up their access routes: from the telegraphic line from Veracruz, to French or British ships (via Havana or New Orleans), and the press of the southern United States, which received news by telegraph. Thus, within a single issue, the freshness of the information reported could vary: for instance, the 10 June issue of *El Siglo XIX* related the news of the bloody recapture of Paris between 23 and 28 May, while in the very next day's issue, the correspondent on the ground described at length the situation on 11 May, analysing the arguments advanced by each side at that point.

But how were these events perceived? Let us once again turn to *El Siglo XIX*, for which I have been able to consult the complete series. The announcement of the French Republic in September 1870 was positively received. But the outbreak of the Commune raised questions, particularly from its Paris correspondent. This, he argued, marked a shift from one extreme to the other – from the tyranny of Napoleon III to the most complete disorder. 'Poor France', he wrote on 19 March 1871, 'all you were missing was civil war, all you needed was the red flag atop the Hôtel de Ville, and the black flag on the palace of Louis XIV.'[51] Initially

50 Some are accessible online, whereas others were consulted at the library of the Ibero-Amerikanisches Institut (IAI, Berlin), with the valuable aid of the library staff.

51 *El Siglo XIX*, 2 May, Paris letter of 19 March.

favourable to Thiers's legitimate government, his analysis gradually became more nuanced:

> It will seem strange in Mexico that an authority such as the Commune . . . can have the support of such a large force of the National Guard, consisting of almost all order-loving people. This anomaly stems from the fact that the Commune defends the Paris municipal franchises, similar to those enjoyed by the people of London.[52]

Over the course of his articles, the author developed what would become his main argument: faced with a parliament that threatened to bring the monarchy back to France, the Paris movement had at least helped to keep alive the institutions of republicanism. The Commune's failing was that it was governed by a 'revolutionary junta' – an expression obviously rich in meaning in the Mexican context – bent on carrying out 'socialist reforms' considered 'a folly'. The Paris secession stood accused of taking things too far, even though its initial programme – municipal franchises – was legitimate. This theme of the Commune's excessive character was widespread. The conservative, Catholic *Voz de México* obviously took an even more severe view of things, especially in matters of religion. 'What about freedom of conscience?' its journalist commented with some anger on 30 May. 'It's unknown to these Reds.' Albeit on very different grounds, *El Federalista* voiced similar distrust, echoing the criticisms of the republican Italian Mazzini, which had been translated and circulated by Spanish newspapers.[53]

Within this flurry of reactions, it is particularly interesting to read the more conciliatory positions, such as those offered by the newly launched *El Socialista*. Edited by skilled artisans, it illustrated the dynamism of Mexico's own workers' movement. In its first issues, the Communards were credited with defending republican and socially just ideas ('tear down the clergy and the Napoleonic nobility, annihilate the propertied'). But here, again, 'They went much further than expected.'[54] Particular attention was directed to the violence of the Parisian events. 'Mexico City does not have the same destructive elements as France',

52 *El Siglo XIX*, 18 May, Paris letter of 10 April.

53 *El Federalista*, 10 August.

54 *El Socialista*, 18 August.

commented an article signed – tellingly – 'Michelet'.[55] 'Here, our customs, even when we are said to be lagging behind, are superior'.[56] A similar idea had been put forward in the 22 July edition of *El Siglo XIX*. For those most inclined to look kindly on the Commune (the radical liberal press, the federalist press, or the workers' press inspired by the associative ideal of 1848), it could indeed offer interesting principles such as communal republicanism or worker-associationism; yet it failed at realising them. A prisoner both of a France and of a Europe crushed by years of submission to monarchy and industrial development, the Commune's endeavour was judged immature, as shown by the unnecessary violence of the Communards and Versaillais. Here emerges the Latin American republican reading, which can now be clarified thanks to the analysis of historian James Sanders.[57] According to him, the Mexican republicans of the day considered themselves as being in the vanguard of a certain political modernity. More precisely, they counterposed a Latin American political modernity – based on the idea of equality, humanity and freedom – to a European one based on economic development and the strengthening of the nation-state, at the cost of big industrial monopolies, racism, and the denial of democracy. In this sense, France lay in the past, while political modernity and the 'real republicans' were to be found on the other side of the Atlantic, despite its tensions and its lesser economic development. This Mexican republican reading – which opens onto a wholly different definition of 'modernity' and the 'Republic' – thus invites a salutary defamiliarisation of our habitual ways of seeing.

The Paris Commune thus prompted a diverse array of readings, centred on a common set of issues. It was as if this event was refracted through debates that had already developed in latent form in the 1850s, particularly in societies characterised by the development of the state and the national question – societies which were, moreover, increasingly questioning the type of interdependency between government and people and the well-being of the nation's inhabitants. The issues to which the

55 The use of the pseudonym 'Michelet' clearly refers to the French historian Jules Michelet (1798–1874), renowned for his republican writings.

56 *El Socialista*, 20 August.

57 Sanders, 'Vanguard of the Atlantic World'.

Commune pointed can thus be organised around two main focuses.[58] First, popular sovereignty: Should it be realised in full, or only in part? By the people, or by the representatives of the people? Within a centralised state, or in a territory which left more room for local governance? Then there was the question of economic relations: Should they be kept as they were, or changed? Was it necessary to retain the existing social differences, or look to a new agreement among the classes – or even a class struggle? These problems were addressed in various ways, sometimes even with contradictions between one country and another. But the Commune did expose these common lines of questioning. Through the debates that took place, this event was thus fixed in different ways. Here emerged a transnational production of the 'Commune' idea, which would contribute to the influence of the Parisian insurrection as well as the power of its myth.

58 Here we take up the approach proposed in Samuel Hayat, 'Souveraineté populaire', in Louis Hincker, ed., *Citoyenneté, république, démocratie en France (1789–1899)* (Paris: Atlande, 2014), pp. 145–59.

4

Strange Species of Spaces: The 'Paris Republic' and the World

Is it possible to identify the effects that these transnational, imperial and global dimensions had on the French and Parisian events themselves?[1] Clearly, the leading actors were at least aware of these dimensions, both in Paris and in Versailles. On 28 April, at the Commune's meeting in the Paris Hôtel de Ville, the delegate for external relations, Paschal Grousset, turned to a problem raised the day before by Gustave Courbet. 'Your delegation for external relations', he explained, 'had already thought of addressing to Europe and the world, not a claim of any kind, but a protest against the infamous violations of the law of war with which the Versailles government has sullied itself.'[2] A few days later in the National Assembly, the intransigent Legitimist MP, the Marquis de Franclieu, raged: 'If we remain stuck in revolution, if we continue to have only governments of chance . . . the dangers that we will bring to the whole world, the fear and repulsion of which we will continue to be the object, will be powerful enough motives to inspire all peoples with the desire to unite against us and to make us disappear as a nation.'[3] These aspects were thus on the protagonists' minds. But they appeared among others

1 The title of this chapter plays on that of Georges Perec, *Espèces d'espaces* (Paris: Galilée, 1974) – transl. and ed. John Sturrock as *Species of Spaces and Other Pieces* (London: Penguin, 1997).

2 Procès-verbaux de la Commune de Paris, 28 April 1871.

3 *Annales de l'Assemblée nationale, Compte rendu in extenso des séances, annexes*, Paris, impr. et libr. du 'Journal officiel', 1871–1872,meeting of 8 May 1871, p. 879.

– first and foremost the national perspective – and they were not granted similar attention by all the different actors. Their effects on the Versailles government have been analysed in the previous chapters: these dimensions imposed interventions and adjustments in the form of economic, diplomatic, technical and symbolic constraints. But, at the same time, they proved to be a resource for preserving the integrity of the national and imperial territories, marginalising the Paris secession, and prevailing in the battle to define the situation. The levels of action did not merge, yet they intersected. How about the Commune? The presence of transnational volunteers and the support of various groups abroad had made it, as we have seen, into one of the banners of the 'Universal Republic'. We should now ask how the Commune fitted (or did not fit) into these networks of interdependence, and how it perceived the spatial horizons of its own activity.

This time, the issue is related to an ongoing debate. Since the decline of the communist historiography, which was attentive to the role of the Commune in the international history of the workers' movement, two opposing visions have gradually taken shape. Some researchers see the Commune, imbued by internationalism, as a moment in which the 'cell of nationality' dissolved – a feature that would explain its persistent relevance.[4] Others, also with some evidence, have placed more emphasis on the patriotic character of an event marked by the war and by the imaginary of the French Revolution.[5] These two perspectives do not in fact stand in flat contradiction. But, to get a clearer view of things, we can begin by looking at the international activity of the Commune's delegation for external relations, which has received curiously little academic attention. We can then ask what was known about this external situation under the Commune, and try to grasp the conceptions of space that emerged in revolutionary Paris. The liberated city is not only an object of attention: it also provides an original observation-post for the vast galaxy of links that is beginning to take shape.

4 See, for example, Kristin Ross, *Communal Luxury* (London: Verso, 2015).

5 Notably in the works of Jacques Rougerie and Robert Tombs.

The Commune's Diplomatic Practices

The proposal made by Courbet on 27 April, to which Grousset gave the above reply, raised a real problem. As fighting raged – with the Versaillais gaining the upper hand – the painter, who was also president of the Artists' Federation and an elected representative of the 6th arrondissement, had asked that the Commune seek to obtain 'belligerent' status. The occasion was provided by an unfortunate comparison between the Commune and the secessionist states of the southern United States, made by Thiers in the National Assembly. Courbet explained, probably with the US Civil War in mind:

> According to the law of all peoples, according to international law, according to the history of civil war, *one is only an insurgent in the first few days*; and the right to fight arms in hand is always recognised for a party that has organised itself militarily and fights in good faith, instead and in place of the state . . . It is therefore time [he concluded] that Europe recognise our rights, and citizen P. Grousset should have begun by demanding from all peoples the formal recognition of our rights as belligerents.[6]

Paschal Grousset replied the next day, pushing back against this. There was no reason, he said, 'to appeal to a court that is manifestly incompetent in the matter'. This war was 'not an ordinary war; it is not a question of the rivalry of two peoples alien to each other and both belonging to what is called the European concert; it is a war in which Frenchmen fight Frenchmen'. So, Europe had no need to intervene; and as for the 'judgment of Europe and the world', it had been pronounced already: 'The facts are known today, the press has popularised them and the opinion of all civilised peoples has been formed.'[7] Two conceptions of civil war thus stood opposed: one acknowledged the secession within the state, and set it within the framework of international law; the other sought to keep it within a national framework and avoid foreign interference. This latter position was finally approved by a vote in the Commune.

6 Procès-verbaux de la Commune de Paris, meeting of 27 April. Emphasis in the original.

7 Ibid., 28 April.

A few weeks later, however, as the Commune's defeats became ever clearer, Grousset declared its official obedience to the Geneva Convention. This came in direct reply to Thiers's ironic retort to the complaints brought before Versailles by the International Society for the Relief of the Wounded: he had argued that the government was under no obligation to respect the Geneva Convention, since the Commune had not signed it; the Commune's adherence to the Convention was in this sense a direct response to his provocation. But the move also served another purpose, affirming a recurring theme of the Communards – one that adapted and extended a leitmotif of the Franco-Prussian War: the opposition between the Commune's 'civilised' war and the 'savage' one waged by the Versaillais. As the text stated, 'it has scrupulously respected all the laws of humanity, in the presence of the most savage acts, the bloodiest challenges to civilisation and modern law'.[8]

Although the Commune tended to respond more to the pressure of circumstances than to a deliberate process of reflection, it did indeed refer to the judgement of foreign countries, and engage with the shifts in international law embodied in the recent Geneva Convention. The combination of the two positions, as articulated by Grousset and the delegation, is rather surprising: the Commune defined a national field of action for itself and, at the same time, mobilised the new forms of international law. But it ought to be remembered that this indeterminacy was a consequence of the civil war striking in the heart of a great European power. A few years earlier, the US Civil War had already seen such a blurring of local, national and international law.[9] The Commune would in turn experience this, albeit on a smaller scale.

Yet even if these decisions were taken rapidly, questions of international law appear to have been important to the Commune. To assume otherwise would be to overlook the discreet but steady work of the delegation and of its representative, Paschal Grousset. Born in Corsica in 1844, he first trained as a doctor, before becoming a journalist.[10]

8 *JOC*, 13 May 1871. Its adherence to the Geneva Convention was referenced on 16 May 1871, when Grousset made clear that this did not prevent the use of the 'new war machines which the Revolution has available to it'.

9 John Fabian Witt, *Lincoln's Code: The Laws of War in American History* (New York: Free Press, 2012).

10 Xavier Noël and Paschal Grousset, *De la Commune de Paris à la Chambre des députés. De Jules Verne à l'olympisme* (Brussels: Les Impressions nouvelles, 2010).

Towards the end of the Empire, he published, under a pseudonym, numerous adventure novels, 'scenes of college life' set in various countries, and translations of Mayne Reid and R. L. Stevenson – skills that would prove useful in his later role. Well turned out in appearance, Grousset was best known for his anti-Bonapartist and socially revolutionary political stance, which he expressed in the newspaper *La Marseillaise*, where he served as editor-in-chief. Notably, he provoked Prince Pierre-Napoleon Bonaparte into a duel – an episode made famous by the killing of Victor Noir, which in turn sparked huge demonstrations in Paris at the end of the Second Empire. After a spell in Sainte-Pélagie prison, he enlisted during the war and, under the Commune, was elected to represent the 18th arrondissement. On 29 March he joined the External Relations Commission, becoming its delegate on 20 April. That same day, the delegation welcomed new members: the flower seller Johannard, the hatmaker's worker Charles Amouroux, and the freethinker and former law student Léo Meillet. All were members of the International Workingmen's Association; the first two were also Freemasons. Despite these affiliations – which did not involve Grousset himself – neither they nor the other figures in his entourage, such as his brother and a certain Lacoste, possessed any real expertise in international law or foreign affairs: they were amateurs. The delegation for external (or foreign) relations was responsible for everything outside the Commune – notably including the *départements* and other cities of France – as a note published in the *Journal officiel* on 4 May reminds us. So it maintained contact with urban centres that might themselves turn into Communes, and it monitored the activities of the Prussian forces established to the north-east of Paris.[11] Of course, international activity was by no means neglected. Both the commission and then the delegation were based in the building of the former Ministry of Foreign Affairs, at 37 Quai d'Orsay (7th arrondissement), completed in 1856. They even adopted some of its working methods, as suggested by Grousset's use of ministerial files, later found by the police at his mistress's home.[12] The delegate was thus prompt to notify foreign

11 On the first of these topics, it conferred with the delegation for war. SHD, 8J, 3e conseil, 29/9, Grousset, Pascal.

12 The list of countries subsequently copied out by the police chief began: the United States, Britain, Austria, Belgium, Denmark and Sweden, Malta, Rome (*sic*), Spain, Russia . . . (SHD, 8J, 3e conseil, 29).

governments of the constitution of the communal government, as announced in the *Journal officiel*. The Paris archives hold the copy sent to Colombia. It reads:

> The undersigned, member of the Paris Commune, delegate for external relations, has the honour of officially notifying you of the constitution of the Communal Government of Paris, he beseeches you to bring knowledge of it to your Government, and seizes this opportunity to express to you the Commune's desire to strengthen the fraternal ties which unite the people of Paris to the Colombian people, Paris, 5 April 1871.[13]

Remarkable here was the suggested equivalence between the 'peoples' of Paris and of Colombia. It is not known whether these missives were received, or even sent. On another front, in Paris the delegation – and through it the Commune – showed great concern for the rights of foreigners and for diplomatic immunity. In mid-April, the intrusion of National Guards from the 218th battalion into the Belgian legation provoked a scandal. The Belgian legation limited itself to reminding those it called 'delinquents' to observe the law of nations. But the Commune reacted in one of its sessions, and then by posting a notice. 'It is a violation of diplomatic immunities', representative Tridon remarked, indignant.[14] To avoid fresh incidents, Grousset had a note published on 26 April:

> . . . the persons and assets of foreign citizens are guaranteed by the rights of neutrals and by the proverbial hospitality of France. Consequently, any movable objects, cars, horses, etc., and any apartment registered in the name of a foreign citizen, enjoying the immunities attached to the sacred title of guest of the Republic, cannot and must not be subject to requisition.[15]

This stance of principle – combining a reference to the law with republican generosity – was reflected in practice. In the delegation's archives

13 Archives de la ville de Paris, AVP, 4 AZ/10.

14 Procès-verbaux de la Commune de Paris, 16 April.

15 26 April 1871 (published in the *JOC*, 27 April).

we find pre-printed letterheads used to inform Parisians of places to be preserved intact:

> Paris Commune, delegation for external relations. In the name of the people, any citizen, officer of the National Guard, or any other, is ordered to respect as neutral and inviolable the . . . of citizen . . . , rue . . . no. . . . Any offender will be prosecuted to the full extent of the law.[16]

Rights based on nationality thus found a place among the Commune's concerns. There were even what could be described as diplomatic exchanges with foreign representatives in France. The latter generally took a cautious approach. At the end of April, a mini-diplomatic crisis broke out. In response to Courbet, Léo Meillet had assured in a session of the Commune that he had been involved in exchanges with the minister of the Republic of Ecuador in order to aid the recognition of the Commune's belligerent status. The publication of this intervention led to an official rebuttal from the vice-consul of the Republic of Ecuador, based in Brussels. In agreement with the president and the foreign minister of his country, the consul published a protest against 'the usurpation of title or the mystification of which the Commune boasted'.[17] Transmitted to Jules Favre on 3 May, the text soon appeared in several Belgian newspapers, and was then reproduced in the French press. The editors of the *Journal officiel* offered a wry response the following day. In any case, when it came to diplomatic relations, caution was necessary. Exchanges with foreign representatives were generally discreet or in response to specific problems. In April, the Spanish consul sent a letter to the *Journal officiel* in order to facilitate the departure of his compatriots; he asked that it be published in Spanish, which was done.[18] On 4 May, the Swiss legation complained to Paschal Grousset about the invasion of the apartment of Mrs Schaffer, a Swiss subject and a widow, at 122 boulevard Pereire (in the 17th arrondissement) by National Guards from the 91st battalion, who had come in search of weapons. The intrusion was perpetrated 'despite the Swiss flag hung from her balcony,

16 CAD, 2QO 83: Commune.
17 CAD, CP, Ecuador, 3 May 1871.
18 *JOC*, 20 April 1871.

despite the writing stuck to the front door of the apartment stating her nationality [the document specified by Grousset]'. In support of his complaint, the legate also evoked 'the law of neutrals, by which foreigners are guaranteed, as was recently recalled by the delegate for external relations in a note inserted in the *Journal officiel* of 24 April.'[19] Tools such as Grousset's declarations thus served as a mediation in such exchanges. Even the US plenipotentiary Elihu Washburne, whose correspondence had no words harsh enough for the Commune, got in touch with the delegation. In diplomatic language, in which he clearly weighed every word, he wrote to Grousset: 'To the delegation for foreign relations of the Paris Commune, 28 April. Dear Minister, This is a small matter, for which I take the liberty, in these exceptional circumstances that deprive us of any direct contact with France's representatives abroad, of appealing to your kindness.' Their exchange had to do with the inheritance of a Miss Dauvergne and the transmission of her mother's death certificate. If the letter was terse, the form of address was just as carefully weighted: 'Please accept the assurance of my most cordial greetings.' Driven by the concern to defend their own nationals' interests, and to this end mimicking diplomatic language, foreign government representatives did maintain relations with the Commune, recognising it at least as a possible interlocutor. The question often arose as to whether the Commune was acting as a government or as a municipality. As we shall see, this uncertainty was impossible to resolve; but on the terrain of 'external relations', it was clear that the Commune was at least partially taking on the trappings of statehood.

Here in Paris: Getting the News from Europe and the World

But in the rebel city, was the population really aware of what was going on outside Paris and France? Even though Paris was surrounded, most press organs remained available, until the banning of several newspapers during April 1871, and especially after the bans imposed on 5 and 19 May.[20] Up to this point, their readers had access to the same information presented above. There was also a republican and a 'Communard'

19 CAD, 2QO 83.

20 Bellanger et al., *Histoire générale de la presse française*, Vol. II, pp. 373–8.

version of this news, accessible in the news-sheets that had proliferated since September 1870. An official version was even provided by the Commune's own press organ. This retained the title *Journal officiel de la République française*, except the 30 March issue, which was entitled *Journal officiel de la Commune*. In order to avoid confusion, we will stick for convenience's sake with this second name.[21] The new version first appeared on 19 March, the day after the occupation of its offices. It was published under the direction of Central Committee delegate Emile Lebeau and part of the previous editorial team. On 24 March, Lebeau was replaced by the journalist Charles Longuet. Long the IWMA's delegate for Belgium, Longuet was a National Guard commander during the siege, a member of the Central Committee, and an elected representative for the 16th arrondissement. He was replaced in turn on 13 May by the man of letters Pierre Vésinier, who was also a Freemason and a member of the IWMA. Men and styles differed, but the 'foreign news' section, which we are about to delve into, was little affected by these changes in the editorial team. This section – the most consistent among the newspapers I have been able to access – gives some insight into how the Commune as a political body perceived the outside world. Appearing daily up to 4 May, this section then disappeared, doubtless under the pressure of military events (though it made exceptional appearances on 16 and 19–21 May). The international news was then moved into the 'various news' section, among many others (news from the provinces, from the courtrooms, and miscellaneous developments).

Reading this section reveals the interesting geography of the *Journal officiel*'s attention. Great Britain was heavily dominant, both in its own right (with thirty-seven mentions in these entries) and as a source of information, especially for countries in Asia and the Americas. Its preponderance reflected both the media influence of the leading power of the day and, without doubt, the editors' own linguistic skills: in the late 1860s Charles Longuet and Pierre Vésinier had lived in exile in England. But their information also came from other foreign titles such as *La Época*, *La Gazette de Cologne*, and so on. The Commune's outlook thus rested on the same textual materials that were circulating around France and in other countries. But the editor added his own processes of selection and interpretation, acting as a kind of filter on the filter.

21 This explains why I have used the latter title here (abbreviated as *JOC*).

Another striking feature of this attention to international affairs was its Eurocentrism. It was especially focused on Northern Europe (beyond Great Britain, Germany was mentioned thirty-four times and Belgium thirteen) and the south of the continent (Italy was mentioned twenty times, Spain thirteen). Apart from Austria-Hungary, central and eastern regions were less present, though there was some mention of tensions in Romania – the sign of a relatively mutual attention. The Asian continent was all but ignored, and the African continent was absent. The territories of the British Empire (Australia, Canada, India), the countries of Latin America, and even the United States (mentioned seven times) – lands which themselves closely followed events in Paris – were hardly mentioned. There was also silence over the French colonies. The exception was Algeria, but its inclusion was linked to the Algiers 'Commune' and its declarations of solidarity.[22] This divergence between the foreign reception of the Commune and its own attention to the outside world explains why echoes of the Commune and their possible repercussions could escape its protagonists' field of observation. Recognising these discrepancies is essential to understanding this event.

Equally instructive was the content of these news pieces. Some entries in this international section concerned foreign states' domestic politics, especially those of countries near to France (Great Britain, Germany, Spain, Italy, Austria-Hungary). The French situation after the defeat to Germany was likewise followed: the fate of prisoners, peace treaties, the annexation of Alsace-Lorraine, the payment of war indemnities . . . A substantial and more original set of texts provided information on outside perspectives, and on foreign expressions of support for the Commune. When it came to the former, the daily especially reported criticisms of Versailles, above all from British sources. As for the latter, the expressions of support coming from Britain, Germany, Austria-Hungary, Spain and Italy heightened the feeling of the growing international influence of the uprising. In another register, oppositional movements in Europe and around the world were also surveyed – on 19 April, the campaign in the Netherlands petitioning for the abolition of the articles of the penal code which punished coalitions of employers and of workers; on 30 April, an uprising in Sinskin against the Japanese

22 Tellingly, while it sometimes appeared in this section, in some editions it appeared in the one regarding the Communes in the provinces.

government's monetary policy; and so on.[23] These references made it possible for the *Journal officiel*'s contributors to set the Commune at the heart of a vast current of contemporary protest, and to present this as an obvious fact. When it came to imperial matters, however, the paper was more likely to reproduce the viewpoint of its sources, adopting the coloniser's perspective: thus it spoke of the battles fought by 'our troops' against the Kabyle insurrection in Algeria (8 May), and took the side of Spain in its war against Cuba – even when the characteristics of this struggle, which had already been known about since 1869, might have suggested an entirely different attitude. Admittedly, an obituary in the 15 April edition paid tribute to the warrior-prophet Iman Schamyl (1797–1871), celebrating the national struggle, anti-imperial fight and holy war waged by 'Abd el-Kader of the Caucasus' against Russia between 1830 and 1860. But this reflected less a sympathy for anti-imperial struggles per se than a characteristic early-nineteenth-century theme: fighting for national liberation against despotic rulers. Finally, a last set of texts fed an imaginary of modernity, such as can be seen through the fascination for nature, new discoveries, and wonderment at technological developments: earthquakes in remote lands, maritime commerce in the South American space, the building of boats meant to travel up the Amazon (8 May). The Commune cast itself as a revolution imbued with the spirit of science. So, what emerges from this section is a particular vision of the outside world: a republican, democratic, socialist one, marked by the metropolitan context of the 1860s. Such was the Commune's quasi-official outlook.

But how much was this vision actually circulated? The *Journal officiel* sold poorly, even after its price was dropped to 5 centimes on 14 May. The most-read dailies of the era were the journalist Eugène Vermersch's *Le Père Duschêne* and, even more so, Jules Vallès's *Le Cri du Peuple*, which printed as many as 100,000 copies on 23 May. The latter offered the various kinds of foreign news mentioned above: on other countries' domestic politics, foreign support for the Commune, their own internal oppositional movements, and so on.[24] But the amount of foreign news

23 Many of the one-off references to countries involved this type of coverage.

24 For this purpose, one in three issues were consulted. The book here referred to is Maxime Jourdan, *'Le Cri du Peuple' (22 février–23 mai 1871)* (Paris: L'Harmattan, 2005).

was rather lower, and no specific section was devoted to it, whereas there was one dedicated to provincial France. 'The World' most often appeared in its pages as a general category: 'To order!' we read on the 28 April front page, 'Cry[ing] out to "free men of good morals", across all France, across all Europe, across the entire world, that Paris is today defending its franchises and the communal ideal against the bombers, just as Palermo defended its rights under bombardment.' Above all, there was a more constant use of patriotic language and concern for national unity. *Le Cri du peuple*, Maxime Jourdan notes, spoke above all of the people, the Republic, and Paris. The presence of the latter especially transpires from the mass of notices, posters and circulars produced by the various authorities in operation, for which *Le Cri du peuple*, in an innovative conception of journalism, became the privileged transmission belt.[25]

While they often had their disagreements, a relatively similar observation could be made with regard to *Le Père Duchêne*, which I have consulted more briefly. Precise information on the international situation was less common in the pages of this paper, known for its crude language, and inspired by its famous ancestor from 1793. Here, Europe and the world above all took on the appearance of a distant horizon, or one consisting of great principles inspired by revolutionary impulses like Federation or the Universal Republic. 'Federation in place of unity! A place in the sun for all, and life, in the name of God, life! Political and social life! . . . In a word, long live the universal federation!', the paper declaimed upon the destruction of the Vendôme Column. 'What should it matter if a man is born in one place or another? Should we have anything against him because he's not from here?'[26] The appeal to patriotism was also particularly present here, as was the invocation of the people and the Republic, in a constant drive towards energy and action.

The relative neglect of this international dimension is owed to the fact that these two titles were combat-publications which sought to feed the dynamism of the Commune. They were pulled along in this movement, and foreign news was used less for the purpose of informing readers than as fuel for the affective and military mobilisation to defend the

25 Ibid.

26 *Le Père Duchêne*, 25 germinal of year 79.

Commune. Here, awareness of the foreign situation proved rather more indistinct, though it was also spread among a wider readership.

A Political-Spatial Project: The Federation of Communes

Conversely, if we want to grasp the perception of space in insurgent Paris, we should perhaps ask how the Commune – or the people involved in its development – understood its scope and the scales on which it acted. Here, a study of the press is completed by examining the statements and discussions coming from the Hôtel de Ville, as well as the mass of posters and proclamations issued by municipalities, battalions, associations, vigilance committees and clubs. Their outlook was anything but homogeneous, even aside from the fact that many of these addresses – urgently written in order to deal with sometimes day-to-day problems – suppose a certain narrowing of attention. Nonetheless, some original perspectives begin to emerge.[27]

The world's judgement and the appeal of the universal Republic

'The World' was not absent from the writings of the Commune's representatives or promoters. Some of them even referred to specific conflicts or political transformations then underway. 'All civilised peoples have their eyes on Paris' – such was the conclusion which one 'appeal to the women citizens of Paris', signed by a 'group of women', wanted to draw. 'This same Germany, whose princely armies devastated our homeland, swearing death to its democratic and socialist tendencies, is itself shaken and agitated by the breath of revolution! . . . Russia itself has seen its champions of liberty perish only to greet a new generation . . .!' Ireland, Poland and Italy were also mentioned, among others.[28] However, references to 'the world' most often retained the generic character indicated above. It was used in this sense right after the creation of the Paris Commune, on 29 March: 'We appeal to the judgement of Europe and

27 I conducted a full-text search by groups of keywords, using the *Journal officiel* as well as the posters collected in *Les Murailles politiques françaises depuis le 4 septembre 1870, vol. II: La Commune* (Paris: Versailles, la Province), *(18 mars–27 mai 1871)* (Paris: Le Chevalier, 1874).

28 *JOC*, 11 April 1871.

the world on these execrable activities [those of the monarchists]'.[29] As well as an arbiter, 'the world' stood as a horizon and index of the scope of the Commune's action. 'The question today is no longer just the emancipation of a particular class', the elected Commune member Gustave Lefrançais explained to the representatives of the Masonic lodges, 'but that of the French people, of the workers of the whole world.'[30] Statements from the Central Committee, from the sections of the IWMA, from the municipalities, and from the National Guard battalions used the term similarly.[31] This 'world' was, more often than not, a possible, projected world. It was that of the revolutionaries of 1789, 1830 and 1848. Above all, it indicated the hoped-for breadth of social-political transformation, and its global scope.

The 'universal Republic', the 'universal federation', and 'universal democracy' were evoked with similar frequency. This idea was paraded right from the inaugural speech of the Commune: the *doyen* Charles Beslay celebrated a Republic capable of making 'France the support of the weak, the protector of the workers, the hope of the oppressed around the world, and the foundation of the universal Republic'.[32] Curiously, this reference seems to have been more often used outside the Hôtel de Ville itself. It had pride of place among the Freemasons, for whom it was a flagship value.[33] It can also be found on many of the posters issued by the various bodies active under the Commune, which often concluded with a 'Vive la Commune! Vive la République universelle!' In these cases, this reference pointed more specifically to previous revolutions: the 'Great Revolution', the European 'Springtime of Peoples', or the republican and democratic struggles of 1848–71. Certainly it seemed more concrete. Insurgent Paris was incontestably a banner of the universal Republic; and it was doubtless here, in the perspective of general emancipation, that the Commune most clearly expressed its international outlook.

29 *Les Murailles politiques*, 29 March 1871 poster; *JOC*, 30 March.

30 *JOC*, 1 May (speech from 30 April).

31 For instance, *JOC*, 7 May 1871.

32 *JOC*, 2 April 1871.

33 Pierre-Yves Beaurepaire, *La République universelle des francs-maçons. De Newton à Metternich* (Rennes: Éditions Ouest-France, 1999).

National unity and the endangered Patrie

But most present was the language of the *patrie*, of the nation, and of France.[34] Citizens were often called 'patriots', and contributions, claims, efforts and duties were termed 'patriotic' . . . The term appeared in the debates at the Hôtel de Ville as well as in the posters and proclamations issued by the Central Committee, the municipalities, or more specific groups such as the republican Zouaves.

This is no surprise. The Paris uprising was an extension of two conflicts, one of them waged against a foreign power. Most importantly, the idea of the *patrie* was intrinsically linked to the French Revolution and to the notion of the Republic, whether democratic and social or otherwise. This appeal to the *patrie* was also a more prosaic adaptation to the situation. On 4 April, the communal delegation of the 11th arrondissement 'appeal[ed] to the patriotic feelings of all able-bodied citizens, in order to constitute new battalions which will have to unite with the already federated ones'.[35] In a city where not everyone joined in supporting the communal government, patriotism was certainly the lowest common denominator for mobilising the population in the face of the siege.

Reading these texts, France appears to have been the horizon of reference for those involved in the Commune, with the horizons of the universal Republic and of the world added to this in a second stage. The famous poster of 19 April, considered its defining document, was indeed addressed 'to the French people'. The same can be said of the other major appeals, including Grousset's call to the 'great cities' at the moment of the Commune's defeat; it was addressed to metropolitan-French cities.[36]

These two horizons did not necessarily stand in contradiction. In the logic of the 'open' nationalism of the early nineteenth century, of which the Commune was also one extension, fighting for the liberation of a nation and against a despotic regime also meant fighting for the

34 The term *patrie* is focused on here rather than 'France' or 'nation' because of the large number of irrelevant occurrences of these latter terms (for instance, in 'National' Assembly).

35 *JOC*, 8 April (dated 4 April 1871).

36 And, without doubt, Algiers (which, as we have seen, had a specific symbolic status). 'Déclaration au peuple français', 19 April 1871; 'Aux grandes villes', 14 May 1871. See also 'La Commune de Paris aux départements', 6 April 1871.

emancipation of other countries, in a universalising perspective. This association took on a particular bent in France, the country of the Revolution, where the *patrie* was supposed to have a universalist calling.[37] Such a notion was also reflected in practice, given that some foreigners had entered the federated National Guard in the name of fighting for the universal Republic. Others, such as Léo Frankel, were even admitted as members of the Commune. This integration was officially justified by the 'consider[ation] that the flag of the Commune is that of the Universal Republic, that every city has the right to give the title of citizen to the foreigners who serve it . . . that the title of member of the Commune is an even greater mark of confidence than the title of citizen'.[38] If the Commune evoked the rights of foreigners, it thus also opened the borders of citizenship – a remarkable trait in a period when definitions of the national were hardening.[39]

Of course, behind these moments of consensus, there were also confrontations. The Communards elected to the Hôtel de Ville did not always agree on this matter: the members of the IWMA (with their diverse positions), together with the Freemasons and the republicans of 1848 or of the struggles of the 1860s, had a sharper awareness of the international dimension than did the Jacobins, who drew solely on the memory of the 'Great Revolution', or indeed the very many Blanquists, who preferred to defend what they called the Commune's 'proletarian nationalism'.[40] Tensions also emerged outside the Hôtel de Ville. On 10 April, a poster was addressed to the National Guard:

> Citizens,
>
> We learn that there is still some concern in the National Guard about citizen Dombrowski, appointed commander of the defences. He is reproached for being a foreigner and unknown to the population of Paris. Indeed, citizen Dombrowski is Polish. [There follows a

37 On the universalism of the French Revolution, see Lynn Hunt, *Inventing Human Rights, A History* (New York and London: W.W. Norton and Co., 2007).

38 *JOC*, 31 March 1871.

39 Laurent Dornel, *La France hostile. Socio-histoire de la xénophobie (1870–1914)* (Paris: Belin, 2004); Gérard Noiriel, *État, nation et immigration. Vers une histoire du pouvoir* (Paris: Belin, 2001).

40 On the Blanquists' ideas, see Patrick Hutton, *The Cult of the Revolutionary Tradition: The Blanquists in French Politics (1864–1893)* (Berkeley: University of California Press, 1981).

> description of his record in Poland, in the Caucasus, and under Garibaldi's leadership]. Citizen Dombrowski is therefore unquestionably a man of war and a devoted soldier of the Universal Republic.
> The Executive Commission of the Commune.[41]

That this had to be specified is an indicator of the concerns of many of these Parisian fighters, then in a situation of war, civil war and revolution. The US consul in Paris, John Read, also reported several incidents of anti-Prussian xenophobia from September 1870 and after 18 March.[42] This is hardly surprising, and nor was it unprecedented (xenophobic disturbances had broken out in 1848). Given the diversity of the groups involved, these forms of belonging were clearly not homogeneous, and often clashed in a fearful besieged city.

The Parisian centre, the 'tree' city

Ultimately, the main territorial reference point was Paris. For the Commune – which claimed to be a citizen government and demanded, as a minimum, municipal 'franchises' and the autonomy of the capital – the city was the primary focus of action. From this base, the other horizons unfolded: on the one hand, the level of the local arrondissement, and on the other those of France, Europe and the world. The posters of the arrondissement town halls, the vigilance committees and the battalions of the National Guard confirmed this structuring of its reference points. Several phenomena accentuated this urban focus: firstly, Paris was a demographic monster, with just under 2 million inhabitants; it was the country's main industrial centre and, up to the beginning of March, the home of all national institutions. Added to this was the existence of a popular Parisian identity, rooted in the everyday fabric of neighbourhood life and marked by the memory of the French Revolution; this undoubtedly played a role in the Commune's mobilising capacity.[43]

41 *JOC*, 11 April 1871.

42 NARA, Washington, RG 84 T1 consul Paris 1870–71.

43 These are lines of inquiry advanced by Jacques Rougerie: 'Le peuple de 1870–1871', in Danielle Tartakowsky and Jean-Louis Robert, eds, *Paris le peuple (XVIIIe–XXe siècle)* (Paris: Publications de la Sorbonne, 1999), pp. 147–57. See also Claude Gauvard and Jean-Louis Robert, eds, *Être parisien* (Paris: Publications de la Sorbonne, 2004).

Moreover, Paris was, after London, the great world city – a banking, imperial and cultural centre that exerted international influence.[44] While not all of these features were present in the minds of the Commune's defenders, they were part of the reason why this urban territory enjoyed such a particular ability to project itself. Other insurgent cities of the time asserted their local, national and transnational scope: Marseille with its Mediterranean perspectives, and Lyon – as we shall see – with its European horizon. This ambition was owed to their status as urban metropoles and to the republican imaginary that had emerged from both 1789 and 1848. But Paris's exceptional situation clearly set it apart.

The urban event had, moreover, crystallised underlying theoretical and ideological positions. Despite their differences, most of the actors involved in the Commune, whether at the Hôtel de Ville or in other bodies, seemed to accept a common perspective of development, if only for want of a better one. The poster of 19 April testifies to this: the Commune did not oppose the unity of France. It claimed to be a model for other cities – and, as per a later correction, for the countryside as well.[45] The project it evoked foresaw the formation of an association of Communes through a process of virtuous imitation that would result from the free will of its members. Once this was achieved, national unity would be all the stronger, because it would be voluntary and not imposed by the state. The integral Republic, driven from below, would then become a reality. Cities outside France – implicitly meaning European ones – could in turn imitate this model; indeed, a priori this was infinitely possible, even if the focus for the moment remained a national one. This perspective was fed by multiple intellectual reference points, as identified by Jacques Rougerie: Proudhonism and its political project of cooperation 'from below'; nineteenth-century Jacobinism, which, drawing on the Constitution of 1793, was also in many respects less centralising than is generally said; the democratic and social republic and the associationism of 1848, which were strongly present; and a revolutionary republicanism founded on popular sovereignty. Also

44 Tyler Stovall, 'Paris and the Making of a World Capital', in Stovall, *Transnational France: The Modern History of a Universal Nation* (Boulder, CO: Westview, 2015), pp. 127–65.

45 André Léo and Benoît Malon, *Appel aux travailleurs des campagnes* (100,000 copies were printed).

present, indeed essential, were the 1840s–50s projects for 'commune-cantons'. The brainchild of figures such as Victor Considérant and Constantin Pecqueur, after the defeat in 1848 it was supposed that these basic cells could give rise to the functional establishment of a direct government on a national scale.[46] The members of the IWMA, more concerned with national-liberation struggles and working-class living conditions, could identify with such a proposal, as could some non-revolutionary but anti-Bonapartist republicans.

Some more sophisticated thinking on this politico-spatial project was even formulated during the event itself. One good example is the writing of Pierre Denis, a cobbler, public employee, Proudhonian and likely author of the 19 April poster. He detailed his views in several articles in *Le Cri du peuple*, to which he was one of the main contributors. He made a declared enemy of centralism, whether under the auspices of the state, the military or the clergy. He deemed this a source of inequality, in the service of the dominant; its 'perfectly symmetrical spiders' web' had a 'suffocating' effect.[47] So, the idea, he claimed, was not to exchange the reins of power, but to transform the *nature* of power itself. And the Commune, or the communal idea, appeared as a solution: encouraging the democratic exercise of autonomy in the fields of politics, education, everyday life and finance, these Communes, whose vocation was to multiply, appeared as genuine units of political life. They were presented as capable of encompassing various 'ways of being' (according to regions, languages, or the size of the communes) while also entering into a free association. Once united, they would allow the emergence of a political and social reality based more on justice, paying attention to the fair organisation of exchanges between individuals, and not only to the structure meant to frame them. The perspective above all concerned metropolitan France (the colonies went unmentioned); but this time, it was more explicitly meant to extend to all the communes 'not only in France, but in Europe'. This conception of the Commune also had a transnational character: its multiple sources were not only French, but included, alongside the reference points just mentioned, the discussions

46 Jacques Rougerie, 'Entre le réel et l'utopie: République démocratique et sociale, association, commune, Commune', in Laurent Colantonio and Caroline Fayolle, eds, *Genre et utopie* (Saint-Denis, Presses universitaires de Vincennes, 2014), pp. 273–92.

47 In the articles 'Fédéralisme et centralisation', 11 May 1871, and 'Centralisateurs', 24 April 1871.

held in London by '48er exiles who likewise favoured a 'Commune'.[48] For Pierre Denis, the future association of Communes could also draw inspiration from other examples of republican federalism. 'The true republican states, which have had lasting existence or still endure: the United Provinces, Switzerland, the United States of North America, and all the republics of the Americas, were or are all organised according to the federal model.'[49] Denis thus proposed a socialist conception of the Commune, in the nineteenth-century sense, and a remarkable effort to give a theoretical consistency to what then seemed an indistinct reality. In appearing in *Le Cri du peuple*, it moreover escaped the circle of initiated militants, and reached a wider audience.[50] This diffusion was also linked to the distinctive social profile of its author. The sociology of the journalists of the Commune is poorly known: many of them, such as Longuet, Vésinier and Vermersch, were former students and publicists, coming from relatively cultured backgrounds, who had been brought into contact with organised labour and working-class circles through their literary, republican or socialist commitments. Others, like Pierre Denis, had a different profile: They were the typical boundary figures of the nineteenth century, both workers and intellectuals, and more located at the junction between the two cultures.[51] They played a particular role as mediators, in this case introducing certain orientations. Thus, original forms of spatial thinking emerged under the Commune, unfolding in the momentum of the event itself. Clearly, such reflection can also explain some of the foreign, republican and federalist readings made at the time.

The coherence of these positions ought however not be overstated. After all, the centrality of the city – and this is the last point – was also owed, more prosaically, to a situational effect. Like most revolutions, the Commune did not start out from a well-thought-out discussion that had preceded it in advance. Paris had been at war since September 1870,

48 Arthur Lehning, *De Buonarroti à Bakounine. Études sur le socialisme international* (Paris: Champ libre, 1977).

49 *Le Cri du peuple*, 11 May.

50 See the discussion advanced in William H. Sewell Jr, 'Response to J. Rancière "The Myth of the Artisan" ', *International Labor and Working-Class History* 24 (Fall 1983), pp. 17–20.

51 See the biography in Bernard Noël, *Dictionnaire de la Commune* (Paris: Mémoire du livre, 2000).

opposed to the Assembly since February, and even the uprising on 18 March surprised the most militant. Those who represented it, or intended to do so, had to adapt to ever-changing conditions, starting from the available points of reference, as well as from the given national and international situation. While specific views and positions did indeed take shape within the 'Paris Republic', the latter was at the same time constructed on an ad hoc basis, taking on more substance over time. Neither a government nor a municipality, it thus appears to have been made up of elements from both: like any insurgent territory, but in a particular way given its roots in the French capital, the Commune blurred the usual categories of the municipal, the national and the global, then in full recomposition. It was also, through this movement, an unidentified territorial form – one that must now be added to the present panorama.

Hence, the Commune did not escape the chains of legal, material or symbolic interdependence of its time. It often suffered from them, and sometimes seized upon them, in a singular way. Specific views and conceptions of territory even took shape. Nevertheless, they also seem to have emerged within a more potent and complex movement. This dynamic of the event and this set of discrepancies must be kept in mind if we are to truly understand the Parisian experience.

Conclusion to Part I: Paris, France, the World, Seen from a Revolution

This is precisely how spring should be. How beautiful the morning is today, what invigorating warmth penetrates the human body, how strongly beats the heart frozen by the winter cold.

N. Nikoladze, evoking the Paris Commune to get around Russian censorship, in the Georgian newspaper *Drobea*, 28 March 1871[1]

Here, we have a first set of answers to our question. Because the Paris Commune was an extension of a war between two of the main industrial powers of the day, because it burst its way into the vast social and republican movement of the 1850s and 1860s, and because it took place in a capital with a particular symbolic force, this event immediately had a global impact.

The word 'global' does not at all imply a homogeneous effect across the whole planet. If the Paris Commune had a global impact, it did so in the sense of global history: not on a global scale, but one consistent with transcontinental levels of interconnection. The event was part of wider movements, the object of multiple connections, appropriations and partial rebound effects. This heterogeneous set of connections maps out the wider constellation – of which I have captured only a

1 Ilya Tabagua, 'La Commune de Paris et la société géorgienne', *Le Mouvement social* 79 (April–June 1972), pp. 263–9.

portion here – that the Commune produced and in which it took place.

In this way, the Commune highlights the global dimension of 1860s France: while it was shaped by domestic dynamics, the country was also enmeshed in far-reaching webs of interrelations, which had become much more tightly knit than at the beginning of the century. This dimension was both transnational (France was connected by multiple links to other European and American countries) and imperial (it had colonies and exercised an 'informal imperialism' which also had a retroactive effect on the metropole). At this level, then, France appears as an important centre, but one among others – acting within other dynamics, and criss-crossed by them.

Two clarifications need to be made. Firstly, within this picture, it is necessary to underline the places not studied, and those where there was no such echo. Some French colonial territories, such as Pondicherry, were hardly affected. Similarly, I have found no traces, from the time of the event, of links between the Commune and Cuba, which was caught up in the Ten Years' War, or between Martinique and the Caribbean space.[2] No doubt media echoes of the Commune can be found in lands such as Australia, India or South Africa, but they were distant. A large swath of the Asian and African continents – the powerful Tukulor Empire, the kingdom of Mandara – do not seem to have been at all concerned by events in Paris. Nor did these events much affect rural areas of most of the aforementioned countries. In this sense, the Commune serves to capture in a particular light one of the 'global figurations' of France in 1871, in its extension, its intersections and its limits.

Examining this dimension, secondly, prompts us to revisit a line of questioning that has emerged from the global history of revolutions concerning the link between revolutionary events. As we have seen, certain readings have emphasised the synchronicities: the idea that there is a link between revolutions because they occur at the same time. Another has identified sequences of revolution and opposition that are more autonomous from one another: in this reading, the so-called Sepoy Revolt (1857), the Taiping Rebellion (1851–64), the European movements of 1848, and the colonial insurrections constitute groups of events which tended to be unaware of each other's existence. Recent

2 NARA, British archives, CAD.

analyses speak of nebulae associating multiple sites with intersecting logics.[3] The present study leans further in this direction, though it grasps the problem in a slightly different way: given the memories rekindled by the Commune, its multiple spill-overs, and its ricochet effects in Algeria, this work shows the existence of clusters of revolutionary or protest events, with ties of varying intensity and nature. This more fractal perspective is undoubtedly linked to the singularity of the Commune. But it has the virtue of remaining sensitive to the structural effects of these chains of interactions, as well as to the chance nature of their intersections and the importance, each time, of the logics on the ground.

Finally, the strength of national and local dynamics cannot be overlooked. With the shock of the event, national logics were constructed and revealed, especially in the context of the dynamics outlined above. This observation applies to the Versailles government as well as to the Commune, though in a different form. As for local logics, the Commune seems to have had a motive force of its own, in addition to the other dimensions.[4] Clearly, we have to grasp these smaller and larger links in combination, as well as the specific logic of the event. It is to this that we now turn our attention.

3 The former is proposed in Christopher Bayly, *The Birth of the Modern World, 1780–1914* (Oxford: Wiley-Blackwell, 2004); the second in Jürgen Osterhammel, *The Transformation of the World: A Global History of the Nineteenth Century* (Princeton, NJ: Princeton University Press, 2014). For the third, see Sujit Sivasundaram, 'The Lived Persian Gulf in the Age of Revolutions', in Kate Fullagar and Michael McDonnell, eds, *Facing Empire: Indigenous Experiences in a Revolutionary Age* (Baltimore, MD: Johns Hopkins, 2018); and Clément Thibaut, 'Idées et pratiques révolutionnaires', in Pierre Singaravélou and Sylvain Venayre, eds, *Histoire du monde au XIXe siècle* (Paris: Fayard, 2017), pp. 123–36.

4 See the discussion on the French Revolution in David Bell, 'Questioning the Global Turn: The Case of the French Revolution', *French Historical Studies* 37: 1 (2014), pp. 1–24.

PART II

The Living Commune (March–May 1871)

> *The truth about the usurpation must not be made apparent [to the people]; it came about originally without reason and has become reasonable. We must see that it is regarded as authentic and eternal, and its origins must be hidden if we do not want it soon to end.*
>
> Pascal, *Pensées*, Br. 294

Citizens
Your presence here attests to Paris and to France that the Commune is a fact, and the emancipation of the Paris Commune is, we have no doubt, the emancipation of all the communes of the Republic. . . . The Republic is no longer today what it was in the great days of our Revolution. The Republic of '93 was a soldier who, to fight both without and within, needed to centralise all the forces of the Patrie *in his own hand; the Republic of 1871 is a worker who above all needs freedom, in order to fertilise peace.*

Peace and labour! That is our future! That is the certainty of our revenge and our social regeneration, and the Republic thus understood can still make France the sustenance of the weak, the protector of the workers, the hope of the oppressed in the world, and the foundation of the universal Republic. . . . Let us say it frankly: the Commune which we are founding will be the model Commune. Whoever speaks of labour speaks of order, economy, honesty, strict control. . . . This, in my opinion, citizens, is the road to follow; take to it boldly and resolutely. Let us not exceed this limit fixed by our programme, and the country and the government will be happy and proud to applaud this revolution, so great and so simple, and which will be the most fruitful revolution in our history.

With these words Charles Beslay, the oldest member of the Commune, opened its first session on 28 March 1871, in a hall inside the Hôtel de Ville. A few moments earlier, the newly elected members were on a platform on the Place de l'Hôtel de Ville, accompanied by the members of the Central Committee. It was a grandiose scene. In front of the podium, machine guns and cannons officiated over proceedings. Around it, the battalions of the National Guard, then the citizens, amassed to the very edge of the square. Red flags fluttered in the wind. A little earlier, the bugles and drums had sounded, along with 'The Marseillaise' and 'Chant du départ'. In the crowd, observers mocked the pointlessly luxurious chairs from the city hall, which had been set out on the platform. When one delegate elected to the Commune, Adolphe Assi, stood up to speak, people joked by shouting out 'Assis!' – a pun on his name, which sounds like 'be seated!'[1] The Parisian sense of humour added a touch of spice to the solemnity of the moment. As president of the Commune's first session, Charles Beslay, a former *commissaire* of the Second Republic, embodied the presence of the principles of 1848 in the Paris of 1871. The summoning of revolutions past, the rush of enthusiasm, the references to France, to the Universal Republic and to other urban Communes were all characteristic of the moment. The restraint of his remarks, the appeal not going beyond certain limits, may seem surprising, as may the only weakly radical or socialist tone of his speech. But his was one voice among others. The seventy-six-year-old patriarch is, it is true, little appreciated in the historiography. He is chided for his bourgeois origins, his controversial role as the 'defender' of the Bank of France, or the fact that in May he obtained permission to flee from the Versailles government.[2] This great speech which began the Commune-event nevertheless makes the tone of the Commune's beginnings clearly audible. And there

1 Cited in Léon Deffoux, *Pipe-en-Bois, témoin de la Commune* (Paris: Éditions de France, 1932).

2 Philippe Richer, *Charles Beslay (1795–1878), le bourgeois de la Commune* (Paris: Dittmar, 2004); Charles Beslay, *La Vérité sur la Commune* (Brussels: Kistemaeckers, 1877).

is no reason to doubt the sincerity of the speaker, as of 28 March: after all, attitudes may vary in the course of 'fluid' situations such as political crises and revolutions. This statement also helps grasp some of the principles that will guide our understanding in Part II of this study – namely, to remain attentive to the diversity of expectations, desires and fears expressed in the event; and to strive, as best we can, to suspend our knowledge of how this crisis ended. By taking these precautions, we can stay as close as possible to what is happening and emerging during these episodes, to find the life in them – before that life is later struck down. By these means it is possible to get a feel for the Communard experience. We will begin by considering it in the plural.

5

From Algiers to Thiers: Insurrectionary Trajectories

As Beslay suggested, Paris was not the only Commune or city in revolution in March 1871. We could almost forget that, for the Russian anarchist Mikhail Bakunin in autumn 1870, the main centres of revolution were to be found in two other French cities: 'If the workers of Lyon and Marseille do not rise up immediately', he wrote on 4 September, 'France and European socialism are lost.'[1] Between September 1870 and June 1871, what could be called a nebula of revolutions expanded at different speeds: a set of insurrections each with its own dynamic, while also being more or less connected to the others (in Marseille, Lyon, Le Creusot and elsewhere). It is important to begin by exploring this nebula, even if the hotbeds of revolution were sometimes fleeting: they help us to identify the plurality of meanings then encompassed by the terms 'Commune' and 'revolutionary Republic', but also give us a better understanding of the wider situation within which the Paris Commune took place. By way of comparison, they will help to identify the specificity of the Parisian event and to get a better feel for its own distinctive movement.

This chapter delves into four of these uprisings, selected on account of their varied profiles and a desire to enrich the existing body of

1 Letter dated 4 September to A. Richard, cited in Maurice Moissonnier, *La Première Internationale et la Commune à Lyon (1865–1871). Spontanéisme, complots et luttes réelles* (Paris, Éditions sociales, 1972), p. 235.

knowledge: a red republic of formerly enslaved people (Martinique), a settlers' Commune (Algiers), a communalist movement of skilled workers (Thiers), and a succession of communal experiments in the country's second city (Lyon).

A Farmers' Republic in the Caribbean: The Southern Insurrection (Martinique)

Thursday 22 September 1870, Rivière-Pilote, southern Martinique. An angry crowd attacked the Codé residence. The caretaker had been killed and the building burned down. A few hours earlier – although the news from Paris had been known already on 19 September – the Republic was officially proclaimed, and welcomed by the crowd to cries of 'Vive la République! Death to the Whites!' This fire was the prelude to a vast movement that set the whole south-west of the island ablaze. During the night of 22 September and the following day, other houses were set on fire despite the troops' intervention. On 24 September, the mutilated body of the house's owner, Cléo Codé, was discovered in a cane field. The insurgents then set up a camp of several hundred people at Morne-Honoré, an elevation that covers the south of the island. Among its leaders were Eugène Lacaille, a mixed-race small landowner, and Louis Telgard, a Black butcher. But their control over the insurgents was limited. The blazes continued, despite their opposition. Among the rebels was a young pregnant seamstress, Lumina Sophie, known as 'Surprise'. According to later witnesses, she distinguished herself by her 'exaltation': 'Nothing must be spared', according to her words, as reported at the trial and translated from Creole. 'The good Lord would have a hut on the ground, and I would burn it, because he must be an old *béké* [a creole word to describe French settlers].' The insurrection took over the centre of the island and threatened the capital, Fort-de-France. Agitated, commander Mourat decreed a state of siege in fifteen communes. The troops, made up of soldiers of the marine infantry, gendarmes and volunteers, tried to contain the movement. The balance of power was reversed on 26 September, during a confrontation at the Aubermesnil estate (the family's plantation). A manhunt followed, taking nearly 500 prisoners, mainly farm workers and day labourers, including 114 women.[2] With thirty-five dwellings burned down and nearly a thousand insurgents, the Southern insurrection was the largest since the abolition of slavery in 1848.

The republican content of the uprising was clear, as shown by the effects of the change of regime being announced. But it was also wrapped up with an earlier local story known as the 'Lubin affair'. This had begun with an altercation on the road from Marin to Rivière-Pilote in February 1870 between a White Creole, Pelet de Lautrec, a white metropolitan Frenchman, Augier de Maintenon, and a Black farmer and entrepreneur, Léopold Lubin. The latter, who was horsewhipped by Maintenon, went to the authorities in Marin to seek justice. But he found no resolution, and two months later he took his revenge by whipping Augier de Maintenon in turn. On 19 August 1870 he was sentenced to five years in prison. The excessive sentence, which reflected the racial prejudices of the magistrates, was strongly felt throughout the island. One of the jurors responsible for the sentence was Cléo Codé, the man who was killed the following month: a rich White landowner with openly monarchist views. Some time beforehand, he had flown a white flag from his residence – which, for the Black population, symbolised a wish to return to slavery. Other people involved in the trial also had their estates burned down during the uprising.

The Lubin affair and the Southern insurrection thus had their roots in the political and social situation on the island following the abolition of slavery in 1848.[3] Universal suffrage, once obtained, was quickly withdrawn, and the Second Empire gave more power to the governors. A few members of the 'mulatto elite' managed to obtain positions in the administration, but the bulk of the positions of power remained in the hands of propertied whites.[4] Fearing a flight of labour after the abolition of slavery, the authorities and plantation owners had also established

2 Accounts and titles taken from Gilbert Pago, *L'Insurrection de Martinique (1870–1871)* (Paris, Syllepse, 2011); Silyane Larcher, *L'Autre Citoyen. L'idéal républicain et les Antilles après l'esclavage* (Paris: Armand Colin, 2014). On Lumina Sophie, see Gilbert Pago, *Lumina Sophie dite 'Surprise' (1848–1879), insurgée et bagnarde* (Matoury: Ibis Rouge, 2008).

3 Paul Butel, *Histoire des Antilles françaises (XVIIe–XXe siècle)* (Paris: Perrin, 2002), Chapter 9.

4 The term 'mulatto' was used in the nineteenth-century sources; I use it here in quotation marks to reflect contemporary usage.

highly unequal employment contracts.[5] Governor du Gueydon – who interestingly, through the imperial circulation of elites, would later become an admiral in Algeria in 1871 – had in 1855 issued a decree to prevent 'vagabondage': it demanded that all individuals aged over sixteen have passports, and its provisions made work effectively compulsory. To compensate for the lack of manpower, and faced with competition from Puerto Rico and Cuba, the planters also resorted to indentured labour, especially from India: just under 10,000 Indians arrived on the island between 1855 and 1862. Finally, many formerly enslaved individuals, who managed to buy land on the margins of the island, particularly in the area known as the Mornes, continued to work on the plantations.[6] These small landowners made up the majority of the insurgents in September 1870.

We can thus better understand the republican sense of the revolt, as demonstrated in the arguments reported at the trial: 'We are in the Republic'; 'Pay up, in the name of the Republic.'[7] Echoing the spirit of freedom that had been expressed in 1848, the Republic appeared as a restoration of rights, the final fulfilment of the promise of justice, as against the unbearable subjection that had preceded it. There is also a direct link with 1848: Eugène Lacaille had been personally involved, and the Lubin family had also distinguished itself in the movements preceding the abolition of slavery. The idea of a recovery of rights is also reminiscent of certain features of the so-called Peasant Republic of 1848 in France, as studied by Maurice Agulhon.[8] At the same time, the movement bore the marks of colonial realities: in its effort to boost its number of fighters, its leaders promised to break men free from the indentured labour to which they were subjected, thus explaining the presence of Indians among the insurgents (even if, pointing to the splits within colonial society, not all followed suit). There is also evidence that sorcery was used: Eugène Lacaille was a practitioner of *quimbois* – a sorcerer

5 On indentured servitude in the Caribbean, see Céline Flory, *De l'esclavage à la liberté forcée. Histoire des travailleurs africains engagés dans la Caraïbe française du xixe siècle* (Paris: Karthala/Société des Africanistes, 2015).

6 Christine Chivallon, *Espace et identité à la Martinique. Paysannerie des mornes et reconquête collective (1840–1960)* (Paris: CNRS Éditions, 1998).

7 *Procès de Martinique, insurrection du Sud, 22 septembre 1870* (Imprimerie Les Antilles, 1870), pp. 57, 63.

8 See especially Maurice Agulhon, *1848 ou l'Apprentissage de la République* (Paris: Seuil, 2002 [1973]).

who, to protect the men in the camp from bullets, made them soak in a mixture of rum and musk gumbo.[9] The insurgent slogans bear the trace of the reference to Saint-Domingue and Haiti, the first Black republic, established in 1804.[10] We can also identify the effects of a more subtle politicisation of the peasant world following the end of slavery, including a club in Rivière-Pilote in which Telgard and Lacaille were active. Given these conditions, it is understandable that the insurgents organised a redistribution of land as soon as they had settled in their camp at Morne-Honoré: in a clash of temporalities, the announcement of the republic on 4 September also stirred up the social republic of the farmers.

Was this revolt isolated? I have not found any link with other Caribbean movements of the 1860s, such as the Jamaican uprising of 1865.[11] The island's French rulers nevertheless asked the governor of the British colony of Saint Lucia to prevent the smuggling of arms to the insurgents. The trans-imperial dynamics that supported the maintenance of the colonial order remained in place. The same is certainly true of the longstanding links between these societies, and inter-island networks clearly escape our view: with the help of the population, for instance, Louis Telgard managed to get away, likely to Saint Lucia.[12]

Terrible repression followed: in December, the main leaders of the insurrection, including Lacaille, were shot. The trial began in April–May 1871. Political tensions increased between White monarchists and republican elites of colour. The outbreak of the Paris Commune in March also had a certain resonance here: at the trial, soldiers and jurors were quick to compare the uprising with the events in the French capital; in April 1871, the authorities even brought in reinforcements of another 200 soldiers, to ward off any problems. In the end, seventy-five convictions were handed down. Lumina Sophie was jailed with forced labour for life. She was released, but according to the principle of *forçats*

9 He confessed this, albeit with an affectation of distance from it, at the trial.

10 Laurent Dubois, *Avengers of the New World: The Story of the Haitian Revolution* (Cambridge, MA: Harvard University Press, 2004).

11 Throughout my research in French, US or UK diplomatic archives.

12 See Ernesto Bassi, *An Aqueous Territory: Sailor Geographies and New Granada's Transimperial Greater Caribbean World* (Durham, NC: Duke University Press, 2016); Clément Thibaud, *Libérer le Nouveau Monde. La fondation des premières républiques hispaniques: Colombie et Venezuela (1780–1820)* (Bécherel: Les Perséides, 2017).

libres ('free convicts'), she was never to leave Guiana, some 1,000 kilometres from the island.[13] The insurrection in the south of Martinique was not directly linked to the Paris Commune itself, but it belongs to the same revolutionary republican dynamic that began in September, and thereby bears witness to its strength. Here it proved to be simultaneously metropolitan, Caribbean and West Indian. It expressed a republic of colonised and formerly enslaved people, driven by a promise of social equality and emancipation, as against a racial, social-political order recomposed since the abolition of slavery.[14]

A 'Colonial Commune' in Algiers

Algiers presents a rather different case. The city also experienced a republican movement, and even a 'Commune' of settlers, briefly addressed earlier. We may now explore it in greater depth. Driven by the ideals of 1792 and 1848, impregnated with the imperatives of freedom and emancipation, it was nonetheless caught up in a relationship of domination and blindness towards the colonised. The upheaval of 4 September was again decisive: the following day, when the change of regime was announced, a tree of liberty was planted and bells were rung.[15] In a climate which – all observers noted – was free of violence, the emblems of the Second Empire were removed to the sound of 'The Marseillaise' and cries of 'Vive la République!'[16] Defence committees were organised, and took on more or less the functions of a municipal authority. Eager to keep up the war effort, they began by organising the dispatch of troops and volunteers to France. They demanded the departure of the governor-general, Baron Durrieu, and the establishment of civilian rule in the colony. The group that gradually took over the functions of the municipal council was socially diverse, consisting of lawyers, merchants,

13 Miranda Spieler, *Empire and Underworld: Captivity in French Guiana* (Cambridge, MA: Harvard University Press, 2012).

14 See Silyane Larcher, L'Autre Citoyen. L'idéal républicain et les Antilles après l'esclavage (Paris: Armand Colin, 2014), pp. 265–85.

15 ANOM, 7G4, report 4–5 September 1870.

16 Ibid. The same facts are related by the British consul Playfair in his reports to the Foreign Office: The National Archives (NA), Kew, FO 27/1834, letters, 5–7 September.

doctors, landlords, teachers, but also carpenters, painters and foremen. All of them were settlers or their descendants. Characteristic of 1848's imperial consequences, they were most often former deportees from 1848 or 1851 (even if many had returned in the meantime).[17] Alexandre Lambert was one such case: this former secretary of the woman writer George Sand and editor of a democratic-socialist newspaper (*Le Travailleur de l'Indre)* had been convicted in 1852 and deported to Algeria. Placed under house arrest (in Blida), he then resumed his journalistic activities in Oran and Algiers, before becoming a figure in the local democratic movement towards the end of the Empire. Similarly, Romuald Vuillermoz, born in Lons-le-Saunier, was deported to Algeria because of his political positions at the same moment. He was interned in Douera until 1865, before being admitted to the Algiers bar.[18] The revolutionary references (to 1793 and 1848) were thus rather more imported from France than in the case of Martinique, even if they were then able to take root locally. Having faced the harshest treatment, these men had a deep-seated hatred of Napoleon III. Favourable to the assimilation of the colony into the Republic, they opposed the Second Empire's 'Arabophile' policy[19] and the division of military and civilian territories associated with the *regime du sabre*: the rule of the sword.

The republican movement in September soon spread to Constantine, Bône and Philippeville. Quickly, the various defence committees sent delegates to the provisional government or asked to join the Ligue du Midi, organised around Marseille. 'The Algiers Committee', we read in a poster from 4 October 1870, 'acclaimed by the public meeting of the 25th day of this past month . . . entered into service following a second meeting . . . The delegates left for France in order to attach Algeria to the Ligue du Midi.'[20]

17 AN, F80/1681, ministère de la Guerre, correspondance générale. On Algeria's role after 1848, see Jennifer E. Sessions, 'Colonizing Revolutionary Politics: Algeria and the French Revolution of 1848', *French Politics, Culture and Society* 33: 1 (2015), pp. 75–100.

18 Bibliothèque historique de Paris, G. Sand papers; ANOM, 12X290, file 'Vuillermoz'; Jean-Louis Reffay, 'Romuald Vuillermoz, avocat bagnard et . . . maire d'Alger. Les tribulations d'un Jurassien peu connu', *Amis du vieux Saint-Claude* 12 (1989), pp. 31–4.

19 The term 'Arabophile' was used by European settlers in Algeria to criticise the Second Empire's policy of granting certain rights and protections to the Arab population. It was not a neutral term but a polemical label.

20 ANOM, FM F80 1681.

The imperial officials were quickly sidelined, and already in September the central *commissaire* of Algiers was arrested. In this city, as in others, there was a proliferation of decision-making bodies (municipal councils, defence committees, and so on), and spaces for political intervention: clubs and public meetings that served as a 'popular sanction' by way of acclamation. Radical newspapers played an essential role.[21] In Algiers, they were called *Le Démocrate*, *Le Petit Colon*, *L'Algérie française* and *La Jeune République*. Petitions, votes, decrees, acclamations, communications to the government, and popular demonstrations set the rhythm of political life. The dilution of power was accelerated by the fragility of the representatives of the central authority, both in metropolitan France and in the colony. The military governor was unanimously rejected and the interim prefect, Dr Auguste Warnier, left in a weakened position even though he had earlier been director of civil affairs in Algeria after the February 1848 revolution. The conflict became more intense as the weeks went by. In October–November, in a climate even more marked by the resurgence of the memory of 1792–93, proclamations and articles increasingly called for the election of 'committees of public safety' (*comités de salut public*) or – as *Le Petit Colon* of 3 November put it – 'revolutionary communes'.

No authority arriving from metropolitan France succeeded in asserting itself here: on 25 October, General Warlin-Esterhazy remained in place for only forty-eight hours after being confronted with a violent demonstration. At the end of October, the important Association Républicaine – present during the Empire and closely linked to the committee – organised a meeting with delegates from the clubs of Constantine and Philippeville, to decide upon a 'Federal Constitution'.[22] In addition to various prominent personalities, this republican movement consisted of journalists, lawyers, skilled workers, shopkeepers and day labourers who had been left unemployed by the interruption of work on construction projects. There is also evidence of women's

21 ANOM, FO 1681, Decree by the prefect of Algiers, 25 September 1870.

22 I have found no more precise information on its constitution and composition, apart from the well-known figures involved (Georges Jourdan, editor of *La Jeune République*, Gédéon Flasselière, presented as a former *commissiare* of the Second Republic in Dijon). While noting its importance, most works presenting this episode are drawing on the indications offered in Claude Martin, *La Commune d'Alger (1870–1871)* (Paris: Heraklès, 1936), p. 23.

presence, but it is not known whether they spoke at the meetings. Other 'Europeans' – as numerous in the city as the French – were also present.[23] In particular this included Spaniards: republicans who had come after the 'Glorious Revolution of 1868', or the impoverished workers from the building sites.[24] This was a political crisis, as sociologist Michel Dobry defines it, with its 'plastic time', the persistence in weakened form of the old sources of power, the competition between different sites of action, a change in the frameworks of intelligibility, and the irruption of other historical references.[25] This together shaped a multiform process that the proclaimed mayor of Algiers, Vuillermoz, repeatedly confessed he was unable to control. Gambetta's reaction clarified, in its own way, the confusion that had arisen: 'We learn that you are playing the dictator', he wrote to the mayor. '[The government] orders you to cease all violations of the law.' The arrival on 17 November of Charles Du Bouzet, editor of *Le Temps* and *préfet* of Oran since September 1870, calmed the situation for a while.

Yet the crisis dynamic was soon set in motion again. Three problems then crystallised the tensions. First was the militia, sometimes called the 'National Guard'. On 18 November, just after the arrival of the new extraordinary *commissaire*, a decree from Tours was published giving either him or the civil governor command of these troops. The Association Républicaine immediately organised a petition, which gathered nearly 1,500 signatures. It recalled that the Algerian militias were above all a municipal-level body. The confrontation thus accelerated the 'communalisation' of Algiers and, on 18 January, a new decree, signed by Vuillermoz, was issued with the heading 'Commune of Algiers'. It insisted: 'Is the Commune not made up of two essential, indissoluble elements: the municipality and the National Guard! How, under the

23 In 1861, for the whole colony, there were counted 112,229 people of French origin and 80,517 'European foreigners' – hence a total of 192,746 'Europeans'; a native Muslim population of around 2.3 million; and 33,952 'Israelites'. In Algiers the census counted 19,477 French, 17,668 European foreigners, 10,616 Muslims and 6,103 Israelites. See Kamel Kateb, *Européens, 'indigènes' et juifs en Algérie (1830–1962)* (Paris: PUF, 2001).

24 See the explanations by the Spanish consul in Algiers, Galbito Cortes: El Archivo del Ministerio de Asuntos Exteriores (AMAE), Madrid, , H-1820. Exp 50.

25 Michel Dobry, *Sociologie des crises politiques. La dynamique des mobilisations multisectorielles* (Paris: Presses de la Fondation nationale des sciences politiques, 2009).

Republic, could . . . one undertake to weaken its authority?'[26] This was no trivial question. Composed of citizens in arms, the National Guard conferred on its members, particularly in a democratic situation, a share of public authority.[27] Yet these militias already had a complex history in Algeria, due to the diversity of social and legal statuses (the French, Europeans, Muslim *indigènes* as well as Jewish ones).[28] The implicit definition of 'citizenship' was particularly problematic, and the communalist movement of 1870 altered this fragile balance. At the time of the events, the Algiers militia was made up of French battalions, foreign volunteers (service was compulsory for 'Europeans', except for those whose countries had signed conventions, as in the cases of Spain and Italy) and the battalion of so-called 'Israelite' National Guards created after the Crémieux decree. At the end of March, Vuillermoz organised fresh elections for officers. After disbanding the companies of foreign volunteers, he took part in the recruitment of new foreign militiamen and brought in guards 'devoted to the municipality', notably including workers and young Spanish republicans – by this point not supposed to be part of it.[29] The moves to take back control of the National Guard thus created new legal boundaries in the social space of the city, accompanying the process of political transformation of the 'Algiers Commune'.

The second point of tension was the political project of the revolt itself, whose clarity varied depending on the actors concerned. On 2 February, three days after the news of the capitulation of Paris, the crowd entered the extraordinary *commissaire*'s offices. It was decided that 'provisionally the commune of Algiers, under the name revolutionary commune, will preside over the fate of all Algeria', and that elections would be held for a 'council of government or committee of public safety'.[30] Du Bouzet responded by declaring a state of siege across the arrondissement of Algiers. However, he was sidelined by the

26 Posters in ANOM, FM F80 1681.

27 Mathilde Larrère, *L'Urne et le fusil. La garde nationale parisienne de 1830 à 1848* (Paris: PUF, 2016).

28 Emmanuel Blanchard, 'La garde nationale "introuvable". La formation de l'ordre urbain en situation coloniale (1830–1852)', *Revue d'histoire du xixe siècle* 50 (2015), pp. 39–56.

29 ANOM FM F80 1682, Report by the prefect Hulot, 1 April 1871; AMAE, Madrid, Exp 50 and Exp 67.

30 ANOM FM F80 1682, confirmed by consul Playfair, 3 February 1871: NA, Kew, FO 27/1888.

government and replaced in mid-February by Alexis Lambert, the *préfet* of Oran (not to be confused with Alexandre Lambert, mentioned earlier). After having lifted the state of siege in a bid to calm the situation, Lambert posted a proclamation which reiterated some of the population's expectations: 'The assimilation of Algeria into France is an established fact. But it will be necessary to obtain administrative decentralisation with the power to colonise Algeria and see to the country's higher interests.'[31] On 27 February, mayor Vuillermoz set out a more precise project in a letter to the interior minister, Ernest Picard. Inspired by the radical ideas formulated at the end of the Second Empire, Vuillermoz adapted them to the current movement: he called for the encouragement of European colonisation 'without distinction of nationality', for doing without subsidies from the metropolis, and for the autonomy of an Algeria that would nonetheless remain 'French'.[32] 'It is autonomy and not assimilation that Algeria needs . . . the autonomy of the commune, and its complete independence, the autonomy of the provinces, in everything that concerns the free disposal of their resources.' A colonial council, elected by universal suffrage, would provide its connection with metropolitan France.[33] This text thus, interestingly, gave expression to what could be called a colonial Commune: a Commune, because it took the name, clearly following (in adapted form) in the heritage of the revolutions of 1792–93 and 1848, and of the municipal republicanism of the 1860s. Moreover, it rejected military government, supported secular schooling, favoured the project of a federation of republican towns and cities, and sought to guarantee political autonomy. But it was indeed also 'colonial', in that the autonomy it claimed still acknowledged a dependence on the metropolitan government, and seemed to ignore the question of any rights that the colonised might have enjoyed.

This brings us to the third and final point of contention. Those labelled at the time as *indigènes*, and particularly the Arab populations, remain strangely absent from our account, even as we know that another great wave of insurrection, the Algerian uprising of 1871, was rumbling. The republican colonists did not totally neglect them: as early as 25

31 NA, Kew, FO 27/1834, letter from 17 February 1871.

32 On radical positions before and after 1870, see Martin, *La Commune d'Alger*.

33 ANOM, FM F80 1682, Algiers, 25 February 1871.

September, Warnier proposed the enlistment of the *indigènes* by means of the decree of 9 November 1859, albeit under specific conditions.[34] But the central point was underlined by Admiral de Gueydon, who arrived at the end of March. In a very severe 29 April statement on the 'demagogic movement', he noted that the Algerians were of little interest to the main actors of the communal movement, while their project consisted of an intensified colonisation of the territory. These men, he commented, 'strove to show that the 2,500,000 Arabs and Kabyles . . . only aspired to become docile servants . . . that the spirit of mistrust was maintained by the presence of the soldiers and that the end of the Bureaux Arabes would lead to the end of insurrections.'[35] Yet they were indeed there. Their presence is attested at the public meetings in January; and during the assault on the governor's palace on 2 February, speeches were made in Arabic, although it is not clear exactly to whom they were addressed.

The Arab population of Algiers in fact broke onto the scene on the day of Eid al-Adha, 1 March. To the sound of tom-toms, a large number of people descended on the governor's square and attacked the post with clubs, while others looted Jewish shops.[36] The Zouaves, the sailors and the militiamen, whose interests had suddenly converged, jointly intervened. By nightfall, the situation was under control. The casualty toll was one dead, ten wounded Arab Algerians, three wounded settlers, and 'several bloodied Israelites', who were not counted. Among the reasons cited by the colonists for this demonstration – which had been repeated in other urban markets (Oran, Mostaganem) – the most common was frustration among the Arab population with the decree naturalising the Algerian Jews. Antisemitic criticism (from Vuillermoz, who was moderate, to Gueydon, who was more outspoken) focused on the 'Israelite' battalion of the National Guard, whose parades were said to have heightened animosities. The movement was also, in fact, a demonstration of anger after a

34 'Milices algériennes, incorporation des indigènes', Algiers, 25 September 1870 (NA, Kew, FO 27/1834).

35 ANOM, F80 1682, Letter from De Gueydon, 29 April 1871. According to the proclamation from late February described by the Spanish consul, 'To get the Arabs' respect, two armed militiamen is enough' (AMAE, Madrid, H-1820, Exp 35, 2 March 1871). The Bureaux Arabes were French military-administrative offices in Algeria (est. 1844) that oversaw local populations; they were dissolved in 1870–71, when civil authorities assumed control.

36 There are many accounts of this: here I draw on those of the newspaper *l'Akbar*, 3 March, and the British consul Sir Robert Playfair.

court ruling the same day following a brawl between members of the Israelite battalion and the Arab Algerians, to the detriment of one of the latter. The historian of the Maghreb Annie Rey-Goldzeiguer cites a further reason: it was also a reaction of these populations to the fact that Du Bouzet – their 'friend', perceived as a defender of Muslim interests – was in trouble. His weakened position was thus also their own.[37] Surely, there were also other motives at work. But this last explanation suggests that this attack was also an intervention by the colonised in the political process in Algiers and the cities of Algeria. If we link it to the simultaneously spreading Arab and Berber protest movement against the 'arrival of civilian rule', it even makes sense. Surprisingly, however, this event did not provoke any reaction from the Algiers insurgents, who considered it anecdotal – only the Israelite battalion was disbanded. The republicans in the towns and cities did not perceive the danger of the Kabyle revolt, though it became obvious in March. As many observers have noted, the newspapers, for instance, denied any such threat, and sometimes denounced it as a military plot to prevent the installation of civilian rule. Perhaps rarely has the discordance of perspectives on justice – and, with it, the discordance of historical dynamics (the Kabyle revolt and the Commune movement) – been thrown into such sharp relief. It conveys the impression of separate planes of reality, only partially aware of each other, yet still interacting.

This disposition explains Admiral de Gueydon's surprise: in mid-April, when the Kabyle insurrection was more than obvious, the revolutionary movement in Algiers and other towns such as Constantine was accelerating. 'I had hoped that the gravity of the circumstances and the dangers . . . would suspend the revolutionary goings-on of the Algiers Commune.'[38] This phenomenon was owed to the invisibilisation of the Arab populations, as well as to the fact that the settlers' attention was caught up in the metropolitan situation. The latter took a dim view of the monarchist victory in the elections to the National Assembly in February and increasingly saw themselves as embodying the country's republican promise, with a duty to preserve the republican regime and its spirit.

37 Jean Meyer, Jean Tarrade and Annie Rey-Goldzeiguer, *Histoire de la France coloniale*, vol. I (Paris: Armand Colin, 1991).

38 ANOM, FM F80 1682, Report from De Gueydon to the minister, 29 April 1871.

In such a context, the outbreak of the Paris Commune in March was well received, particularly by the radicals of Algiers and Constantine. The Paris event had its defenders in the newspapers, which reported on its every move, as well as in public meetings. The Paris Commune often appeared to them as the a posteriori confirmation of the movement that had been set underway in September – and some newspapers even reversed this perspective, judging it more accurate to say that the radicals in Algiers had opened the way for their Parisian counterparts.[39] An address of congratulations and support for the Commune was sent to Paris, and reproduced in its *Journal officiel*.[40] Alexandre Lambert, the figure from the Algiers movement who was then in metropolitan France, presented himself in Paris as a delegate of Algiers's Association Républicaine. He was promoted to the role of Algerian delegate to the Commune, after the ratification of his mandate by *La Solidarité* (the organ of the Association Républicaine).[41] There, he was installed in an improbable 'Committee of General and Interior Safety, Department for Algeria and the Colonies, Place Beauvau', then becoming 'chief clerk at the Interior Ministry (press section)', before being killed during the assault on the capital.[42] He thus embodies a direct connection between the movements in Algiers and Paris. Back in Algiers, Admiral de Gueydon had to compromise. On 25 March, he established a state of siege in the colony, taking care to avoid the republican cities so that 'one could not see in this any political measure against their hostile tendencies'.[43] After March, surveillance of migration movements was intensified.[44] At this point, after a long period observing how events unfolded, a final actor intervened: foreign consuls. The consuls of Spain, Great Britain and Italy met to protest against the possible mobilisation of their nationals in the militia, and to protect the interests of their countries from the Arab uprising. In April they asked their governments to send long-range warships. Here again, we see active trans-imperial

39 Note from the prefect Roussel.

40 *JOC*, 29 March 1871.

41 As described in Michel Cordillot's entry on it for the *Maitron* dictionary.

42 *JOC*, 8 April 1871 (announcement in which he calls for opposition to De Gueydon's nomination).

43 ANOM, FM F80 1682, De Gueydon's report to the minister, 29 April 1871.

44 ANOM, FM F80 1682 Letter from the prefect Hélot, 16 March 1871, note from the war ministry, 28 March.

cooperation in the colonies. The frigates *Roma*, *Arapiles* and *Defence* arrived in May to support the French authorities taking back control with their presence.[45] On 7 May, De Gueydon finally received authorisation from the government to dissolve the city council and the National Guard, and to ban clubs and newspapers.[46] He declared a state of siege at a moment when the population was becoming aware of the gravity of the threat and the political experiences in the main cities were unravelling. The news of the defeat of the Paris Commune in May, followed by the fires, caused the movement to subside.

Historians have been harsh in their judgements on the events in Algiers, deemed a 'farce' or 'pantomime Commune'. From the perspective adopted here, however, it emerges as a fascinating experience: for its republican dimension in a colonial context; for its dynamic of unsettling an Algerian society divided between communities; and for the astonishing project, imbued with the ideals of the Great Revolution and of 1848, of what can still, despite everything, be called a 'colonial Commune'.[47]

A Cutlery Makers' Commune (for a Few Hours): The City of Thiers

The republican and communalist movements in metropolitan France were, of course, more numerous. Their tone was rather different, even if we find similar rhythms in many of them; and they are better known, including such cases as Le Creusot, Narbonne and Marseille. Some of them, however, remain to be explored, like the strange communalist movement in Thiers (Puy-de-Dôme), reported in the parliamentary enquiry on 18 March, which piqued my curiosity. We could only be disappointed to find that the 'Commune' amounted to an occupation of the town for a few hours by the National Guards of the working-class neighbourhoods. Having said that, many 'provincial communes' had a

45 AMAE, Madrid, H-1820, Exp 78, Spanish consul, letter from 16 May 1871.

46 ANOM, FM F80 1682, Telegraphic dispatch, Interior Ministry, 7 May 1871.

47 This re-evaluation corresponds to the renewal of historiography on nineteenth-century Algeria. See Hélène Blais, Claire Fredj and Emmanuelle Saada, 'Introduction – Un long moment colonial: pour une histoire de l'Algérie au xixe siècle', *Revue d'histoire du xixe siècle* 41 (2010), pp. 7–24.

similar fate; and the results of the investigation carried out in the departmental archives seemed rich enough to be analysed here.

Thiers was a sub-prefecture of 16,000 inhabitants, located in a rural area between the Limagne and the Forez mountains. The series of events begun by the 1870 war and the proclamation of the Republic seems to have taken the local economic and administrative elites by surprise as well. Their control of the town seemed assured, as the pages of the *Album de Thiers*, a sort of official local newspaper, would suggest. The Empire had imposed itself thanks to a tried and tested arsenal: support for official candidates during elections, the ties between the mayor, the sub-préfet, the big manufacturers and merchants, and the creation of structures to help the workers and the destitute sponsored by these elites (the town's mutual aid society).[48] The local memory of 1848 nevertheless remained vivid among the population: after February 1848, the town council had been replaced, liberty trees planted, and religious services interrupted. The town's workers continued to invoke the 'democratic and social republic' throughout the Second Republic.[49] Louis-Napoleon Bonaparte won the December 1848 elections, as in other working-class towns. But the coup d'état of 1851 prompted resistance. Thus, after a period of stabilisation, the rise of opposition forces made itself felt during the 1870 plebiscite: the 'No' vote carried the town, even though the *département* overall returned a 'Yes' majority, thanks to the rural vote. The war and the call-up of the National Guard in August – whether mobile or not – further destabilised the existing order. And on 4 September, when the change of regime was announced, a red flag appeared in Thiers.[50] Aware of the town's republican aspirations, the authorities quickly appointed a sub-prefect, a moderate republican from 1848, as well as a mayor known for his attention to workers' hardships. At this point, interesting connections appear between our different cases. The two main leaders of the republican movement were

48 Archives départementales (AD), Puy-de-Dôme, 8 BIB 294/2, *Album de Thiers* (a sort of official organ of the sub-prefecture), 1868–71.

49 AD, Puy-de-Dôme, 4M 116, reports from the sub-prefect, March 1848 to October 1849; 4M 96 'correspondance générale, 1848'; *Album de Thiers*, 1848–49 and 1869–71. The events in Limoges, 300 kilometres further west, bore a major influence. See John Merriman, *The Red City: Limoges and the French Nineteenth Century* (Oxford: Oxford University Press, 1985).

50 AD Puy-de-Dôme, U 10811, dos 6003: 'Procès de Thiers', indictment, 10 August 1871.

Jean-Jacques Chomette, aged fifty, and François Chauffrias, who was forty-six. They were former participants in the 1851 resistance; the latter had been deported to Oran, Algeria. In addition, the mobile National Guard was sent, according to the principle described above, to the same colony, to Médéah, where it remained for the bulk of the conflict. Finally, here as elsewhere, the course of the war set the pace of opposition movements. At the end of October, during the surrender of Metz, a crowd invaded the sub-prefecture, during which Chomette briefly declared himself the 'people's delegate'.

Tensions remained high over the winter, but the advent of the Paris Commune once again had a powerful echo. The work of republican militants in public meetings since October, among other things, had also borne fruit. On 2 April, upon one of these meetings, Chomette was appointed delegate of the town. He went to a public meeting in Clermont-Ferrand, where a federation project was discussed and where the *département*'s delegates to the Paris Commune were elected.[51] Chomette was in Paris from 5 to 10 April, where he met Delescluze and Lefrançais. Could it be that he crossed paths with Alexandre Lambert, the Algiers delegate, at the Hôtel de Ville? In any case, upon his return to Thiers he organised further public meetings, visited the houses in the working-class neighbourhood of Boulay, and began a subscription to send volunteers to defend the Commune. Jacques Vedel, an engraver and iron merchant, who had also been convicted in 1851, accompanied him. On 18 April, Chomette went to Lyon, officially to prepare the municipal elections set for 30 April 1871. He agreed with two 'advanced' Lyon newspapers – *Le Défenseur des droits de l'homme* and *Le Cri du peuple* – to have 500 copies of each publication delivered to Chauffrias's address. They were distributed via Thiers workers' own channels of communication.[52] The copies of these newspapers galvanised the opposition. Worried, the sub-prefect had them seized.[53] This intervention was taken negatively by the town's working-class population, who saw it as the confiscation of what was rightfully

51 Facts confirmed by the *Enquête parlementaire sur le 18 mars*, report by the first president of the court of Riom, Achille Moisson, 8 September 1871, p. 124.

52 'Procès de Thiers', indictment, 10 August 1871 (reports unchallenged by the defendants).

53 Report from the brigadier Berry and De Planche, country rangers, 24 April 1871.

theirs: cries of 'We want our newspapers!' were heard from the crowd on the evening of these events.[54]

Like other communalist movements in the province, the attempted insurrection took place on 30 April, the day of the municipal elections. At three o'clock in the morning, the blacksmith Suquet, who had come to vote, hit an officer posted at the town hall, shouting: 'I want to join the Commune, not Versailles!' A crowd formed, went to the adjoining sub-prefecture, and prevented the sub-prefect from entering.[55] Guillaume Saint-Joanis, known as Lancelot, a thirty-five-year-old cutler, went through the town shouting 'To arms, citizens, it's time to go and proclaim the Commune in the town hall and fly the red flag!'

This sedition was helped along by the chance rotation of the National Guard: the 8th Company – known as 'de Boulay', in reference to the neighbourhood populated by cutlers and tinsmiths – arrived to take over in this very moment, singing 'The Marseillaise'. It swelled the ranks of the crowd in front of the prefecture and the town hall. The cutlery makers clearly played a particular role in this political dynamic, as well as in these echoes of the Paris Commune. When they went to trial, the majority of the fifty-four defendants belonged to this world (cutlers, blacksmiths, tinsmiths, and so on), with the exception of those whom the prosecutor called the 'ringleaders': Chomette, Chauffrias and Vedel. All three were distinguished by their trade (surveyor, shoemaker, iron merchant, respectively), their age, and the fact that they could read and write. These observations deserve some clarification. Thiers was at that time the French and European capital of cutlery making: as of 1866, some 108 foundries and 557 cutlery workshops were operating in the district.[56] The manufacture of knives required several operations (working with wood and bone, assembling the knife), and several types of skilled workers coexisted, with elaborate knowhow: cutlers, tinsmiths, assemblers, polishers, and the famous grinders who, lying with their hands in the Durolle river, shaped the metal using a grinding wheel

54 Cross-examination of Mr Blais, secretary of the sub-prefecture, 8 May 1871, in 'Procès de Thiers', indictment, 10 August 1871.

55 The two buildings stand side-by-side on the square in front of the city hall (AD Puy-de-Dôme, U. 10 811° 'extrait du plan d'ensemble des rues', 15 May 1871).

56 AD Puy-de-Dôme, 10 M9, 'Enquête parlementaire sur les conditions de travail', 1872.

driven by a mill.[57] There were strong social stratifications among the different types of worker, but also between workers, bosses and merchants. These social divides were likewise inscribed in the town's geography: the grinders worked at the bottom of the valley, while the big manufacturers were located on the heights. The workers' worlds were diverse, but they found a certain coherence in the unity of the town, their endogamy, and their mutual acquaintances: except for Chomette and Chauffrias, all the defendants were born in Thiers. They all knew each other, including the witnesses, and during the exchanges in court they identified themselves by their activity ('there was a group of tinsmiths'), their neighbourhood ('Faye from Boulay'), their nickname ('Suquet, called the Zouave'). These were the workers' worlds that had been marked, twenty-two years earlier, by the 'democratic and social republic' of 1848. They had also faced financial difficulties at the end of the 1860s, and the crisis was particularly acute in the winter of 1870, when a drought made it impossible for the grinders to do their work. Social grievances were mounting.

That afternoon, at the sub-prefecture, the sub-prefect handed back the newspapers. But the crowd harried the National Guards, who had stuck by their orders, and disarmed them. At the town hall, the guards refuse to obey. The provisional mayor of Thiers fled after being struck in the face by a stone. When the gendarmerie arrived, a hail of stones fell on the sub-prefecture building. Part of the crowd occupied the town hall. Another group headed to the nearby Saint Genès church and tried to break into it using an axe. For a few hours, the town was in the hands of the workers in revolt: 'We want to support our brothers in Paris, there are no more police, we can do what we want!' Yet, the adventure was short-lived: summoned by telegraph, the reinforcements arrived from Clermont-Ferrand during the night. They were delayed by the insurrectionary movement in Lyon, which had started that very day, after that city's authorities asked Clermont to muster the available forces. By ripple effect, the insurgencies could once again feed into each other.

If Thiers was only briefly occupied, these events are not without interest. The occupation unfolded in a festive atmosphere. It took place on an election Sunday, and all those involved had been drinking. No doubt,

57 Dany Hadjadj, ed., *Pays de Thiers. Le regard et la mémoire* (Clermont-Ferrand: Presses universitaires Blaise-Pascal, 1999).

referring to this could offer a post facto defence, faced with the courts: but the role of drunkenness in such moments is well established.[58] As a testament to the local sociability, everyone had made a stop at the inns of Courtial or Marius. Women and children were part of the festivities – especially the former, who were also a driving force in events. Songs were sung several times over ('The Marseillaise', 'Mois de Mai') and certain outfits suggested a carnival atmosphere, such as the red cap worn by the ex-Zouave, Suquet. This festive moment, however, was also a time of political expression, as the recurrent invocation of the Paris Commune indicates. Here the reference, in its republican sense, was indeed a claim to right: shouts of 'You are having our brothers in Paris murdered!' and 'We want our rights!' rang out in front of the sub-prefecture. This was also an opportunity to assert one's status as a 'citizen', such as the woman called 'La Grande Douris' proudly repeating 'I am a citizen', as she faced a gendarme who had unsheathed his sword. The social dimension of the reference to the Commune is also present here, and more specifically working-class than in the two previous cases: on arriving on the square, the 8th Company mixed the cry of the Lyon *canuts*' revolt (1831) with the adventure of insurgent Paris by chanting 'Live by working or die by fighting, long live the Commune!' In front of the town hall, the crowd expressed its demand for equality and social justice by shouting: 'We want our rights, we have suffered enough, we have been hungry long enough, now the rich must pay, long live the Commune!' 'We are the masters', the cutler Lancelot is said to have shouted, inverting the hierarchies with the manufacturers, 'we will establish the Commune.' The presence in the crowd of a banner of Saint Eligius, the patron saint of cutlers, carried by the grinder Brun, known as 'Pelade', confirms, if any further proof were needed, the working-class identity of this revolt.

Obviously, one must be cautious with the words reported during a trial. But if each person denied having uttered them, none of the participants or witnesses challenged them. Thiers thus offers the example of a brief communalist movement led by skilled workers, marked by the reference to 1848, structured by both an old republican culture and the local logics of labour.

58 Here again, the analysis has many overlaps with the ones regarding 1848. For instance, Peter McPhee, *The Politics of Rural Life: Political Mobilization in the French Countryside (1846–1852)* (Oxford: Clarendon, 1992).

The Lyon Communes: From La Croix-Rousse to La Guillotière

Yet, without doubt, we should also examine a 'Commune' in one of the larger centres outside Paris. Here I have chosen Lyon, the second-largest city in France – this time drawing rather more on existing studies.[59] One particularity of Lyon is immediately striking: on 4 September 1870, for the first time in the nineteenth century, the change of regime was proclaimed there in the morning – before Paris – indicating the capital's lesser pre-eminence. Simultaneously, a first 'Commune' and municipal autonomy were also announced in Lyon. The city was considered a rebel city in the nineteenth century (with the federalist movement of 1793, the *canuts* struggles of the 1830s and February 1848). It was thus closely monitored by the Second Empire: Lyon was placed under special measures (state control of the police, abolition of the mayor's office); the police force was expanded, and the surrounding communes annexed (Vaise, Croix-Rousse, Guillotière, and so on).[60] Other changes had taken place in the 1860s: the urban fabric had been transformed, religious institutions had established themselves, and the silk manufacturers had weakened the *canuts* by developing an original form of proto-industry in the countryside.[61] In parallel to this, new metallurgical and chemical industries had developed in La Guillotière, downstream from the Rhône, in workshops that counted up to 400 workers.[62] However,

59 Jeanne Gaillard, *Communes de province, Commune de Paris 1870–1871* (Paris: Flammarion, 1971); Julian P. W. Archer, 'The Crowd in the Lyon Commune and the Insurrection of La Guillotière', *International Review of Social History* 17: 1 (1972), pp. 183–8. Archer's PhD dissertation, 'The First International and the Lyon Revolutionnary Mouvement, 1864–1870', University of Wisconsin (1970), was never published; Moissonnier, *La Première Internationale*. For a new analysis that also incorporates the war and the republican movement, see Inès Ben Slama, 'En République. Une histoire matérielle de la guerre franco-prussienne et des communes dans les grandes villes du Sud de la France (Lyon, Marseille, Toulouse, Bordeaux), 1870–1871', PhD dissertation, Université Paris Cité (2024).

60 Law of 19 June 1851 and decree of 24 March 1852; Florent Prieur, 'Dompter une ville en colère. Genèse, conception et mise en oeuvre de la police d'État de Lyon (1800–1870)', PhD dissertation, Université Lyon-2 (2013); John Merriman, *The Margins of City Life: Explorations on the French Urban Frontier 1815–1851* (New York/Oxford: Oxford University Press, 1991).

61 Philippe Dujardin and Pierre-Yves Saunier, eds, *Lyon, l'âme d'une ville (1850–1914)* (Lyon: Éditions lyonnaises d'art et d'histoire, 1997).

62 Yves Lequin, *Les Ouvriers de la région lyonnaise (1848–1914), vol. I: La Formation de la classe ouvrière régionale* (Lyon: Presses universitaires de Lyon, 1977).

the city still had one of the highest concentrations of workers. Republican sentiment was widespread, in various forms, among the members of the liberal upper bourgeoisie – artisans as well as factory workers. Significantly, the 'No' vote had won in the plebiscite of May 1870, and the city had been marked by a wave of public meetings, as well as by the strike movement of 1869–70. So, on 4 September 1870, a 'Committee of Public Safety [salut]' was established. It included men like the weaver Chépié and Dr Hénon, one of the few republican MPs elected in 1852. Red flags were raised over official buildings, the city took the name 'Commune de Lyon', and a 'Committee of General Security [sûrété]' arrested certain local exponents of the fallen regime. The Committee of Public Safety decided to continue the war by entrusting the command of the volunteers to Garibaldi. It decreed the suppression of religious congregations, instituted the election of *commissaires* by universal male suffrage, and decided to elect a municipal council. Set up on 15 September, this council proved a little more moderate and less working-class, even though it included several members of the former Committee of Public Safety.

At that moment, an actor we have not yet met entered the scene: the International Workingmen's Association (IWMA) – or, rather, its Lyon section. The International was indeed well established in Lyon, among the workers of the neighbourhoods of La Croix-Rousse and Guillotière. Despite numerous dissensions, the group was particularly influenced by Bakuninite anarchism and the Alliance for Socialist Democracy, whose links with the First International had been complex and full of twists and turns. Its members wanted to eradicate the existing order, in favour of building a fairer society that would allow the 'forces of life' to express themselves. The section thus stood far from the positions of the General Council in London. The Russian leader arrived in Lyon in mid-September, having set off from Switzerland, where he had been living for five years. Bakunin, then fifty-seven years old, was an important exponent of anti-authoritarian socialism. After having participated in the Springtime of Peoples in 1848, and in particular in the Dresden uprising (1849), he was long imprisoned in Austria, and then in Russia. His anarchist ideas became clearer on his return and after.[63] With the Committee for the

63 Mathieu Léonard, *L'Émancipation des travailleurs. Une histoire de la Première Internationale* (Paris: La Fabrique, 2011).

Salvation of France, created on 17 September, he set off a riot against the Hôtel de Ville on 28 September. A small group took the building, and one of the leaders declaimed: 'I declare, in the name of the people, that the municipal council is required to accept and sign the radical programme immediately', which called for 'dismissal of all officials, without exception, who belonged to the Empire; dismissal of all army officers . . . finally, in a word, the overthrow of the existing order, and its reconstruction on radical and revolutionary foundations'.[64] But the attempt failed after the intervention of the battalions of National Guards from La Croix-Rousse, and faced with criticisms from construction workers, who had initially come to a demonstration to defend the Republic.

The IWMA temporarily took a step back. The republican dynamic and the displacement of the sites of power, however, did not falter. The new prefect, Challemel Lacour, was sidelined. The municipal council continued to defend the city's autonomy, stepped up its anticlerical actions and asserted its policy of secularisation. It also tried to municipalise the police and pursued military preparations. The republican committees remained active. To these were added a central federative committee, which supported the formation of the Ligue du Midi, and a revolutionary committee of La Guillotière, marked by the presence of Dr Crestin and constituted around a radical, egalitarian programme. The editorial lines of the newspapers, for their part, changed little, but public meetings were also now held, while the sites for building defences set up by the Committee of Public Safety served as a site of politicisation, before they were closed down in December. The shadow of the war remained omnipresent. The defence of the Republic, the city and the country were intermingled, in a rumour-filled climate. The climax came when the crowd killed the National Guard commander Antoine Arnaud, after news became known of the defeat in the Battle of Nuits-Saint-Georges on 19 December.

This event provided an opportunity for certain elites and authorities to react. The defeat against Prussia, the appointment of the hard-line prefect Edmond Valentin and the elections of February 1871 led to a first resumption of control.[65] The National Guard remained active,

64 Cited in Moissonnier, *La Première Internationale*, p. 259.

65 Garibaldi was elected, but far behind the moderate republicans and conservative candidates like Trochu.

however, and in La Guillotière the revolutionary committee, elected by acclamation, began a radical local-level reorganisation: it took charge of the police, arbitrated disputes in the arrondissement, and so on. It was in this context that Paris's '18 March' burst onto the scene, and its echo was strongly felt here as well: on 22 March, the democratic central committee of the National Guard asked Mayor Hénon to support Paris. Faced with his refusal, its members forced their way into the Hôtel de Ville, had a provisional commission appointed by acclamation, and proclaimed a new Commune. Albert Leblanc, an emissary sent by the Paris Commune on 11 February, was appointed 'delegate from Paris' (he was only able to follow the march of events). However, the new provisional commission did not succeed in establishing its authority. Noting the erosion of its authority, it resigned. The municipal council took over the city hall while reaffirming its attachment to the Republic and, once again, to the autonomy of the 'Commune'.

The situation in the capital, however, continued to attract attention in Lyon. Public meetings rallied support for Paris. Newspapers favourable to a revolutionary Commune were created, such as *Le Cri du peuple lyonnais* on 5 April – doubtless the one that Chomette had come from Thiers in search of. A delegation from the municipal council then went to Versailles, to attempt a reconciliation with Paris, and surely also to calm the situation in Lyon. It was now that the third uprising was launched. This time it was led by Blanquists, members of the International, and militants such as Louis Berthet, from the metalworkers' circle. Unlike in the previous attempts, the group behind it remained discreet. An indication of the transnational connections evoked in this book's first part, it received at least formal support from Swiss Internationalists: both 'the Jura group', close to Bakunin's positions, and the 'Geneva group' – even if these labels do not convey the real complexity of the situations.[66] The action was planned for 30 April – again, the day of the municipal elections in the arrondissements.[67] On the day in question, two conspirators charged with eliminating the prefect were arrested. In La Guillotière, which for weeks had been in a state of quasi-self-government, a riot broke out. This prompted a wider movement,

66 See Marc Vuilleumier, 'La Première Internationale en Suisse', *Revue syndicale Suisse* 9 (September 1964).

67 Lyon still could not elect its mayor after the law of 14 April 1871.

and a group of National Guards seized the Guillotière town hall in the name of the Commune. A mob formed, consisting of local residents, National Guards and striking workers. Faced with this situation, after much hesitation, the military authorities sent in the cavalry at 7 p.m. Terrible fighting unfolded at the barricades erected around the city hall. Thirty people were killed. A few barricades were then erected in La Croix-Rousse, without much effect. The reaction of the authorities was not long in coming: the National Guards were disarmed and newspapers were shut down. This marked the end of Lyon's communal adventure, even if events in Paris continued to be followed closely there.

Lyon thus offers a remarkable example of the interlocking nature of the Communes, as the municipality never ceased to bear this name throughout this period. It thus sheds a particular light on the competing meanings that this word could take on. The cycle of events in 1870–71 also served as a catalyst in the city's history: the Commune is generally considered to be a moment of transition in Lyon's oppositional cultures, between the silk workers of La Croix-Rousse and the new metalworkers of La Guillotière. It also reminds us that, both for social reasons and because of urban changes, communalist movements involved not only the skilled workers of the so-called traditional sectors, but also the less-skilled workers of the new industries.[68]

Epilogue: Entering into Paris's Revolutionary Dynamic

A revolutionary nebula

Each of these trajectories thus led to a singular, localised result. At the same time, they present an obvious family resemblance with one another. To resolve this paradox, we can follow the analyses of the political scientist Boris Gobille. Indeed, he invites us not to reduce the study of such events to a set of predefined causes, but to examine them as processes in the course of which, given the various possible conditions, some became operative and others do not; in turn, these generated

68 Pierre-Yves Saunier, *L'Esprit lyonnais (XIXe–XXe siècle). Genèse d'une représentation sociale* (Paris: CNRS Éditions, 1995).

interdependencies, which gradually give the crisis its specific traits.[69] Through this perspective, it is possible to understand this interplay of proximities and differences.[70]

This way of understanding critical conjunctures is interesting for several reasons. Firstly, it highlights the shared conditions of possibility: the economic transformations and political struggles at the end of the Second Empire, the shock of the war, the proclamation of the Republic, the resurgence of revolutionary memories, the local competition for power, the weight of the defeats, and then the February elections. Moreover, it allows non-static comparisons to be made. Each time, the process of crisis or revolution accentuates or redistributes social and political divisions. However, it seems to take more ambiguous forms in colonial situations, no doubt because of the greater number of cleavages that run through these societies (be they economic, social, political or legal, and including religious and racial ones). The colonial terrain also highlights the ambivalence of a revolutionary and republican movement with multiple profiles: sometimes, when mobilised by formerly enslaved people, it led to moments of subjectivation and political emancipation (as in Martinique); sometimes, when associated with a 'European' experience, it resulted in phenomena of exclusion (as in Algeria). Nineteenth-century republican universalism here reveals its variations. Finally, this approach makes it possible to grasp both the autonomy of these scenarios and their interaction effects. Many are indirect (the zone of influence of regional urban centres, the biographical trajectories of deportees, and so on). Others are direct, and are mobilised by actors who observe what is happening elsewhere in real time, revealing richer-than-expected local frames of reference.

69 Boris Gobille, 'De l'étiologie à l'historicité des crises', in Myriam Aït-Aoudia and Antoine Roger, eds, *La Logique du désordre. Relire la sociologie de Michel Dobry* (Paris: Presses de Sciences Po, 2015), pp. 153–76. See also Boris Gobille, 'L'événement Mai 68. Pour une sociohistoire du temps court', *Annales. Histoire, Sciences sociales* 63: 2 (2008).

70 A problem raised in Louis M. Greenberg, *Sisters of Liberty: Marseille, Lyon, Paris and the Reaction to a Centralized State (1868–1871)* (Cambridge, MA: Harvard University Press, 1971); Ronald Aminzade, *Ballots and Barricades: Class Formation and Republican Politics in Nineteenth-Century France* (Princeton, NJ: Princeton University Press, 1993).

Paris, September 1870–March 1871: notes on the mole's path

This analysis could clearly be taken further. But these perspectives and trajectories lead us back to Paris, whose position stands out more clearly. Although these movements are above all local, the Paris Commune is the only event to be consistently mentioned (except for the insurrection in Martinique), and the only one to exert a tangible influence on these trajectories – beyond the possible presence of emissaries whose role turned out to be secondary. Even though it began after certain other experiences, it remains the obvious centre of gravity of the revolutionary nebula. The comparison brings out other distinctive features: Paris, the former capital, is the only one to have had a quasi-government that broke with the other national institutions. And it is the only one whose crisis and then revolutionary dynamic, once set in motion, lasted for so long: the process of transformation was surely pushed further there, which justifies a closer look at this exceptional experience.

This multi-site exploration also makes it possible to clarify certain features of an origin-narrative that has been repeated countless times, yet never settled. First of all, though this nebula of revolutions did not have any direct effects on Paris, it surely helped to fuel its hopes and energies to some degree. The sheer breadth of the military and political context in which the path to the Paris Commune began to take shape also becomes clear. So, too, is the particular way in which it did so in this city, with its status as a capital, its demographic mass, its working-class and republican character, and the spread of radical and socialist ideas within it. We could also consider factors such as the siege of the city, the role of organisations parallel to the government of National Defence (IWMA sections, vigilance committees, National Guard battalions), or even the feeling of anger after the National Assembly's vexatious measures.

Finally, and most importantly, such a perspective invites us to look back at the advent of the Paris Commune, particularly its processual dimension. The Commune, as we know, came about at the end of a slow 'slide' from September 1870 to March 1871, which has been re-evaluated in recent years.[71] The choice of narration has long allowed historians to underline the multiple sources of this process, and to break the Commune out of the theoretical and political generalisations to which it often used

71 See the accounts of Rougerie and Tombs, cited in previous chapters.

to be reduced.[72] Yet it also has the disadvantage of suspending analysis and neutralising part of the interpretation itself. So, despite everything, perhaps we should try to clarify the consistency of this process. Faced with the plurality of scenes of action and their rhythms, as well as the impossibility of accounting for them, the historical and social-science studies of political crises and revolutions no longer seek to establish origins. After having identified the general conditions of possibility, they are now more interested in the phenomena of emergence, and to this end they identify documentable moments of inflection. In this way, it becomes possible to approach the dynamics of the crisis itself, in addition to the persistence or replaying of old elements. This allows us not to identify an origin or a root cause, but to gain a proper feel for the movement's own effectiveness. This is what I am aiming to do now. The sociologist and historian Ivan Ermakoff has proposed a device for this purpose. It consists of starting from decision-making arenas whose actions can be observed, and then assessing their repercussions on the chains of relations – even if they are at the crossroads of fluid and plural relations of force.[73] Given the documentation and the studies available to us, it is possible to conduct such an investigation for the Paris Commune. We can start from the week of 18–26 March, bracketed by the movement to reconquer the city and the Commune elections: the week that historians have aptly called the 'week of uncertainty'.

The week of uncertainty, under the microscope

Let us focus on one scene and one small group of actors. We are in Paris on 19 March 1871. On that day, Parisians could read these opening words on a poster of the Republican Federation of the National Guard: 'If the Central Committee of the National Guard were a government, it could, for the dignity of its voters, feel no need to justify itself. But [it has] the simple honesty to remain exactly within the express limit of the

72 On this, see Jacques Rougerie and Robert Tombs, 'La Commune de Paris', in Michel Pigenet and Danièle Tartakosvky, eds, *Histoire des mouvements sociaux en France (de 1814 à nos jours)* (Paris: La Découverte, 2011).

73 Ivan Ermakoff, *Ruling Oneself Out: A Theory of Collective Abdications* (Durham, NC: Duke University Press, 2008), Chapters 7–9. The author offers a more theoretical exposition in 'The Structure of Contingency', *American Journal of Sociology* 121: 1 (July 2015), pp. 64–125.

mandate which has been entrusted to it . . .' After 18 March, the members of the Central Committee of the National Guard who occupied the Hôtel de Ville building hesitated.[74] Planned for 10 March and constituted on 15 March, this Central Committee was essentially composed of elected workers, and represented the majority of the Parisian battalions. It was not the only actor in play in the capital. There was also the intervention of the 'Central Committee of the twenty arrondissements', uniting the vigilance committees created in September, which was composed of members of the IWMA, Blanquists and radical republicans. They had experienced repeated ebbs and flows during the autumn and winter and were, a priori, more favourable to a social revolution. In addition, there were the National Guards, 200,000 of them, whose profile varied according to district, who elected their delegates. If the Central Committee was the emanation of these forces, it did not control them. The population, of course, cannot be forgotten: not all Parisians were revolutionaries, and attitudes varied according to neighbourhood or the specific moment: but in general they were incensed by the defeat and the reactionary policy of the National Assembly. Finally, there were the 'legitimate elected representatives', the arrondissement-level mayors elected in November and the MPs of the Seine elected in February, who were generally republican. Opposed to all these was the National Assembly, elected in February, with a monarchist and conservative majority, which was then on its way from Bordeaux to Versailles (it had its first session there on 20 March). It was accompanied by the government led by Adolphe Thiers, appointed by the Assembly, which included several members of the former Government of National Defence.

At the time, all the protagonists agreed on two points: the need to hold elections, and the rejection of civil war – each having in mind the spectre of June 1848.[75] But the same words did not have the same meaning. In Paris the mayors, of various political leanings (from the most

74 Here we draw both on various post facto accounts – *l'Enquête parlementaire sur le 18 mars*, and Prosper-Olivier Lissagaray, 'La semaine de l'incertitude', in his *Histoire de la Commune de 1871* (Paris: Dentu, 1896), Chapter 4 – as well as a systematic study of the *Journal officiel de la Commune* (starting 20 March), of the debates in the National Assembly, and of the minutes of the secret meetings of parliament, whose publication the National Assembly authorised in 2011: Éric Bonhomme, ed., *De l'Empire à la République. Comités secrets du Parlement (1870–1871)* (Paris: Perrin, 2011).

75 This spectre was evoked at the Central Committee as early as 18 March, and upon the opening sessions of the National Assembly.

moderate to the socialists), were in favour of municipal autonomy and the Republic, i.e. the holding of municipal elections, the recognition of elections within the National Guards and the postponement of rent payments (until after the war period).[76] The Central Committee, for its part, also intended, using these same terms, the abolition of the army and the police prefecture. Moreover, several mayors, including the republican socialist Louis Blanc, felt that they did not have to negotiate too much with those who had not been anointed by universal male suffrage. This sentiment was not shared by members of the Central Committee elected by the National Guards and installed after a popular insurrection. In other words, at this moment, several conceptions of legitimacy in the Republic stood opposed. And, after an abortive attempt at consultation, two competing electoral processes were organised: that of the Central Committee, announced for 22 March, and that of the mayors, which they saw as more official, and intended to have validated by the National Assembly.[77] They went to Versailles for this purpose on 20 and then 21 March.

In the Assembly, the material, administrative and political framework was quite different. This institution followed its own rhythm – an 'urgent procedure' had to be requested, while, as one MP said, 'in this moment, minutes count for centuries'.[78] Here, the MPs from the Seine were unable to get their side of the story heard, due to repeated interruptions from other MPs. The session of 21 March and the beginning of that on 22 March nevertheless marked a moment of hesitation. Everyone wanted to avoid civil war. Thiers hesitated and, if certain monarchist or Bonapartist MPs wished to raise volunteers against the capital, many agreed with the idea of elections, provided they were held within the framework and the proper timescales of the national parliament. The situation was suspended.

The breaking point came on 22 March – and came not from the monarchists but from the government. That day, Favre gave a speech in

76 Including those who aspired to a social revolution or a Commune, like Varlin and Malon.

77 See the two posters from 21 March, published in the *Journal officiel* the next day: one by the Central Committee and the other by the Paris MPs.

78 Comte de La Rochethulon, 23 March session – *Annales de l'Assemblée nationale. Compte rendu in extenso des séances, annexes* (Paris: A. Wittersheim, 1871–72), p. 67.

the harshest tones: 'I would like those who are throwing the *Patrie* into such an abyss of evil to understand the responsibility that weighs on them, before history.'[79] His intervention changed positions and united monarchists and moderate republicans against Paris. The rupture was confirmed by the discussion in secret committee which took place that evening from 9.45 p.m. to 2 a.m., the minutes of which have recently been published.[80] Thiers had clearly made his choice, as had the president of the Assembly, Jules Grévy. Why? As Favre indicated in the session, Prussia had meanwhile made it known that it did not want the events in Paris to call into question the preliminary peace agreements. The international dimension continued to weigh heavily. But that alone was not enough. In addition to the Versailles MP's hatred for the Parisian revolutionaries, likely also in play, on the government's side of things, was the recognition that the more time passed, the more the process of political dislocation in Paris would be intensified. The choice thus seemed to make itself. It was therefore decided to hold elections, but for the whole of France and in April. Paris had no exceptional status, and would not even get a mayor. The break was clear.

Meanwhile, in Paris, the process had indeed run its course in parallel: as the planned elections approached, the number of National Guards increased, positions became more radical, and socialist rhetoric became clearer. But this reciprocal game of decisions also accelerated matters. On 24 March – after the Assembly's decision – the Central Committee mentioned for the first time in a poster the expression 'advent of the workers' world', and evoked a political and social revolution.[81] The social nature of the Committee and of the National Guards, who were mostly artisans and skilled workers, became more evident from this moment onwards. It was not that this dimension had ever been absent: there had been talk of revolution since June 1868, and 18 March 1871 was indeed a popular movement born of the peripheral neighbourhoods. But here it crystallised, openly asserted itself, and became a driving force behind the secession.

The mayors and MPs continued, for their part, to seek conciliation in Versailles. However, after a demonstration in Paris on 22 March by the

79 *Annales de l'Assemblée nationale*, 22 March session, p. 52.

80 Bonhomme, *De l'Empire à la République*.

81 *Les Murailles politiques*, poster, 'Aux gardes nationales', 24 March 1871.

so-called 'friends of order', which caused the first deaths in the Commune, the group split. Some of them then switched to the opposition, and tried to organise resistance to the insurgent city. The most radical, such as the Internationalist Benoît Malon and the republican Millière, quit their ranks. Political divisions now took precedence over what had been their shared legal role in previous days: to represent Paris itself. The process thus gradually drew and reinforced the dividing lines between revolutionaries, radical republicans, moderates and liberals, as well as between the 'common people' and the 'bourgeois'. While in some cases these lines would continue to be blurred, from this point onwards they seemed unmistakably clear.[82] In the Assembly, the voice of the MPs from the Seine was no longer audible, and there was a systematic rejection of the 'rabble' (*la populace*) and the 'Reds'. In Paris, the revolutionary and popular identification of the Parisians and the denunciation of a 'White' Assembly (the monarchists) were strengthened. Even so, most of the mayors ended up accepting elections for Paris only. The final choice was made with the elections of 26 March. The abstention rate was high, particularly in the bourgeois districts, but the vote brought revolutionaries and very radical republicans to the head of the capital by legal means. The choices had now been made, and the responsibilities assigned by each side. There was no going back.

This sequence is, once again, only one impulse within a more complex movement. The other scenes, perhaps even the one in Lyon, are surely not absent from it. But this examination provides a way into the situational logic of the event. Beyond the interplay of transnational and national connections, beyond the earlier oppositions and conditions of possibility, there were logics specific to the time of crisis itself. This important point must be added to the previous picture: the Paris Commune had a movement of its own. And with that movement, the perception of history and of the space of possibilities gradually shifted. It is now time to cross to the other side of the Paris ramparts.

82 Tolain, the worker-founder of the IWMA, remained on the side of the mayors; Clemenceau would regret to the last the failed attempts at reconciliation; and so on.

6

The Paris Commune 'from Below'

Let us head back to the Place de l'Hôtel de Ville, and the moment when Charles Beslay was about to deliver his rousing speech. In declaring its existence with such pomp, the Commune was turning into something else. Following many others before us, we must now delve into the maelstrom of insurgent Paris – into its organisations, its arrondissements, its barricades and its streets.

There is no need to go back over what is already well known: the commissions with their changing remits; the seventy-nine elected representatives gathered at the Hôtel de Ville; the high proportion of skilled workers; the diversity of political positions (Blanquists, Internationalists, Proudhonians, Jacobins, and so on); the main measures taken (abolition of conscription, separation of church and state, the ban on wage deductions); or the pulling-down of the Vendôme Column and the importance of the reference to previous revolutions, especially the 'democratic and social Republic'. All these elements matter. But, as noted above, it is on this basis that a long series of studies have also emphasised how meagre the Commune's achievements were, how it managed only to 'stammer out a system', or the fact that, ultimately, its mere existence sufficed to make it an exceptional moment.

This last observation may indeed be accurate. But is it really enough to grasp the 'Commune' moment? Recent works invite us to explore what was going on beyond the Hôtel de Ville, out in the arrondissements and the neighbourhoods.[1] Some local field studies do exist. But for the Commune, unlike for the revolutions of 1789 or 1848, we do not yet have any microhistorical studies of neighbourhood organisation, analyses of combatants' careers, or examinations of what it meant to 'become a revolutionary' – in short, elements that would show the 'revolution at work'.[2]

Yet this dimension is essential in two respects. Insofar as the Commune sought to hand power to all citizens, and given its relatively brief existence, much of its life did surely play out at this level. Added to this is a certain methodological imperative: as we have seen, with the end of the grand paradigms, researchers in history and the social sciences have developed more process-based approaches, which are attentive to events and to the practices of the actors, as well as to the combination of the social, cultural and organisational dimensions. This approach, which represents the micro-analytical level of the overall configuration-based analysis used here, also makes it possible to observe what happens in the time of crisis or revolution, before offering an interpretation. These two considerations render such an analysis 'from below' especially appropriate.

Three sites of observation are used for this purpose, with an emphasis on practices: the administration of the extra-ordinary, the army, and economic relations. Heading down to 'ground level' in this way will allow us to grasp the shifting web of relations in a city that was, we should not forget, immersed simultaneously in revolution, war and a siege. The focus of study here is not so much the Commune, in the sense of what was going on at the Hôtel de Ville, but rather the multiform set of interactions and frameworks of meaning that characterised the 'Paris Republic'.

A final comment is required on the term 'from below' itself. Sometimes it refers to the action of popular groups, whether they self-defined or were defined as such by others, and sometimes to situations that played

1 See, for example, Jacques Rougerie and Robert Tombs, 'La Commune de Paris', in Michel Pigenet and Danièle Tartakosvky, eds, *Histoire des mouvements sociaux en France (de 1814 à nos jours)* (Paris: La Découverte, 2011).

2 Among a wealth of literature, see Timothy Tackett, *Becoming a Revolutionary: The Deputies of the French National Assembly and the Emergence of a Revolutionary Culture (1789–1790)* (Princeton, NJ: Princeton University Press, 1997); Haïm Burstin, *Une révolution à l'oeuvre. Le faubourg Saint-Marcel (1789–1794)* (Seyssel: Champ Vallon, 2005). On 1848, see Louis Hincker, *Citoyens-combattants à Paris (1848–1851)* (Villeneuve-d'Ascq: Presses universitaires du Septentrion, 2008).

out beyond the Hôtel de Ville's own field of action. But 'from below' most often refers to the examination of composite situations that developed in combination with the Hôtel de Ville or other bodies.[3] Above all, it is an angle of observation. As such, it allows us to grasp what concrete change occurred in everyday institutions, sociopolitical relations, and modes of apprehending the world, during a moment that many Parisians no doubt considered remarkable.

Public Functions and the Administration of the Extra-Ordinary

In insurgent Paris, the city administration quickly became a major issue. The newly elected members of the Commune had to prove their capacity to keep the city running and establish a form of communal government that broke with the *ancien régime*. Beyond the political differences mentioned above, there was a consensus on some points: the dismantling of the Bonapartist state and certain of its institutions (the police prefecture, the army); and the transfer of power to citizens, regarded as directly possessing a share of sovereign power.

But these ambitions had to be adapted in parallel to a situation that was largely outside of the Hôtel de Ville's control. Some districts had seen alternative modes of governance as early as autumn 1870. And on 18 March 1871, Thiers took the entire Paris administration with him: a significant proportion of the tens of thousands of civil servants and employees of the state and city administrations left Paris.[4] While it is impossible to know exactly how many of them did leave, the functions in closest contact with the public were hit hard. The city experienced a remarkable administrative *tabula rasa*, to which the Commune had to

3 On this usage, see Simona Cerutti, 'Who Is Below?', *Annales. Histoire, Sciences sociales* 70: 4 (2015), pp. 931–56.

4 It is impossible to provide any precise estimate. By combining various works covering the period 1869–1900, we can arrive at an indicative figure of 11,500 people employed at the police prefecture, 1,700 in the fire department, 17,900 in the services of the Seine Prefecture, and 4,000 in the central state administrations. See Louis Girard, *Nouvelle histoire de Paris, vol. IX : La Deuxième République et le Second Empire, 1848–1870* (Paris: Hachette, 1981); Pierre Casselle, *Nouvelle histoire de Paris. Paris républicain, 1871–1914* (Paris: Hachette, 2003); François Burdeau, *Histoire de l'administration française* (Paris: Montchrestien, 1989); Bernard Marchand, *Paris, histoire d'une ville, XIXe–XXe siècle* (Paris: Seuil, 1993).

adjust: day labourers, cobblers and clerks became tax collectors, police chiefs and excise officers.

The archives do offer us an opportunity to observe what was going on in Paris; some of these 'officials' were later tried and convicted for 'usurpation of office' following a judicial process that ran either parallel to or in combination with that of the military tribunals. Out of just over 320 verdicts recorded between 1871 and 1872, I have been able to reconstruct 256 cases from the procedural files.[5] It is difficult to say how many there really were: the definition of 'public service' fluctuated under the Commune, and many posts changed hands. Moreover, the archives offer no access to the cases that were dismissed, and some of them were evidently handled internally, within the administrations themselves. Clearly, this is a small sample. Even so, it offers an exceptional opportunity to study up close a part of the power shifts that took place under the Commune, together with what it changed in the 'ordinary' administration of an 'extra-ordinary' situation.

Occupying Posts: The Polynomy of the Commune

These alleged 'usurpers' were mainly men. Women were few in number and generally confined to functions considered 'feminine', such as schoolmistresses for primary-age children. These men were generally at least approaching middle age (thirty-eight years old on average), and belonged as much to the world of skilled workers (typographers, cabinetmakers, engravers, and so on) as to that of the petty and middling urban bourgeoisie (white-collar employees, artists, students, teachers). Most were married (77 per cent of those whose marital status is reported). In comparison, their profile is slightly more 'popular' than that of the men elected to the Hôtel de Ville, and less than that of the standard portrait of the Communard, such as can be established based on military records:

5 Survey conducted starting in 2009, in collaboration with modernist historian Jérémie Foa. The first estimate comes from consulting the registers of judgments between June 1871 and February 1872 (AVP, D1U6-8-16). It was interrupted when the percentage of usurpation cases relative to the total number of cases judged became very low (0.5 per cent). So, the full number of usurpation cases must be slightly higher. The case histories are taken from the case files for the years 1871–73 (AVP, D2U6 5-17). Some have been supplemented by the archives of military councils (SHD, 8J), as well as by pardon application files (AN, BB 24).

those were generally younger, more likely to be unmarried, and most often working-class.[6] The occupants of these posts were therefore men with families, from various backgrounds, who looked for or had been directed towards these positions more than towards service in the National Guard, which was initially dedicated to combat. But to speak only of the averages scarcely reflects the diversity of situations.

A closer look at this sample reveals different ways of arriving at these positions in insurgent Paris, which, together with historian Jérémie Foa, I have termed 'investment formulae'.[7] Four in particular stand out. The first is the *revolutionary calling* – the choices made by political militants. We find this especially often in connection to leadership roles. The Blanquists, particularly Raoul Rigault, monopolised such positions at the police prefecture. We also find Proudhonists and militants of the IWMA in important posts, such as André Bastelica, director of indirect taxes. This same phenomenon was echoed at lower levels, whether in the cases of seasoned activists or individuals who had become politicised and committed to political action during the wave of public meetings, or the movement following 4 September 1870. A second way of attaining such posts was through *recommendation*, thanks to a certain degree of proximity to those who held office. Marius Fabre, a quantity surveyor, reported that he had approached Massard, director of the Estate and Stamp Office, for a post as *commissaire de police* of the Arts and Metiers district: 'I asked Massard, who I had got to know at the café, for this post'.[8] Surely, we should look with some caution on this version

6 Jacques Rougerie, 'Portrait du communard', in Rougerie, *Paris libre 1871* (Paris: Seuil, 2002). This profile corresponds relatively closely to general demographic data. See Jacques Dupâquier, ed., *Histoire de la population française* (Paris: PUF, 1988), pp. 425–8.

7 See Luc Boltanski and Laurent Thévenot, eds, special issue 'Justesse et justice dans le travail', *Cahiers du Centre d'études de l'emploi* 33 (Paris: PUF, 1989). On this usage, see Quentin Deluermoz and Jérémie Foa, 'Titulatures, positions sociales et mouvement révolutionnaire: les "usurpations de fonctions" communardes (1871)', in Quentin Deluermoz and Jérémie Foa, eds, *Usurpations de fonction et appropriations du pouvoir en situation de crise (XIXe–XXe siècle)*, online edition of the Centre d'histoire du XIXe siècle (2012), pp. 59–74.

8 As Anglophone specialists on France's social history have insisted, the English term 'commissioner' does not work as a translation of *commissaire*. It is standard practice to keep the latter. See John Merriman, *Police Stories: Building the French State, 1815–1851* (Oxford: Oxford University Press, 2005). AVP, D2U6/14, Fabre Marius Joseph, usurpation de fonction (13.7.1871); AN, BB 24/770.

of events emphasising personal acquaintance, which tends to retroactively depoliticise the assumption of such roles. But many requests were made, and webs of acquaintances were an important resource to draw on in such situations. The recommendation could come from friends of friends; sometimes it was a matter of filling some position that had otherwise found no takers. In April, Claude Lafont – a white-collar employee who was infirm and in need of cash – went to the director of public assistance after being 'recommended to him by Mr Collin under the government of 4 September'. He wanted a job in the 5th arrondissement's firewood depot. But the director, Treillard, offered him the post of *commissaire de police* in the Saint-Germain-des-Prés district, which he eventually accepted.[9] The third important mode of reaching such posts had to do with *local district and neighbourhood-level relations*. Residents of a district, often local personalities, held positions with or without the support of other residents. At this level, vacancies became public knowledge: if a functionary departed for Versailles, or was otherwise absent, this was easy to see. Such appointments were also a way for residents to gain – or keep – some control over their local environment. Pierre Chauvet, a forty-four-year-old white-collar employee, said that he had accepted the position of *commissaire de police* in the Chaussée-d'Antin neighbourhood 'at the request of the residents' – a fact that seems to be confirmed by the letters of support later sent at the time of the trial.[10] From some cases we can also see the influence of connections among neighbours or relatives (fathers and sons, brothers, etc.).

The final route is a little different. Perhaps curiously, once the first few weeks had come and gone, the Communards sought to organise recruitment on the basis of competence, whether this was expressed by some objective yardstick – by a title or qualification ensuring that personnel were interchangeable – or in terms of concrete experience in the field. This can be called an *institutionalisation* process. From April 1871, the Commune's public services commission opened recruitment offices. On 1 April, Bastelica, director of the Indirect Taxation Department of the Seine, issued a poster indicating that 'due to the absence or dismissal of a large number of employees, the administration is calling on citizens

9 AVP, D2U6/7, Lafont Claude, usurpation de fonction. Letter dated July 1871 from Claude Lafont.

10 AVP, D2U6-7, Pierre Chauvet, usurpation de fonction.

able to serve in the various branches of the service. They are to present themselves, *with supporting titles*, at the directorate's headquarters, rue Dupont, 12.'[11] This was how the accountant Charles Paradis – who was obviously far removed from political partisanship – became the tax collector for the 6th arrondissement. Finally, there were those, perhaps many, who continued to carry out their duties during the Commune, despite orders from Versailles.[12] Some did so at the request of their superiors, to protect their premises and documents. Others remained in their jobs out of inertia, choice or ideological commitment. In many cases, staying in post allowed them to obtain a higher rank, which enabled the clerks, a real administrative proletariat, to become first-class clerks or office managers, with a higher salary. This marked a real change, given that those with careers in the lower ranks of the administrations typically ran into hard limits.[13] These various routes into administrative posts could, of course, intersect.

The filling of public functions thus responded to identifiable logics. There was neither anarchy nor spontaneous order, but a genuine Communard polynomy. However, these considerations should also be set in the context of each neighbourhood and the particular moment in the Commune's development: they correspond to a patchwork of heterogeneous social-political orders, each seemingly obeying its own rhythm.

The public authorities in action

But what did these people actually do with the public authority they held? Given the unstable remit of their functions, their room for manoeuvre varied. These officials (let's call them that) had to adapt their work to the multiple sites of power (vigilance committees, clubs, municipalities, the National Guard, city hall), and to the combinations as well as the frictions between them. The abundance of distinctive markers of authority in the city (uniforms, medals, scarves, armbands) also altered

11 *JOC* (my emphasis).

12 On 5 April 1871, a decree promised an indemnity to those who did not yet have any work but agreed to leave their posts.

13 On the social situation of civil servants, see Jean Le Bihan, *Au service de l'État. Les fonctionnaires intermédiaires au XIXe siècle* (Rennes: Presses universitaires de Rennes, 2008).

the content of the functions themselves. According to the historian Robert Descimon, this substance does indeed partly depend on the controlled number of such markers.[14] Finally, these officials dealt with local residents who, given the 'citizen imperium' now in place, themselves possessed a share of public authority. These individuals were more easily able to solicit, oppose or challenge officials' interventions. More than in the previous period – where these functions were based on stable recruitment, regulations, rules and institutions – officials were somehow cogs in these ever-changing situations. Depending on opportunities, political choices or temperaments, they could maintain the status quo, or slow down or amplify the revolutionary movement. Under such conditions, we would struggle to present any coherent overall picture of these supposed usurpers' actions. But when we read the sources, we find logics of action that show the effects of their interventions – or, through them, the effects of the conjuncture of crisis and of the revolution itself.

The first corresponds to a sort of clean-up of the normative environment, as can be seen in the vast administrative literature preserved in the judicial records (reports, minutes, notes): echoing the previous revolutions, formal modes of address were replaced by 'Salut et Fraternité', and citizens addressed each other as 'citoyen' and 'citoyenne'. Many neighbourhoods bearing the names of saints were renamed, as during the French Revolution: the name of Saint-Denis was partly crossed out, to read simply 'Denis'. These practices – anodyne in appearance, but vast in scale – belong to what historian Philippe Artières calls an undermining of the ordinary writings of power.[15] They are also testimony to the everyday presence of the French Revolution, and contributed to the symbolic alteration of urban space that was now underway.

The second logic of action refers to the imperatives of survival in a state of siege and civil war. In a city whose social life had been disrupted for more than seven months, many sought to preserve an appearance of

14 Robert Descimon, 'La vénalité des offices et la construction de l'État dans la France moderne. Des problèmes de la representation symbolique aux problèmes du coût social du pouvoir', in Robert Descimon, Jean-Frédéric Schaub and Bernard Vincent, eds, *Les Figures de l'administrateur. Institutions, réseaux, pouvoirs en Espagne, en France et au Portugal (XVIe–XIXe siècle)* (Paris: Éditions de l'EHESS, 1997), pp. 77–97.

15 Philippe Artières, *La Police de l'écriture. L'invention de la délinquance graphique (1852–1945)* (Paris: La Découverte, 2013).

continuity. Some previous functionaries continued in their work. Others made more proactive efforts to respond to popular expectations. Taxes were collected – or, in other words, some taxpayers paid, whether out of vocation, fear, duty, patriotism or habit. Registers were maintained with more or less meticulousness, inventories of the deceased were drawn up, proofs of identity were issued, and housing was found for those whose homes had been destroyed. Re-establishing routine procedures was a real challenge, at both the local and city-wide levels. The director of Post Office administration, Albert Theisz, provided some evidence of this when he announced on a poster: 'letters can be deposited in full confidence': restoring such faith was also a way of managing uncertainty.[16]

The third element was the Communards' remarkable concern for legal niceties, particularly among the most committed. There was constant reference to the law: on the pre-printed reports from the Empire, some *commissaires de police* crossed out the line 'by virtue of article . . . of the code' and replaced it with a more general one: 'in the name of the law'. The same goes for administrative procedures and deeds. On 28 April 1871, after the tax collector Dupont fled the city, the new inspector, Pistre, had the Clichy revenue office opened up. He drew up an official report, whose tone was itself telling: 'We, the undersigned . . . had the locksmith Lesourd, also undersigned, carry out the procedure'.[17] Seals were also affixed. After 18 March, many neighbourhood policemen's apartments were searched. Such devices were often used when the previous legal and regulatory structures were no longer in place, and everyone knew that the dwellings were going to be visited by the population. Such concern may be surprising. Yet, as Jacques Rougerie reminds us, this was ultimately quite normal for republicans influenced by the memory of the French Revolution – during which 'the rule of law', the product of the nation as against the monarchy, was a fundamental value – and in this sense it did not stand opposed to the idea of a revolutionary transformation of the world. Indeed, the reappropriation of law was an enduring characteristic of the moral economy of the crowd, both in the eighteenth and nineteenth centuries: it was just

16 Poster dated 8 May, in *Les Murailles politiques françaises depuis le 4 septembre 1870, vol. II: La Commune* (Paris: Versailles, la Province), *(18 mars–27 mai 1871)* (Paris: Le Chevalier, 1874).

17 AVP, D2U6-13, Legent file.

that this no longer meant the customary law of the *ancien régime*, but rather the rationalised law and regulations of the nineteenth century.[18]

The use of more technical processes (minute-taking, seals) invites us to ask whether these also served as markers for the inhabitants – that is, as familiar reference points which made it easier to negotiate the legitimate and the illegitimate in the 'plastic' time of insurgent Paris. What was at stake, then, was not statutory law or the legal theories likely to be deployed by seasoned professionals, but rather law and the legal process as they were embodied in everyday routines. These elements thus point to the persistence of what we might call state practices and state thinking, even in this time of crisis.[19] This does not mean, of course, that they had retained the same content.

This observation is linked to the fourth logic – namely, the emergence of other normative registers. In April, the hairdresser Gautret, on the rue Oberkampf, had his neighbour, the wine merchant Lalande, arrested by the National Guard. Lalande was quickly released, and Gautret was himself soon apprehended by other members of this unit. In each case, the intervention was made in the name of the Commune. But the investigation file shows that the two men had long been at loggerheads, partly as a result of the fact that Lalande would no longer go to Gautret for a shave.[20] This is an extreme case, yet it is clear that many personal quarrels were pursued in this manner (for instance by jealous husbands or wives), again on the Commune's authority. With the undermining of codes and regulations, the distinctions between the judicial and extra-judicial, the public and private, no longer held, or were displaced in new ways. Without doubt, vast fields of social activity were now being politicised. The sociopolitical order of each neighbourhood was also becoming more densely structured. We can here define these as spaces of mutual acquaintance, whose boundaries could vary but which were drawn together by a shared sense of place: in some areas, wine merchants or concierges took it upon themselves to keep watch

18 E. P. Thompson 'The Moral Economy of the English Crowd in the Eighteenth Century', *Past and Present* 50: 1 (February 1971), pp. 76–136. For nineteenth-century France, see François Jarrige, *Au temps des 'tueuses de bras'. Les bris de machines à l'aube de l'ère industrielle (1780–1860)* (Rennes: Presses universitaires de Rennes, 2009).

19 Pierre Bourdieu, *Sur l'État. Cours au Collège de France (1989–1992)* (Paris: Seuil, 2012).

20 AVP, D2 U6-18.

over the comings and goings of others in the local area.[21] Other normative references were deployed, as can be seen on the posters and in the minutes: for instance, 'patriotic duty', 'sincerity', 'common sense' and 'sound justice'.[22] These terms are not neutral. For instance, the last of these echoes *bon droit*, a sense of rightful justice and legitimate claim that was very present among skilled workers and working-class circles in the latter half of the nineteenth century. Rooted in the search for negotiation and reconciliation, it was especially used in industrial tribunals, if not only there.[23] 'Morality' was also invoked. This is a polysemic term: historians have shown how important it was to worker solidarity in the late Second Empire, as well as against the competition imposed by the bosses.[24] Other normative models emanating from the world of work or from other social universes also asserted themselves in the space of the Commune, either in favour of or against the holders of public functions.

The individuals who deployed these references may have considered them as sites of transformation. But there were also logics of more properly revolutionary action: arresting priests, house searches, enforcing compliance with rental decrees, and so on. Two examples will help us understand how diverse these logics could be. The first is the activity of Démophile Coussat in the 8th arrondissement. Coussat was a militant shoemaker of long standing – as evidenced by his change of name, from 'Theophile' (friend of God/lover of God) into 'Démophile' (friend of the People). A militant in the IWMA and a member of the vigilance committee of the 18th arrondissement, he was appointed secretary, and then *commissaire*, of the Goutte-d'Or police station.[25] In May, the head of the 'ex-Prefecture of Police', Théophile Ferré, who had succeeded Raoul Rigault, sent him to take

21 For 1848, see Laurent Clavier, '"Quartier" et expériences politiques dans les faubourgs du nord-est parisien en 1848', *Revue d'histoire du xixe siècle* 33 (2006), pp. 121–42.

22 *Les Murailles politiques françaises, vol. II.*

23 Alain Cottereau, 'Droit et bon droit. Un droit des ouvriers instauré puis évincé par le droit du travail (France, XIXe siècle)', *Annales. Histoire, Sciences sociales*, 6: 6 (2002), pp. 1,521–57.

24 Alain Cottereau, 'Vie quotidienne et résistance ouvrière à Paris en 1870', Introduction to Denis Poulot, *Le Sublime, ou le travailleur parisien tel qu'il est en 1870, et ce qu'il peut être* (Paris: Maspero, 1980), pp. 7–104.

25 SHD, 8J, 3e conseil, dos 976, and APP, DB 511.

over the Champs-Élysées police station. His migration across the city shows that there was an administrative circulation of 'trusted' figures even between distant districts. This decision is more properly located in the competition between projects and powers that played out across the space of the Commune: Ferré, following on from Rigault, sought in this way to resolve a local conflict with the mayor, Jules Allix, who was a Fourierist-inspired socialist, radical republican.[26] A strong supporter of self-organisation, he wanted to appoint the agents of his arrondissement himself. As he had explained to Raoul Rigault, they 'will work for you as *commissaires de police*, but they will have the civilian character which I want in the arrondissement'.[27] Upon the death of the incumbent *commissaire de police*, a local resident close to Allix, Coussat, was sent to replace him. Coussat and his men, operating out of the police station, thus found themselves strangers in a 'hostile' arrondissement. But they quickly implemented a more aggressive policy of searching – the Versaillais called it 'looting' – the homes of wealthy dignitaries of the Second Empire. The residence of the duke of Rivoli, chamberlain of the Empire, bore the brunt of this. Coussat had the house's interiors destroyed and its riches seized, handing them over to the Commune. As for the horses, 'I am sending them to you [the ex-Prefecture of Police] so that you can use them for a public service, since they are not doing anything.' Alongside the raising of funds necessary for the Commune's survival, this gesture also amounted to a political act. As a common slogan in the clubs put it, it was about 'pulling down the castle and raising up the thatched cottage': in this way, the democratic and social republic was realised in the concrete, practical and immediate sense in which it was understood by many actors.

This dynamic took on other aspects, for example within the administrations, such as at the Hôpital Sainte-Eugénie (12th arrondissement), renamed the 'Hôpital des Enfants du peuple' ('Hospital of the Sons and

26 Rigault certainly continued to follow this affair. On the situation at the Ex-Prefecture of Police from the end of April, see Alain Dalotel, 'Maintien de l'ordre public à Paris et polices en 1870–1871', in Société d'histoire de la révolution de 1848 et des révolutions du XIXe siècle, *Maintien de l'ordre et polices en France et en Europe au XIXe siècle* (Paris: Créaphis, 1987).

27 APP, DB 511, VIIIe arrdt. Letter from the mayor of the 8th arrondissement to the Ex-Prefecture of Police, 30 March 1871.

Daughters of the People'), where the republican doctor Rieder transformed the chapel into a club and raised the nurses' salaries.[28] But here we shall focus on the case of the Post Office administration under the direction of Albert Theisz. This administration was essential to the economic and social life of Paris at the time, through the circulation of letters and money orders. The former director Rampont, who remained in place after 18 March, had initially tried to evacuate as much material as possible to Versailles. He was replaced on 5 April by Theisz, a thirty-two-year-old bronze chiseller. A member of the International and a participant in the movement to bring together the trade-union chambers at the end of the Empire, he was a perfect example of the 'tradesmen's socialism' of the nineteenth century. As soon as he arrived, he confronted the problem of the unauthorised occupation of post-service jobs, and proposed to 'abolish everything superfluous'.[29] 'Let us not forget that the Commune is poor and that it has other things to do . . . than to pay men who smoke cigars . . . as it was criticised for doing under the Ancien Régime [i.e. the Second Empire].'[30] Theisz sought to get the institution back on track: he carried out a selection from among the new officials, and tried to get the old ones to return. To those who hesitated, he indicated that 'by making the post office for all, we are not playing politics, we are fulfilling a duty of good citizenship'.[31] He also sought to collect money orders, combat counterfeiting, and respond to the spread of private postal networks. He even accepted some of their help, responding positively to an offer from the civil engineer Barbier, made in the name of a meeting of merchants and traders.[32] Finally, the internal service was restructured. As part of this reorganisation, 'considering that the revolution of 18 March was a democratic and social revolution, and that in a good democracy it is right to help the neediest', the former agents received a 100 franc raise.[33] Post Office officials were named on a 'provisional' basis, and their salaries were frozen. Experience and on-the-ground knowledge were particularly valued: new officials were taken on one month's probation, and the more

28 SHD, 8J 4e conseil, doc. 831.

29 Archives de la Poste (Paris), D 7100-7102 – undated letter.

30 Ibid. – undated letter on the reorganisation of the Post Office.

31 Ibid. – letter, 9 April 1871.

32 Ibid. – Postes, letters to Paris, 20 April 1871.

33 Decree, 'après délibération du conseil des Postes', n.d. (archives de la Poste, D 7100–7102).

senior positions were offered to the longer-established. Hierarchies were also changed. Military-sounding names ('brigadier' and suchlike) were abolished and replaced by 'simpler and more logical' titles such as 'agents' and 'delegates'.[34] A 'postal council' with an essentially deliberative role was established. On several occasions, Theisz also sought to justify his own place in the hierarchy. He especially emphasised relations of cordiality and fellow feeling, rather than strictly professional ones, and set a premium on reciprocity: 'Your assistance, by facilitating my work, has created relations of sympathy between us . . . I am thus convinced that you, for your part, will take proper note of the recommendations which I am addressing to you.'[35]

This 'revolutionary' transformation of a public service may be grounds for surprise. We can surely point to the contradictions of an institution being reshaped in the name of the revolution, while at the same time seeking 'not to play politics', upholding relations of cordiality while also maintaining hierarchical ones. In reality, the service itself had to adapt to a delicate situation: the hesitations among the former postal workers, private competition, the lack of funds, the urgent need to get its work back on track, the difficulty of circulating letters . . . But this is not the end of the matter. This work of reorganisation can equally well be read as an attempt to democratise the bureaucratic order: bureaucratisation and democratisation were two of the major trends of nineteenth-century in France. The previous regime, the Second Empire, had linked them in a distinctive way, making, for example, the agents of the administration into representatives of the state who had both to monitor and listen to the population.[36] What emerged in the Commune was, by contrast, something like an inverted articulation of these same tendencies: a trend towards a democratisation of a bureaucracy. The most committed Communards, or those who identified themselves as such, have been criticised for their lack of a specific political project. This is to forget – if one considers for example the debates about credit systems or the organisation of work in the 1860s – that many workers, militants or otherwise, often devoted particular attention to problems of status and

34 Ibid. – Decree, 7 May 1871, for the telegraphs.

35 Ibid. – 'Lettres aux employés' (around April 1871).

36 On this trend under the Second Empire, see Pierre Rosanvallon, *La Démocratie inachevée. Histoire de la souveraineté du peuple en France* (Paris: Gallimard, 2000).

organisation. These questions, while apparently technical, in fact overlapped with real political issues.[37] This way of running public services thus corresponded to what we would today call a 'real utopia': those institutions or experiences that prefigure an alternative mode of social and political relations, while also being anchored in the present and the constraints of reality.[38] The Post Office administration is surely an exceptional case, being one of the few services that managed to reorganise itself. But it does allow us to see many of the shifts that were taking place at the local level, which also need to be properly understood.

Surely, these different dynamics could be combined in various ways. At this stage, it is still difficult to grasp how they intersected, and what their spatial distribution was. A look at police activities in three neighbourhoods will help us to get a clearer picture.

Variations: Policing Insurgent Neighbourhoods

The archival centre of the Service Historique de la Défense holds the activity registers of the Commune's *commissaires de police* – an exceptional source on everyday life in revolution.[39] As these registers form a considerable body of material, we will here focus on three of them, belonging to *commissaires* who supported the Commune (which explains why their records are more fully preserved), each set in a very distinctive context. In this way, we can approach these local configurations more closely.

The situation was quite distinctive in the 16th arrondissement, where Commissaire Delaire had been in office since mid-April.[40] The wealthy population was hostile to the Commune, and made its interests felt through the provisional municipal commission of the arrondissement, which acted as a buffer between the Commune and the neighbourhood.

37 See the remarks in Michel Cordillot, *Eugène Varlin, chronique d'un espoir assassiné* (Paris: L'Atelier, 1991). The Workers' Commission of 1867 offers one proof of this attention.

38 Erik Olin Wright, *Envisioning Real Utopias* (London: Verso, 2010).

39 SHD, Ly 17, 18 and 19. On police–society relations in Paris, see Quentin Deluermoz, *Policiers dans la ville. La construction d'un ordre public à Paris (1854–1914)* (Paris: Publications de la Sorbonne, 2012).

40 SHD, Ly 18, 16th arrondissement.

In the political and administrative context described above, with the practice of universal male suffrage, the arrondissements that were less sympathetic to the Commune could thus secure or create authorities of their own. This also generated tensions. With regard to the decree on rents of 29 March 1871, for instance, citizen Oudet of the Commune invited the 'citizen members of the town hall commission' of the 16th arrondissement 'not to waste [their] time through ignorance of the law'. Delaire, an ardent republican, also tried to intervene against anti-Communard attacks, but his efforts were hindered from various directions. One difficulty came from isolated radical groups arriving from other districts, such as the Communard *turcos*, who occupied the Convent of the Assumption and, for a time, held the *commissaire* himself under detention. Another, larger challenge came from conservative local residents. Nor did some of the National Guards respond to his pleas. 'But it is necessary' – he magnanimously explained to his inspector – 'that everything should be done by the book.' So, although Delaire was a long-time resident of the neighbourhood and was well known there, he found himself being kept at a distance even in his own field of activity. But the situation was transformed in early May, when the bombardment by the Versaillais struck this arrondissement. This changed the whole balance of tensions and urged a greater degree of mutual assistance. The *commissaire de police* issued more requisition orders, supplied certificates of destruction, sought replacement housing, and dealt with many cases of thefts from abandoned or gutted homes. The various actors in the arrondissement now moved towards greater coordination, on different bases: no longer based on political opinions, but on the need to organise the survival of a neighbourhood under a state of siege, faced with a threat that had become critical. Confronted with this danger, the opposition between friend and enemy was therefore reframed.

Further north, in the Épinettes district (in the 17th arrondissement), the activity of Commissaire Lubert took on rather different features. Lubert, a former upholsterer appointed by the communal council of the 17th arrondissement, offers a remarkable example of activity governed by the *bon droit* of the workers.[41] The tone of his reports well reflects this type of language, for instance:

41 Before being submitted to Rigault for approval (letter from the municipal council of the 17th arrondissement, 16 April 1871, APP, DB 511).

> By virtue of a decision taken by me, the *commissaire* of the judicial police, and given that a transaction and intervening immediately [*sic*] in the name of humanity which it is my duty as a magistrate not to disregard, I order that the Mamiers couple will pay their mother's pension until the Commune has fulfilled the fraternal duty that it will have to accomplish, and I say that the decree will be respected towards and against all and that the law will prevail.[42]

Unlike his colleague in Auteuil, he also acted as a justice of the peace.[43] The exercise of policing and delivering justice was here embodied and personalised, as shown by the use of the first-person singular, even in official situations ('the individual freedom for which I bear responsibility', he says in another report). The reasons are always recalled and explained; and the intervention is based on the agreement of the parties, the search for conciliation, and the 'just' decision: 'I have done justice as far as possible and made a proposal to Messrs. Duval and Bastien, who, at my instigation, have agreed to conform to my ideas. Compensate Langlois for the sum of 5 francs which was agreed by all parties.' On the other hand, for those who refused the proposal, punishment followed.[44] Unlike in other arrondissements, this *commissaire de police* carried out little political surveillance. At most, he arrested draft dodgers, generally on moral grounds (being in the company of 'girls of ill repute'). Acting in the name of 'conciliation' and 'at the request of the inhabitants', he thus shows how the workers' *bon droit* could be mobilised on a daily basis in the field of policing and justice.

The 19th arrondissement – one of the hotbeds of the insurrection since September – presented a different profile. In the district of La Villette, Pierre Elloy remained *commissaire de police* throughout the period.[45] He took up his post on 25 March with a mandate from the

42 SHD, Ly18, report, 27 April 1871.

43 APP, DB 511.

44 SHD, Ly18, Note the arrest of a certain Larouze, who refused conciliation. Written report, 8 May.

45 This district is studied in Iain Chadwick, *Revolutionary Neighbourhoods and Networks During the Paris Commune of 1871* (Oxford: Oxford University Press, 2011). The author emphasises the tensions around the town hall, but neglects to look at the wider neighbourhood. On Belleville, another perspective can be found in Alain Dalotel, *Gabriel Ranvier (1828–1879), le Christ de Belleville, blanquiste, communard et franc-maçon, maire du XXe arrondissement* (Paris: Dittmar, 2005).

Central Committee of the National Guard of the 19th arrondissement, information which he himself reported to the 'ex-Prefecture of Police'.[46] Here, the articulation of different authorities seems to have gone further. First of all, he was a 'delegate attached to the communal police station in the district of La Villette', and declared himself 'municipal commissaire of the 19th arrondissement' while remaining very close to the 'administrative commission of the 19th arrondissement'. Although there was still some friction, the commission, the National Guards and the *commissaire de police* seemed to work together more closely, as the minutes show. With the municipal delegates and some of the National Guards, he opposed other groups such as the 'Marseillaise' committee, which had begun to conduct 'illegal searches'.[47] The administrative environment here was more all-encompassing. Thus, although many aspects of its activity do resemble the previous cases (certificates, thefts, application of the decree on rents, and so on), it also took a particular twist. The preparation of defensive measures was more intensive, with both the *commissaire de police* and the National Guards actively searching for weapons caches. Particular attention was paid to foodstuffs, no doubt also because of the proximity of the slaughterhouses at La Rotonde and La Villette. But at a time when wartime rationing was maintained, albeit less severely than in autumn, the particular concern here was to avoid 'wastage' and to 'guarantee fair consumption'.[48] The inhabitants themselves played a more active role in monitoring draft dodgers and attempted escapes, since the arrondissement bordered the north-eastern fortifications surrounded by the German lines.[49] They also intervened to sanction insults against the Commune.[50] The district was thus more politicised, with a strong orientation towards the Commune. In La Villette, the structures of authority seem to have been more integrated into the fabric of local society and the everyday habits of its residents: so, we can say that there were neighbourhoods or parts of them that were more clearly revolutionary and in which, albeit not without friction, the transformation of daily relations ran deeper. In the 11th arrondissement, for example, we again find this articulation between the

46 SHD, Ly 19, 19th arrondissement, Villette, minutes, 25 March 1871.
47 SHD, Ly 19, minutes, 18 April 1871.
48 SHD, Ly 19, minutes, 29 March 1871.
49 SHD, Ly 19, 14 April 1871, 327; 17 April, 336.
50 SHD, Ly 19, log of reports, 11 April 1871.

commissaire de police, the 'municipal citizens of the 11th' and the ex-Prefecture of Police, along with an emphasis on the 'republican' character of the inhabitants. Elsewhere, as in the 6th arrondissement, there were sharper divisions.[51]

Thus, we can see several ways in which orders coalesced – more or less linked to the Hôtel de Ville, sometimes in interaction, sometimes at a distance. Together they nevertheless produced a gradual yet profound shift from previous routines and habits.

In the City and on the Ramparts: The National Guards' Military Activity

The ordinary administration of the extra-ordinary was not the only domain involved in the preservation or modification of sociopolitical space. Doubtless one of the most important institutions in this respect was the National Guard. Active since the siege of 1870, it had an essential role under the Commune, where it was responsible both for maintaining order and the defence of Paris. Initially based on voluntary service, membership of the National Guard became compulsory for all individuals between the ages of nineteen and forty after the Cluseret decrees of 4 and 6 April. Composed of citizens-in-arms and commanded by democratically elected officers, it assembled around 180,000 men (one-tenth of Paris's population).[52] It was organised by arrondissements and districts, although there were also professional battalions, such as the ones on the railways (the 251st battalion of the Orléans railway) – giving some sense of how far it shaped the city, both politically and militarily.

Here, too, the profiles and commitments of these battalions varied according to location and social parameters, though they never straightforwardly reflected them.[53] We can take the examples presented in Part I. In the 8th arrondissement, where support for the Commune was low,

51 SHD, Ly 17, 6th arrondissement, Odéon; and Ly 18, 11th arrondissement, in particular Ambroise and Folie-Méricourt.

52 Around a third of the population, 600,000 people, had fled the capital in May 1871 (a figure that was probably lower in April).

53 Robert Tombs, '"Prudent rebels": The 2nd Arrondissement during the Paris Commune of 1871', *French History* 5: 4 (1991).

the companies of the 3rd battalion were, according to the muster rolls, made up of carpenters, upholsterers, launderers and charcoal burners, but half of them also belonged to more affluent professions such as rentiers, veterinarians, pharmacists and clerks.[54] The legion commander had to cope with the men's refusal to go into battle, and on his 'sheets of situations and reports' the words 'de marche' (combat-ready) in the expression 'marching company' were crossed out, indicating the determination of these guards to remain 'sedentary': to avoid leaving their district.[55] The 184th Battalion of the 13th legion, on the other hand, was led into battle by Commandant Mercier, a mason living in the arrondissement nicknamed 'Cul d'ours' – 'Bear's Arse'.[56] There were tensions also in this case. In a complaint made on 27 April, officers from the sedentary companies accused him of forcing guards over forty, normally assigned to those companies, to march to the Hautes-Bruyères redoubts (he was said to have called them 'cowards and idlers', and to have threatened to disarm them). Here, the fracture line was drawn more by age than by social status.[57] The National Guard companies were indeed a site of constant discussion of the rules of authority and their justifications. While some obeyed simply because of the military-type framework, others left without explanation, or played on the multiple rules of legitimacy (election, combat experience, local or popular origin) to act in certain ways, and even refuse to act. Still others made the conscious choice to obey, in the interest of the common cause: the 137th battalion declared, for example, that 'to strengthen order and discipline *they would submit to passive obedience*, but only on condition that the leaders were elected by a majority of votes'.[58] This remarkable expression is indicative of the strength of the desire for autonomy within many companies. This diversity of ties and attitudes largely explains the difficulties encountered by the staffs of Cluseret and then Rossel in reorganising this army from April onwards: forming war companies,

54 SHD, Ly 46 (3rd battalion, 8th legion), roll-call for the 5th company.

55 SHD, Ly 46, Letter to the citizen-war delegate from Commandant Duclos, 29 April 1871.

56 SHD, Ly 85 (184th battalion, 13th legion), on Mercier, APP, BA1180.

57 The letter came from the 5th, 6th and 7th sedentary companies, and was perhaps addressed to the Central Committee.

58 SHD, Ly 36, Comité central de la garde nationale, March–May 1871. My italics.

introducing compulsory military service, and creating councils of war and courts-martial – whose decisions, significantly, were repeatedly overturned by the Commune council. The Paris National Guard was 'this real citizen army, in which citizens had the obligation to serve, but without the high command ever resorting to forcible means; incapable of serving but having the sense of duty and solidarity'.[59]

These National Guards both kept up neighbourhood-level surveillance and fought the Versaillais forces. The first of these activities followed the same logic we have seen for district policing, in which these forces were also an important actor. Others headed into battle. Some studies have emphasised the tiny proportion of the National Guards who became combatants, properly speaking: as few as 20,000, or around 6.7 per cent of a total of close to 300,000.[60] But we may also consider that, if 20,000 or 25,000 men were fighting on the ramparts at any given moment, these were not always the same individuals. And we tend to forget that these few tens of thousands of men experienced enemy fire – for the first time, for some of them, or once again in the case of veterans. Given the difficulties that the mobilisation faced, the fighting involved the most revolutionary battalions, those from the working-class neighbourhoods close to the front lines, and those deemed 'bourgeois', who were sent into combat as a form of punishment or trial. These National Guards took part in siege warfare, which blended very old forms of combat (such as the emphasis on the warrior ethos) and new ones like the use of trenches and the unprecedented concentration of firepower in the hands of both sides.[61] The 13th legion – consisting of the men from the 'Bear's Arse' battalion – itself attests to these battlefield conditions. At the Hautes-Bruyères redoubt, its correspondence speaks time and again of the 'urgency' of the problems encountered: the lack of food, of clothing, of weapons – and of soldiers to relieve them. The 11 May report states, in exasperation: 'The 133rd battalion has the greatest need to return for rest. It has been at the outposts at Villejuif since *22 April*'.[62] Further

59 Robert Tombs, *La Guerre contre Paris* (Paris: Aubier, 1997), p. 182 (passage added in the French version).

60 William Serman estimates the actual number of combatants at 50,000 in April and 40,000 in May. William Serman, *La Commune de Paris (1871)* (Paris: Fayard, 1986), p. 474.

61 Following the first siege, Paris had a large arsenal.

62 My emphasis.

north-west, on the ramparts of the 17th arrondissement, Dr Rieder's medical reports describe the terrible physical damage inflicted by the fighting: 'Béju, double amputation; Artémar, amputation of the left arm, shrapnel; Lucat, double amputation of both legs.'[63]

Nor was the rest of the city cut off from this experience. Combatants' displays of defeatism or acts of courage received public exposure within the legions as well as in the *Journal officiel*, which presented daily extracts from military reports with an exaggeratedly enthusiastic or euphemistic tone.[64] The National Guards' attitudes, particularly in the local arrondissement, were often a topic of conversation in the clubs, also indicating the almost horizontal link between the battalions and their neighbourhoods.[65] A culture of war permeated insurgent Paris and the – often virile and patriotic – martial language fed into posters, proclamations and discussions in the clubs. This was also a culture of weaponry itself. On sunny days, crowds of people would come with their families to pass their judgement on the cannons in Montmartre or – more often, on the Place de l'Hôtel-deVille.[66] The beleaguered population of Paris placed great hopes in the creation of extraordinary weapons which, spurred on by modern science, were meant to ensure swift and total victory. Louis-François Parisel, director of the Délégation Scientifique, had the task of building them – and indeed, collecting all the projects dreamed up by 'citizens', from 'aerial machine guns' to 'locomobiles' and the incendiary weapons known as 'Greek fires'.[67]

Everyday life in the city was even more affected by the conflict. Ambulance services multiplied, mobilising many people (doctors, nurses, and so on). Some of these were major initiatives, such as that of the Magasins Réunis. Others were more makeshift: a Mrs Nivet, a midwife, set up her own ambulance service in her flat on the Avenue

63 SHD, Ly 94, 17th legion, daily medical report, 20 April 1871.

64 Published military reports had first been used for such propaganda purposes in the bulletins of the Grande Armée. See Jean-Paul Bertaud, 'Napoléon journaliste: les bulletins de la gloire', *Le Temps des medias* 4 (2005), pp. 10–21.

65 SHD, Ly 22, minutes of the Saint-Ambroise club.

66 Malvina Blanchecotte, *Tablettes d'une femme pendant la Commune* (Paris: Didier, 1872). We can speak of a 'culture of arms'. See Hincker, *Citoyens-combattants*.

67 Éric Fournier, 'Louis-François Parisel: un acteur oublié, au centre de la culture de guerre communarde', in Marc César and Laure Godineau, eds, *La Commune de 1871. Une relecture, actes du colloque 'Regards sur la Commune de 1871 en France' (Narbonne, 24–26 mars 2011)* (Paris: Créaphis, 2019).

de Clichy.[68] At the end of April, moreover, a real 'hunt for draft dodgers' was organised at the neighbourhood level to pressure able-bodied men to go into battle. But the presence of the fighting was particularly evident because of the funerals that pockmarked the city's activity. The most famous were those organised after the first deaths on 3 April: led by the Commune's elected representatives, 'three very large hearse carriages, decorated with red flags and green palms' paraded along the Grands Boulevards, surrounded by a large crowd.[69] They then came in ever greater numbers, whether organised by the Hôtel de Ville, the arrondissement town halls, the battalions, or the families of the dead. The practice was generally accompanied by collections, patriotic subscriptions and donations of all kinds. Assistance campaigns were organised by means of posters, in newspapers, or in the arrondissement town halls, whose role had become essential. On 8 April, the town hall of the 18th arrondissement posted an 'appeal to good citizens' which invoked 'Liberty . . . the only heritage that the People intend to leave to their children . . . Office open at the *Maison communale*, for fraternal donations. Long live the Commune! 8 April.' Although the victims were killed on the ramparts or outside Paris, their funerals and the ceremonies that followed thus repatriated the experience of death to the heart of the city, making it palpable. Moreover, these practices both followed on from the first siege and offered a gesture of support for the second – whether the support was directed towards the Commune itself, or more simply to relieving the suffering of the besieged city.

The military conflict thus dominated the capital. For many Parisians, as we can see, the siege and the presence of war undoubtedly constituted an experience in itself, prompting appropriate reactions and gestures. For others, it was inseparable from the defence of the Republic, whatever the meanings attached to this word. Doubtless, this was particularly the case for combatants, who sometimes forged their devotion to the Republic or the Commune in the heat of battle.

In her *Souvenirs d'une morte vivante* ('Memories of a Living Dead Woman'), Victorine Brocher tells of such a bond being established. A canteen worker and ambulance driver in the 'defenders of Paris' corps,

68 SHD, 8J 74 (affaire Bédiet).

69 Blanchecotte, *Tablettes d'une femme pendant la Commune*, p. 44.

she fought in Neuilly and Issy, and at the end of May she was on the barricades. This text – composed of impressions that were perhaps sometimes transcribed on the spot, but mostly rewritten later – has to be treated with a certain caution. But it offers a rare viewpoint which well renders the various stages of the solidarity among combatants: the effect of being in a larger group, the importance of the judgement of one's fellow fighters, the identity of the unit as embodied in its flag and its uniforms, the exchange of gifts, and the bonds of friendship and respect, particularly with regard to the 'most beloved' commander, Martin. The ordeals of combat also included waiting in the trenches, the test of fire, and the shared experience of exhaustion. Then came the cause that gave meaning to the group as well as to the fight itself. 'We were avenging our beloved France, which had been trampled upon and sold out', Brocher explains in her account of 7 April, a moment when she was under a hail of bullets and shells. 'We gave our blood, our lives for freedom, at each bloody stage we shouted "Long live the Republic"'. Ultimately decisive was the encounter with death: on 1 May, seventy-two of her comrades-in-arms were killed. Brocher accompanied them through Paris, with the battalion's flag enveloped in black, urged on by the crowd. These demonstrations of support – whether collective or official (at the Hôtel de Ville) – as well as the expressions of hatred coming from the moderate inhabitants of her corner of the 7th arrondissement, were doubtless not negligible, either. The description of the meagre, exhausted group which sought on 19 and 20 May to reunite its members, while also keeping up the fight from one barricade to the next, illustrates how small collectives could bond around values, acquaintances old or new, and the ordeals in which they had shared.

These emotional, political and military cells were formed in parallel with other situations: on 20 or 21 May, in the Place de l'Hôtel de Ville, a woman in a short skirt with a kepi on her head offered to join her group. 'It was Louise Michel', noted Victorine Brocher. 'I didn't know her, I didn't know the women's movement either, I'd never set foot in a public meeting.'[70] Michel, the republican former teacher from Haute-Marne, who had become a revolutionary in the Paris of the 1860s, was already one of the great female figures of the Paris insurrection. She was a leader

70 Victorine Brocher, *Souvenirs d'une morte vivante* (Paris: Delesalle, 1909), p. 190.

of the Club de la Révolution, an ambulance driver and a fighter, and asserted her right to fight arms-in-hand, subverting gender barriers, in the name of the 'social revolution'.[71] Their meeting was no mere accident. But, as Brocher said several times: 'I had only one idea, to be useful and to save the Republic' – a term she described as a 'magic word'. Of course, these statements have been reworked after the facts, but they also make explicit what we dimly perceive when we read the laconic 'Long live the Republic!' or 'Long live the Commune!' on these registers of battalion correspondence, sometimes after some dramatic situation has been described. This was a different kind of Republic altogether, one forged in flesh and blood and in the real battle as it took shape – and this, too, was a living, active reality of insurgent Paris.

The Shifting Frameworks of Property and Labour

There remains the question of social and economic relations – although, as we have seen, the distinction between different domains of activity tended to blur. We are dealing here less with institutions than with sets of practices. The Commune also claimed to be a social revolution. Its record in this respect has been widely discussed: commentators and historians have remarked the paucity of real achievements, and the many procrastinations of the representatives elected at the Hôtel de Ville. On 2 May, even as the pressure of the military combat was bearing down on them, they discussed the question of credit at some length. This might seem disconnected from the urgency of the moment, yet this debate drew on the thinking of the 1840s–60s on industrial and workers' credit, and expressed the speakers' desire to establish an industrial order built on justice, over a longer period of time.[72] Beyond this example, however, certain shifts were taking place – some more concrete and visible than others. Given that it is impossible to cover everything, I will concentrate here on questions of property and labour, which are more widely present in the archives consulted.

71 Xavière Gauthier, *La Vierge rouge. Biographie de Louise Michel* (Paris: Éditions de Paris-Max Chaleil, 2013).

72 *JOC*, 4 May (2 May session). An overview of these debates can be found in the issue 'L'intelligence de la pauvreté' of the journal *Les Études sociales* 164 (2016).

Contrary to what a strand of twentieth-century historiography long hoped to find, the Communards taken as a whole did not seek to abolish private property. The idea was rather, in the words of the famous poster of 19 April 1871, to 'universalise power and property' – in other words, to ensure that everyone had the means to live in dignity, the basis of independence and equality. Although they differed on the means, this was the position of many nineteenth-century socialisms, except of course for collectivism in the strong sense. One of the main authors of the poster, Pierre Denis, is, for example, known as a Proudhonian.[73] Contrary to what is sometimes thought (articulated in the famous words 'Property is theft'), for Pierre-Joseph Proudhon, property was the basis of freedom (one must have something of one's own in order to be independent), and cannot be dissociated from labour. What he rejected, rather, was the capitalist system, which encourages accumulation and monopolisation, depriving workers of precisely this 'just' property.[74] This was not the only cluster of ideas at work. Jacobins may have had in mind Robespierre's 24 April 1793 speech 'On property', which has been republished ever since; followers of Pierre Leroux may have thought back to his great contrast between 'tyrannical' and 'legitimate' property; and still others, inspired by Louis Blanc's principles from 1848, may have held that individual and associative ownership of the means of production could go hand in hand, as part of a movement for the emancipation of workers – a movement not directed, but rather supported, by the state.[75] These texts and their principles had circulated among militant groups and beyond: their tone was undoubtedly familiar to those who had participated to some degree in the movement of public

73 On the debate over the authors of the poster of 19 April 1871, see Michel Cordillot, 'Le programme de la Commune de Paris, 19 avril 1871', in Michel Cordillot, ed., *La Commune de Paris. 1871* (Paris: Éditions de l'Atelier, 2020), pp. 224–6.

74 Pierre-Joseph Proudhon, *Qu'est-ce que la propriété ? ou Recherches sur le principe du droit et du gouvernement* (Paris: Brocard, 1840), then *Théorie de la propriété* (Paris: A. Lacroix, Verboeckhoven & Cie, 1866), which were reprinted several times in the 1860s.

75 On the 'rereading of Jacobinism', see Jacques Rougerie, *La Commune de 1871* (Paris: PUF, 2009), p. 83. On nineteenth-century socialism, see Thomas Bouchet, Vincent Bourdeau, Edward Castleton, Ludovic Frobert and François Jarrige, eds, *Quand les socialistes inventaient l'avenir. Presse, théories et expériences (1825–1860)* (Paris: La Découverte, 2015).

meetings from 1869 onwards.[76] Finally, for those who remained more distant from these circles, there were many other reasons to be attached to one's assets, economic independence, and sense of social justice upon such an occasion as the Commune.

Two arguments from the Hôtel de Ville, also present in the arrondissements, justify what can be called the bounds of 'legal' attacks on property – that is, legal in the eyes of the Communards, albeit not in those of the Versaillais. The first was the rejection of 'speculators' and 'hoarders'. The Commune presented itself as the defender of the 'people of Paris'– a floating notion, but one that was then embodied in the time of revolution: generally, it included workers, the world of commerce, small administrations and small businesses.[77] And it stood opposed to its 'enemies', who had to be fought: the Versaillais, the Prussians, priests, gendarmes and magistrates, but also industrialists, large landowners and monopolists. The other argument stemmed from the military context: the city had to adapt to the imperatives dictated by the conflict and carry out war requisitions.

The first shift in the definition of legal attacks on property was a result of this latter need. As the Commune's leaders saw things, in cases of requisitioning the goods had to be returned to their owners if they came back. On 25 April, Benoît Malon had a decree passed making vacant hotels and housing available to the victims of the bombardment of Paris. It stipulated: 'The taking of possession must be preceded by an inventory of the premises, a copy of which will be delivered to the representatives of the runaway owners.'[78] Nevertheless, the Commune also 'communalised' – that is, brought under its control – some already state-run establishments, such as the Imprimerie nationale and the tobacco manufactory. Workshops that had been left abandoned were occupied. They were requisitioned by a decree of 16 April, issued in the name of the resumption of work 'essential to communal life' and the bosses'

76 Alain Dalotel, Alain Faure and Jean-Claude Freiermuth, *Aux origines de la Commune. Le mouvement des réunions publiques à Paris* (1868–1870) (Paris: Maspero, 1980).

77 On this construct, see Jacques Rougerie: 'Le peuple de 1870–1871', in Danielle Tartakowsky and Jean-Louis Robert, eds., *Paris le peuple (XVIIIe–XXe siècle)* (Paris: Publications de la Sorbonne, 1999), pp. 147–57.

78 Procès-verbaux de la Commune, 24 April 1871.

refusal to fulfil their 'civic obligations'.[79] In this case, the decree envisaged the transfer of the premises to workers' societies, in exchange for an indemnity which would be paid to the bosses. The practice affected a series of assets: carriages, horses, bedclothes, clothing, and so on.

The second encroachment on property concerned the searching and destruction of certain buildings. An exemplary case was the fate of Adolphe Thiers's house in May 1871: after being emptied of its contents, the building was destroyed stone by stone. After the initial fighting in April, a decree had decided, 'considering that the men of the Versailles government have ordered civil war, [and] killed women and children, the property of Thiers, Favre, Dufaure and Simon will be sequestered'.[80] On 15 April this measure was extended to all Versaillais and to the 'bad citizens' who fled Paris.[81] As we have seen, other dwellings were also affected. The collective destruction of houses responded to multiple interlocking logics. As historians of the war remind us, the home was a tangible enemy presence in the heart of the city, and destroying it was a means of striking at that enemy.[82] At the same time, as the example of the Duke of Rivoli's house showed, the attack was both social and political. Whether they acted on the invitation of the Commune, that of the local town halls, or more spontaneously, the Communards intended to attack the material trace of an injustice. In doing so, they highlighted the reality that property is not only a market value, but also the bearer – through its form or usage – of symbolic force and economic hierarchy. The fate of the objects thus sequestered was telling in this sense: in some cases their function was changed (for example, horse-drawn carriages were turned into taxis); other types of confiscated goods (silverware, decorative items) could be sent to the Finances Commission and then melted down at the Mint. This last transformation – a change in the nature of the object – was surely a means of providing the Commune with money. But it also constituted, even without this being clearly formulated, a symbolic undermining of the previous social and cultural order. The violations of homes – which were often uncoordinated and more spontaneous – followed a similar logic: it was part of the desire to purify the urban space and destroy the

79 Ibid., 16 April 1871.

80 Ibid., 2 April 1871.

81 Ibid., 15 April 1871.

82 John Horne, 'Corps, lieux et nation: la France et l'invasion de 1914', *Annales. Histoire, Sciences sociales* 55: 1 (2000), pp. 73–109.

dross of the old order. In fact, although the principle of private property was not itself called into question, its scope was changed, and its definition repeatedly chipped away at.[83] Particularly revealing of this phenomenon – by putting it in counter-relief – is the bill tabled in the National Assembly on 29 April 1871 declaring 'inalienable the public or private properties which have been seized or removed in Paris since 18 March last'.

The labour question took on a similar dimension. The general balance sheet seems so meagre that even the men elected to the Commune wryly derided its efforts. Such was the case of Léo Frankel, who bitterly observed that the Commune's decree on night work for bakers was basically the only truly socialist measure it had taken. While many abandoned workshops were requisitioned, only one of these – according to historians of the Commune – was really placed under workers' self-management.[84] Here again, we have to grasp the wider situation: with the reigning political instability and the two sieges it had suffered, Paris's economic fabric had been severely damaged. It was no mere post facto justification by those concerned to say that service in the National Guard or some public function had provided a useful means of laying one's hands on some money. Similarly, several businesses and trading houses tried to establish links with the Communard authorities, in order to continue their activity as best they could. The Communard definition of the 'people of Paris' included the world of shops and small businesses; and the boundary drawn against its 'enemies' was always in flux. Madame Lefèvre, a landlady in the rue Dunois, 'in a position close to poverty', thus asked the *commissaire de police* of her district – that of the railway station – to be paid by her tenants, 'at least those who can afford it'. The report was accompanied by a list of names, next to which the *commissaire* noted: 'Answer tomorrow at 8 p.m.'[85] For many, this period meant a halt to their work, and a complex jumble of efforts to keep their family or their economic activity going from one day to the next.

83 On the social variations of these definitions, see Maurice Godelier, *L'Idéel et le Matériel* (Paris: Fayard, 1984), pp. 104–12; and Viviana Zelizer, *La Signification sociale de l'argent* (Paris: Seuil, 2005).

84 Robert Tombs, 'Harbingers or Entrepreneurs? A Workers' Cooperative during the Paris Commune', *Historical Journal* 27: 4 (1984).

85 SHD, Ly19, daily reports from the police captain of the neighbourhood of the train station, no date (May 1871).

Yet, coinciding with these economic doldrums, the rise in the number of workers' union halls, which had already begun towards the end of the Second Empire, continued under the benevolent gaze of the Labour and Trade Commission. This body was mainly composed of IWMA members, and indeed aimed to promote workers' self-organisation by giving an important role to trade unions, cooperatives and associations.[86] It received several interesting proposals that shed light on certain traits of the phenomenon at work.[87] Consider an unsigned proposal on 'women's work'. Gender norms held firm under the Commune: women did not have the right to vote, and were often confined to jobs considered 'feminine' (canteen workers, ambulance women, and so on). However, major cracks in these norms also opened up during the revolutionary period, for example through the bearing of arms and the wearing of uniforms, publicly speaking out in female or mixed clubs, and claiming the status of 'woman citizen'. Historian of feminism Caroline Fayolle calls this process a 'revolution within the revolution'.[88] The same was true in the field of the organisation of work – a key focus of the Commune's attention, at the time considered as relevant to the meaning of 'citizenship' as voting rights themselves. In April the Internationalist in exile Élisabeth Dmitrieff and the bookbinder Nathalie Le Mel created the 'Union of Women for the Defence of Paris and the Care of the Wounded' with this aim in mind – notably, through an initiative, probably already underway, to set up 'productive associations' for women in the Parisian textile trades. Perhaps this project itself fitted into this framework.[89] In any case, it took note of the effects of the war: the government 'of lawyers and capitulationists . . .

86 It was created on 29 March. Rougerie, *Paris libre 1871*.

87 For example, this project by the typographers arrived in April, to create a workers' 'association for production'.

88 Caroline Fayolle, 'Femmes. Féminismes et révolutions, une approche mondiale (XVIIIe–XXIe siècle)', in Ludivine Bantigny, Quentin Deluermoz, Boris Gobille and Laurent Jeanpierre, eds, *Une histoire globale des revolutions* (Paris: la Découverte, 2023).

89 SHD, Ly 22. 'Notes. Travail des femmes'. On the Women's Union, see Gay L. Gullickson, *Unruly Women of Paris: Images of the Commune* (Ithaca, NY: Cornell University Press, 1996); and Carolyn J. Eichner, *Surmounting the Barricades: Women in the Paris Commune* (Bloomington, IN: Indiana University Press, 2004). Women's military activity is discussed in Quentin Deluermoz, 'Des communardes sur les barricades: les femmes-soldats de la Commune de Paris (1871)', in Coline Cordi and Geneviève Pruvost, eds, *Penser la violence des femmes* (Paris: La Découverte, 2012), pp. 106–19.

had understood . . . what danger there would be in giving work exclusively to entrepreneurs who exploited last winter's unprecedented destitution at will'. Of course, it was necessary to go further, towards an organisation of work that would also not be too expensive: 'Does this mean that we should fall back on the system of national workshops [as in 1848]?' No. The project proposed to organise 'categories' or 'guilds' of workers around the municipalities, which would be responsible for putting the various groups of workers in touch with each other. Its aim was to 'produce marketable objects of current value which can be easily sold', following a circuit of production and marketing that would be able to compete with others: fairer in terms of cost and the organisation and price of labour, it was meant to be able to 'do battle with commerce', and ultimately conquer it. Such an approach had already been developed in 1848, and set to work in Paris and Lyon. The initiative was also based on a detailed knowledge of the world of women's work, particularly sewing, since the plans for organisation were wedded to the existing forms of work: one of the guilds included lingerie and children's clothing; another concerned the production of clothing for the National Guard – an activity that had come into being after 4 September 1870; and another concerned 'feathered flower fashions'. The project shows the influence of the reference to the democratic and social Republic inspired by 1848.[90] It also points to the persistence of job organisations during this time of crisis, and the way they continued to structure the social space while also being transformed by it.[91] These examples remind us that, amid the disorganisation and attempts to survive, there were real tendencies towards a socialist or 'associationist' change in labour relations.

Some of these endeavours remained at the planning stage. Others resulted in small but concrete steps, full of meaning for the workers and employees. Sometimes constrained by circumstances, partial in scope, or limited to some specific point, they are nonetheless visible in the archives: the filing of job lists with town halls to combat haggling (which led to competition between crews of workers); the raising of salaries

90 On its relationship with the forms of organisation established in 1848, see Maurizio Gribaudi, *Paris, ville ouvrière. Une histoire occultée (1789–1848)* (Paris: La Découverte, 2014).

91 An entanglement of temporalities (of social space and crisis) highlighted in William H. Sewell Jr, *Structure and Mobility: The Men and Women of Marseille (1820–1870)* (Cambridge: Cambridge University Press, 1985).

except for management positions; changing recruitment standards; price-fixing; election of delegates; establishment of cooperatives, and so on. Taken together, these initiatives constitute a phenomenon of no small importance.

These examples do not run the full gamut of trading relations. In such conditions as these, many exchanges were non-mercantile transactions. We can observe countless gestures of solidarity at the local level: loans, offers of shelter for the night, exchanges of goods, helping hands. When such acts were carried out in the name of the Commune, the people involved generally called upon the intervention of the authorities that had been created. But they could also obey older solidarities among neighbours or family relations, or belonging to the realm of actions to be expected in a city under siege. Upon their return from the front, Brocher and her fellow fighters found succour among the priests of the minor seminary, who offered them a meal and a bed. 'Whatever their opinions', she explains, 'they were kind to us.' There were surely many negative responses and abuses: the existence of 'hoarders' was no mere Communard myth. The same can be said of thefts: the archives are brimming with such cases. In April, the young Alexandre Lepileur, aged seventeen, was arrested by a corporal of the National Guard for stealing copper filter rolls from the premises of a sugar refiner.[92] The young man was surprised because, he said, 'everyone does it'. Theft under the Commune has long been a matter of debate. We cannot subscribe to the Versaillais reading which, based on such examples, presents the Commune as a world open to all kinds of plunder. 'Death to thieves' remained a common revolutionary slogan.[93] Yet nor is the Communard version tenable according to which, thanks to the spontaneous virtue of the citizenry, there was no theft under the Commune. During certain raids, many valuable objects disappeared. But what did change in this period, when legal provisions were no longer in force, was the assessment and treatment of theft. For example, theft by officials could cost them their jobs. If some held out against all odds, and others were no doubt never detected, being caught in the act of theft – however minor it might appear – meant having to resign.

92 SHD, Ly19, rapport du commissaire Piéron, April 1871 (day impossible to read).

93 *JOC*, 23 March 1871, placard posted on the doors of the Hôtel de Ville.

Frédéric Force, secretary-general of the town hall of the 10th arrondissement, learned this the hard way. During a search, two or three woollen ties from this same town hall were found in his home. 'Since my wrongdoing makes it hard for me to discharge my duties', he concluded, he quit the board of delegates.[94] This was an effect of the Commune's practice of binding mandates, in which – as per this empirical definition of democracy – the agents of public authority had to be immediately accountable to 'the people'.

Of course, there was also theft by citizens. Doubtless many such cases are untraceable. But the culprits were sometimes brought before the competent authorities, whether by the injured party, the crowd, or the National Guards. On 14 May, a young woman was arrested for having a meal without paying. 'She told us that she had committed this offence', noted the *commissaire de police*, 'because she was hungry and without lodgings'. She 'asks to live by some work, please provide her with some, as she is without shelter and without bread'. The outcomes depended on the circumstances or the judges' dispositions. Here we can see a trace of the clemency which, as legal history shows, is more easily granted to women in such circumstances. But this mode of resolution was no isolated case. The judgments of the prosecutor Aubry, a former *clerc de notaire*, offer an interesting insight into the possible decisions that could be taken. He received persons who had already been imprisoned and subjected them to an interrogation, which was quickly noted down on deposition sheets.[95] Of the twelve cases found in the archives, half concern theft. The prosecutor also made his choices explicit, and exercised the sense of judgement discussed above. This attitude also proves that recourse to *bon droit* was not confined to the working class, and suggests that such judgments probably also served, in return, as a site for the validation of these popular juridical norms in insurgent Paris.[96] Faced with this, defence strategies adapted to the perception of what was and was not deviant behaviour. The cart driver Charles Sponsan, brought in for having stolen a horse, tried to justify his actions by explaining that he had 'taken it from a gendarme whom he had killed'. If this excuse was

94 AVP, D2U6-13, November 1871, Frédéric Force.

95 SHD, Ly 7. On Aubry, see Jean Maitron, ed., *Dictionnaire biographique du mouvement ouvrier français, vol. II*, at maitron.fr/aubry-charles-auguste/.

96 Cerutti, 'Who Is Below?', p. 951.

a bit far-fetched (responding to the assumption that the gendarme was an 'enemy' of the Commune), it also did not work – though the judge found Sponsan 'honest and sympathetic'. Shortly afterwards, the shop boy Pierre Champenoys confessed to having stolen a pair of sheets from a lodging house in the rue des Amandiers: 'He said that he was driven by poverty and asked to join the National Guard' – which the judge recommended. Again, we get the same decision referred to above, which was not uncommon. Dealing with cases of theft by integrating the culprits into the Commune (as a workshop worker, National Guardsman, and so on) thus seems to have been a fairly common practice. Theft was considered an antisocial act, but when driven by poverty it could be redeemed by joining the National Guard – both as a source of income and an act of commitment to the collective good. Such arrangements made sense in this period, when the fields of social activity were no longer disjointed but instead tended to merge. Above all, they confirm one of the phenomena noted in this chapter: the undermining, under the Commune, of the previous boundaries between social spheres, and the emergence of new, active collective forms.

The Commune was a civil war embedded in a war against another country, as well as a political crisis and a revolution. It was thus made up of cases of conflict, resistance and competition, according to ever-changing configurations, which varied according to time and place. The central authorities also added their own dynamics: the Hôtel de Ville and the ex-prefecture of police tried, as in the 8th arrondissement, to regain control of the local administrations by installing men considered to be safe pairs of hands. Moreover, most of the posts held were described as 'provisional', before other modes of recruitment could be established, while some commissions tried to set up examinations and competitions (for National Guard officers and for *commissaires de police*, for example).[97] These efforts met with no success, for lack of time. But from this point of view, the Hôtel de Ville also gained some degree of consistency and efficiency during the time of crisis, despite its increasingly sharp internal divisions.

Under the influence of these many impulses, there gradually developed a profound change in social relations. In certain places, or on

97 SHD, Ly 36; and APP DB 420.

certain occasions, a social, political and economic reorganisation took shape, which affected even the most embedded features of the everyday order: the division of social activities, the delegation of authority, the definition of property, labour relations, and so on. This was the result of decisions by the Hôtel de Ville, the initiatives and ideas of militants, the practices of the working class, and a desire for justice and a better world – but also of gestures intended to cope with the uncertainty of the situation, attitudes imposed by the war, and reactions to the suspension of economic activities. Irregular, heterogeneous, often contradictory, these movements were nonetheless manifest. And in a context of communal government, the whole picture certainly took on a particular force.

We can now better understand the variety of meanings that different actors gave to the word 'Commune', as can be seen on the posters covering the walls of Paris. The word always refers to the defence of the Republic. For some, it implied a return to the capital's trampled-on municipal franchises. For others, it included the autonomy of the city, the principle of election in the National Guard, the levying of taxes, or the abolition of the police prefecture and the army. Some saw it as a site of freedom, others as an unbearable world of new rules and constraints. For still others, the word Commune referred to a space for transforming the world as it was – a promise yet to be realised. To grasp precisely what this meant, we must now examine the change that was also taking place in the ways people experienced time and space.

7
A Revolution in Time and Space: Emancipation in Action

After several days' absence, Malvina Blanchecotte, a woman of letters, returned to the capital on 21 March. She was struck by the city's strange appearance. National Guards had replaced soldiers, life in the streets seemed to have come to a standstill, and the rumble of cannon fire echoed through the city. 'What a change in eight days! . . . Red flags are flying almost everywhere; Lamartine is no longer there to protect the tricolour flag; the squares are empty, Paris is abandoned'.[1] Like many personal reflections on the Commune, Blanchecotte's diary was rewritten after the fact, based on notes she had taken at the time. But most contemporary observers broadly agree: the city – its landscape as well as its appearance – was transformed after 18 March. The insurrection had altered the perception of lived space itself.

Historical study and the social sciences have, in recent times, re-evaluated the sensory, symbolic and affective aspects of political events – not merely as a cosmetic addition to lived realities, but as a full-fledged component of the revolutionary experience, which requires distinct documentation and a methodology of its own.[2] Indeed, this dimension

1 Malvina Blanchecotte, *Tablettes d'une femme pendant la Commune* (Paris: Didier, 1872), p. 17.

2 Some of the many titles regarding the eighteenth and nineteenth centuries include: Haïm Burstin, *Révolutionnaires. Pour une anthropologie politique de la Révolution française* (Paris: Vendémiaire, 2013); Guillaume Mazeau, 'Émotions politiques: la Révolution française', and Emmanuel Fureix, 'Les émotions protestataires', both in Alain Corbin,

of events is essential for understanding the phenomena of mobilisation and demobilisation and the processes of political subjectivation, as well as for grasping the breach of meaning that characterises such moments.

The most straightforward approach is here to consider directly the parameters of experience, space and time – to which we can add the actors' self-perception – in order to see how they were shaken, then transformed over these three months. Bit by bit, the Commune produced another space-time. It changed Parisians' ways of living or situating themselves in history, and in many cases gave them the impression that possibilities were opening up as never before.

A Commune in the City

The Commune took place in Paris. This would be a mere truism, except that it also reminds us of the importance of the urban setting. The city is understood here in its material, social, political, symbolic and sensory dimensions. In this sense, it was both 'produced' and 'productive', including in the Commune-event, in which it played the roles of both force of inertia and vector of transformation.[3]

Let us start with this first role. First of all, the urban fabric: Haussmann's Paris with its twenty arrondissements, its main arteries, its barracks and its department stores. Reading the minutes of the debates at the Hôtel de Ville shows that the Communards had little interest in urbanism per se. Surely, 18 March was a moment when the city, as the saying goes, 'reconquered itself', as the populations of the periphery, recently displaced by Haussmann's works, reclaimed the central districts of Paris. But as a whole, the Communard mode of occupying the capital fitted into the mould of this existing urban structure, and thus appeared out of step with these new forms of political and social control.

Jean-Jacques Courtine and Georges Vigarello, eds, *Histoire des émotions* (Paris: Seuil, 2016), 2 vols; Micah Alpaugh, *Non-Violence and the French Revolution* (Cambridge: Cambridge University Press, 2015). From the other social sciences, see the considerations Tarragoni reminds us of in *L'Enigme révolutionnaire*. I am here following the path of a history of sensibilities, in the broadest sense, ranging from sensory perception to feelings and emotions. See Quentin Deluermoz and Hervé Mazurel, 'L'histoire des sensibilités: un territoire-limite?', *Critical Hermeneutics* 3: 1 (2019), pp. 125–70.

3 Bernard Lepetit, *Carnets de croquis. Sur la connaissance historique* (Paris: Albin Michel, 1999), pp. 120–46.

Urban rules and customs also endured. Historians have remarked with some amusement on the persistence, even under the Commune, of Paris's Ham Fair.[4] We could similarly cite the regulations on horse-riders, restored on 15 April, or those on the sale and illicit peddling of fuel, on traffic, or, at the beginning of May, on fishing.[5] This regulatory routine, which was preserved even as the legal order itself was swept away, was owed partly to the concern among the men elected to the Hôtel de Ville to maintain some stable parameters for insurgent Paris. This was, moreover, justified by the Commune's primarily municipal character, and indeed a necessity in a demographically and economically unique city that required certain practical rules to function. Also relevant here were the informal rules of the street. In the 6th arrondissement, in the Odéon neighbourhood, Commissaire Lelièvre ran into difficulties. To 'enforce compliance with the Commune', he noted on 20 April, 'we went into the streets around the Saint-Germain market to prevent sales on the public thoroughfare'. In the margin, a note specifies: 'Quite a difficult mission, as most of these street vendors are very rude. We have implored them to comply and have ordered them to do so and are determined to act severely against them if they defy the decree.'[6] Intervention by officers – even Communard ones – faced the same resistance and street customs as neighbourhood policemen had encountered under the previous regime. Informal rules coming from the streets themselves still had a certain force – doubtless even more so in a context where authority had been undermined.[7]

Lastly, the city exuded cultural practices that reflected the spectacularisation of everyday life so typical of the 1860s.[8] Whether elected

4 Decree from Raoul Rigault, 30 March 1871 (published in the *JOC*, 7 April).

5 All in the *JOC*.

6 SHD, Ly17, report from 20 April 1871.

7 On this, see Quentin Deluermoz, *Policiers dans la ville. La construction d'un ordre public à Paris (1854–1914)* (Paris: Publications de la Sorbonne, 2012); and Howard S. Becker, *Outsiders: Studies in the Sociology of Deviance* (New York: Free Press of Glencoe, 1963). The expression 'neighbourhood policemen' refers to the uniformed police force established in Paris in 1854, modelled on the London Metropolitan Police (the 'bobbies'), and known as 'sergents de ville' under the Second Empire and as 'gardiens de la paix' under the Third Republic. They were the police officers most visible and active at the neighbourhood level.

8 Vanessa Schwartz, *Spectacular Realities: Early Mass Culture in Fin-de-Siecle Paris* (Berkeley, CA: University of California Press, 1998).

representatives and officialdom found it charming or bothersome, Parisians still strolled along the boulevards on sunny days or sought out privileged vantage points to watch the spectacle of the fighting. The unprecedented photographic work carried out during this revolution is partly owed to this new logic of the staging of the self and the urban environment.[9] This does not mean that nothing had changed: but these elements also gave the event a distinctly Parisian tone.

For, at the same time, the very face of the city was being transformed. Economic activity was disrupted, as we have seen, and the same was true of material and sensory space. The sonic and visual environment was clearly affected by the fighting: on 3 April, 'It was a great surprise to hear the voice of the cannon' – a sound that had disappeared since February. 'Since 28 March', Victorine Brocher continues, 'we seemed to be living . . . in an atmosphere of confidence and hope.'[10] In the most intense moments, Malvina Blanchecotte tells us, the brightness of the explosions gave such different taints to the Paris skyline that 'it no longer has its natural colour'.[11] The city increasingly bore the scars of the material destruction that came with the second siege, in addition to that already seen in the first.

Above all, however, the capital underwent a symbolic transformation. Right from 4 September 1870, symbols, statues and street names had been destroyed, subverted or changed. In such moments, the historian Emmanuel Fureix has shown, the ordinary and almost invisible markers of power take on new significance, again becoming a site of conflict: their destruction allows for a local-level transformation of political parameters.[12] This phenomenon accelerated after 18 March. Unlike in previous revolutions, Fureix notes, Communard iconoclasm did not respond to any overall plan. It was more a matter of spontaneous individual and collective gestures, according to the rhythms of the

9 Quentin Bajac, ed., *La Commune photographiée* (Paris: Réunion des musées nationaux, 2000).

10 Victorine Brocher, *Souvenirs d'une morte vivante* (Paris: Delesalle, 1909), Chapter 22.

11 Blanchecotte, *Tablettes d'une femme pendant la Commune*, 15 April.

12 Emmanuel Fureix, 'L'iconoclasme: une pratique politique (1814–1848)?', in Laurent Le Gall, Michel Offerlé and François Ploux, eds, *La Politique sans en avoir l'air. Aspects de la politique informelle (XIXe–XXIe siècle)* (Rennes: Presses universitaires de Rennes, 2012), pp. 117–32.

conflict with Versailles.[13] Perhaps suggesting a less properly destructive intent – or indeed the desire to mark a temporary suspension – black veils and drapes were especially widely used to cover up images or statues of religious figures or politicians. Yet the combined alteration of the symbolic context and the sensory space was no less sharp for that. The colour red had imposed itself across the landscape, noted the dismayed 'bourgeois' – as he called himself – Henri Dabot back in Paris after the proclamation of the Commune: 'When I open my window I see the red flag flying at the door of the Sorbonne; I am struck as by a dagger right to the heart' (28 March).'[14] Flags adorned official buildings, town halls, and the masts of boats on the Seine.[15] These transformations of course affected the space of the city to varying degrees – probably more so in the central, north-eastern and south-eastern neighbourhoods, and in certain areas within each arrondissement.

They also took varied forms. For instance, the interiors of official buildings were not spared such changes. At the renamed Hôpital des Enfants du Peuple, the crucifixes were removed and the statues of the saints veiled in black.[16] At the Hôtel de Ville, corridors were renamed after Communard heroes such as Blanqui and Barbès. In some places, the social and regulatory barriers, which took the material form of thresholds and doors, were undermined. One recurrent presence in the archives is the locksmith, indeed a key figure in the Commune: the doors and drawers of ministries, as well as those of certain police stations and tax offices, were opened up. Such transgressions also concerned buildings, or areas inside them, that were generally closed to the 'public' (what sociologists aptly call 'backstage areas').[17] Xavier-Édouard Lejeune, for a time an enthusiastic participant in the Commune, recalls how he was able to enter the town hall of the 1st arrondissement, and, later, to 'use his privilege as a National Guard' to climb up into the towers

13 Emmanuel Fureix, *L'Œil blessé. Politiques de l'iconoclasme après la Révolution française* (Ceyzérieu: Champ Vallon, 2019), pp. 315–40.

14 Henri Dabot, *Griffonnages quotidiens d'un bourgeois du Quartier latin (1869–1871)* (Paris: Mercure de France, 2011), p. 67.

15 Léon Deffoux, *Pipe-en-Bois, témoin de la Commune* (Paris: Éditions de France, 1932), p. 9.

16 SHD, 8J, 4e conseil, dos 381: Joseph Rieder, 'Rapport sur l'affaire', 13 March 1872.

17 TN: In French, the word translated as 'public' also has the sense of 'audience'; Erving Goffman, *The Presentation of Self in Everyday Life* (New York: Anchor, 1959).

of Notre-Dame de Paris. There he gave full vent to his joy.[18] As in 1848, Parisians from the popular classes occupied the sites of power – the Tuileries, the Hôtel de Ville – or at least took the chance to ramble through them. The same was true of cultural spaces, in particular theatres and concert halls, which some Parisians discovered for the first time. In this sense, too, the city was taken back by its 'people'.

The material reality of the city was also reshaped. Surely the most famous example is the felling of the Vendôme Column. This memorial erected by Napoleon I was ceremonially destroyed as 'a monument to barbarism, a symbol of brutal force and false glory'.[19] This tangible trace of the fallen regime and its principles had to be erased. Doubtless, a more striking case was that of the barricades – pieces of the city turned into walls in defence of the revolution. They took on more monumental and symbolic dimensions than they had before and, in 1871, there was even a special commission dedicated to them.[20] They were also performative spaces in the streets. As Lejeune remarked, in front of a barricade on the Butte Montmartre, 'Everyone had to lay a paving stone on this wall made of paving stones and planks, as proof of their civic-mindedness.'[21] Outraged by what he considered excessive demands, Charles Desplats, professor of medicine, stated in a letter that he had 'managed to avoid this'.[22] Often, however, the call to join in building barricades was insistent – not infrequently under pressure from the women of the neighbourhood – and those who refused might risk being enlisted in the National Guard.

Even the words of the everyday environment were affected. Situations of civil war and revolution, Jérémie Foa reminds us, raise doubts over language and its capacity to give things their proper name.[23] This doubt may have been owed to the uncertainty which now plagued the world of before, but it might also have been the product of certain actors'

18 Xavier-Édouard Lejeune, *Calicot. Enquête de Michel et Philippe Lejeune* (Paris: Arthaud-Montalba, 1984), p. 8.

19 Decree, 12 April 1871.

20 Mark Traugott, *The Insurgent Barricade* (Berkeley, CA: University of California Press, 2010).

21 Lejeune, *Calicot*. The existence of such a practice is also confirmed by many witness statements to military tribunals.

22 Victor Desplats, *Lettres d'un homme à la femme qu'il aime pendant le siège de Paris et la Commune* (Paris: Lattès, 1980).

23 Jérémie Foa, *Survivre. Une histoire des guerres de Religion* (Paris: Seuil, 2024).

world-changing ambitions. The many fields affected included the words defining the city. Hence the Parisian police institution on the Île de la Cité was renamed the 'ex-Préfecture de police' – the prefix suggesting that previous conventions had been suspended. Popular witticisms – a weapon able to expose and attack the symbolic dimension of power – played an essential role in this process.[24] They were used even on church doors, some of which were emblazoned with the words *baraque à louer* (a play on two meanings of *louer*: 'to rent' and 'to praise') – a pun also heard in the heated debates in the clubs. This undermining of names for places and titles introduced instability into the political space, and sometimes it even shook the legitimacy of the bodies seeking to establish themselves. Other aspects of urban space were affected, such as communication and its functions. Rumours spread through the neighbourhoods, propagated by newspapers and word of mouth. Based on easily identifiable patterns (plots, attacks on innocent victims, miracles), they altered the perception of the situation, fed Parisians' fears, and contributed to collective reactions. They could also function as a call to order and vigilance: the posters that lined the walls were full of stories of canteen girls who had been raped and of innocent nurses murdered by the troops, who had to be avenged. Citoyenne Querver at the Saint Ambroise club expressed her deeper distress, reminding us of how, in such circumstances, hitherto seemingly anodyne places could become focuses of threat: 'They dig right into the sewers in the main neighbourhoods and even into the Bois de Boulogne to blow us up.'[25]

It is thus possible to identify certain distinctive features of this Parisian Communard space – bearing in mind that their intensity and the conflicts that run through them varied according to the given place and moment. First of all, the frames of reference that ordered the functioning of the city became blurred. Paris became a source of collective emotion, even for the most recalcitrant. The 'Latin Quarter bourgeois' Henri Dabot, mentioned above, wrote in his diary on 6 April: 'The fédérés' National Guard is defeated; but it has great courage.' When these words were published, he added as an aside, 'I am sorry to catch myself in the act of writing a Communard note once again. But is not what anxiety and apprehension have made me write precisely the expression

24 Georges Balandier, *Le Pouvoir sur scenes* (Paris: Balland, 1980).

25 SHD, Ly 22, Proceedings of the Saint-Ambroise patriotic club.

of the truth?'[26] Similarly, this space was often performative, and not only for those standing in front of the barricades. In many neighbourhoods, to be in the streets was already to participate, to be caught up in the Commune, and this became ever the more clearly the case over time. Finally, the space of interactions – in the sense developed by sociologist Erving Goffman – tended to change in accordance with the fragmentary geography noted above. An unknown person's posture or the impression they gave could easily serve to connect them to some assumed political attitude, based on the friend/enemy opposition (man or woman of the people, worker, republican, patriot, socialist, versus Prussian, Versaillais, property owner, neighbourhood policemen). The office boy Alexis Bourguignon was arrested after being taken for a neighbourhood policeman (*sergent de ville*) by the National Guard, evidently on account of his height.[27] As institutional routines weakened, the rules of self-presentation in the streets tended to be reconfigured, with both a certain reduction of roles and identities, and the appearance of new social divisions.[28] Even if we set aside the more extreme cases, such redefined boundaries prompted individuals to make complex adjustments or disclosures on the spur of the moment. While this contraction made the passage from one social role to another more delicate, it also facilitated, on the one hand, processes of denunciation and rejection, and, on the other, gestures of solidarity and collective action in the name of 'the Commune'. Space was thus both politicised and politicising.

Becoming a Communard

This conclusion leads to another problem: apart from the well-known figures, who were the men and women who sided with the Commune, and how did they do it? This is a classic question, and the answer to it is hardly self-evident. There have, indeed, been many analyses of the

26 Dabot, *Griffonnages quotidiens*, p. 180.

27 AVP, D2U6-9, 'Bourguignon Alexis, complicité d'arrestation illégale', 5 September 1871.

28 This phenomenon is analysed in Cyril Lemieux, 'L'hypothèse de la regression vers les habitus et ses implications. Dobry, lecteur de Bourdieu', in Myriam Aït-Aoudia and Antoine Roger, eds, *La Logique du désordre. Relire la sociologie de Michel Dobry* (Paris: Presses de Sciences Po, 2015), pp. 71–92.

relationship between the individual, the event, their commitment and their consciousness of the extra-ordinary. Some of them are especially worth mentioning, here.

For example, sociologist and historian Roger Gould suggested in the 1990s, on the basis of network analyses drawing on civil-register sources, the importance of neighbourhood connections and urban identity in the mobilisation of Paris in 1871. In this account, class identity corresponds more to 1848. In reality, the Commune was both urban and political, but the role of community relations and the association between neighbourly ties and the defence of citizenship was real.[29] Other more recent studies have been less interested in the factors behind the irruption of the revolution than in its effects on individuals. For the sociologist Michel Dobry, in such times of 'fluid' conjunctures, we can observe a 'regression to *habitus*': when there is great uncertainty about the situation and it is no longer possible to rely on institutional routines, he explains, individuals tend to turn to what they know best, their embodied dispositions (their habitus). Or else – and the two phenomena go hand in hand – they are pointed towards such dispositions by their counterparts, who expect them to provide clues as to their position: as an 'aristocrat', 'worker', 'patriot', and so on.[30] Yet other works, often those focusing on the French Revolution, emphasise the dimension of 'becoming a revolutionary'.[31] These studies, which are particularly attentive to the processes of political commitment and radicalisation, address the way in which actors – be they leaders or anonymous figures – move from one identity and consciousness of action to another, revolutionary one, often as a result of open political

29 Roger Gould, *Insurgent Identities: Class, Community and Protest in Paris from 1848 to the Commune* (Chicago: University of Chicago Press, 1995), taken to task in Robert Tombs, 'Les Communeux dans la ville: des analyses récentes à l'étranger', *Le Mouvement social* 179 (1997), and Jacques Rougerie, 'Autour de quelques livres étrangers', in C. Latta, ed., *La Commune de 1871, l'événement, les hommes et la mémoire: actes du colloque organisé à Précieux et à Montbrison, les 15 et 16 mars 2003* (Saint-Étienne: Publications de l'université de Saint-Étienne, 2004).

30 Michel Dobry, *Sociologie des crises politiques. La dynamique des mobilisations multisectorielles* (Paris: Presses de la Fondation nationale des sciences politiques, 2009), pp. 153–4.

31 On the MPs, see Timothy Tackett, *Becoming a Revolutionary: The Deputies of the French National Assembly and the Emergence of a Revolutionary Culture (1789–1790)* (Princeton, NJ: Princeton University Press, 1997).

conflict. Haïm Burstin has coined the notion of 'protagonism' to describe the way in which so-called ordinary individuals, often from humble backgrounds and who have not been especially mobilised, are struck by a revolutionary event, become conscious that they are actors in history, contribute to the revolutionary movement, and then associate themselves with it in their deeds, attitudes and writings – a process that can then be documented and studied.[32] The historian and sociologist Mark Traugott has alternatively suggested an 'organisational hypothesis' to explain this self-transformation. It refers to the effectiveness of certain military organisations – in his study, the Mobile Guard of 1848 – which, through the interplay of solidarity and values within the group, motivate initially indifferent individuals to join the cause and participate in the fight. Traugott also reminds us that in the nineteenth century, more than in the eighteenth, it would have been a difficult time to be a true political novice, and to set aside the influence of past socialisation.[33] These different approaches do not necessarily stand opposed: rather, they offer many ways of apprehending the individual complexity of the irruption of the event, and of examining the revolutionary dynamics of 1871. With their help, five journeys through the Commune – each corresponding to a type of displacement – will allow us to get a better grasp of what the crisis and the revolution did to the actors involved, but also what these actors did to the crisis and the ongoing revolution.[34]

First, I must first say a word about the indifferent: those who, stuck in the capital, tried to procrastinate, to stay out of things, or to maintain an awkward neutrality, sometimes amid others who were rather like them. By chance, on a police register we meet the *citoyenne* Briardel, coming from Clichy-la-Garenne to her sister-in-law's house to escape ill-treatment by her husband.[35] Political issues seem

---

32 Burstin, *Révolutionnaires*. For its use in other fields, see Quentin Deluermoz and Boris Gobille, 'Protagonisme et crises politiques. Individus "ordinaires" et politisations "extraordinaires"', *Politix* 112: 4 (2015).

33 Mark Traugott, *Armies of the Poor: Determinants of Working- Class Participation in the Parisian Insurrection of June 1848* (Princeton, NJ: Princeton University Press, 1985), and 'Les limites du protagonisme: une anthropologie politique de 1848', *Politix* 112: 4 (2015), pp. 83–110.

34 A good example of such personal paths through the event appears in John Merriman, *Massacre: The Life and Death of the Paris Commune* (New York: Basic Books, 2014).

35 SHD, Ly17, Odéon *commissariat*.

distant from her case. Barely visible because of the weaker traces they have left behind, many such individuals populate the blind spots of the archives: parents concerned about the fate of their children, philosophical vagabonds, prostitutes distrustful of politics, more cautious-minded workers, and so on. These cases suggest the limits of the previous approaches. One lies in the difficulty of correlating the infinite gradation of individual attitudes with a sociology of the population, itself in need of greater refinement (since it would be necessary to consider in each case their social position, whether they had experienced 1848, whether they considered themselves Parisians or were just passing through the city, and so on). Another is the risk of relying on overly rigid sociopolitical identities or forms of habitus, given that these individuals' trajectories were also influenced by chance, family history, or personal dispositions that remain beyond view. Surely, such paths are not without interest for us: they are part of the retraction and expansion of the revolutionary process. These men, women and children of varied profiles, who could swing to one side or the other, were not necessarily opposed to the Commune. They might participate for a moment, out of inertia, to avoid problems for themselves or to take advantage of the situation to their own benefit, before then changing tack. In this way, they contributed to the unexpected, and to what we might call the restrained form that the plasticity of a time of crisis could take. This dynamic was indeed present. Let us now turn to our five journeys through the Commune.

First of all, not everyone's bearings were shaken by this event, and this was especially true when it came to those who wanted to push the Commune further. The Blanquist Raoul Rigault was one of them. Born in Paris in 1846, this son of a councillor at the Seine prefecture was in the 1860s one of the young men studying in the Latin Quarter.[36] A bachelor of arts and sciences and a student of mathematics, this young man of lofty intonations turned to political and revolutionary activity. He organised rallies and took part in civil burials, which were also political actions, earning him a dozen arrests. He contributed to several newspapers, including the famous *La Marseillaise* (for which Paschal Grousset

36 Here I draw on the entry in the *Maitron* biographical dictionary. See Luc Willette, *Raoul Rigault, 25 ans, communard, chef de la police* (Paris: Syros, 1984).

and Arthur Arnould also wrote), in which he penned a number of articles on the administration and functioning of the imperial police.[37] With his Hebertian tendencies, he was close to Blanqui: for the latter, dubbed 'l'Enfermé', the revolution would have to come from a *coup de force* prompted by organised and trained militants, and then energetically carried through to its conclusion.[38] As an actor in the revolutionary days of the first siege of Paris, at age twenty-six, he became an elected member of the Commune (in the 8th arrondissement), a member of the Commission de Sûreté Générale and a civil delegate to the ex-prefecture of police. He found himself at ease there, through his knowledge of this institution as well as out of political conviction. From there, Rigault organised the hunt for Versailles's agents and carried out several arrests: those of Archbishop Darboy, Councillor Chaudey and the Commune members Cluseret, Assi, Allix, and so on. After resigning from his post, he became prosecutor of the Commune on 26 April. Inspired by the French Revolution, and especially by 1793, on 1 May 1871 he declared himself for the Committee of Public Safety. 'Hoping that the Committee of Public Safety in 1871 will be what it is generally – but mistakenly – believed to have been in 1793', he said in a famous remark , 'I vote in favour.'[39] He was also the one who signed the decrees for the killing of the hostages. Arrested on 24 May in the rue Gay-Lussac, he was shot by a sergeant of the Versailles Army, though not before he had shouted 'Long live the Commune, down with the murderers!' So, in Rigault's case, far from his previous dispositions being undermined by the revolution, they were strengthened and actualised by it. While there was nothing automatic about this process, it explains why he was able to find an important place in the Commune's institutions so quickly, and why he became both a key player in and an accelerator of the Communard revolutionary dynamic.

The journey of Eugène Varlin, sometimes considered a true 'secular saint', was rather different. He, too, had long been a political militant.

37 Antoine Schwartz, 'La Marseillaise, ou la formation d'une critique révolutionnaire et socialiste à la fin du Second Empire', in Marc César and Laure Godineau, eds, *La Commune de 1871. Une relecture, actes du colloque 'Regards sur la Commune de 1871 en France' (Narbonne, 24–26 mars 2011)* (Paris: Créaphis, 2019).

38 On Auguste Blanqui, see Maurice Paz, *Un révolutionnaire professionnel, Auguste Blanqui* (Paris: Fayard, 1984).

39 Procès-verbaux de la Commune de Paris, 1st May 1871.

Like Theisz, he is a typical representative of the influential Parisian workers' movement of the 1850s–70s.[40] He was born in 1839 in Claye (Seine-et-Marne), into a family of republican workers and day labourers, and – unusually for the time – attended school up to age thirteen. Like many autodidact workers, he kept up his ongoing education throughout his life, in fields as varied as accounting, geometry and singing. He quickly became one of Paris's most renowned bookbinders. Early in his working career, he became involved in the mutual-aid society movement, and took part in the committees heading the strikes in the capital from 1864, as well as in the cooperative movement (in 1868 he founded the cooperative restaurant 'La Marmite'). He distinguished himself in each case, whether through his organisational skills or the diligence of his account-keeping, and gradually established himself as a recognised figure. Attracted by the international dimension of the 'workers' question', he joined the IWMA. Varlin was also concerned to promote unity between the trades' organisations, and took part in the Workers' Commission of 1867. As he explained in a letter of January 1870 to the Belgian socialist Eugène Hins, 'what we want to organise is the representation of the trade organisations [*corporations*] – in other words, of the various specialisations of the workers – with the aim of regulating social relations, that is, of organising production and exchange'.[41] Like other worker-activists, he had multiple political influences: Michel Cordillot notes that in Varlin we find Proudhonism, mutualism, Fourierism (regarding women's place in society), collectivism, and a healthy dose of pragmatism. A prison spell in 1868 convinced him of the need to overthrow the existing society, but his primary objective remained the emancipation of labour and working-class federation, with a stronger focus on social issues than Rigault's.

During the siege, Varlin worked in the arrondissement-level committees, the National Guard and the vigilance commissions. He was even one of the few members of the IWMA to be part of the Central Committee of the National Guard, and played a significant role during the 'week of uncertainty' explored above. His negotiating skills opened up a variety of different

40 On what follows, see Michel Cordillot, *Eugène Varlin, chronique d'un espoir assassiné* (Paris: L'Atelier, 1991).

41 Letter, 28 January 1870. Quoted in Jacques Rougerie, *Eugène Varlin. Aux origines du mouvement ouvrier* (Paris: Éditions du Détour, 2019), p. 136.

options, including the possibility of reconciliation with the mayors: clearly, his aim was to do everything to favour the emergence of a collective dynamic. Under the Commune, he was elected for the 6th arrondissement, and took part in the meetings at the Hôtel de Ville. But he was more discreet than others, concentrating on more administrative or accounting-related tasks, within the Finance, Subsistence and War committees, which he exercised diligently. Opposed to all authoritarianism, on 1 May he declared himself on the side of the 'minority', and rejected the Committee of Public Safety. He then focused on the administration of his arrondissement, which he had never completely abandoned. Could this be seen as a kind of 'regression towards habitus'? Irritated by infighting in the Hôtel de Ville, worried about growing disaffection, and indifferent to the communal festivities, perhaps Varlin simply relied on what he knew best: the tasks of the administrative organisation of the social movement. That is – and these options are clearly not mutually exclusive – unless he considered that it was precisely in this way, from the bottom up, and by focusing on concrete questions, that this communal revolution could truly be realised. When the Bloody Week came, he, too, showed no hesitation in taking up arms and defending his arrondissement on the barricades, then at the Panthéon. He ended up in Belleville, exhausted, still calling on his comrades to keep up the fight. When he was recognised, the thirty-two-year-old was brought before General Laveaucoupet, and then shot in front of a crowd baying for his blood. Varlin, too, may have shouted: 'Long live the Republic! Long live the Commune!'

Hence, there was more than one way of being a Communard. But each of these two men, from different social backgrounds, had become revolutionaries before March 1871. What about those who became so during the event itself? This is an essential question since, even if these socialist and republican revolutionary militants – from the most long-standing to those converted after 4 September 1870 – played a decisive role, they are simply not enough to explain the entire movement. So it is necessary to see how so-called ordinary individuals, those who were at first barely mobilised, and who may or may not have had previous experience, became 'protagonists' in the course of the event – that is, conscious actors in history making deliberate choices. Useful for this purpose – indeed, a seemingly exceptional document – is the private diary that Martial Senisse supposedly wrote during these events.[42] It

42 Martial Senisse, *Carnets d'un fédéré de la Commune (1871)* (Paris: Saint-Just, 1965).

tells the story of a journeyman mason from the Creuse *département*. He came to Paris at the start of January 1871 to declare his love for his cousin Élise, who worked for a property owner on the rue Monge. Senisse at first took a cautious stance towards the political events of winter and spring. His entry into the Communard movement had more of a social character, as an act of solidarity with his fellow masons who had taken him in. But then, his diary tells of his political apprenticeship, through meetings and reading newspapers, and his arrival at conscious political commitment. On 11 April, he wrote in a letter to his uncle who had remained in Limousin: 'I don't know how the adventure will end for me, but at least I would like the republicans back home to know that if I do lose my life, it was for the Republic that I took the side of the Commune and the people when I arrived in Paris.' He then joined several official bodies of the Commune, and his diary reveals a real process of revolutionary subjectivation. Through its pages, Senisse becomes aware of his status as a political subject and of the motives for his struggle – which were, more generally, to fight against the injustice of the ruling order and for an ideal of emancipation. The problem is that this text, though possibly based on real facts or testimonies, is a forgery. We have not found any such private diaries, nor have we found any sources such as those studied by Haïm Burstin for the French Revolution. The men and women transformed by this event were surely too caught up in the action, not to mention the fact that many of them died during the Bloody Week. However, some suggestive shadows do appear in the judicial and military archives.

Jeanne Bigeau, a fifty-six-year-old seamstress, lived at 102 rue de Sèvres in the 15th arrondissement. Since 1866 she had worked stably for the same upholsterer, but had never attracted notoriety before September 1870. 'She had no political opinion as such', stated a report by the police *commissaire* after the events. This observation is a little hasty: she had in 1845 been convicted of interrupting a religious service in the village of her birth, Saint-Servin – an anticlerical act that may have been republican in inspiration; as for Victorine Brocher, the courses of action taken in 1871 often did not come from nowhere. Still, in her time living in Paris there had been nothing to distinguish her. But everything changed, as the witnesses in court confirmed, with the war and the Commune. After 18 March, she became 'exalted', as they put it, frequenting clubs and joining in the production of cartridges for guns. We shall see later why the judge did not convict her. In any case, here we find in faint outline one of those processes of 'becoming a revolutionary' to which a reading of Senisse's diary can help to give greater human depth.[43]

François Michot, a clerk, provides an illustration of the organisational hypothesis: this thirty-year-old former soldier, who became an employee of the Belle Jardinière clothing emporium in 1867, was described by his entourage and his neighbours as a 'good comrade' without any 'exalted opinions'. In September, along with other employees of the store, he enlisted in the battalion of *francs-tireurs* for the city of Paris, before taking up his old position once the peace had been signed. At the end of March, the commander of his former battalion, with whom he had become close, came looking for him. By this point, this other man had become a lieutenant-colonel for the Commune: attracted by camaraderie and military recognition, Michot followed him, and fully took part in his battalion's activity.[44]

These cases are surely illustrative of the insurgent trajectories that existed among the great masses who took part in the Commune. This commitment could be more or less radical or measured, definitive or temporary. But it was essential: much of the Communard adventure played out here, among the workers, the small employees, the intellectuals, the journalists, the artists, the republicans by family tradition, the local figures, acquaintances from one's patch, neighbours, and others. The creative and existential dimension of the event here explodes like a shower of sparks. For many of these men and women, this choice left an indelible mark.

It is also necessary to consider those who, while sometimes enthusiastic at the outset, withdrew at some point during the event. One such case was Xavier-Édouard Lejeune.[45] Born in Laon in 1845, and raised by a republican grandfather, at age thirteen this seamstress's son began his working life in a store selling the latest fashions – hence his nickname 'Calicot', a rather pejorative term for 'shop boy'. An autodidact, passionate about learning, he began writing in his personal notebooks at the age of fifteen. He stopped writing in 1868, and resumed in 1870–71 (and again in 1891). He described himself as a republican, anticlerical and patriot. He joined the National Guard in 1870, and greeted the

43 AVP, D3U6-2.

44 SHD, 9J, 3e conseil, dossier 30.

45 Lejeune, *Calicot*.

'memorable day' of 18 March with some enthusiasm. As soon as the first battles and the first deaths occurred, doubts began to set in. However, his retreat from the fight was owed to a quite different factor: at the beginning of April, when Gustave Flourens died, a delegation from the Place Vendôme headquarters came to the shop where he worked to buy black crepe fabrics for the mourners. The officer handed the owner a money order for 900 francs, which the latter was unable to obtain payment for at the Hôtel de Ville. The next day, this same captain was present for the funerals of Duval and Henri. The shop-owner demanded his due, and the officer retorted: 'You refuse to hand over what I ask you for in the name of the Republic? Very well, tomorrow you'll give it by force.' Immediately the owner, the shop girls and the young *calicot* put the goods in safe storage. Then they left Paris, and Lejeune fled with a Dutch passport. Once safe, the shop boy concluded: 'I send the Commune, Versailles, and all political combinations to hell. The main thing is to save one's skin and have a little peace of mind.'[46] The connection that had initially been made was here broken by the contradiction between the hope of a just existence, respectful of the rules of trade, and an exclusivist republicanism upheld in the name of pressing higher interests – two of the possibilities under the Commune. Indeed, as this episode progressed, many took a turn which cut across their previous one: no longer wanting to be part of the adventure, they returned home, left the city, or even shifted from one stance to another.[47]

There were also all those labelled as enemies, and denounced or pursued as such: priests, neighbourhood policemen, aristocrats, bankers, the rich and propertied. Many of them fled or managed to escape, either by drawing on pre-existing networks (parishioners, servants, those in their debt, and so on) or by disguising themselves and mimicking what they imagined to be typical Communard behaviour. Clearly, these different reactions and self-definitions (commitment, radicalisation, withdrawal, opposition) fed into each other: they contributed to the fluidity of the situation, and account for the ebb and flow of the revolutionary dynamic. Some of these 'enemies' were arrested, and

46 Ibid., p. 301.

47 See, for example, the paths which Émile Maury took after early May, as unearthed by Alain Dalotel, in Émile Maury, *Mes souvenirs sur les* événements *des années 1870–1871*, ed. Alain Dalotel (Paris: La Boutique de l'histoire, 1999).

their reactions are no less interesting. On 17 May, at 5.30 a.m., the Notre-Dame-des-Victoires church, in the 2nd arrondissement, was invaded by National Guards. Abbé Amodru and three other vicars were arrested. In a letter published just after his release, the abbot recounts that, before being taken to the Roquette prison, he had seen no more than an indistinct crowd of people.[48] While he only knows what happened next from the rumours that reached him, or from what he was told when he was released, he does give some useful information about the hostages' own reactions. Amodru reports the words of an abbot who was preparing to die, written on 19 May on a breviary, in Latin, to escape his jailers' attention and surveillance: 'I die with joy, because I die for having remained, to the last, a servant of God and the Virgin Mary.' This is a fine example of self-assertion in a situation of constraint. This observation is only strengthened by the priests' main activity during their stay – namely, prayer. In the face of adversity, these men of God collectively affirmed the identity for which they had been arrested. The somewhat affected expression of Christian compassion was thus itself a focus of struggle. It is therefore possible that, in these dramatic circumstances, some of these men of the Church also felt themselves to be actors or heroes of history – at least their side of it. Their defensive gesture is perhaps more significant than we might realise: faced with the sense that a revolutionary transcendence was inevitably on the march, did their prayer not aim to oppose this precisely with another, religious one?

Bringing Forth 'the Dawn of a New Future'

Indeed, even more decisive than the transformation of space was the revolutionary transformation of time. To grasp this dimension, we must look more closely from the perspective of the most politically committed, within the phases of ebb and flow revealed by the revolutionary dynamic.

The transformation began with 4 September 1870, before taking a radical turn after 18 March 1871. At first, this time was designated as a revolution. The official proclamations, speeches and posters put up in the streets spoke of the 'Revolution of 18 March', the 'Communal

48 Laurent Amodru, *La Roquette, journées des 24–28 mai 1871 par M. l'abbé Laurent Amodru, vicaire à Notre-Dame-des-Victoires* (Paris: Laroche, 1871), p. 17.

Revolution', the 'Social Revolution' and even the 'Administrative Revolution'. They were accompanied by a series of dates – '4 September', '31 October' – which indicated an immediate historicisation of the event, and the feeling of living in a time strongly charged with history.

'Citizens!' proclaims a poster issued by the Federation of the National Guard shortly after March 26:

> Today, we were given the opportunity to witness the most grandiose popular spectacle that has ever struck our eyes . . . Paris greeted and acclaimed its Revolution; Paris opened the book of history to a blank page and wrote its powerful name upon it. . . . Hindered in our march by the loyalty which forbade us to act as a government, we were nevertheless able, by relying on you, to prepare a radical revolution in eight days.[49]

Added to the acceleration of history was the resumption of the chain of revolutions. The Commune was deeply influenced by 1789, 1792, 1793, 1830 and 1848. This presence was reflected in the ceremonial policy at the Hôtel de Ville. On 5 April 1871, for example, there was a 'democratic ceremony' reappropriating the church of Sainte-Geneviève (the Panthéon): in front of an imposing crowd, two workers sawed off the branches of the cross perched at the top of the building, replacing it with a red flag. The transfer of sovereignty is obvious here, as is the revival of the revolutionary memory: eighty years earlier, on 4 April 1791 to be precise, the building had been titled the 'French Panthéon' by the National Assembly. The plan to demolish the chapel of expiation for Louis XVI – a symbol of Restoration-era France's repentance for the 'crimes' of the Revolution – obeyed the same logic. According to the decree of 5 May, 'the building known as the *Chapelle expiatoire de Louis XVI*' was an 'enduring insult to the first Revolution and a perpetual protest by Reaction against the justice of the People'. Destroying it was an act of reparation towards the revolutions of the past, and, again, a way of reactivating its memory in insurgent Paris.

49 *Les Murailles politiques françaises depuis le 4 septembre 1870, vol. II: La Commune* (Paris: Versailles, la Province), *(18 mars–27 mai 1871)* (Paris: Le Chevalier, 1874), no 37. All posters cited here are drawn from this collection.

The living past of revolutions

Since the work of the German historian Reinhart Koselleck, researchers have become increasingly interested in modes of being in time – or, to put it another way, in the relationship between past, present and future, and the way in which they are articulated according to different societies or periods.[50] Indeed, the revolutionary moment induces a rupture in the order of time itself. Inspired by other works, such as those of Walter Benjamin, historians are now better able to reconstruct this breakthrough moment where a qualitative time, a time of possibilities, replaces the quantified and measured time of the ordinary world: the experiences of past struggles, with their unrealised promises, become current again. They break with the previous situation, serve as a call to action, and make it possible to conceive the advent of a new world to come.[51]

In this discontinuous time in which the new is arriving, certain pasts are merged and presented as belonging to one same world of before: the 'old world', the 'former world', or the *ancien régime*, as the language of the moment had it. The description of the Commune's enemies testifies to this, when it combines 'the *Chouans*, the paunchy Orleanists and the men of December'– that is, 1790s counterrevolutionaries, the July Monarchy, the Second Empire and Versailles.[52] We also find this collusion when the industrial development of the Second Empire is equated with 'industrial feudalism', a term that arose in the labour struggles of the 1840s. This old world is contrasted with the time of revolutions and

50 Reinhart Koselleck, *Futures Past: On the Semantics of Historical Time* (New York: Columbia University Press, 2004); François Hartog, *Régimes d'historicité. Présentisme et expériences du temps* (Paris: Seuil, 2003). See, more recently, Christophe Charle, *La Discordance des temps. Une brève histoire de la modernité* (Paris: Armand Colin, 2011); Dan Edelstein, Stefanos Geroulanos and Natasha Wheatley, eds, *Power and Time: Temporalities in Conflict and the Making of History* (Chicago: University of Chicago Press, 2020).

51 Walter Benjamin, 'On the Concept of History', in *Selected Writings 1938–40* (Cambridge, MA: Belknap, 2003). On Benjamin, see Stéphane Mosès, *L'Ange de l'histoire. Rosenzweig, Benjamin, Scholem* (Paris: Gallimard, 2006). On his use by historians, see Michèle Riot-Sarcey, 'Temps et histoire en débat', *Revue d'histoire du XIXe siècle* 25 (2002), pp. 7–13; Ludivine Bantigny, 'Le temps politisé. Quelques enjeux politiques de la conscience historique en Mai–Juin 68', *Vingtième siècle. Revue d'histoire* 117 (2013), pp. 215–29. For work by sociologists, see Federico Tarragoni, *L'énigme révolutionnaire* (Paris: Les Prairies ordinaires, 2015).

52 Poster, 16 April.

hoped-for futures. Here, it is not a matter of memories or recollections, but rather of living references to the past – particularly that of previous revolutions.[53]

The commander of the National Guard of the 18th arrondissement expressed this spirit when he proclaimed, shortly after 18 March: 'May we prove that we are the worthy sons of 1789.'[54] Elements of the more distant past could also be associated with this – for instance, the medieval Communes, described as a 'truly popular tradition' of the city's struggle against the powerful, which was simultaneously mobilised in support of Paris's self-government in the present.[55] Others referred to the timeless struggle of all oppressed people across all eras. 'Close ranks around the *Patrie*,' read an (undated) poster issued by the 6th legion, 'around this red banner, red with all the blood that the people have shed over countless centuries.' These actualised pasts were thus articulated as blocks of raw meaning that burst into the present of 1871. Revolutionary time is a time of upsurge, of becoming.

Inevitably, this development extended beyond the discursive fabric of decrees, newspapers and posters, permeating daily life in the city.[56] It expressed itself in institutions such as the National Guard, in everyday forms of address such as *citoyens* and *citoyennes*, and in references to the 'Universal Republic', echoing 1848. It affected what might be imagined to be mere details, including the forms of address in letters of candidacy: 'Recommend that these servile formulas, of monarchical mores, are no longer used', noted the official in charge of selecting future schoolteachers for the 12th arrondissement, under the phrase 'I beg you to accept, sir'.[57] Of course, this development was strikingly apparent in the revolutionary calendar, which the Committee of Public Safety re-adopted the day after 1 May – that is to say, in Floréal, year 79. But some newspapers, such as *Le Cri du peuple*, and some of the protagonists themselves, had already used it before, in fits and starts. Although its use was rather

53 On this idea, see Michèle Riot-Sarcey and Claudia Moatti, eds, *Pourquoi se référer au passé?* (Paris: L'Atelier, 2017).

54 Poster, 20 March.

55 For instance, *JOC*, 6 April and 18 April 1871 ('Une Commune au Moyen Âge').

56 On this discursive fabric, see Simon Guérot, 'Les Références à la Révolution française chez les élus de la Commune de Paris (1871)', master 2 dissertation, Université Paris-4 (2013).

57 AVP, VD 3/15.

limited, it did have real importance: the organisation of the calendar is also bound up with power, and the counting of months and years was one of the clearest manifestations of this revolutionary resurgence. It also recalls – together with the Chinese and Muslim calendars discussed in Part I – the plurality of counting systems and experiences of time that can coexist in one single moment, both within and outside Europe.

Churches: spectres of the spectres of the past

This irruption of political time was also expressed in certain individual and collective practices. The slotting-together of different pasts is sometimes dizzying, as shown by the example of the destruction of churches. Religious buildings suffered two waves of attacks during the Commune: the first at the beginning of April, when priests were arrested and the separation of Church and State was decreed (2 April); the second in mid-May, as the Communards' defeats of the Versailles forces mounted. In total, across the sixty-six parishes of Paris, some fifty-two churches were affected, whether they were raided, used as storage space, or transformed into clubs.[58] Twenty-two buildings were especially disturbed. These raids could be organised by the National Guards, or by police *commissaires* (Benjamin Le Moussu, from the 18th arrondissement, made a speciality of it), or else were more spontaneous affairs. At Notre-Dame-des-Victoires, in the 2nd arrondissement, the tabernacle and altars were stripped out. The confessionals and flagstones were broken, and the furnishings removed. The coffin of the founder of the archconfraternity, Desgenettes, was opened up. His body was exhumed, while the wax-covered body of the young saint Aurélie, brought back from the catacombs of Rome after 1843, was said to have had its head cut off and put on display at the back of the church – though this last piece of information is rather less reliable.[59] At Notre-Dame-de-Bonne-Nouvelle (in the 2nd arrondissement), the altar was ripped open, the statues broken, and the

58 Numbers suggested by Stéphane Rials, *De Trochu à Thiers (1870–1873)*, vol. XIV of *Nouvelle Histoire de Paris* (Paris: Hachette, 1985), p. 457. See also Olivier Marion and Luc Perrin, *La Commune et l'Église*, master's dissertation, Universités Paris-10 and Paris-12 (1981).

59 Alfred Rastoul, *L'Église de Paris sous la Commune* (Paris: Dillet, 1871), p. 325. See also l'abbé Giraudet, '12 heures de captivité sous la Commune, lettre au juge d'instruction du 20 juin 1871', reproduced in *La Semaine religieuse*, 22 July 1871.

paintings scattered. Further north, at Notre-Dame-de-Lorette (in the 9th arrondissement), the insurgents decapitated the statue of the Virgin. In several places, objects of worship were desecrated during raids: National Guards spat on the consecrated hosts, urinated in the fonts, and so on. Carnivalesque practices are also reported. Communards donned priests' clothing and imitated the mass: at Saint-Jacques-du-Haut-Pas, according to several accounts, the delegate Rose, dressed in sacred vestments, carried out a mock consecration. The most famous raids remain the ones on the Picpus convents and the Saint-Laurent cellars. There, officers and National Guards found skeletal remains. The discovery of a strange 'lock of blonde hair' was quickly interpreted as the remains of girls who had been raped and killed by the priests. *Le Cri du peuple* was indignant:

> Do you see this horrible scene, these young women, these girls, attracted by promises or by the hope of pleasure, who woke up here, sealed off, walled in, alive? . . . Mothers of credulous families, you who entrust the honour and the life of your children to priests . . . here is Catholicism doing its work. Behold![60]

These practices may seem strange. Yet they were hardly senseless: in many respects, they echoed the gestures and slogans of the French Revolution, and to a lesser extent the demonstrations of 1831. Back then, many churches had been used as sheds or clubs, and many buildings desecrated: Notre-Dame-des-Victoires had been transformed into a stock exchange, and Saint-Jacques-du-Haut-Pas into a 'temple of Reason'.[61] In attacking the churches' stonework, the Communards again actualised this revolutionary time. Moreover, in the Paris of 1871 they resumed the struggle between the fanaticism of the Church, blamed for keeping the people in a state of ignorance, and the Reason of the Enlightenment, taken as a source of emancipation.

In contrast to the French Revolution, however, in 1871 the churches were not turned into 'temples of Reason'. The Paris of the 1860s was more

60 *Le Cri du peuple*, 12 May (article later produced as a poster).

61 Michel Vovelle, *La Révolution contre l'Église. De la Raison à l'Être supreme* (Brussels: Complexe, 1988); Stéphane Baciocchi and Dominique Julia, 'Reliques et Révolution française (1789–1804)', in Philippe Boutry, Pierre-Antoine Fabre and Dominique Julia, eds, *Reliques modernes. Cultes et usages chrétiens des corps saints des Réformes aux Révolutions* (Paris: Éditions de l'EHESS, 2009), pp. 483–586.

industrial and literate, the working-class population was already more de-Christianised, and political anticlericalism was on the rise. If these assaults on churches had some element of transferring the sacred from the religious domain to that of popular sovereignty, these efforts look rather more like an attempt to secularise public space. At the same time, these gestures did not refer to those of the French Revolution alone (especially as the latter themselves harked back to earlier precedents). Analysing them is surely a delicate problem, insofar as we do not have access to the exact words used at the time of the events. But these acts irresistibly bring to mind the iconoclasm of the Wars of Religion.[62] We find a similar gestural grammar, which helps to interpret these actions: the destruction of the altar and the collection box is designed to prevent worship taking place; the profanation of hosts denies transubstantiation; decapitation targets the supposed home of the soul – and so on. In this sense, these attacks made up part of a reversed ordination, meaning: God is not where you think, and the space of the sacred is not to be found in such places as these. The perpetrators may not have been entirely aware of this symbolic logic; nonetheless, as they performed these acts, they knew their gestures were not devoid of meaning: this implicit framework is by no means negligible.

It is perhaps possible to go back yet further. The destruction of churches during political revolts is attested even in the eleventh century. But here we will follow the intriguing trail of the strands of blonde hair, and the figure of the lustful, defiling priest, which we came across in Saint-Laurent and which can be found also elsewhere. In 1871, they clearly referred to the romantic and gothic literature of the eighteenth and nineteenth centuries, best illustrated by Victor Hugo's *Notre-Dame de Paris*, a bestseller throughout Europe. This gives us a sense of the wide circulation of such literature within many segments of Parisian society. But, as the medievalist Alain Boureau reminds us, this figure is in fact much older. It was probably first created by twelfth-century clerics opposed to the Gregorian reforms and the growing power of the ecclesiastical institution.[63] In the sixteenth century, this once-salacious figure took on a more threatening guise, before the Wars of Religion gave it fresh notoriety. As is so often the

62 Especially Olivier Christin, *Confesser sa foi. Conflits confessionnels et identités religieuses dans l'Europe moderne (XVIe–XVIIe siècle)* (Paris: Champ Vallon, 2009).

63 Alain Boureau, *Le Droit de cuissage. La fabrication d'un mythe (XIIIe–XXe siècle)* (Paris: Albin Michel, 1995).

case, the mental frames and instruments of such opposition had been moulded within the Christian world itself: this imaginary was a figure of resistance to oppression by a stronger, central power, which had been regularly updated since then, including in the nineteenth century. However, the medievalist notes, these actualisations also echo one another, according to 'virtualities of representation', which result from their imperfect realisations, from conflicts of interpretation between social groups, or from the discrepancies left by earlier hopes and fears. Far from appearing as 'mentalities', an overly homogenising term, they appear as discontinuous references of uncertain status, which actors seized upon according to the demands of the situation, and which themselves offer an open-ended wealth of meanings. This is to say that the references invoked here could involve an even greater collision between times: the most obvious spectres, such as the French Revolution, also concealed other, more obscure and distant ones. And these pasts of pasts certainly contributed to their evocative and attractive power in insurgent Paris. We can thus better grasp the breach and the depth of field that opened up at that moment. Belonging at once to revolutionary practices and to popular forms of resistance, they also help explain the strength of this feeling of immediate justice.[64] Certainly, not everyone shared in this perception: often, local residents, and even ones favourable to the Commune, tried to oppose these invasions of church buildings. The same goes for the authorities: while some, perhaps Le Moussu, may have seen the mobilisation of this resource as a means of drawing people into revolutionary participation, others worried about a deviant, overly aggressive process that risked dragging the Communard cause into disrepute, or its slipping beyond the control of the institutions then trying to establish themselves. There are, of course, several competing ways of being in revolutionary time.

Realising a new era: messianism and the spirit of science

In any case, a time perceived as new or regenerated appeared to the protagonists as the bearer of alternative futures. This hope could

64 The term 'popular' does not refer here to a fixed and pre-given group. See Roger Chartier's critique in *Culture écrite et société. L'ordre des livres (XIVe–XVIIIe siècle)* (Paris: Albin Michel, 1996). It refers to actions of opposition or affirmation in which groups define themselves as belonging to 'the people', and then give flesh-and-blood reality to this notion. See Tarragoni, *L'Énigme révolutionnaire*.

simultaneously be expressed both by the most revolutionary and by those who hardly dared believe in it, and in either a reflective or an unmediated manner. The channels through which it was voiced were various: the Commune's central institutions, municipalities, National Guard battalions, newspapers, clubs, vigilance committees, unions of all kinds, cabarets, neighbourhood discussions, and so on. This flourishing of horizons and expectations surely has to be understood in its properly polyphonic character. To take just a few examples: 'The happiness of the country, the future of the whole world, are in your hands; lying in wait for you are the blessings or the curses of the future generations' (poster issued by the Central Committee); 'Deeply convinced that the Commune, representative of the international and revolutionary principles of the people, carries within it the seeds of the social revolution, the women of Paris will prove to France that they, too, will know how to . . . give their blood and their lives, like their brothers' (manifesto of the central committee of the Union of Women for the Defence of Paris and the Care of the Wounded); 'the right ideas will come to take their place, they will no longer suspect their fellow man, they will become republicans' (words transcribed from the minutes of the Saint-Ambroise club); 'the Central Committee entreats you to march united in progress . . . [It] is conscious that the heroic Parisian population is going to immortalise itself and regenerate the world' (poster, 5 April); 'we want to emancipate the proletariat, so that each will live from his labour; no more lazy, no more parasites, no more exploiters, no more exploited, live working or die fighting' (notice from the communal delegation of the 1st arrondissement, 13 April); 'Let's take up arms again and push these Prussians out of our *Patrie*, and through the enthusiasm we put into that, we will probably take things further' (speaker in a club); 'it is necessary to live, not speculate' (letter from the captain commander of the 16th legion); 'let us establish the financial federation' (speaker in a club); 'regenerate France through the Republic and the municipal franchises' (public letter from Charles Beslay to Thiers); 'lay the foundations of a positive peace, as the dawn of a new future' (manifesto issued by the Freemasons).[65]

65 SHD, Ly22; SHD, Ly18; SHD, Ly22. On this diversity of expectations and perspectives under the Commune, see also the remarks in Jean-Louis Robert, 'Une histoire politique de la Commune', in Robert, ed., *Le Paris de la Commune (1871)* (Paris: Belin, 2015).

With their conjugation in the imperative and the future tense, these expressions used personification and a solemn tone to express this desire for the absolute and to call for the application of grand principles. They are, we can see, marked by both reference to circumstance (the siege) and ideas that had been circulating for some years: hatred of the Second Empire, municipal republicanism, the socialist currents of the nineteenth century, proposals for the reorganisation of labour, the improvement of the individual. Patriotism, Parisian identity and more general expectations such as putting an end to poverty, also appear. This is not to forget – and this is essential – the outbursts of joy. 'We have never been as happy as today', a certain Mr Aber recalls having heard the officer who came to search his home repeat.[66] These appeals give us a feel for the horizon of enfranchisement – in the strong sense of the term, of liberation and emancipation – that the Commune carried with it. If we add to this the concrete practices identified in the previous chapter in certain clubs, National Guard battalions, municipalities and workshops, we can understand that this enfranchisement took on a particular heft: here, the Commune takes its place as a multiform, concrete ideal of personal and collective autonomy.

Insurgent Paris thought of itself in the future tense: 'the struggle of the future against the past' was surely the most widely used expression of the day. Various qualities of future time seem to have blended together, in hybridisations that are sometimes difficult to pick apart. Messianic expectations sprang forth, imbued with eternity and the absolute: 'The Revolution of 18 March will triumph . . . and humanity will owe us its improvement and its independence' (poster issued by the War Administration, 9 May). In this, we can see the revolutionary messianism of humanity, a messianism without a messiah. Marked by a religious conception of time, it draws on a time-out-of-time that allows for the immediate advent of a radically different world. Another aspect of this future-oriented imagination was the new importance accorded to the 'sciences' and the 'positive' spirit, characteristic of the positivist discourse that had established itself over the past decade.[67] The poster issued on 19 April read: 'The communal revolution . . .

66 SHD, 8J 3e conseil, dos 976, Coussat Démophile, Rapport du 12 février 1872 par le commissaire de police de la Goutte-d'Or.

67 On messianic time, see Michael Löwy, 'Temps messianique et historicité révolutionnaire chez Walter Benjamin', *Vingtième siècle. Revue d'histoire* 117: 1 (2013), pp. 106–18. This intrusion of the promise of justice into reality is magnificently captured in

ushers in a new era of experimental, positive, scientific politics. It is the end of the old governmental and clerical world.'[68] But more gradual perspectives were also expressed, as suggested by the emphasis placed on the 'provisional'. Perhaps this emphasis may have been linked to the siege situation that so shaped the revolution, or to the development of the idea of progress and modernity that had consolidated itself over the 1860s. It could also mean that the immediate emergency had to be addressed while securing this future for later. In any case, there was a sense of a gap between the present moment and the promise still to be fulfilled. 'While awaiting the solution to the social problem of the *organisation of labour*, with which the Paris Commune is occupied', says a poster from the municipality of the 8th arrondissement, 'we would like to be able to satisfy all urgent needs: subsistence, clothing, housing'.[69] Did this represent a difference compared to 1848, when these other futures appeared immediately at hand? It seems the 1871 revolution is indeed set apart by this intrusion of temporal distance into the heart of revolutionary becoming. This hypothesis could explain why, after the fact, the Paris Commune could appear 'modern' when invoked by the revolutionary movements of the twentieth century – even if this involved significant, and sometimes substantial, distortions.

The Mechanics of Intensity: Sustaining the Revolution

But there is nothing self-evident about this politicised and affective time. It had to be nurtured – and it demanded struggles that themselves contributed to its rhythm and texture. Surely, the more weeks passed by, the more the fact of the revolution and its irreversibility appeared to find confirmation. But even the most enthusiastic Communards did not spend these seventy-two days in a constantly febrile state. Diaries, letters and eyewitness accounts tell of alternating times of hot and cold, of excitement and exhaustion.[70] Uncertainty and doubt weighed heavily. This sense of communion and possibility therefore needed to be repeatedly recharged. The Commune

---

Ernst Bloch's classic analysis *Thomas Münzer als Theologe der Revolution* (Frankfurt: Suhrkamp, 1969 [1921]).

68 Guillaume Carnino, *L'Invention de la science. La nouvelle religion de l'âge industriel* (Paris: Seuil, 2015).

69 *JOC*, 12 April 1871, emphasis in original.

70 Mazeau, 'Émotions politiques'.

seems to have had its own mechanisms for keeping this charge alive: communal ceremonies, such as the one on 28 March in front of the Hôtel de Ville, are one such case. But there were many others: ceremonies in the municipalities, demonstrations, assemblies, clubs, discussions in the National Guard or in certain workplaces. These acted as 'emotional rituals': in these times of relative lethargy, of the disintegration of social ties, and of a desire to transform all that existed, they allowed for a momentary rekindling of enthusiasm, the feeling of belonging, and its redefinition of good and evil.[71] As Michèle Riot-Sarcey has aptly emphasised, these assemblies, battalions and clubs, which were inseparable from voting practices, also expressed the popular-sovereignty-in-action that was so characteristic of the revolutions of the nineteenth century. At the same time, they were a site for the creation of a collective – the one that took 'Commune' for its name.[72] These different dimensions clearly went hand in hand: here again, the political took on a different substance.

This was why this revolutionary time also prompted such opposition and resistance. The Commune was also a struggle between temporalities – and between possible worlds. Those who refused to be part of it, out of fear or out of choice, developed their own strategies to escape it. For example, Professor Desplats wrote (on 29 March): 'I am taking advantage of it all to stay shut in at home next to a good fire, far from the din and the sight of this third-rate revolutionary mob.' The banker Émile Lehideux explained in his letters that during the siege he had gone back into the office and pretended to work, to give meaning to his days even despite the lack of real activity. He continued this practice after the Commune – even though, as he put it, 'one spends one's time rather bored' – before then fleeing.[73] In reaction to the revolution and what they perceived as anarchy, these individuals reproduced ordinary routines in order to keep alive the old times – the times perceived as 'normal.' Sociologists have well described this conflict in the uses of time: that between what might schematically be called 'bourgeois' time – an anticipated, organised, regular time (significantly, Lehideux was

71 Randall Collins, *Interaction Ritual Chains* (Princeton, NJ: Princeton University Press, 2004).

72 Michèle Riot-Sarcey, *Le Procès de la liberté. Une histoire souterraine du XIXe siècle en France* (Paris: La Découverte, 2016); Mazeau, 'Émotions politiques.'

73 Virginie Lehideux-Vernimmen, ed., *Le Siège de Paris (1870–1871). Les 141 lettres d'Émile Lehideux à son épouse (6 septembre 1870–25 mars 1871)* (Paris: Éditions familiales, 2002).

still signing a deed of stewardship even in January 1871) – and the prophetic time of the most destitute, who under 'normal' circumstances literally have no future.[74] There were many such tactics, at both the individual and collective levels. They could be banal: Malvina Blanchecotte liked to remember poems, as an escape from the chaos unfolding before her eyes. Others wrote letters to their families: Émile Lehideux noted, 'Excuse me if the letters are short, and if they continue to be, but I have very little to say to you apart from politics, about which the newspapers must inform you at great length.' Some made their letters deliberately banal: this expressed the concern, through the act of writing, to construct a fictitious space as a place of comfort, a link to the other, and a brief escape from the 'hot' time of the event. These practices were sometimes a matter of social struggle, and sometimes of simple survival: this is how we can understand, at least in part, the reaction of those who, as certain defeat loomed, abandoned their posts, tried to flee, and retreated to the cellars. According to memoirs and legal depositions, many Parisians hid in these underground refuges during the Commune's final weeks. These closed and buried places were the ideal destinations for escaping from the space and time of the Commune – for removing oneself from the history that was playing out therein.

Far from being merely internal, this struggle turned outward. The military struggle, too, operated on the terrain of time. The telegrams of the head of the Versailles government, Adolphe Thiers, are perhaps the best illustration of this:

> Versailles, 11 April 1871, 10:30 a.m.
> Nothing new. The greatest calm reigns in our quarters. . . . The army is getting organised and increasing its forces each day . . . Let the good citizens, sincere in their alarm, be reassured. Not a single event will occur without it being made known to them, and there is nothing disastrous to be foreseen or feared.

These telegrams were intended for the whole population, and the head of the Versailles government knew they were read in Paris. His formulations also aimed to kill off the very idea of revolutionary time. These terse texts minimised the event (reduced to the work of a 'factious'

74 Pierre Bourdieu, 'The Plurality of Times', in Bourdieu, *Pascalian Meditations* (Stanford, CA: Stanford University Press, 2000).

minority), and from one week to the next heralded the looming end of a 'fight whose outcome is not in doubt' (26 April). The counting of hours and sometimes minutes ('Versailles, 2 p.m.') also narrowed the horizon, hammering home the determination to return to 'reality'. This military-administrative language had a constraining effect. It produced a reaction from the Commune side, with an intensification of revolutionary time by those who remained in Paris. The Alliance Républicaine des Départements thus replied to Versailles on 23 April with a poster insisting 'that the Paris of 1871 must not be slandered, that the current movement is not just a miserable insurrection; it is perhaps – despite deplorable incidents – the greatest revolution of modern times'. As the weeks passed, the tone became more emphatic:

> The People that brings down kings from their thrones, that destroys the Bastilles; the people of '89 and '93, the People of the Revolution, cannot lose in one day the fruits of the emancipation of March 18. Parisians, the struggle now underway must not be deserted by anyone; for it is the struggle of the future against the past, of Liberty against despotism . . . of the Solidarity of the peoples against the egoism of the oppressors.[75]

On 15 May, in an appeal to the republican towns and cities, Paschal Grousset thundered: 'Paris has made a pact with death. Great cities of France, will you look on motionless and impassive at this duel to the death of the Future against the Past, of the Republic against Monarchy?'

May 1871: chronicle of an apocalypse foretold

These wars over time had an accelerating and transformative effect. At the beginning of May, as the Communards' defeat loomed, the references took on an apocalyptic tone, in keeping with the hopes that had been raised. 'At this hour of extreme peril', we read on 18 May in a full-page advertisement calling for recruits for the Commune's riflemen, 'we call for the devotion of those ready to die for the social revolution.' In this we see another characteristic of the Commune: it was a revolution whose actors knew relatively early on that it was doomed to a terrible

75 Poster issued by the Committee of Public Safety, 2 prairial of year 79 – *Les Murailles politiques françaises*, p. 563.

end. Popular language quickly found the appropriate formulas. '[The National Guards] continue the struggle for what they call the honour of the cause', noted Malvina Blanchecotte, 'but they are taking, as they themselves say, *a funeral ticket*'. The awareness, in the Commune's final moments, that death was likely coming also explains its radicalisation, the hunt for the recalcitrant, and the attempt to absolutise the struggle. It gives a tragic dimension to the event, in the eyes of Parisians as well as those who followed developments: the revolution moved inexorably forward even while it heard the footsteps of its own approaching demise.

These considerations help shed light on already known but only dimly interpreted facts about the moment of the final battle. Telling in this regard are the 20,000 fighters, according to the most common estimates, who remained at their posts at the time of the final struggle. Even after the dissolution of the communal authority, these Parisians held their barricades, as isolated local groups welded together by their mutual acquaintances. The inertia-effect of their commitment to the struggle ought not to be disregarded. But this attempt to keep up the fight also illustrates the reality of this 'Commune', rooted in the existence of a communal government, in its members' paths to becoming revolutionaries, in its different forms of self-organisation, in the resurgences of past revolutions, in the battalions' pull on their members – or, more simply, in the determination to defend one's neighbourhood or one's dignity as a citizen, sometimes as a family. These insurgent pockets of Paris, even when cut off from any coordinating authority, perhaps stand as the clearest outcrops revealing the depth and resilience of the movement that had built up over the preceding months.

The Commune produced its own space-time. Probably the best illustration of this comes in the rival accusations of anachronism. For the Versaillais, the Commune was unquestionably anachronistic: it pointed back to a bygone era of revolutions, to violence and the unleashing of popular passions. The Versaillais considered themselves to be on the side of true progress: reason, moderation, the regular functioning of institutions, respect for universal male suffrage, and awareness of political and economic issues. But for the Communards – those who identified as such – the Versaillais were the anachronistic ones: were these representatives of rural France not monarchists, conservatives, defenders of order and religion? For them, the Commune alone embodied the future: the Republic, equality, science, education, secularism, complete emancipation, the end of economic injustice and of social antagonisms. In a letter-poster addressed to Thiers, the elder Beslay wrote that he had blinded himself to 'all the work of social transformation that has been accomplished in Europe these last fifty years . . . The world is marching on, and you persist without taking a step forward as you continue stalling on one spot'.[76] While it drew on prior elements, the Commune-event thus opened up a fault-line in the perception of historical becoming.

This conclusion ties in with the previous one concerning the interpretation of the Commune. The military dimension and the effect of the two sieges must not be overlooked. Neither must its brevity, its apparent ideological confusion, or the meagreness of its achievements. It is understandable that historians have questioned the real scope of the event, and at times its revolutionary nature. Perhaps, however, given the conditions under which it unfolded, they have not always looked in the right place. If we consider not only the Commune's government and its measures, but also the activity in the neighbourhoods, the mobilisation of various more or less formalised groups, the initiatives in the organisation of labour, the changes in social and gender relations, the transformation of the frameworks of historical experience, the pursuit of real, albeit fragmented, utopias, or the institutions that began to be created, we can indeed make out the outline of a genuine revolutionary process, and the expression of a will to transform the world. This was anything but homogeneous; it was made up of conflicts and remained largely unfinished. But, to adopt an expression already used for 1848, there was a Commune 'movement' – a concrete, multiform, advancing one.[77] What remains to be seen is what this movement corresponded to.

76 *JOC*, 26 April 1871.

77 Rémi Gossez, *Les Ouvriers de Paris, book I, L'Organisation (1848–1851)* (La Roche-sur-Yon: Imprimerie centrale de l'Ouest, 1967).

8

Neither Dawn nor Twilight: An Essay on the Temporalities of the Commune

Posing the question of what this movement might have corresponded to may seem surprising. Has the answer not long been understood? After all, if we think in terms of historical positioning, few revolutions can lay claim to such a clearly defined place as the Commune. It has indeed long been axiomatic to say that the Commune represents both the 'twilight' of the revolutions of the nineteenth century, because of its tie with the Great Revolution, and the 'dawn' of modern revolutions, given that it produced a majority-working-class government. On this view, the Commune marked the end of the French and European revolutions of the nineteenth century, and ushered in the era of modern revolutions, with what was perceived as their more highly developed ideological and organisational structure, starting with the Russian Revolution of 1917. Originally a Marxist reading, this positioning of the Commune at the junction of two periods then spread more widely. Yet it has also been challenged by historical research, particularly regarding the second moment of this supposed binary. The idea of the 'last of the revolutions of the nineteenth century' has retained broader currency, even if historians soon registered that this appears out of step with the real complexity of the event. In recent decades, many questions have even been raised over the implicit perspective behind this binary formulation, with its underlying idea of progress and of the contrast between the old and the modern. How, then, should the Commune be situated?

The effort behind the long intellectual tradition to locate the Commune's place in history should not be denigrated. With its concern to establish a hierarchy of causes and to mobilise coherent theoretical models, and with its thirst for generalisations (which today is considered excessive), it nonetheless situated the Commune within a chain of temporalities, in order to suggest a robust interpretation of the event. There are clear advantages to more recent analyses, which place greater emphasis on the complexity of processes; but one of the risks is that they may go no further than that, leaving the more properly analytical dimension unaddressed. Today, just like spatial models, temporal models of history surely need to be further enriched. The analyses in the previous chapters have indeed shown that the Commune was above all characterised by a layering of temporalities, in the sense of dynamics that each responded to their own rhythms. Is it not worth trying to delve further into them? To this end, should we not try to adopt more of an external vantage point, in order to grasp the cyclical, deep, short, medium and long temporalities that made themselves felt within this event? The aim of doing so would not be to place the event once again within some supposed temporal order, but rather to discover which more or less long-range histories played out, and were refracted and projected in and through it.

Unlike the rest of this book, this chapter is an interpretive essay. It does not have the same investigative rigour as the other chapters, and is based on hypotheses. It is also, unavoidably, selective in scope: since it is impossible to grasp all of the temporalities at work, the essay will look in depth at only a few of them, selected from the preceding study. Once again, it is the Commune's own movement that prompts the perspectives to follow. We will then be able to revisit the question of what was at stake in the Commune; address the problem of its temporal layering and cross-comparability; and, finally, explore what, beyond the succession of events, constituted its deeper significance.

The Third Revolution of the Nineteenth Century

To begin with, the Commune was inseparable from the military and political circumstances in which it arose. It also unfolded according to its own dynamics and temporal sequences: the fragmentation resulting from the war with Prussia and the political transition were followed, in short order, by the week of uncertainty; the raising of hopes and expectations after 28 March; the first fighting and tensions in April; and, in early May, the acceleration of the revolutionary process and of doubts in the Commune. These sequences then fractured into many different rhythms across the various neighbourhoods and arrondissements of Paris. In doing so, they ushered in other temporalities and tendencies, of shorter or longer duration, which we will examine more closely below.

For instance, the Commune also revived the cyclical time that had been typical of the revolutionary modes of action of nineteenth-century France. This is not exactly the same thing as the qualitative time of possibilities. The perspective in question more closely echoes the famous 'repertoires of collective action' identified by the sociologist Charles Tilly, and then applied to the revolutions of the nineteenth century by other authors.[1] As Mark Traugott explains, this category refers to 'a set of behavioral templates which exert an influence, at once constraining and enabling, over the activities of whole groups, with demonstrable, objective consequences'.[2]

These repertoires are made up of watchwords, scripts, patterns of behaviour and institutional practices inherited from previous revolutions. They offer actors dealing with situations of uncertainty and insurrection the possibility to coordinate their actions, thereby making them more effective and meaningful; in so doing, they give these critical moments a routinised character. In the Commune, this was evident in the fact that various watchwords and mechanisms could almost be taken for granted. These ranged from established terms (revolution, citizen, vigilance committee, committee of public safety), to the importance of the Hôtel de Ville (which the crowd spontaneously headed towards on 18 March, as in 1830 or 1848), or the presence of the National Guard, the barricades and the clubs. Yet the repertoire of collective action never has just the same elements across different individual cases. Appropriations, poaching and inventions are common. For instance, unlike in 1848, the Commune of 1871 widely mobilised the soldiers of the revolutionary Year II, especially during the first attempts at Communard sorties from the city: officers hoped that these initiatives

1 Charles Tilly, *From Mobilization to Revolution* (New York: Random House, 1978), and *La France conteste. De 1600 à nos jours* (Paris: Fayard, 1986); Mark Traugott, *The Insurgent Barricade* (Berkeley, CA: University of California Press, 2010).

2 Mark Traugott, 'The Limits of Protagonism: A Political Anthropology of 1848', *Politix* 112: 4 (2015), pp. 83–110, at p. 109.

would result in a mass levy or *levée en masse*.[3] This connection was also owed to an objective fact – namely that, in 1871, the country was again in the midst of a civil war that followed a military defeat against a foreign power, a fact that encourages comparisons with 1792. The discrepancies with the revolution of 1848 were rather more numerous. Anticlericalism – inspired by the Great Revolution and reinvigorated by the republican discourse of the 1860s – expressed itself especially intensely in 1871. The red flag prevailed over the tricolour, and the question of labour was more central, as was discourse around science and positivism. Moreover, the Commune introduced elements that would provide reference points for later insurrections, such as an understanding of the possible steps to be taken by an insurgent urban government. These observations explain why the notion of a repertoire of action has been so widely debated: its elements are never fixed, the 'past' to which it refers is never clear, and it turns out to be difficult to establish the modalities or stages of the transformations that take place.[4]

Still, this notion also allows us to emphasise that, even within the volatility that revolutionary action generates, it also possesses a certain stability. And it explains why, in 1871, this revolution was so quickly able to take shape and gain specific connotations, even though it existed so briefly. Lastly, it reminds us that the Commune was the third revolution of the nineteenth century: and that the actors involved, whether militant supporters of the Commune, sympathisers, opponents, or indifferent observers, had in a sense already become accustomed to revolution. All of them knew what it meant; when one broke out, it was considered as one possibility among others; and, even if they did not foresee the ultimate outcome, they did have frameworks for anticipating what would come next. If the Commune began from 'time's degree zero', this was not the same as that of the French Revolution.[5] More precisely, it fitted into a mould bequeathed by the Revolution of 1789, which, as

3 The term *levée en masse* refers to the general mobilisation of the population to defend the Republic during the French Revolution in 1793.

4 Michel Offerlé, 'Retour critique sur les répertoires de l'action collective (XVIIIe–XXIe siècle)', *Politix* 81: 1 (2008), pp. 181–202.

5 On this, see Lynn Hunt, 'The French Revolution: Time's Degree Zero' (in Russian), in Elena Višlenkova and Denis Sdvižkov, eds, *Izobretenie veka. Problemy i modeli vremeni v Rossii i Evrope XIX stoletija* (*Die Erfindung des Jahrhunderts. Probleme und Modelle der Temporalität in Russland und Europa im 19. Jahrhundert*) (Moscow: Deutsches Historisches Institut [*studia europaea* 3], 2020), pp. 40–55.

some of its historians have emphasised, had the unique flavour that went with being the first, irreversible occurrence of revolution. This did not make the lived reality of the Commune any less intense; and, as we have seen, for many insurgent Parisians this was an extreme experience. Rather, the interpretive divide between analyses based on the historicity of revolutionary time and those grounded in the routines of collective action is owed to divergent approaches towards such events. The first emphasise the singularity of each upsurge, and are reluctant to draw comparisons: they seek to understand the protagonists' capacities for action in their own present. The second, for their part, identify the inherited and ever-shifting forms that provided the mould into which these experiences fitted, the better to analyse their forms and effectiveness. The two approaches must be considered in combination.

For it is indeed valuable to examine both the differences between revolutions and the elements of repetition. One such element is 'protagonism' – a productive notion in the study of revolutionary dynamics from below. The Commune was not the French Revolution studied by Burstin. In 1871 (as in 1848), there were no massacres like the ones of September 1792, with their decapitations, eviscerations and eye-gougings.[6] Before the massacre of the hostages, the only collective killing by the crowd in 1871 was the putting-to-death of a sub-brigadier of the Préfecture de Police, upon the commemoration of February 1848. Spotted by demonstrators while he was taking notes on what was happening, he was beaten, garrotted and thrown into the Seine.[7] He drowned under the hail of stones. A terrible death, to be sure, but one that remained distanced, preserving the integrity of the body. This difference with the type of massacres seen in the Great Revolution is owed to the change that took place over the nineteenth century in terms of sensitivity to violence. It was also connected to an explicit desire not to repeat previous acts of cruelty, in a revolution that purported to be more mature and humane. Typical elements of the past were sometimes evoked the better to distinguish the present from it: for instance, early in the event, two guillotines were symbolically burned in the 11th

6 See Alain Corbin, 'Le sang de Paris. Réflexions sur la généalogie de l'image de la capitale', in Corbin, *Le Temps, le Désir et l'Horreur. Essais sur le XIXe siècle* (Paris: Flammarion, 1998).

7 See Quentin Deluermoz, *Policiers dans la ville. La construction d'un ordre public à Paris (1854–1914)* (Paris: Publications de la Sorbonne, 2012), pp. 151–3.

arrondissement. The aim was to denounce the 'monarchical domination' under the previous regime, but also, as in 1848, to overtly reject any new Terror. The clubs, likewise, did not speak out with the same vigour or political effect as they had at the end of the eighteenth century. At the height of their activity during the French Revolution, they had constituted a site of direct surveillance, able to influence the members of the Commune or the Assembly.[8] In 1871, they were again a space where a horizontal, popular, political voice took form, but without the same intensity as during the 1789–1794 period. This political dynamic was different – because of the circumstances; because of this routinisation of revolutionary practices; and, no doubt, because of the regular practice since 1848 of male universal suffrage, which had altered the forms of public expression. Parisians' gestures, consciences and expectations were thus informed by the succession of revolutions and their respective outcomes – even if the revolutionary energy did not have quite the same tenor as on earlier occasions.

The 1850s and 1860s: The Big Cities Against the Second Empire

Clearly, other, more tendential temporalities also found expression – and took on peculiar inflections – in the Commune, allowing for a better understanding of some of its features. They could span a relatively short period, as in the case of the Second Empire – more precisely, the 1850s and 1860s. We will explore three such cases. Let us start with male universal suffrage. Proclaimed on 2 March 1848, and enacted nationwide on 23 April that year, it was maintained under the Second Empire for both parliamentary and municipal elections. In the subsequent two decades, the norms of legitimacy changed, and electoral competition profoundly reorganised the political sphere. This transformation also had real and multiple effects on the Commune. It made itself felt in the demands formulated during the 'week of uncertainty', particularly after 18 March when, worried about their legitimacy, the members of the Central Committee of the National Guard proposed that the members of the Commune be elected by male universal suffrage. Its connection is

8 Haïm Burstin, *Révolutionnaires. Pour une anthropologie politique de la Révolution française* (Paris: Vendémiaire, 2013).

less clear with the electoral practices within the National Guard and certain administrative bodies: these were more closely related to democratising practices that had been developed during the Great Revolution and February 1848. At the same time, the political combinations that the system of election had produced under previous regimes could only fuel Parisians' distrust towards overly far-removed delegations of power. Napoleon III's 'illiberal democracy' had demonstrated that universal suffrage, diluted by various provisions such as 'official candidacies', could be compatible with a highly personalised exercise of power.[9] In a similar vein, for many sincere republicans, the fact that the previous experiment of the Second Republic had proved so short-lived was partly to be blamed on universal suffrage and the poor preparation of the bulk of the country. As early as 1850, exiled 'Montagnards' had concluded that the republican principle had to take precedence over the type of suffrage, and argued for the merits of direct government.[10] Given the election results of February 1871, with the advantage they awarded to conservatives and monarchists, it is understandable that, in 1870–71, many Parisians took the 'immediate Republic' and its use of binding mandates as at least one among several credible solutions. This backdrop may also explain why the women involved in the Commune did not demand voting rights as vigorously as their sisters in 1848 had: universal suffrage no longer enjoyed the same aura it once had.[11] In 1871, they saw the organisation of Labour as a more important political and social issue, and one just as closely linked to the functions of citizenship. Together, these observations help us to understand the plurality of registers of political legitimacy at work during the Commune.

Another of the most important social transformations under the Second Empire was the Haussmannisation of Paris. We encountered its influence earlier on, when examining the 're-conquest of the city by

9 On illiberal democracy, see Pierre Rosanvallon, *La Démocratie inachevée. Histoire de la souveraineté du peuple en France* (Paris: Gallimard, 2000); Patrick Lagoueyte, *La Vie politique en France au XIXe siècle* (Gap: Ophrys, 1997).

10 The Montagnards were radical republicans, heirs of the so-called Mountain of the 1790s, who, in exile after 1851, advocated prioritising republican principles over universal suffrage. (The 'Mountain' refers to the radical republican faction in the National Convention (1792–1795) during the French Revolution.)

11 Jacques Rougerie, 'Les femmes de 1871', in Christine Fauré, ed., *Encyclopédie politique et historique des femmes (Europe, Amérique du Nord)* (Paris: PUF, 1997), pp. 405–31.

itself', the incipient challenge to hierarchical segregation, and the absence of rival urbanism projects. But we can also note that, with the Commune, a revolutionary Paris with twenty arrondissements (no longer twelve) now took shape, and that Belleville joined the ranks of great revolutionary neighbourhoods.[12] It is likewise worth considering the unexpected effects of the Second Empire's religious policy: when the Communards attacked churches, they were not only trying to revive the revolutionary time of 1789–99. These attacks were also a reaction against the recent construction of new religious buildings in Paris. Under the Second Empire the city had, in Jacques-Olivier Boudon's words, been the 'religious capital': twenty-three new churches were built, and others were restored. In truth, such an image is more clear-cut than the reality: the Second Empire had distanced itself from the Church in the 1860s.[13] But in March 1871, this association prevailed without hesitation. The denunciation of the Second Empire, which was seen as complicit with the forces of the Church, was only encouraged by the presence in Versailles of a 'rural' monarchist and conservative Chamber. Attacks on churches and religious institutions were thus also targeted at this socio-political order of the 1850s. In addition to resurgences of 1789 and 1831, they likewise corresponded to the practices of urban reappropriation that had followed the transformations of the French capital. This points to an interesting entanglement of temporalities.

But more important still were the recompositions of the workers' and republican movements during the 1860s.[14] Brought to its knees at the beginning of the Second Empire, the labour movement regained strength with the regime's liberal turn – sometimes with the regime's support, sometimes in opposition to it. Between extensions, rediscoveries, alterations and adaptations, this period saw a diversity of socialist thought (Proudhonism, Fourierism, collectivism, mutualism, and so on). This flurry of ideas in the 1850s–60s remains too little-known, at

---

12 For Belleville, see Gérard Jacquemet, *Belleville au XIXe siècle. Du faubourg à la ville* (Paris: Éditions de l'EHESS, 1984). See also Jeanne Gaillard, *Paris, la ville (1852–1870)* (Paris: Champion, 1977).

13 Jacques-Olivier Boudon, *Paris, capitale religieuse sous le Second Empire* (Paris: Cerf, 2001).

14 See, for example, the research project 'Utopie 19: Une tradition oubliée – intellectuels et expérimentateurs socialistes, 1830–1870' (ANR, 2012–2015), funded by the French National Research Agency (Agence Nationale de la Recherche).

least apart from the distinct renewal of Proudhonian thought in this same period, stimulated by the posthumous publication of *De la capacité politique des classes ouvrières* (1865).[15] As far as organisational projects were concerned, the skilled trades reinvigorated their associationism by using or subverting mechanisms that existed already (mutual-aid societies, the labour halls tolerated after 1868, and so on). Labour's drive for stronger association found particular expression in the Workers' Commission of 1867, created against the backdrop of the International Exhibition.[16] Similarly, strikes became a more established practice after the 1864 law. And the IWMA, as we know, gradually established itself in the Parisian social landscape. It enjoyed a remarkable rise in the capital, where many workers' societies joined the First International – though its scale should not be overstated: in 1869, the Association had a few tens of thousands of members in France, and repression by the imperial authorities remained quite effective. Finally, in 1868–70, after further liberalising measures, a vast movement of public meetings unfolded, during which a radical or outright revolutionary discourse could be voiced.[17]

To this was added, moreover, the 'republican moment' of the 1860s, driven by a new, more positivist and anticlerical generation (that of Gambetta and Clemenceau). It found outlets in para-state institutions (the university, the bar), the recently established opposition press (*Le Réveil, La Lanterne*), leagues (of educators), and the resurgence of republican rituals (symbolic funerals, anniversaries). In this period, it also particularly took the form of municipal republicanism.[18] This trend, which was sometimes connected to the labour movement but also sometimes opposed to it, was especially influential in Paris. It is

15 See Samuel Hayat, 'The Construction of Proudhonism within the IWA', in Fabrice Bensimon, Quentin Deluermoz and Jeanne Moisand, eds, *'Arise Ye Wretched of the Earth!': The First International in Global Perspective* (Leiden: Brill, 2018). On Proudhon, see also Edward Castleton's many useful insights.

16 Michel Cordillot, 'La Commission ouvrière de 1867', in Cordillot, *Aux origines du socialisme moderne. La Première Internationale, la Commune de Paris, l'exil. Recherches et travaux* (Ivry-sur-Seine: L'Atelier, 2010).

17 Alain Dalotel, Alain Faure and Jean-Claude Freiermuth, *Aux origines de la Commune. Le mouvement des réunions publiques à Paris* (1868–1870) (Paris: Maspero, 1980).

18 Philip Nord, *Le Moment républicain. Combats pour la démocratie dans la France du XIXe siècle* (Paris: Armand Colin, 2013 [1995]).

always difficult to assess the importance of these dynamics without retrospectively making them the principal point of origin of all that followed. Yet they did play an obviously important role in the emergence of the Commune, to which they provided many cadres, as well as intellectual frameworks and ideological themes. The Commune, too, belongs to this 1850s–1860s temporality.

The Long Nineteenth Century: The Democratic and Social Republic, Capitalism, and the Nation-State

Still, we can hardly stop there. Let us return to the workers' movement. This is, surely, only one temporal thread among others. But there are good reasons for choosing it: in 1870, half of working Parisians lived off industrial labour, and they had the potential to be a considerable social force. Terms we often find in the mouths of the men and women who identified with the Commune, such as 'association', 'democratic and social', and 'industrial feudalism', made reference to a wider movement dating back to the post-revolutionary 1820s.

In this moment, an outright working-class voice had emerged through newspapers (such as *L'Atelier*), songs and poetry. The first currents of socialism were also being developed by Saint-Simon, Fourier, Cabet, and many others. Such figures saw themselves not as 'utopians', but as the founders of a new social science that attempted to provide both concrete and ambitious solutions to the problems posed by the new industrial order.[19] At first they reached only a limited circle of workers, but over the 1830s and 1840s their ideas and slogans increasingly percolated beyond these limits. At that time, working-class language was enriched by a new vocabulary. The eighteenth-century terms 'tyranny', 'despotism' and 'slavery' were supplemented by 'proletarian' and the watchwords 'dignity', 'fraternity' and – especially after 1830 – 'liberty.'

At the organisational level, after the end of the guilds of the *ancien régime* (*corporations*), sociability in the streets, in cabarets, and in

19 Among many other works, see Alain Dewerpe, *Le Monde du travail en France* (Paris: Armand Colin, 1996); Jacques Rancière, *La Nuit des prolétaires. Archives du rêve ouvrier* (Paris, Fayard, 1981) – published in English as *Proletarian Nights: The Workers' Dream in Nineteenth-Century France* (London: Verso, 2012).

popular leisure societies was, for some, joined by Freemasonry and *compagnonnage* – the craft-based brotherhood centred on passing on knowhow to apprentices. More common, though, were mutual-aid societies and workers' societies, which could take various forms. This movement was especially present in Paris. Rémi Gossez, Jacques Rougerie and Maurizio Gribaudi have shown how deeply these new practices were rooted in the labour process, and in the very morphology of the city.[20] They were accompanied by a particular morality, the 'popular collective democratic ethic' that we have already seen in insurgent Paris.[21] This took shape in projects for 'association', in the strong sense of a 'great movement of emancipation' in favour of the union of classes, and the ending of the exploitation of man by man. While initially local in character, the movement gained greater consistency and scope in February 1848, a moment when it was also fed by the advent of universal male suffrage and projects for 'associations of associations'.[22] Cut short at the beginning of the 1850s, the movement continued through the recomposition processes of the 1860s, adjusting to conditions under the Second Empire, before spreading again under the Commune. It surely did not mobilise all workers (for instance, day labourers and factory workers were rather less involved). Instead, it centred on workers in the most skilled trades; and even in their case, there were internal tensions. But this movement was deeply rooted in the Parisian space, and expressed many of the conceptions, expectations and organisational practices that also prevailed under the Commune. For Jacques Rougerie, with the intellectual and political changes of the 1860s and the desire for municipal autonomy, the Commune found its most reliable moorings in this 'popular majority's [aspiration] for true democracy, for what had since 1848 been called a democratic and social republic'.[23] The present study corroborates this claim: the words 'Republic', 'freedom', 'People' and 'justice' had, at that time, a particular meaning, which is largely forgotten today.

20 Maurizio Gribaudi, *Paris, ville ouvrière. Une histoire occultée (1789–1848)* (Paris: La Découverte, 2014).

21 Jacques Rougerie, 'Le mouvement associatif populaire comme facteur d'acculturation politique a Paris, de la Revolution aux années 1840. Continuité, discontinuités', *Annales historiques de la Révolution française* 297 (1994), pp. 493–516.

22 Rémi Gossez, *Les Ouvriers de Paris, book I, L'Organisation (1848–1851)* (La Roche-sur-Yon: Imprimerie centrale de l'Ouest, 1967).

23 Jacques Rougerie, 'Commune et démocratie', in Jean-Louis Robert, ed., *Le Paris de la Commune (1871)* (Paris: Belin, 2015), p. 80.

This observation invites us to consider other, broader social dynamics in which this history took place, such as economic changes and the rise of the so-called 'modern' state. Researchers tend to underestimate these slower dynamics on which the Commune worked, but which also, of course, themselves shaped the Commune. They provided an important part of the framework within which individuals operated. Let us consider the case of industrialisation, or rather industrial capitalism. I prefer this second term, despite the many debates it generates, because it more clearly indicates a social relationship.[24] A brief summary of its history is in order. At the end of the eighteenth century, and even more so with the industrialisation process of the nineteenth century, Northern Europe saw a tendency towards the emergence of an economic and social system based on the free market, competition, the private ownership of the means of production, and the imperative of profitability and profit. This tendency was accompanied by the increased circulation of standardised, manufactured products, facilitated by transformations in both technology and the sources of energy. This had far-reaching effects on social organisation: the economy tended to become a domain unto itself, a primary factor in the organisation of social life; and there was increasing commodification: the transformation of objects, resources and services into commodities.[25] These operational logics did not appear on the scene already fully formed: they were linked to other cultural changes, and were constantly affected by power struggles and state interventions. In most cases – indeed, quite often at the behest of the employers themselves – there was a mixture of the free market and market regulation, as well as a constant play of tensions between local,

24 Among the points of debate: on the 'origins' of capitalism, see Fernand Braudel, *Civilisation matérielle, économie et capitalisme (XVe–XVIIIe siècle)* (Paris: Armand Colin, 1979), 3 vols; Giovanni Arrighi, *The Long Twentieth Century: Money, Power, and the Origins of Our Times* (London: Verso, 1994). On the difficulties of definition, see Alexia Blin and Nicolas Barreyre, 'À la redécouverte du capitalisme américain', *Revue d'histoire du XIXe siècle* 54: (2017), pp. 135–48. Useful considerations also appear in Patrick Verley, *L'Échelle du monde. Essai sur l'industrialisation de l'Occident* (Paris: Gallimard, 1997).

25 On these classic notions, see, for example, Karl Polanyi, *The Great Transformation: The Political and Economic Origins of Our Time* (New York and Toronto: Farrar & Rinehart, Inc., 1944); Moishe Postone, *Time, Labor, and Social Domination: A Reinterpretation of Marx's Critical Theory* (Cambridge: Cambridge University Press, 1993); W. H. Sewell Jr, 'The Temporalities of Capitalism', *Socio-Economic Review* 6: 3 (2008), pp. 517–37.

national, colonial and global trends.[26] Nevertheless, from the 1830s onwards, these logics took on greater consistency in the Atlantic and imperial spaces, but also in countries like France.[27] By the middle of the century new players were emerging: merchant banks and joint-stock companies, for example, whose number increased from ten in 1850 to 200 in 1869. Although these were only small islands in a sea of more diverse forms of production, their effects made themselves felt. The activity of the shop-boy Lejeune in the novelty stores was a sign of these changes: indeed, one of their very symbols was the department store, with its illuminated windows, its use of 'single prices', and indeed its role in the circulation of 'ephemeral fashions'. Its emergence also points to the growth of the world of clerks and shop employees, and to the appeal of this offer to a varied public, including the working classes. It further reminds us that this change brought a trend towards higher wages.[28] This surely had paradoxical elements: the cycle of economic crises did not cease (as in 1866); a new industrial elite consolidated and gained political power; and while chronic destitution in Paris greatly declined, occasional poverty grew strongly, particularly in the peripheral arrondissements. This peculiar precariousness of the populations in the most fragile position is surely another factor that needs to be considered if we want to understand the Paris revolt: the call for the 'end to misery' was very common during the Commune.[29] Similarly affected was the world of work in the French capital, although it remained largely artisanal and made up of small, scattered workshops (out of 100,000 Parisian bosses in 1860, 31,000 employed between two and ten employees, 62,000 one or none). Some historians emphasise the ability of these small bosses and skilled workers in Paris to adapt, and sometimes turn the situation to their advantage. Others, like Alain Cottereau, instead emphasise the mark that the 'invisible threads' of capitalism left on working practices: the concentration of capital, a new division of labour tasks, competition

26 Alessandro Stanziani, ed., *Dictionnaire historique de l'économie-droit (XVIIIe–XXe siècle)* (Paris: Libraire générale de droit et de jurisprudence, 2007).

27 Verley, *L'Échelle du monde*.

28 Michael B. Miller, '*Au Bon Marché*' *(1869–1920). Le consommateur apprivoisé* (Paris: Armand Colin, 1987 [1981]).

29 Gaillard, *Paris, la ville*, p. 165; Alain Cottereau and Maurizio Gribaudi, *Précarités, cheminements et formes de cohérence sociale au XIXe siècle* (Paris: Éditions de l'EHESS, 1999).

between types of workers (for example, those employed in workshops and those engaged in the putting-out system in their own homes), a tendency to lose control over prices and rates, and so on.[30]

The Commune found its place within this *longue durée* trend – a trend marked by shifting power relations, contradictions, and the weight of the inheritance it bore. It was a reality that had to be dealt with, sometimes pragmatically: in mid-April, in search of funds, the men elected to the Commune tried to sell City of Paris bonds, issued in 1869, on the London stock exchange.[31] Similarly, given the urgent pressures faced, orders were placed with private companies – firms which could be called capitalist – to make the National Guard's uniforms. But this framework was more generally present. It made its mark on everyday language, with its 'bosses' (*patrons*), 'bourgeois', 'proletarians' and 'workers'. It strongly influenced many of the Commune's elected officials: as shown by the debates on machinery, credit and the freedom of trade, they were not necessarily opposed to industrialisation and its tools. But they did seek to reorientate this process radically, in the diversity of political positions already mentioned.[32] This trend also explains the vigour behind the criticism of hoarders and speculators in insurgent Paris, the strengthening of the language of class, and the emphasis placed on the problem of labour organisation. Present already in 1848, these questions had a concrete meaning for many skilled workers, but also for clerks and employees, who were greater in number in 1871 than they had been in the revolution two decades before.[33] The Commune was also a result of this complex industrial transformation.

The other major social change was the development of the state in its so-called modern variant. This political form is just as difficult to define as capitalism itself: in its broadest sense, the state is both a symbolic category and a type of moulding of the social dimension.[34] Here I will

30 Yves Lequin, 'Les métiers', in Jean-Jacques Becker et al., *Ouvriers, villes et société. Autour d'Yves Lequin et de l'histoire sociale* (Paris: Nouveau Monde Éditions, 2005); A. Cottereau, 'Vie quotidienne et resistance ouvrière à Paris en 1870'.

31 CAD, CP, England.

32 An example of such debates can be found in Pierre-Louis Poyau, 'Le Pain pendant le siège de 1870 et la Commune de Paris. Approvisionnement et organisation de la répartition des denrées: une permanence de l'économie morale', master 2 dissertation, Sciences Po (2017).

33 Jacques Rougerie, *La Commune de 1871* (Paris: PUF, 2009), pp. 99–102.

34 Pierre Rosanvallon, *L'État en France, de 1789 à nos jours* (Paris: Seuil, 1990).

focus on one of its expressions: the state administration. This can be defined as the bodies and institutions, organised by law, responsible for the exercise of public power and constituting the concrete expression of the state in society. To this end, I will draw on my earlier analysis of the holders of public office.

For the example of these figures already places us within a long-term perspective: to understand the order underlying these public functions during the Commune, one must indeed go back to the sixteenth century. In that period, under the influence of doctrinal work, the development of the state administration, and the impulse of the Wars of Religion, a more properly political domain tended to detach itself from the cosmic-religious sphere in this period. In terms of power, this phenomenon manifested itself in the transition from offices ('dignity with a public function', as jurist Charles Loyseau had it) to public titles and functions. These amounted to a more defined apportioning of power, within circumscribed boundaries, as identified and underwritten by the state.[35] This shift, far from being linear, nonetheless represented a fundamental change: the forms of delegation of authority under the Commune were part of this *longue durée* political universe. But the nineteenth century also brought clear inflection points. Despite constant uncertainties (there are no cut-and-dried definitions of 'state employee'), the parameters of public functions and their holders became more clearly defined: from new rules for recruitment to the codification of conduct, the structuring of careers, and the right to retirement. The same was true of modes of organisation, often influenced by the military model. The weight of state administrations on society likewise grew, while long-distance power relations intensified – through communications, administrative papers, and the practice of voting.[36] Sociohistorical research has shown that, as regimes succeeded one another and as more or less autonomous spheres took form, these state presences crept into the

35 Robert Descimon, 'La vénalité des offices et la construction de l'État dans la France moderne. Des problèmes de la representation symbolique aux problèmes du coût social du pouvoir', in Robert Descimon, Jean-Frédéric Schaub and Bernard Vincent, eds, *Les Figures de l'administrateur. Institutions, réseaux, pouvoirs en Espagne, en France et au Portugal (XVIe–XIXe siècle)* (Paris: Éditions de l'EHESS, 1997).

36 Guy Thuillier and Jean Tulard, *Histoire de l'administration fran-çaise* (Paris: PUF, 1994); Gérard Noiriel, *État, nation et immigration. Vers une histoire du pouvoir* (Paris: Belin, 2001).

population's everyday lives. Gradually, either harmoniously or through conflict, they reshaped the dynamics of social relations: in Paris, the rising importance of administrative documents and markers of the state was one of many signs of this trend.[37]

This long-term change was thus still visible in insurgent Paris, and provided part of the framework within which the event played out. The Commune retained most of the city's public functions, including the institution of policing. A comparison with the police *commissaires* during the French Revolution allows us to clarify what exactly this entailed.[38] In several waves during this period, individuals assumed the function of police *commissaire* (first created in 1699). They also drew on other normative registers and elements of the previous institutional environment. In other words, earlier forms of state were in play in the French Revolution. But if we compare 1789–99 with 1871, taking into account the contrasting durations of each experience, we can see distinctive features of this latter case: the lack of elections in 1871, the projected competitive examinations, the reference to the codified, national law typical of the nineteenth century. In other words, it incorporated several of the innovations that accompanied the nineteenth-century transformation of the policing function. The Commune built on these developments. This is what I meant by the persistence of state practices and state modes of thought, here revealed in their full anthropological depth. Karl Marx noted this peculiar situation in two distinct assessments in his famous analysis of the Commune, *The Civil War in France*. On the one hand, he criticised the Commune for having remained within the bourgeois state apparatus rather than dismantling and replacing it; on the other, he praised the implementation of what he saw as a frugal Republic and a lean state, suited to the freedom of individual action.

Let us turn back to the example of public functions. They indeed did not always have the same content as they had before the Commune. The difference lay in recruitment methods (even if these had remained

37 As attested in Masai Mejiaz, *Les Frontières du Paris insurrectionnel (1870–1871)*, master 1 dissertation, Université Paris-13 (2011).

38 Discussion between Vincent Denis, Vincent Millot and Emmanuel Blanchard at the 'Police et crises politiques (XVIIIe–XIXe siècle)' workshop, ANR 'Systèmes policiers européens (XVIIIe–XIXe siècle)', 2013–2015. See also Vincent Denis, *Policiers de Paris. Les commissaires de police en Révolution (1789–1799)* (Ceyzérieu: Champ Vallon, 2022).

malleable under the Second Empire) as well as in the source, use and implicit definition of the power thus held. In this perspective, whether it was the result of mature political reflection, spontaneous decisions or the situation itself, the Commune did, through small shifts, bring about a transformed relationship to the state. If we add to this the uncertain nature of the Commune as a political form – halfway between a government and a municipality – we can see how it could produce a significant change in the relationship to authority and to the state that had gradually taken shape through this long historical construction of the administration.

The Intertwining of Historical Times: Arts of Resistance and Communal Autonomy

Should we not go back further, then, to before the French Revolution? Studies on the 'arts of resistance' invites us to do just this – and the Commune has already been set within a long and enduring history of so-called popular resistances.[39] This avenue can be explored anew, this time drawing on recent studies in both modern and medieval history. Indeed, such research has shaken off the chimera of unearthing origins: scholars no longer delve into the depths of the Middle Ages in order to track down the 'origin' of later institutions and promises, such as those of the nineteenth century. Similarly, they have discarded the Marxist-inspired interpretive lenses which, while having the undeniable merit of restoring dignity to past movements of popular resistance, also often cast them as revolts driven by archaic impulses.[40] These works instead seek to identify the resources and forms of political expression in action within their own proper context. Feudal societies or estates-based societies have gradually taken on a different face. While these societies were strongly hierarchical, and based on inequality and a diversity of legal statuses, they were at the same time endowed with various mechanisms that ensured a certain fluidity of social life: assemblies, voting, designation, the drawing of lots – not to mention the experiments that took

39 James Scott, *Domination and the Arts of Resistance: Hidden Transcripts* (Yale: Yale University Press, 1990).

40 Michel Mollat and Philippe Wolff, *Ongles bleus, Jacques et Ciompi. Les révolutions populaires en Europe aux XIVe et XVe siècles* (Paris: Calmann-Lévy, 1970).

place across rural, urban and ecclesiastical spaces.[41] Through these tensions and struggles, the notions of recognition, autonomy, equality, freedoms, franchises and 'the people' were broadly advanced. They did not have the same meaning as they would later, in the nineteenth century, after the French Revolution, and the assertion of the principle of the legal equality of individuals. But these terms were already present, charged with meaning and the desire for reform, acting within the structures of medieval and early modern forms of power.

It is worth considering here some of the major urban revolts in which rebels managed to occupy the cities in question. In fourteenth-century Florence, the wool carders, known as the Ciompi, revolted and then occupied the city for a month between 18 July and 31 August 1378: during the insurrection that marked that summer, they ravaged the Palazzo dell'Arte della Lana (the centre of the wool trade), produced petitions that expressed their demands in an institutional register (criticism of the tax system, the demand for equality), organised a militia, formed a guild, and tried to govern the city – albeit without success. Equally interesting are the revolt of the Maillotins in Paris (1382) and the uprisings in Ghent (1338–1349, 1379–1382, 1449–1453) – both at the heart of the movement for autonomy and communal representation in the thirteen to fifteenth centuries; or, later, the 'revolt of snowballs' in Venice in 1511.[42] Historical studies remind us of the extreme diversity of actors involved (rulers, elites, artisans and common people), as well as of their demands. Our knowledge of them comes to us only in bits

41 For the Middle Ages, see Jacques Dalarun, *Gouverner c'est servir. Essai de démocratie médiévale* (Paris: Alma, 2012); Patrick Boucheron, *Conjurer la peur (Sienne, 1338). Essai sur la force politique des images* (Paris: Seuil, 2013); Denis Menjot, 'Le mouvement des libertés dans les villes de l'Occident médiéval', in *Belfort 1307, l'éveil à la liberté*, proceedings of the symposium (Belfort, 19–21 October 2006), Belfort, Belfort town hall, 2007, pp. 9-30; Jan Dumolyn, Jelle Haemers, H. R. Oliva Herrer and Vincent Challet, eds, *The Voices of the People in Late Medieval Europe: Communication and Popular Politics* (Turnhout: Brepols, 2014). For the fifteenth to eighteenth centuries, see Olivier Christin, *Vox populi. Une histoire du vote avant le suffrage universel* (Paris: Seuil, 2014).

42 Alessandro Stella, *La Révolte des Ciompi. Les hommes, les lieux, le travail* (Paris: Éditions de l'EHESS, 1993); Claude Gauvard, *Le Temps des Valois (1328–1515)* (Paris: PUF, 2013); Jelle Haemers and Jan Dumolyn, 'A Bad Chicken Was Brooding: Subversive Speech in Late Medieval Flanders', *Past and Present* 214: 1 (2012), pp. 45–86; Claire Judde de Larivière, *La Révolte des boules de neige. Murano face à Venise (1511)* (Paris: Fayard, 2014).

and pieces, which renders tenuous any comparison with the subsequent period. However, some of the elements we do have inevitably arouse curiosity: the role of craftsmen and guilds, which introduced frameworks for action, norms of justice, a sense of order, and the pressing of demands; the existence of a desire for equality, often based on actors' Christian-inspired outlooks; and a multifaceted definition of autonomy and of the 'commons'. Turning to practices, these revolts reveal the destruction of the homes of the wealthy and of churches, strikes, collective assemblies, and examples of legitimacy being conferred through popular acclamation. Added to this are the importance of rumours, irony, manipulations of the calendar, the retrieval of almost forgotten memories, the politics of immediacy, and the desire to mould the real substance of politics.[43]

All this also existed under the Commune in 1871, from the destruction of the Duke of Rivoli's residence to the subversive use of wordplay and puns, carnivalesque practices, and the role played by skilled tradesmen. Does this tell us that the 'roots' of many of the Commune's forms of revolt lie in the twelfth to fifteenth centuries? Such a proposition entails a significant risk of depoliticising the actions of the Paris insurgents, while also flattening out the differences between eras. These same studies show, on the contrary, how far these practices belonged to their own contemporary worlds: a Christian world governed by God, a universe of orders made up of multiple estates and rights, a society largely structured by sociability and practices of personal acquaintance. It was also a world organised around a cyclical relationship with time, or in any case one less inclined towards the idea of 'progress' that would develop after 1750. These practices and expectations were thus effective in their proper context. We are far from the world of the mid-nineteenth century. There seems, then, to be no continuity.

One useful approach to understanding such relations across different eras is hinted at in E. P. Thompson's masterful work on the making of the English working class. He shows in particular how the vocabulary of eighteenth-century artisans was enriched by words stemming from their original rural environments, thus keeping part of their earlier

43 On the retrieval of memories, see Andy Wood, 'History, Time and Social Memory', in Keith Wrightson, ed., *A Social History of England (1500–1750)* (Cambridge: Cambridge University Press, 2017), pp. 373–91.

cultural and political universe with them even as they arrived in a new world.[44] The constant entanglement of references and interlocking of times and universes are surely essential to grasping the problem at stake. The model that seems most effective in accounting for this may be that of 'survivals'. This notion, which refers to a 'being of the past that never ceases to survive', was coined by the art historian Aby Warburg, and subsequently employed by several other researchers, including Georges Didi-Huberman.[45] Initially concerning graphic forms, it was from the outset intended to have a broader scope. In this perspective, these different words, gestures, practices and conceptions that run through time carry meanings that are not fixed, but crystallise differently depending on the context. At the moment of their realisation, they awaken a 'fossilised' meaning and energy, revealing themselves to be both anachronistic and wholly contemporary. Each actualisation thereby simultaneously extends this meaning, adds new possibilities to it, and may also conceal another which, though buried for the moment, may later resurface. These gestures, words and graphic forms appear as a reservoir of action and meaning whose exact origin is no longer of much interest, but which, through their repeated reappropriations, acquire a kind of legitimacy. The attacks on churches were one example of this. These practices of politics are plurivocal, intertwined, discontinuous – ones that can resist both the established authorities and subsequent scholars' attempts to impose formalising frames upon them.

Again, these ideas and practices do not invariably come 'from below'. They may also be age-old traces of confrontations between authorities and subjects, which are subsequently reappropriated by populations (or marked by trans-border circulations before eventually coming to appear 'vernacular' within these spaces and societies). The notion of *bon droit* used among skilled workers in insurgent Paris offers one such example. Some of its features greatly resemble the 'summary justice' of the

44 E. P. Thompson, *The Making of the English Working Class* (London: Victor Gollancz, 1968 [1963]).

45 Georges Didi-Huberman, *L'image survivante. Histoire de l'art et temps des fantômes selon Aby Warburg* (Paris: Éditions de Minuit, 2002), p. 33; Aby Warburg, *Essais florentins* (Paris: Klincksieck, 1990); *L'Atlas Mnémosyne* (Paris: L'Écarquillé, 2012); Carlo Ginzburg, 'De A. Warburg à E. H. Gombrich. Notes sur un problème de méthode' (1966), in Ginzburg, *Mythes, emblèmes, traces. Morphologie et histoire* (Paris: Flammarion, 1989), pp. 39–96.

seventeenth century: a search for conciliation and fair judgement, based on the perceived legitimacy of action, and on the actors' acknowledged lack of formal competence in the law. Anchored in an older legal tradition (natural law), and particularly employed at the time by skilled urban craftsmen, this justice only appeared 'popular' at the end of a long process of social and juridical readjustments.[46] Far from a marginal normative practice, *bon droit* was thus the object of beliefs and conceptions drawn from a long-forgotten past, yet tried and tested, and retaining a solid place in nineteenth-century society. This helps explain its credibility and force at the moment of its wider use under the Commune.

But, if it is necessary for the historian to restore this temporal depth, it is evident that the link is not that of a continuous thread. Rather, it takes on the form of fossilised fragments of the past: more or less connected, fixed for a time and then detached, marked by earlier realisations without being reducible to them, and above all gaining meaning in the moment of action. In the Commune's case, such survivals are visible, for example, in the demand for popular justice, in the ideal of urban autonomy, in the representations of the people – and in the weight of words. Consider the term 'municipal franchises', so heavily laden with medieval resonances, yet so often neglected in analyses of the event. Nor should we overlook the word 'Commune' itself. It has been defined countless times. But in this perspective, it appears as one of those 'Urwörter' (original words) – not in the sense of its etymological origin, but denoting words that are repeatedly borrowed, masked, cross-fertilised, and overloaded with meaning.[47] Attending to this ever-remoulded word, which keeps generating new meanings, helps explain its remarkable evocative power. It is capable of creating a symbolic space – and in the Paris of 1871, its significance exceeded the sum of its usual references (municipal commune, community, the Commune-canton of the 1850s–60s, the revolutionary Commune of 1792–93, the *petit peuple* of the sixteenth century, and the medieval communes – among others).

This way of following the threads of gestures and words seems to offer one of the most convincing means of explaining their presence. It avoids both the analyses that overly reify them – as if they had preserved the same content over centuries – and, worse still, those that refuse to

46 Simona Cerutti, 'Who Is Below?', *Annales. Histoire, Sciences sociales* 70: 4 (2015).

47 In Warburg's and Didi-Huberman's terms.

pause over them at all. By focusing on the way in which the event itself crystallises its own past, it becomes possible for us to acknowledge the preceding worlds with their open trajectories, while at the same time underlining the essential historical depth of these gestures, words and discourses in insurgent Paris in 1871. We may call these 'historically situated depths'.[48]

This perspective therefore allows us to understand those 'popular' practices that are too often – and in fact mistakenly – regarded as 'archaic' or 'outdated'. There remains the question of their transmission. Without doubt, this operates in myriad ways: through these traces of traces, through oral memory, or through the temporal palimpsest of places and buildings. It may also persist through intergenerational family memory, whose original events are long forgotten yet endure in the unspoken or in the form of 'family recipes'. There is likewise an institutional or group memory: skilled trades are well known for reappropriating old elements while simultaneously metamorphosing them – banners, processions, the word *corporation* (guild), and so on. Such transmissions also operated through oppositional writings, or through the folds of official memory and scholarly history, which played a significant role in the nineteenth century. Nor should we overlook the channels of literature and images – from canonical paintings to stereotyped reproductions from the age of mechanisation – or yet others forms closer to practices without discourse. These reprises may occur without any guiding intention. In any case, they seem to be the vehicles for what historians have called 'subterranean memory', in order to account for these latent pasts before taking form in flesh and blood, and in energy once mobilised. The fact that the Communard newspapers invoked these medieval and modern pasts, even only in fragments, shows how available they were for reactivation. And, of course, we must not forget Paris itself: the centuries-old capital bore the imprint of successive social and legal configurations (let us recall that the Hôtel de Ville stands on the site of Étienne Marcel's former Maison aux Piliers, emblem of the Parisian

48 By 'historically situated depths', I mean historically sedimented layers of meaning and practice that resurface within specific contexts. The expression translates the French *profondeurs situées*, which refers not to an unbroken continuity but to fragmented survivals of the past, reactivated and re-signified in the moment of action.

revolt of 1358 and lasting symbol of municipal liberties); it made such plunges into memory possible in 1871.

These practices, with the meanings they carried, allow us to place the Commune within a *longue durée* interlacing of temporalities, which can be pinned down using multiple indices. They give account of the depth and intensity of this event. They can even help to identify mechanisms of politicisation that I have noted too cursorily: if certain actors, for example, turned to iconoclastic or carnivalesque gestures because they had the French Revolution in their memories, others undoubtedly joined in with less deliberate intent – through imitation, or through the need to vent their passions against an imaginary enemy (the real one being out of reach). But, through such gestures, they were aware that they were *doing something*; and this appeal to meaning was certainly not negligible in their access to politicisation, as in their grasp of the references to 1792 or 1793.

Lastly, it is important to note that these gestures and words were significant in the insurgent Paris of 1871, in a twofold sense. First, in terms of their situational relevance: in a revolution, crisis or civil war – particularly in a besieged city – action can often only be directed at one's immediate surroundings. This means confronting the weight of symbols, implicit hierarchies, and the social order woven into the material environment, everyday language, ordinary relations, and even bodies. Second, in terms of their political relevance: many of these features – the embodiment of politics, the interweaving of the economic, social and political spheres of life, and the capacity to create a meaningful experience of time – appear as a fitting response to some of the social dynamics of the nineteenth century mentioned above: the specialisation of different fields of activity, the professionalisation of politics, the growth of long-distance relations, and the mechanisation of time. Such features might indeed have taken form within political projects, such as that of a democratic and social republic, but they also reached beyond it. The insurgent Parisians thus mobilised a resource that both belonged to them and was effective in the struggle. These 'historically situated depths', therefore, found special meaning in insurgent Paris: their apparent anachronism can be read as the expression of plural paths of history, and as an attempt – even if only a temporary one – to reappropriate the alternatives then available through action.

The Untimely Depths: Millenarianism and Democratic Possibilities

Perhaps we can look even further, even deeper? Certain traces suggest so. Take the example of some of the millenarian and apocalyptic tones that emerged within this event. Do they not stem from the millennia-old Christian culture whose long persistence, in various forms, medievalists have constantly pointed out, even into the nineteenth century?[49] Such a reference may seem curious for a revolution that was so imbued with anticlericalism. But while this was indeed a characteristic of the Commune, it did not suppress the need for the sacred. This connection also seems less incongruous if we consider the shifts that took place through the 'mutation of beliefs' in the nineteenth century. This term refers to a cultural shift in which spirituality left the sole purview of the Church, and which also found channels of transmission in republican and socialist movements (utopian socialism, spiritualism, worker rituals, the cult of the Mariannes, and so on).[50] In this sense, with the fracture of the event, the Commune can be included in what the historian Alphonse Dupront has called the phenomenon of 'returns' – more precisely, of the returns of millenarianism, making it possible to feel this shift in time and to think about the breakthrough of another, more just world into the present.[51] Can we add to this the 'dream of equality', also carried by part of this Christian culture – perhaps also a more ancient one, arising occasionally yet recurrently over the course of time?[52] The medievalist Georges Duby, for his part, speaks of this 'very old utopia . . . a society that would no longer divide the classes, and which would not thereby cease to be orderly'.[53]

Should we not follow this lead, up to the very edges of the investigation? It comes up implicitly when researchers speak of the Commune

49 Jacques Le Goff, *Un long Moyen Âge* (Paris: Tallandier, 2004).

50 For the 1850s–70s, see Philippe Boutry, 'Les mutations des croyances', in Jacques Le Goff and René Rémond, eds, *Histoire de la France religieuse, vol. III: Du roi Très Chrétien à la laïcité républicaine (XVIIIe–XIXe siècle)* (Paris: Seuil, 2001), pp. 440–74.

51 Alphonse Dupront, 'Temporel et éternel, anthropologie religieuse et histoire', *in Du sacré. Croisades et pèlerinages* (Paris: Gallimard, 1996), pp. 467–537.

52 Ernst Bloch, *Thomas Münzer als Theologe der Revolution* (Frankfurt: Suhrkamp, 1969 [1921]).

53 Georges Duby, *Les Trois Ordres ou l'Imaginaire du féodalisme* (Paris: Gallimard, 1978), p. 425.

having a 'libertarian' or 'anarchist' character – suggesting its extension beyond the ideas and actions of those who explicitly claimed such political stances. But what does this really mean? Conscious of the problem this poses, Jacques Rougerie spoke of the 'true democracy' of the Commune. Referring to the type of politics at work during the Commune, he also evoked – in the form of an interpretive challenge – a 'first degree of politics'. In any case, observers, historians, sociologists and philosophers have long thought they might perceive something more fundamental at work in the Commune, thus suggesting possible points of contact with other – even distant – societies. This needs further exploration.

So, let us try – with all possible caution – to 'compare the incomparable', within the framework of 'an experimental and constructive type of comparison'.[54] Let us travel to more distant shores. In the depths of the Latin American forests lies the territory of the famous Guayaki Indians, the nomadic hunters in the Paraguayan forest studied by Pierre Clastres.[55] The anthropologist tells us that these people live in an immanent state of freedom and anarchy, in essentially egalitarian relationships – with the exception of women, which is no minor caveat. In Clastres's analysis, these people have, if not necessarily consciously, developed real strategies to avoid being turned into a society with a state: rejecting any leadership set apart from the community, and practising exogamy, self-surveillance, flight, and so on. There are abundant examples of this type of society: the Iroquois confederation, the 'ordered anarchy' of the Nuer, the Kachin of Burma, and the Amazonian Achuar peoples studied by Evans-Pritchard, Edmund Leach and Philippe Descola, respectively. To these can be added the vast, mountainous region stretching from north-east India to the Annamese Cordillera, which James Scott called 'Zomia'.[56]

54 Marcel Detienne, *Comparer l'incomparable* (Paris: Seuil, 2009), p. 173 – transl. into English by Janet Lloyd as *Comparing the Incomparable* (Stanford, CA: Stanford University Press, 2008).

55 Pierre Clastres, *La Société contre l'État. Recherches d'anthropologie politique* (Paris: Éditions de Minuit, 1974) – transl. Robert Hurley and Abe Stein as *Society Against the State: Essays in Political Anthropology* (New York: Zone, 1989).

56 Edward Evans-Pritchard, *The Nuer: A Description of the Modes of Livelihood and Political Institutions of a Nilotic People* (Oxford: Oxford University Press, 1940); Edmund Leach, *Political Systems of Highland Burma* (London: Athlone, 1954); Philippe Descola, *Les Lances du crépuscule. Relations jivaros. Haute-Amazonie* (Paris: Plon, 1993); James

The evidence is thus that many societies far removed (in time or space) from modern Western history have developed practices of decision-making by assemblies, horizontal relations, a concern for equality, or a desire for autonomy – as under the Commune, we might say. It is tempting to establish a connection between them. But what exactly is this relation? Some caution is in order here. The implicit evolutionism of some of the works cited has since been criticised, as has the somewhat instrumental, romantic mobilisation of so-called 'authentic' societies as a political model for the researcher's own present or future. Far from representing the supposed infancy of human society, these forms of organisation are distributed across the planet in both a diachronic and a synchronic manner. Moreover, close observation shows that these societies do not offer complete equality (particularly in terms of age or gender), and they also show more or less enduring tendencies towards hierarchical or vertical relationships.[57] Several studies have also emphasised the precarious conditions on which they are said to depend: communities of limited size; small surpluses preventing social differentiation; the absence of groups defined by inalienable rights; the early internalisation of the values of sharing or friendliness – and so on. Some have suggested that such forms, which correspond to one form of power among others, can only exist outside the state, and more particularly outside the modern state.[58] Here again, no clear link seems to readily present itself.

However, this last claim has itself been contested. According to the prehistorian Alain Testart, a 'democratic tone' is set, over the *longue durée*, in regions marked by truly ancient forms of 'primitive democracy'. Following no predetermined pathway, this democracy can express itself in the most varied forms. For example, in the area that would later be called 'Europe', such forms range from those of ancient Greece to those in contemporary liberal democracies, via the French Revolution.

C. Scott, *The Art of Not Being Governed* (New Haven, CT: Yale University Press: 2009); Thomas Gibson and Kenneth Sillander, eds, *Anarchic Solidarity: Autonomy, Equality, and Fellowship in Southeast Asia* (New Haven, CT: Yale University Press, 2011).

57 For a recent overview, see Riccardo Ciavolella, 'Alterpolitics or Alterotopies: A Critique of Nomadology and Resistance (with Reference to West Africa)', *Focaal. Journal of Global and Historical Anthropology* 72 (2015), pp. 23–36.

58 On these debates, see Bernard Formoso, 'Les sociétés libertaires existent-elles ?', *L'Homme* 209 (2014), pp. 153–70.

In that case, why not the Commune too?[59] For the anthropologist of contemporary alternative movements David Graeber, democratic practices – understood as the egalitarian taking of power in the form of an assembly and, by extension, the rejection of all forms of verticality and hierarchy – are neither a recent nor a Western phenomenon. They can be found throughout human societies, across time. Indeed, Graeber argues, they emerge in the course of specific political and historical circumstances, marked by 'cultural improvisation': forced to make arrangements for themselves, groups of individuals set such processes in motion, resulting in highly variable subsequent realisations.[60] This argument is surely debatable: these situations of improvisation can just as easily lead to other outcomes, such as domination by a charismatic individual, or the formation of some dominant group. But it also has the merit of suggesting that these practices, too, form part of the possible historical configurations of human organisation, often in the form of a tendency. The Commune could then be seen as an actualisation – always an impure and specific one – of this 'potentiality of historical becoming'.[61]

This dimension can be discerned in insurgent Paris – for example, in the incessant debate over the legitimacy of the bearers of authority, in the Commune's forms of local self-organisation, and in the search for equality and fair exchange. It obviously appeared more blurred and uncertain in 1871, amid the flow of events. But perhaps it also helps us to understand why some Communards felt they were experiencing something essential – a kind of eternal justice retrieved from the depths of time – while the Versaillais, conversely, thought they were witnessing the expression of infantile desires, a regressive form of politics that threatened the foundations and the achievements of civilised society. Some of the Versaillais spoke of a 'combination of appetites'; others of a menace to the social, even natural order.[62] Looking beyond their linguistic excesses and conventional metaphors, can we not read in these

59 Alain Testart, *Éléments de classification des sociétés* (Paris: Errance, 2005).

60 David Graeber, 'On Cosmopolitanism and (Vernacular) Democratic Creativity: Or, There Never Was a West', in Pnina Werbner, ed., *Anthropology and the New Cosmopolitanism: Rooted, Feminist and Vernacular Perspectives* (Oxford: Berg, 2008), pp. 281–308.

61 Expression borrowed from Patrick Boucheron, 'L'expérience communale', Collège de France seminar, 2016–2017.

62 Maxime Du Camp, *Les Convulsions de Paris, vol. II: Épisodes de la Commune* (Paris: Hachette, 1879).

characterisations an awkward attempt to express the feeling that something of vast magnitude was unfolding before their eyes – an eruption that struck at part of what philosopher Cornelius Castoriadis calls the 'imaginary institutions' that underpinned established society?[63] In other words, the role accorded to the economic sphere, the hierarchy of positions, the delegation of power, the determination of what is reasonable and what is absurd , and so on. This therefore had to do with part of the 'first degree' of politics, which is manifestly not really 'first' in any strict sense.

For these characteristics did not appear ready-made out of some supposed 'dark night of time', nor out of a fortuitous display of exoticism. Whether ancient or representing a possible form of organisation, these modes of access to power and resources, as the anthropologist Maurice Godelier reminds us, were not in fact entirely erased in Europe by the rise of industrial capitalism and the modern state. Quite the contrary: as an idea and as a possibility, they lodged themselves within these new social, political and cultural structures. As we have seen in the case of industrial capitalism, their emergence consisted of conflicts and constant power struggles. Other structures, born before or alongside them, then continued to coexist. At once persistent, updated and recomposed, these elements were thus intrinsically part of these societies, in diverse guises and through unexpected entanglements.[64] They took shape, probably through the transmission belts and latent forms discussed above, precisely on these occasions. And thus, following the reformulations I have just discussed, they also took form even within the Commune.

This observation has crucial implications. It helps explain the 'family resemblance' that sometimes seems to connect the Commune to other experiences of the 1860s–70s, such as the so-called Kabyle forms of 'democracy', or the egalitarian forms of organisation seen in the Taiping Rebellion (1850–64).[65] At the same time, it explains why these

63 Cornelius Castoriadis, *The Imaginary Institution of Society* (Cambridge: Polity, 1997).

64 Maurice Godelier, 'Karl Polanyi et la "place changeante" de l'économie dans les sociétés', in Godelier, *L'Idéel et le Matériel* (Paris: Fayard, 1984), pp. 231–67.

65 A discussion of these Kabyle political practices, which have given rise to much debate, can be found in Alain Mahé, *Histoire de la Grande Kabylie (XIXe–XXe siècle). Anthropologie historique du lien social dans les communautés villageoises* (Saint-Denis:

experiences appear absolutely incomparable, each being powerfully marked by its own particular historical trajectories. These dimensions always present themselves in this way, as concretions in which various elements are interwoven: it is up to researchers to decide what to examine, and at what level they wish to conduct their inquiry.[66] In any case, these observations suggest that this democratic dimension was present during the Commune; and that something of the 'non-modern' exists within the 'modern' – not in the sense that the former is embedded as such within the latter, but in the sense that the two are always intertwined in multiple combinations. Finally – and most importantly – this may explain why the Commune was later appropriated in other, sometimes very different contexts (in Europe as in Asia, in urban as in rural contexts), through a process of retranslating this experience. In this sense, the Commune can be seen as a short-lived but possible and significant alternative within a movement of 'modernity' that proves more complex than it may appear. Perhaps I have taken this exploration too far. But this was the only way to give a more robust form to what would otherwise have been no more than an impression.

Assessment: The Commune, or the Fractures of the Event

All of these elements, along with the dynamics of the crisis, the projections and the plural perception of the future, fit together. For this reason, they do not take the form of a homogeneous whole, but rather that of a tearing-asunder, of eruption, of contradictions, of concertina-effects. Given such considerations, it makes little sense to insist on firm distinctions between the old and the new. The Commune is a heterochrony – a different, singular and unstable arrangement of time. And therein probably lies the last temporality to be addressed: that of the seismic. Given

---

Bouchène, 2001). Élisée Reclus was one early proponent of such comparisons: see Reclus, 'La solidarité chez les Berbères', *Le Travailleur*, September 1877. On the Taiping Rebellion, see Stephen Platt, *Autumn in the Heavenly Kingdom: China, the West and the Epic Story of the Taiping Civil War* (London: Atlantic, 2012).

66 Examples of such 'family resemblances' can be found in S. Cerutti and I. Grangaud, 'Comparer par cas. Esquisse d'un projet comparatiste', in Antoine Lilti, Sabina Loriga, Jean-Frédéric Schaub and Silvia Sebastiani, eds, *L'Expérience historiographique. Autour de Jacques Revel* (Paris: Éditions de l'EHESS, 2016), pp. 151–62.

its seventy-two-day lifespan, the Commune was above all a movement, a revolution in the making, which was brutally cut short. This is why it is impossible to assign it any simple or fixed meaning. The Paris insurrection was marked by a collapse of the previous form of social organisation, several of whose features persisted even as other dynamics and possibilities arose. Here and there, they took the form of rough outlines or partial realisations. It is as if, on this occasion, the time of history described by Cornelius Castoriadis was made manifest – that time of societies' self-alteration which shakes up the instituting work of instituted things and can open up unprecedented spaces of action.[67] Here, indeed, lies the creative dimension of the event: amid this turmoil, something new emerged – this Paris Commune, with its uncertain contours and original practices – an alternative political form after which there is no going back to the past. For now, the Commune should perhaps be left in this state of tremor. Only this can account for its contradictions and oppositions, the persistence of its routines and its inventiveness, its alternating periods of atony and intensity, its richness of action, its moments of hatred and hope. Only this can make sense of this government of Paris and of the singular breakthroughs that took place.

67 Castoriadis, *Imaginary Institution of Society*.

Conclusion to Part II: The Creation of Worlds, on Both Sides of the Ramparts

We have all risen up en masse
For you, it is a time of danger.
We will hunt you down;
You are foreigners to us;
France has risen up against you,
Along with its red flag.
Our Republic is saved:
Tyrants, descend into your graves.

Song written during the Commune,
lyrics by Ferré Léger, to the tune
of Pierre Dupont's 'Chant des soldats'

It is now easier to understand why many Parisians felt they were living through an extraordinary – and, for others, incongruous – moment. But is such a combination of elements not to be found in all insurrections and revolutions, particularly in the nineteenth century? The conditions that made them possible can always be identified after the event; each of these revolts has its own logic of crisis, and includes an emergence of new perceptions of historical time, a crystallisation of expectations, or a hybridisation of historical dynamics. And the result is invariably unique – due to interdependence effects, the ways in which things play out and are replayed, power struggles, and the ultimately unpredictable outcomes.

Such is the case with the Commune: steeped in the circumstances of war and the political transition, marked by the social, political and intellectual context of the latter half of the nineteenth century, as well as by the coalescence of the times just described. It therefore, of course, had its own specific features, including the active and distinctive definition of 'the people', its international dimension, the importance attached to the question of labour, and its popular sovereignty *in actu* – a creative process that paradoxically also hindered its organisational capacity. Two additional elements must be taken into account, however: first, its abrupt interruption, which leaves its interpretation particularly open; second, its confinement to the Parisian space, which undoubtedly gave its dynamic a remarkable intensity. This, in turn, recalls a third point: the Parisian event unfolded in the face of a clearly identified external world and actors. This fact, and the interactions that followed from it, are a final important element. It is as if two dynamics were at work: one 'from within' (the Commune) and one 'from without' (Versailles and, with it, the other governments in power at the time). These two factors were connected, defining and influencing each other; yet each also had its own rhythms, accentuated by their opposition. Thus, over the course of the conflict, the Commune gradually became the site of one of the temporal 'discordances' of the nineteenth century identified by Christophe Charle – one that also tended towards a discordance between worlds, at once close and alien.

This may explain why even those who were initially sympathetic to the Commune, but did not share the Parisian experience on the ground, could remain circumspect, or even turn hostile. More generally, it may help to explain the persistent impression that the Commune seemed both small in itself, and yet an extraordinarily powerful moment.

Here, some light is shed on one of our initial questions: if the Commune had such an impact despite its brevity, this was because the event, while fleeting, was also politically meaningful, open and profound. To this we can add – to pursue the previous conclusion – the fact that it took place in the era of mass media, in a city that was the capital of revolutions and of the world's second-greatest power. The clash of worlds was then inevitable. Everyone sensed the dramatic scope of the struggle to come. Even the return to order forced the winning side and its supporters into difficult arrangements, which in turn would have clear effects at the local, national and transnational levels.

PART III

The Commune Transformed (1871–1880)

Police and thieves in the streets, oh yeah
Scaring the nation with their guns and ammunition
Police and thieves in the street, oh yeah
Fighting the nation with their guns and ammunition
From genesis to revelation
The next generation will be, hear me

'Police and Thieves'
Junior Murvin (1976) / The Clash (1977)

7:45 a.m. – I have just witnessed the darkest fury, caught doing its sinister work. I headed into this magnificent city as it was hauled before the firing squad. Architectural glory disappearing in the flames and fires. Moscow amid the noise of cannons, machine guns, projectiles, the magnificent sunshine. Many buildings remain untouched. This luckless city – covering the light of the civilised sun – is surrendered to the implacable scourge of fire. The newspapers are saying that the Foreign Minister is expressing his emotion, after the events of the moment, without any outburst. Smoke, metal and stone . . . The

> Versaillais army advances, much more as rebels than apostles. We know the terrible drama of this ill-fated city which protested an existing power, watched on by the population with stupefied silence. Freedom – a claim on the right to advance, as the last watchword and way of expression, condemned for centuries. Everything is weeping, and not just the major buildings or public edifices. Its cause: not only mature consideration, but also a means as simple as it is frightening: by emptying the city through adoration and by a brief but fruitless enthusiasm, it has set it ablaze *with a match of brute force.*[1]

As the final engagement began, both in France and abroad attention to events in Paris intensified. With this came a surge of commentary. We can only be impressed, overwhelmed even, by the flood of discourse that accompanied and then followed the struggle between Paris and Versailles. The above text is created from newspaper reports of the Bloody Week, using the cut-up technique developed in the 1950s by the poets William Burroughs and Brion Gysin. For its two creators, this practice of cutting up and randomly reassembling texts was meant to smash the implicit mechanisms of the dominant media discourse, to reveal its unconscious imaginaries, and ultimately to use the poetic breaches thus created to break through them.[2]

It is up to the reader to judge this effect. For the historian, this exercise itself helps to recreate the impression of being crushed by words. By its tropes and their variations, it also reveals in a raw fashion the discursive continent of the post-Commune, which buried the event without ever exhausting its meaning. Narration is often somehow linked to order, and the narrative that took the Commune at its word after May 1871 had a particular solidity. In this same movement, however, the fragmented text above hints at the internal contradictions of the clichés that have been repeated in so many different ways. In places, it tears away their veil, and as the absurd comes to the fore it sheds a light on the threads and knots that so clumsily attempt to tie together words and things. The attentive observer then sees a sap that still runs beneath the

1 My emphasis.

2 William S. Burroughs, 'The Cut-Up Method of Brion Gysin', 1962 (robertspahr.com/teaching/map2/cutup_gysin_burrough.pdf). The papers used here are *The Times*, 25 May 1871; *L'Indépendance belge*, 27 May 1871; and Giuseppe Mazzini's article 'The Commune in Paris', published in the *Contemporary Review*, June 1871.

petrified roots. Powerful on the Versailles side, the flood of discourse also has its counterpart on the side of the rebellion.

The focus of Part III is this strange interplay of order and disorder. After looking back to the end of the Commune, it will address the recomposition of the French political space, the adjustments in European and imperial power relations, and then the way in which the Commune's still-vivid past was expressed across several parts of the world. Getting to grips with the aftermath and the effects of an event is no easy task: the further we move away from the starting point, the more artificial the connections seem. Hence our archival investigation, properly speaking, has focused on the 1871–72 period, before drawing connections as late as the 1880s on certain themes. Many studies consider this period as a turning point in the history of France, Europe and the world. This is confirmed here. It brings to a close the first phase of this 'Commune moment', in the broadest sense – before, of course, other stories and intersections begin once again.

9

Putting an End to the Civil War: France

At 3.00 in the afternoon on 21 May 1871, a company of the 37th March battalion, supported by artillerymen and some soldiers from the 91st, crossed into Paris via the Porte de Saint-Cloud. The reconquest of the old capital had begun. The troops' march through the city would be held back by the barricades, especially once they reached a line running from Montmartre to Parc Montsouris; they were also slowed by their own caution, born of the fear that a mined street or sewer could explode at any moment. But given the sheer number of troops and cannons on the Versaillais side, their victory over a disorganised National Guard was almost certain. Their recapture of Paris was a bloody affair, punctuated by killings behind the barricades and summary executions. It ended in the early afternoon of 28 May, with the defeat of the barricade on the rue de la Fontaine-au-Roi.

This reconquest of Paris, known as the *Semaine Sanglante*, or 'Bloody Week', is one of the major symbolic moments in French history. Each of its episodes – the execution of the hostages, the burning of the city, the large-scale massacre of the insurgents – has been widely examined and analysed. But the debates are still ongoing. And despite the abundance of books on the subject, there has not yet been a study of the dual *sorties de guerre* from both the international and civil wars on a scale comparable to those that exist in the cases of the Napoleonic Empire, the American Civil War, or the Great War.[1]

1 Recent works focus more on memory: Karine Varley, *Under the Shadow of Defeat: The War of 1870–71 in French Memory* (Basingstoke: Palgrave Macmillan, 2008);

Without claiming to fill this gap, this chapter focuses on the way in which order was gradually re-established, and what this 'order' entailed. First, however, we must look back at the key moments of the recapture of Paris, in flames and bloodshed.

Paris in Flames, or the Urban Apocalypse

When the troops entered Paris through the Porte de Saint-Cloud, the soldiers discovered the men and women who had in previous weeks taken on the appearance of an absolute enemy. The encounter worked both ways. The information on the atrocities committed by one side, magnified by rumours, generally pushed the other side to a new and higher threshold of violence, with each side in turn stepping up the brutality of the conflict. Only on the morning of 22 May did the insurgent Parisians learn that the Versaillais had made their way into the city. They then discovered the existence of special units scouring the neighbourhoods of Paris, which arrested people on the slightest suspicion and then killed them. In response, alongside the building of barricades, the Communards began, from 23 May onwards, the execution of hostages taken in previous weeks – churchmen, gendarmes, neighbourhood policemen, judges and bankers. The most famous were the archbishop of Paris, Monseigneur Darboy, who was put to death on 24 May, and in particular the fifty hostages in the rue Haxo on 26 May. There were a hundred in all, put to death sometimes on the orders of the members of the Commune, sometimes by a frenzied crowd. These acts, against men

---

Stéphane Tison, *Comment sortir de la guerre? Deuil, mémoire et traumatisme (1870–1940)* (Rennes: Presses universitaires de Rennes, 2011). A work of social and political history is Jean-François Chanet, *Vers l'armée nouvelle. République conservatrice et réforme militaire* (Rennes: Presses universitaires de Rennes, 2006).

TN: *sorties de guerre*: A term of art in French historiography – literally, the study of the 'the ways out of wars'.

For the Empire, see David A. Bell, *The First Total War: Napoleon's Europe and the Birth of Warfare as We Know It* (Boston: Houghton Mifflin, 2007); Natalie Petiteau, *Lendemains d'Empire. Les soldats de Napoléon dans la France du XIXe siècle* (Paris: La Boutique de l'histoire, 2003). For the US Civil War, see Drew G. Faust, *This Republic of Suffering: Death and the American Civil War* (New York: Knopf, 2008). For the Great War, see Bruno Cabanes, *La Victoire endeuillée. La sortie de guerre des soldats français (1918–1920)* (Paris: Seuil, 2004).

who were soon held up as martyrs, surely stirred many fears. Yet, especially in the press outside the French capital, these killings made less of an impact than did the simultaneous burning of several Parisian monuments: the Hôtel de Ville, the Palais de Justice, the Cour des Comptes, the Palais des Tuileries, and so on.[2] While these fires were objects of fascination, they were long overlooked by historical research, until the recent works of Jean-Claude Caron, Éric Fournier and Bertrand Tillier.[3]

We now know that the idea of setting these fires did not come out of nowhere. Threats of such actions had begun in Paris with the first defeats in April, and then became more frequent. 'Paris is determined to do anything', warned *Le Cri du peuple* on 16 May. 'Paris will win or, if it succumbs, it will engulf the victors in an appalling catastrophe.' As police archives and the participants' memoirs reveal, this same imprecation echoed through the debates in the clubs and in ordinary discussions. Speakers and journalists of the Commune habitually associated this threat with other famous fires: the Moscow fire that interrupted Napoleon's campaign (1812), the blaze at a theatre packed with spectators in Zaragoza (1778), or the fire in Rome in the first century AD, blamed on Nero, which destroyed a large part of the city. These references were another reminder of the Communards' desire to set their experience within a grand History, as well as expressing the apocalyptic tone of the last days. The Délégation Scientifique aux Armes Nouvelles, set up on 22 April under the direction of Louis-François Parisel, breathed further life into this idea of destruction. As we have seen, its mission was to create the ultimate weapon – whether a so-called 'Greek fire' or some alternative – which would enable a rapid and total victory. But its work proved to be in vain. No more was achieved than to establish the location of several oil depots. At this stage, the fire still belonged to the Communard imagination.

The turning point came later, with the Versaillais assault. On 23 May, the Hôtel de Ville gave the order to burn houses. This decision was part

2 Jean-Claude Caron notes that military archives say little about this: Jean-Claude Caron, *Les Feux de la discorde. Conflits et incendies dans la France du XIXe siècle* (Paris: Hachette, 2006).

3 Ibid.; Éric Fournier, *Paris en ruines. Du Paris Haussmannien au Paris communard* (Paris: Imago, 2008); Bertrand Tillier, *La Commune de Paris, révolution sans images? Politique et représentations dans la France républicaine (1871–1914)* (Seyssel: Champ Vallon, 2004).

of the fight against the traitors, but it was also a military tactic: insofar as the Versaillais could get around the barricades by passing through the adjoining houses, these fires were meant to serve as a protective barrier.

From 23 to 24 May, the Hôtel de Ville was no longer in control of the situation. An erratic period began, in which units of National Guards kept up their resistance despite their increasing isolation, while many Parisians hid in buildings. It is difficult to say, amid such confusion, whether orders were being followed or whether the initiatives taken were spontaneous ones. We do know that the butcher's assistant Bénot and General Bergeret participated in the burning of the Tuileries. In many cases the decisions were intertwined, not to mention the fact that these blazes surely had a 'signal effect' on each other. Historians have recorded 238 fires, ignited by the most varied means. To these could be added those others that were prepared but not set. On 24 May, Father Prampain described the college where he taught, Vaugirard, as it was found after the departure of Gustave Flourens's avengers: 'In the room, in the classrooms, there were torn up books and straw sprayed with oil or petrol and packages of cartridges. Trails of gunpowder linked all these pyres to the stairs. All that was needed was a flame, and the building would have turned to dust.'[4] The destruction struck at various targets (rue de Rivoli, rue de Lille, the warehouses at La Villette), but the most notable were the prestigious buildings mentioned above.

Not all of Paris was set ablaze. But the fires gave the army's penetration into the city the tone of an extreme end-times, which was felt by contemporaries both inside and outside Paris. Shortly after these events, Malvina Blanchecotte used her literary talent to convey her own impressions. Here, the fires merged with the war against the *fédérés*: 'This is the extermination of the world', she wrote on 23 May.[5] 'Who has not witnessed this game of chance from such an observatory [she was perched on a belvedere], that of bombs hurled furiously at a city, cannot imagine this frightening spectacle. . . . And all of a sudden, the sky is ablaze! The Tuileries are burning, the Hôtel de Ville is burning.' Outside

4 R. P. Édouard Prampain, *Souvenirs de Vaugirard. Mon journal pendant le siège et pendant la Commune*, 2nd edn (Paris: Lecoffre, 1888). The events took place on 22 May.

5 Malvina Blanchecotte, *Tablettes d'une femme pendant la Commune* (Paris: Didier, 1872).

the ramparts, in Argenteuil, where he was taking refuge, the *calicot* Xavier-Édouard Lejeune was taken aback. On the night of 26–27 May, the entire population, awakened by a tremendous explosion, headed to the banks of the Seine. 'Then we saw sprays of flame rising above Paris into the clouds. . . . We stayed till dawn, in front of this terrifying spectacle.'[6] One common theme of these accounts is the burned pieces of paper that blew out of the windows of the torched ministries and rained down several miles away. Everyone – first and foremost men of letters – spoke of how powerless words were to convey what seemed a quite unspeakable experience.

This feeling, to be sure, was voiced at each of the great political and social dramas that shook France, including after the terrible scenes of June 1848. The impression of exceptionalism that clings to such extreme situations ought not to mislead us: the history of paroxysmal moments teaches that they were more frequent than historians have often believed.[7] But is there something to be said about these actions taken amid the turmoil – these fires which were long associated with pure madness? We can surely not overlook the fact that there was some measure of irrationality involved, owing to fear. Nor can the fires' defensive significance be ignored. The chronology of the blazes followed the defeats of the *fédéré* troops – and, clearly, one of their objectives was to shield these combatants' retreat. But such observations do not alone explain everything. In his meticulous study of the methods of destruction, Éric Fournier speaks of 'buried rationalities'. Enlightened by the knowledge of the previous weeks, perhaps we can now attempt to unearth them. Three elements are especially worth highlighting.

The first is *sensory and psychological*. With civil war, revolution and war, the atmosphere of the insurgent city was transformed, notably through the effects of popular exaltation, anxiety and disorientation. Far from being a merely individual matter, this psychological dimension

6 Xavier-Édouard Lejeune, *Calicot. Enquête de Michel et Philippe Lejeune* (Paris: Arthaud-Montalba, 1984).

7 Christian Ingrao, *Le Soleil noir du paroxysme. Nazisme, violence de guerre et temps present* (Paris: Odile Jacob, 2021); Malika Rahal, 'From One Civil War to Another: A History of Paroxysms', *History and Memory* 24: 1 (Spring/Summer 2012), pp. 118–51. I also refer here to the seminar 'Explorations of Paroxysm: Traces, Objects, Perspectives (19th–21st Century)', which I organised with Christian Ingrao and Hervé Mazurel in Paris between 2013 and 2017.

was an integral part of the event itself. It contributed to the qualitative mutation of historical time discussed earlier. In certain places and times, as we have seen, the texture of the city changed, and this made a different future a conceivable possibility, particularly for those most committed to the Commune. Yet these same conditions probably allowed for an inverse state of mind that made conceivable the outright destruction of the city as the troops advanced.

The second element is more *sociological and political*. These attacks concerned emblematic sites of power or culture. These were central, monumental and symbolic places, which were usually off-limits to a large part of the capital's population. After 18 March, many Parisians of various social profiles had challenged these hierarchies by visiting or occupying these same places: the Commune was a time of appropriation – albeit partial – of the buildings from which the population was generally excluded. This reconquest of the city by the 'people of Paris' was, moreover, one of the certainties of an episode whose content could sometimes appear blurred. So, it is quite conceivable that in this supreme moment, for some of the final combatants, it was unbearable to give up what had earlier been reconquered. These same places – the Hôtel de Ville, the Louvre, the Cour des Comptes, the ministries – were precisely the sites through which the world of the past, with its litany of political, social and cultural barriers, was to be re-established. Since these places were such a palpable sign of the return to the previous state of things, it perhaps made sense to resort to the desperate act of erasing them.

The last perspective is an *anthropological* one – even if this risks launching us into overly general considerations. The element of fire is hardly absent from the imaginary of the 'modern soul'. Rather than having a simple and vague 'purifying' role, it fulfils several functions. First of all, it is a moment of division: it destroys odours, separates the elements, and leaves impurities.[8] Perhaps the fires in Paris played this role: for the buildings concerned were associated with a certain Parisian identity, as indeed the Versaillais and international press noticed at the time. In this sense, these fires could function as a way of appropriating this Parisian identity one last time, which would be – as it was – brought to a halt with the Commune, leaving the victors with nothing but a pile

8 Gaston Bachelard, *La Psychanalyse du feu* (Paris: Gallimard, 1938); 'L'incendie', special issue of the *Revue d'histoire du XIXe siècle* (1996).

of impurities, in the form of ashes. Fire, moreover, has a temporal function, as a means of access to transcendence. In the face of defeat, it could appear to have marked an attempt to *stop time* – in other words, a desire to freeze in flames what had been and was irretrievably going to disappear after the defeat: namely, the experience of the Paris Commune itself. These 'crazy' gestures can thus be read as a way of reasserting control, once failure was already certain, over the erasure-effect that the winners' history was bound to impose. These acts appear here as another aspect of the *war over time* identified above.

These dimensions go together. Once again, the fire-starters did not need to be specifically aware of this to know that their actions bore a great deal of meaning. The preparation necessary for the fires (making the wicks, transporting the turpentine, and so on) suggests this, as does the reaction of the rest of society, both French and international, which was clearly aware how significant these acts were. Such an interpretation may seem exaggerated; but to view these flames only from a distance would be a mistake. These fires were evidence of the rivalry between the different worlds identified above, and can thus be read as a trace of the last impulses of the Communard dynamic, in particular among those for whom the fight was an unavoidable duty. At the same time, however, they would become the focus of the irreversible mutual incomprehension between the Communard adventure and the rest of the so-called 'civilised' world.

Trouble in the Civilising Process? The Bloody Week

In the heat of battle, the fires further heightened the ferocity of the Versaillais forces. Yet this was not the only factor, and the massacre of the hostages also fuelled this process. For the soldiers, the fact that the barricades had been placed under the stewardship of women, the elderly, and the youngest – also indicating that the Parisian struggle was a popular, family and neighbourhood affair – confirmed the worst stereotypes about their opponents' barbarity and lack of humanity. These Versaillais fighters were not, as has long been said, drunken and boorish country folk. In his classic study, Robert Tombs has reconstructed the steps taken by the government to build up the forces that would be deployed to reconquer the city. It mobilised soldiers from the Franco-Prussian conflict, liberated prisoners of war, *francs-tireurs*, National Guardsmen and some volunteers. In April, Germany had agreed to an increase in the number of soldiers in the French army: 130,000 men could be assembled at Versailles. The command, made up of officers defeated in the Franco-Prussian War and anxious to regain their legitimacy, was slowly reorganised. The troops, reluctant to wage civil war against their French compatriots, were then placed under strict control. At the same time, they were subjected to targeted propaganda that portrayed the Communards in the darkest possible light. Despite the short intervals of time involved, the force that finally made its way into Paris was, indeed, an army.

The killings were terrible. They constitute the other great historical issue posed by the episode. They were fuelled by fear, by the heat of the action, and by a hatred renewed upon encountering the insurgents. The rumours of terrifying *pétroleuses* eager to set the city ablaze, or the disturbing spectre of women bringing the soldiers drinks spiked with poison, doubtless stirred animosity.[9] But the brutality of the killings was also owed to the culture of following orders and the battalions' driving effect, sweeping the men along. Executions were carried out sometimes with bayonets behind the barricades, mostly in the form of summary executions or shootings. They are indicative of a change in the methods of repression that had taken place since the early nineteenth century, methods increasingly carried out in series and from a distance – in other words, more industrial.[10] Finally, the command on the spot, and their political orientation, was also decisive. The worst abuses took place under the orders of the most conservative officers, driven by hatred for the lower orders of society, such as Captain Garcin or General Galliffet. In the north, the operations headed by the republican General Clinchant showed greater clemency.

The massacre proceeded in several stages. First came the deaths in battle, which were relatively few in number given the crushing superiority of the Versailles army, at least until it reached the bastions in north-eastern Paris. Then came the massacre of Communard fighters behind

---

9 Loïc Cadiet et al., eds, *Figures de femmes criminelles* (Paris: Publications de la Sorbonne, 2010).

10 Alain Corbin, 'Le sang de Paris. Réflexions sur la généalogie de l'image de la capitale', in Corbin, *Le Temps, le Désir et l'Horreur. Essais sur le XIXe siècle* (Paris: Flammarion, 1998).

the revolutionary barricades, and with it the mopping-up operations conducted by the Versaillais special units mentioned above. In this context, having blackened hands – a likely sign of having handled gunpowder – was a death sentence. Others were subjected to impromptu trials, under the authority of sector-level officers, and in a later phase brought before more properly constituted military tribunals, the most fearsome of which was set up the Palais du Luxembourg. Here again, after a selection process, men, women and children were shot at various sites (the École Militaire, the Place Vendôme, the Mazas prison, and so on). The bodies were buried in a hurry, often without identification, or were heaped up, burned, and buried in mass graves. The executions continued until June. They were halted under the pressure of protests from moderates and radicals within France, but also of international criticism, including a campaign orchestrated by *The Times*.

How should this massacre be interpreted? The question may begin at a simpler level: How many people died? This assessment has recently been the subject of debate among historians. Initially, the figure of 30,000 deaths was used, although several researchers have lowered this estimate to between 17,000 and 25,000 deaths. A first downward revision was proposed by Robert Tombs at the end of his investigation into the 'war against Paris', at around 12,000 dead. In 2011, after a careful examination of the sources, the British historian suggested a death toll of between 6,500 and 7,500, all the while emphasising that this massacre remains 'the worst single episode of civil violence in Western Europe between the French and Russian revolutions'.[11] This reduced estimate nonetheless caused a stir among specialists, before it was subjected to challenge.[12] This war of numbers is mainly of interest for its underlying assumptions. According to Robert Tombs, the reduced number better corresponds to the result of a war between two armies. It re-evaluates the action of the *fédérés* who, despite their disorganisation, were at times able to put up solid resistance, and suggests that, despite the atrocities

11 Robert Tombs, 'How Bloody Was *la Semaine Sanglante*? A Revision', *H-France Salon* 3: 1 (2011), pp. 1–13 – subsequently 'How Bloody Was the *Semaine Sanglante* of 1871? A Revision', *Historical Journal* 55: 3 (2012), pp. 679–704. Citation from the author's reply to comments in pdf available at h-france.net, p. 3.

12 John Merriman, *Massacre: The Life and Death of the Paris Commune* (New York, Basic Books, 2014). See also the remarks in Jean-Louis Robert, 'Une histoire politique de la Commune', in Robert, ed., *Le Paris de la Commune (1871)* (Paris: Belin, 2015), p. 46.

that obviously took place, the Versaillais army was relatively restrained by its superior organisation and command. In this light, the massacre could be deemed more akin to a purge mounted and controlled by the state – and, in a sense, this makes it no less terrible.[13] According to Tombs, this new figure should in turn allow for a more detached reflection on the exercise of violence at that time. In particular, he claims that it offers an opportunity to distinguish the massacre itself from the 'myth' of the Bloody Week.[14] From this perspective, the idea of absolute violence which has so captivated historians seems more of a discursive reconstruction bound to the logics of memorial in the two camps, though they adopt it for opposite reasons; beyond that, the sense of apocalypse is, for Tombs, also the product of the gradual transformation of sensitivities to violence in the later nineteenth century, also finding expression here.[15] But critics of the reduction of the estimated death toll point to the scientific and political risk of normalising a massacre that truly was exceptional. In their view, a high figure would better reflect the social war that took place, fuelled by the hatred of bourgeois newspapers and MPs since the beginning of the nineteenth century. Other arguments have been advanced: the new government had to put a definitive end to revolutionary activities in the capital; and finally, in anthropological terms, after an acute time of crisis, the use of such extreme violence is one of the possible means of refounding the regime, and indeed the idea of law itself.[16]

May 1871: State violence and 'dyscivilisation'

Once again, Robert Tombs is to be credited with opening up the important question of state violence – a discussion that has been stifled by the repetition of one same horrified narrative. But it may be that the interpretation of this episode is not limited to this one dispute, and that perhaps more clarification is needed as to what made this massacre unprecedented. Firstly, the fact that the army was better organised and commanded, in a

13 Tombs, *The War Against Paris*.

14 Tombs, 'How Bloody Was the *Semaine Sanglante* of 1871?', pp. 699–704.

15 Alex Dowdall, 'Narrating *la Semaine Sanglante* (1871–1880)', MPhil thesis, University of Cambridge (2010); Corbin, 'Le sang de Paris'. The number of homicides fell from 1.24 per 100,000 in 1826 to 0.69 in 1861–65.

16 Corbin, 'Le sang de Paris'.

context of rising thresholds of tolerance to violence, may – paradoxically – have led to a more intense exercise of violence. This is what Norbert Elias, whose analytical framework here serves as a point of reference, called the 'decivilisation' process. The idea was later honed further by the sociologist Abram de Swaan, who proposed the term 'dyscivilisation'.[17] By this he meant the fact that, in societies, such as 1860s France, where the state was asserting itself in its so-called modern form – where the ties of interdependence were growing, and serving as a restraint of affects – this so-called 'civilising' process could in some circumstances be reversed, particularly when a population designated as oppositional or outside the body of society was targeted. This kind of case entailed especially intense violence, because the state could draw on unprecedentedly powerful technical and organisational means. Such violence could also be confined within circumscribed boundaries, even as the rest of society continued to live according to its usual norms or, in – as in this case of the end of a war – its expected norms. This definition corresponds well to the Bloody Week: the spatial confinement, the co-construction of a despised figure of the Other, the media's propagation of hateful speech, the government's assertion of the maintenance of 'normality' – and so on. The damage done to the newly asserted norms of sensibility, or unease at the sheer scale of the killings, did not derail this overall trend. On the contrary, they correspond to what the sociologist has called a 'compartmentalisation' process. As twentieth-century history has shown, the greater control of the army and the reduced abundance of interpersonal attacks in ordinary situations do not together guarantee a lower number of victims in such contexts. Significantly, the most recent re-evaluations once again place the number of killings at between 10,000 and 15,000.[18]

17 On decivilisation, see Norbert Elias, *La Société des individus* (Paris: Fayard, 1991 – first German edition 1983), and *Les Allemands. Luttes de pouvoir et développement de l'habitus aux XIXe et XXe siècles* (Paris: Seuil, 2017). On 'dyscivilisation', see Abram de Swaan, 'La dyscivilisation, l'extermination de masse et l'État', in Yves Bonny, Jean-Manuel de Queiroz and Erik Neveu, eds, *Norbert Elias et la théorie de la civilisation. Lectures et critiques* (Rennes: Presses universitaires de Rennes, 2003), pp. 63–73 – and more recently his *Diviser pour tuer. Les régimes génocidaires et leurs hommes de main* (Paris: Seuil, 2016).

18 See, for example, Michèle Audin, *La Semaine sanglante. Mai 1871, légendes et comptes* (Montreuil: Libertalia, 2021).

Social repression, colonial repression

Yet the intensity of the social war in Paris, and of the associated determination to annihilate the enemy, can be put into perspective if we make a comparison with the colonial war – which was also a racial war – taking place at the same time in Algeria. The comparison is justified because these operations took place on two pieces of French territory, they overlapped in time (from the last week of May to early June, in one case; the period from May to October, in the other), and they were in some ways directly connected. Indeed, some of the troops required to contain the Algerian insurrection were held up in metropolitan France because of the events in Paris and the other Communes (Lyon and Marseille). Rather less consequentially, many of the Versaillais soldiers least willing to fight were sent to Algeria as punishment. However, the two battlefields were hardly the same. In Algeria, more than in the Parisian case, several different forces were involved (both European and native-Algerian local units, the regular army from France, and urban militias that committed many abuses).[19] They operated in 340 short and localised confrontations, spread over a period of five to eight months, and across vast territory. In Paris, the struggle mobilised a more coherent military force, lasted less than a fortnight, and remained confined to the city or around its ramparts.[20] For the purposes of direct comparison, I will concentrate here on the methods and intensity of the killings.

The insurgents' ways of fighting were markedly different in these two cases. The Algerian insurgents cut up and mutilated the bodies of some of their victims after the fighting, in this following a precise aim and grammar that historians of combat have shown us how to examine.[21] It was not that they acted beyond the laws of war: indeed, more often than not, the combatants seem to have respected the prescriptions of Islamic law in sparing non-combatants, as recalled by Sheikh El-Haddad upon the proclamation of the jihad. In Palestro, for example, where the most publicised killings took place, the mutilated bodies belonged to male

19 *Rapport fait au nom de la commission d'enquête sur les actes du gouvernement de la Défense nationale. Algérie*, by Monsieur de La Sicotière, a member of the National Assembly (Versailles: Cerf & fils, 1875).

20 An estimated 600,000 people fled the city in May.

21 Stéphane Audoin-Rouzeau, *Combattre. Une anthropologie historique de la guerre moderne (XIXe–XXe siècle)* (Paris: Seuil, 2008).

combatants in the prime of their lives. A total of forty-two women, elderly people and children were taken prisoner.[22] The Parisian *fédérés* carried out no attacks of this type – they did not have the time to do so. Most importantly, even if such acts remained part of the imaginary of the massacre, inspired in particular by memories of the French Revolution, they did not belong, or no longer belonged, to the repertoire of insurrectionary action in metropolitan France, and particularly its cities.[23] Two different cultures of combat operated here, on either side of the Mediterranean. Ultimately, in both cases the number of soldiers killed by the insurgents was rather limited, not least given the military superiority of the regular army: around a thousand regular troops died in Paris, and 2,686 in Algeria (more than half of them from disease).

Of more direct interest to us here are the repressive practices used in the two cases. Counting the number of insurgent victims in Paris is a delicate task, much as in the Algerian context. Using the lowest of the new range of figures, the number of Parisian deaths is estimated at 10,000 out of a population of a little less than 2 million inhabitants, faced with a force of some 110,000 men (and then faced with the courts). In Algeria the data are more volatile: the minimum estimate of the number of Algerian victims of summary executions is 2,000 dead for 200,000 combatants, against a force of around 90,000 men at the height of the uprising. However, some counting methods multiply this figure tenfold or consider the insurgent populations as a whole: some 800,000 individuals.[24] Any comparison is tricky.

---

22 Louis Rinn, *Histoire de l'insurrection de 1871 en Algérie* (Villers-Cotterêts: Ressouvenances, 2016 [1891]), p. 310. The fact is mentioned in several works on the insurrection.

23 The case of the countryside is different, although this change in the forms of recourse to violence is also perceptible. See Alain Corbin, 'La violence rurale dans la France du XIXe siècle et son dépérissement: l'évolution de l'interprétation politique', *Cultures et conflits* 9–10 (1993), pp. 61–73.

24 Figures taken from Mohammed Brahim Salhi, 'L'insurrection de 1871', in Abderrahmane Bouchène, Jean-Pierre Peyroulou, Ouanassa Siari-Tengour and Sylvie Thénault, eds, *Histoire de l'Algérie à la période coloniale (1830–1962)* (Paris: La Découverte/ Algiers: Barzakh, 2012); Charles-André Julien, *Histoire de l'Algérie contemporaine, Vol I: La Conquête et les Débuts de la colonisation (1827–1871)* (Paris: PUF, 1964); Jean Meyer, Jean Tarrade and Annie Rey-Goldzeiguer, *Histoire de la France coloniale*, vol. I (Paris: Armand Colin, 1991); Charles-Robert Ageron, *Histoire de l'Algérie contemporaine (1830–1999)* (Paris: PUF, 1999 [1964]); Djilali Sari, *L'Insurrection de 1871* (Algiers: SNED, 1972); Kamel Kateb, *Européens, 'indigènes' et juifs en Algérie (1830–1962)* (Paris: PUF, 2001).

That said, the main method of killing outside of combat seems similar in the two cases: summary executions and mass shootings. The currently existing research on the Algerian context does not detect a mimicking of acts of cruelty, such as had been the case in the 1840s and 1850s, when French troops hung the decapitated heads of rebels from the city walls.[25] There are indicators, such as the trophies taken from enemy infantrymen and brought back by the Spahis. But these practices seem to have been less mass-scale.[26] Perhaps they attracted less attention, which would be surprising given the rival authorities and the subsequent concern of Algerian militants to counter official French narratives.

In the same vein – and this question is worth asking – it is difficult to say whether some of the violence in Paris had been learned on Algerian soil. Several of the colonels and generals involved had indeed taken part in the so-called 'pacification' operations in this colony (Mac-Mahon was, we should remember, governor-general of Algeria from 1864 to 1870). But these career soldiers had also done battle in the Second Empire's other theatres of operations, and were especially shaken by the Franco-Prussian conflict.

Remarkably, as far as the archives can tell us, the only explicit lesson circulated between metropolitan France and Algeria headed in the opposite direction, in the sense of a supposed greater control of violence. Indeed, Governor Gueydon insisted on 'acting as in Paris: we judge and we disarm'.[27] This comment in fact demonstrated his ignorance of the situation in the French capital. Above all, this call for a legal frame of action, albeit a fictitious one, ought to be seen in the context of the sharp rivalry between the military and the republican colonists, who themselves called for the most extreme solutions. So, this idea of setting limits was undoubtedly a way for the military to keep control of the situation. On the ground, it was quite evidently not put into practice.

The clearest and most remarkable difference between the two cases in fact lay in the attacks on the environment – both social and ecological. In Algeria, property and crops were destroyed. The troops

25 SHD, 1H192.

26 Cited in Kateb, *Européens, 'indigènes' et juifs en Algérie*, p. 45. However, most accounts of atrocities focus on summary executions (parliamentary inquiry report, La Sicotière).

27 Julien, *Histoire de l'Algérie contemporaine*, vol. I, p. 491.

practised *razzias* – an old technique borrowed by French troops from what they called the 'indigenous war'. There is plentiful evidence of the burning of villages, the destruction of crops, and the cutting down of fruit trees. The intention behind these acts is only confirmed by the subsequent deliberate effort to undermine the indigenous social and economic structures. The aim was to weaken these belligerents in the long term: 'Confiscation is a punishment capable of leaving a permanent mark', said the government's High Council at the beginning of 1872: this 'dispossession, which is perfectly justified by the persistent recurrence of the crime, will do enough to strike at the minds of the guilty'.[28] So, while in Paris there were quasi-systematic executions, the range of other abuses remained limited compared to what happened in the two other conflicts of the year: the Prussian occupation and the repression in Algeria. For instance, unlike in the former case, there is no trace of rape (or else they comes only from subsequent accounts that seem unreliable).[29] Moreover, unlike in the Algerian case, while some thefts were recorded, we find no looting or wilful economic destruction as such.[30] Is this a sign of the kind of restraint suggested, above, which the army ultimately exerted on Parisian soil? Or of the fact that civil war, even social war, was nevertheless waged in the nineteenth century 'between the French', thus limiting the permissible range of attacks?[31] But there was also a political calculation: the Versaillais government sought to limit the economic impact of the conflict, keep a lid on social destitution, and ensure a rapid resumption of economic activity in metropolitan France, particularly in the capital (not least as reparations still had to be paid to the Germans). What happened after the massacre,

28 Conseil supérieur du gouvernement, meeting of 22 January 1872, quoted in André Nouschi, *Enquête sur le niveau de vie des populations rurales constantinoises, de la conquête jusqu'en 1919. Essai d'histoire économique et sociale* (Saint-Denis: Bouchène, 2013 [1961]), p. 375.

29 Olivier Berger, 'Les "Crimes de guerre" et exactions de l'armée prusso-allemande dans les départements de l'Essonne, des Hauts-de-Seine et du Val-de-Marne (1870–1871)', master 2 dissertation, Université Paris-4 (2006).

30 Corroborated in Tombs, *The War Against Paris*.

31 This obviously does not apply to all civil wars, as shown by the atrocities committed during the Wars of Religion in the sixteenth century. Still, the role of religion in the conflict surely creates its own particular dynamics. See Denis Crouzet, *Les Guerriers de Dieu. La violence au temps des troubles de religion (circa 1525–circa 1610)* (Seyssel: Champ Vallon, 1990); Jeremie Foa, *Tous ceux qui tombent: Visages du massacre de la Saint-Barthélemy* (Paris: La Découverte, 2021).

once the prisoners had been removed from Paris, is significant here. The government had the police *commissaires* issue the sum of 100,000 francs to widows and to women whose husbands had been arrested, in order to prevent them and their families from falling into poverty.[32] This decision to channel the aid through these women also continued a policy that the government and employers had pursued in the 1860s, the idea being to try to make wives and partners allies of the authorities in their attempt to 'civilise' their male companions.[33] Ultimately, this is where we find the main difference between the colonial massacre and the massacre in metropolitan France in 1871: the attack on economic and social structures. If Paris saw terrible repression, the social and economic fallout was much less than it was in colonial territory. In other words, the Bloody Week can be defined as an exceptional massacre, which was driven by the sociopolitical antagonisms of the time, but remained within the framework of a metropolitan society. These clarifications also help to shed some light on the first moments of the post-Commune period.

Rebuilding a 'Normal' World

After the daunting and terrible reconquest of Paris came the time for regular justice. Over four years, from 1871 to 1875, some 40,000 people were processed by the military tribunals; the number of such courts rose from four to twenty-six in this same period, in what was the largest judicial operation in nineteenth-century France. For the government and its leader, Adolphe Thiers, this was a way of maintaining the criminalisation of the movement while reintegrating the repression of the Commune into the legal framework. 'Monsieur Thiers', as he was called, enjoyed great prestige in the France of the time. He had repeatedly contrasted the revolutionaries' so-called 'dictatorship' with the

32 APP, DB 420, Circular dated 5 January 1872 from the Prefect of Police, Renault, to the police *commissaires* of the city of Paris. Further, more limited, assistance was offered in January 1873.

33 Mentioned in Alain Cottereau, 'Vie quotidienne et résistance ouvrière à Paris en 1870', Introduction to Denis Poulot, *Le Sublime, ou le travailleur parisien tel qu'il est en 1870, et ce qu'il peut être* (Paris: Maspero, 1980).

legitimate representation of an entire country at Versailles.[34] 'Now we have material strength. When one has material strength, one must follow a policy of moderation. I do not mean weakness, God forbid! But when one is strong, one is allowed to be moderate.'[35] While the nature of the regime remained unclear, Thiers had to prove its solidity both inside and outside of France, and to guarantee its legal and regulatory basis. It is now known that the head of government had initially given orders for clemency, which were not respected, before he then deliberately both concealed and endorsed the evident ferocity of the repression. But Thiers's position – between harshness, acceptance of extra-legal violence, and the call for respect of the law – was probably not simply the result of circumstance. It also corresponded to a growing theoretical reflection among the liberal currents of the late 1860s: politicians and intellectuals, marked by the memory of June 1848 and the American Civil War, sought to conceive a state that would respect the Constitution and fundamental political freedoms, and even accept universal male suffrage, yet remain capable of withstanding political and revolutionary convulsions. This combination of concerns could be realised through arrangements such as the provisional suspension of civil liberties within a state of exception, which they hoped could be kept under control. For these liberals, *raison d'état* somehow demanded the maintenance at all costs of political freedoms – and, paradoxically, in exceptional circumstances it was possible to temporarily set aside these very freedoms precisely in the name of protecting them. The repression during the Bloody Week was, in this sense, an important step in the constitution of a new kind of liberal state in France.[36] More prosaically, this position also allowed Thiers to build a consensus. He had to compromise with the military and the monarchist right wing of the Assembly, which considered France's redemption incomplete, and with the moderates and republicans, especially those of the 'third party', who denounced illegal abuses

34 Marc Calmon, ed., *Discours parlementaires de M. Thiers* (Paris: Calmann-Lévy, 1879–1889), vol. XIII, p. 203.

35 *Histoire de la révolution du 4 septembre et de l'insurrection du 18 mars. Dépositions de M. Thiers devant les commissions d'enquête parlementaire* (Paris: Garnier, 1873), p. 152. The session took place on 24 August 1871.

36 Stephen Sawyer, *Demos Assembled: Democracy and the International Origins of the Modern State (1840–1880)* (Chicago: University of Chicago Press, 2018), pp. 99–132.

and acts of violent mistreatment.[37] He also kept an eye on the political situation in the country, given the victories for republicans – albeit moderate ones – in the by-elections.

Battle cries and conflicts: the Assembly and the press

Other aspects of this return to order after the Franco-Prussian War and the Commune need to be considered before we look at the judgments that were handed down. In the National Assembly, the conservatives, who were in the majority, hoped for the return of the monarchy, whereas both moderate and radical republicans tried to preserve the young Third Republic at all costs. The uncertainty and the tug of war between them would last some seven years. Yet all of them, or almost all of them, rejected the Commune, in different ways depending on the given speaker's political preference.[38] 'I believe', the Legitimist MP for Morbihan, Armand Fresneau, quipped in 1872,

> that below the surface . . . there are two great parties[:] the party of those . . . who want, through persevering, honest, stubborn work, to keep what they have and acquire what they lack; then the other party, which resorts to expedients consisting . . . in setting the collective against the individual — in other words, in appropriating, by means known only to the International, a good they have not earned (*Very good! on the right*). That, for me, is the division: the two great parties facing one another today, one which, with its nuances and divisions, constitutes conservative France, and the other, revolutionary France (*Very good! Very good!*).[39]

These positions were amplified, not without discrepancies, by the media. The main features of how these events were received, first in Versailles and then in France – a reception which is itself the subject of numerous

37 Jeanne Gaillard, *Communes de province, Commune de Paris 1870–1871* (Paris: Flammarion, 1971).

38 The groupings in question could be complex: Jean Garrigues, 'Les groupes parlementaires aux origines de la IIIe République', *Parlement(s). Revue d'histoire parlementaire et politique*, March 2003, pp. 51–68.

39 Session of 12 March 1872.

studies – can be summarised as follows.[40] Some 298 pamphlets and brochures were published in response to the events: a figure that indicates both a windfall for publishers and a need to put words – most often insulting ones – to the event. The press was hardly free of this. As the conservative *Le Figaro* had it, 'In 1871, barbarian hordes invaded Paris.'[41] The same tone was found in the moderate republican *Le Siècle*. Paul Lidsky long ago analysed the positions of 'writers opposed to the Commune', often journalists. On the monarchist and Catholic right there were several readings.[42] A religiously inspired interpretation saw in the Commune a consequence of the defeat of 1870, proof of God's punishment. The second, more political interpretation saw the Commune as the inevitable consequence of the ills introduced by the revolution of 1789. For Louis Veuillot, 'All these forces and systems [the Republic of 1870, the Second Empire] are but different figures of the same ulcer, stemming from the same vitiated blood. We are dying of the Revolution.'[43] The guilty parties thus needed punishing, and the path of death opened in 1789 would have to be definitively set aside. The 'non-committed', in Lidsky's terminology, were less interested in the complete expiation of the Communard bandits. They preferred to turn away from the horror, which they saw as driven by frustrated appetites, which had taken place before their eyes. 'From open cages', wrote Théophile Gautier, 'the hyenas of '93 and the gorillas of the Commune leapt forth.'[44]

The republicans were here counted among the 'moderates' even when they had been radicals at the end of the Second Empire. They offered a more nuanced reading: they were opposed to the merciless military and then judicial persecution of the Parisians, and continued to consider the capital's initial recriminations against Versailles

40 In addition to the works cited, see Paul Lidsky, *Les* Écrivains *contre la Commune* (Paris: Maspero, 1970); John M. Roberts, *The Paris Commune from the Right* (London: Longman, 1973).

41 *Le Figaro*, 5 June 1871, quoted in Jean-Claude Caron, *Frères de sang. La guerre civile en France au XIXe siècle* (Seyssel: Champ Vallon, 2009), p. 213.

42 J. M. Roberts, *Paris Commune from the Right*. An overview in French appears in Roberts's 'La Commune considérée par la droite. Dimensions d'une mythologie', *Revue d'histoire moderne et contemporaine* 19: 2 (1972), pp. 187–203.

43 Louis Veuillot, *Paris pendant deux sieges* (Paris: Palmé, 1872), p. 160 – cited in Roberts, 'La Commune considérée par la droite', p. 190.

44 Théophile Gautier, 'Paris-capitale', October 1871 – cited in Lidsky, *Les Écrivains contre la Commune*.

legitimate. But their criticism of the Commune was just as sharp. 'You are nothing but rioters', said Catulle Mendès indignantly, 'and rioters whose main aim is to plunder under the cover of night.'[45] For figures like Émile Zola, George Sand and Catulle Mendès, the Commune had no social or political significance. Above all, they absolutely had to reject the association that the monarchists consistently made between the Commune and the republican system itself. 'It is time', clarified the novelist and chronicler Jules Claretie, 'that the republican cause be freed from the Communard cause.'[46]

In this torrent of indignation, voices sympathetic to the Communards were marginal. Illustrative of this was the reaction to the neutral position taken by Victor Hugo, who was sensitive to the fate of the executed. Despite his prestige, this attitude itself caused a scandal. Only a few poets from the Paris bohemian milieu, such as Rimbaud or Verlaine, detected the humanity and social significance of this revolt. For Lidsky, this is an indication of the class character of the position of the other writers and journalists, all of whom were either in a relatively stable position or hoped to gain one. A few popular songs, such as '*La Lutte, chant des communeux*', or graffiti on the walls of the capital, point to the enduring presence of Communard sentiments in Paris.[47]

So, after May 1871 the Commune was roundly condemned, and this stigma endured for the rest of the decade. A series of crude or more nuanced clichés fixed themselves in the collective memory, and these too structured how the event was subsequently interpreted. The revolutionaries were lumped together with all the ills of the day: alcoholism, criminality, prostitution, hereditary diseases, urban disorder, and so on. Critics had a special distaste for the female Communards, who – spat Alexandre Dumas *fils* – 'look like women when they are dead'. They focused on the factionalists or foreigners involved in a revolution that

45 Catulle Mendès, *Les 73 Journées de la Commune (du 18 mars au 29 mai 1871)* (Paris: Lachaud, 1871) – quoted in Lidsky, *Les Écrivains contre la Commune*, p. 50.

46 Jules Claretie, *Histoire de la Révolution de 1870–1871* (Paris: L'Éclipse, 1872–75), p. 620 – quoted in Lidsky, *Les Écrivains contre la Commune*.

47 Philippe Darriulat, *La Muse du peuple. Chansons politiques et sociales en France (1815–1871)* (Rennes: Presses universitaires de France, 2011); Éric Fournier, *'La Commune n'est pas morte'. Les usages du passé de 1871 à nos jours* (Paris: Libertalia, 2013), pp. 34–5.

was subsequently deemed a cosmopolitan affair. There was nothing systematic about such attitudes hardening. But in that moment, under the shock of the blazes and the massacres, this reading was dominant, and cast its veil over the event.

The graphic representations studied by Bertrand Tillier highlight this veiling of the Commune.[48] On 11 March, Vinoy had restored censorship. The circulation of images of the Commune was banned for the Paris area on 28 December 1871, and for the whole of France on 25 November 1872. Only images of ruins and photographs of insurgents, approved by the interior ministry officially for identification purposes, could be published. This policy was coupled with a form of self-censorship among painters, photographers, engravers and cartoonists. But the problem went deeper: those, like Manet, who did wish to portray the Commune, were unable to depict it. The revolution seemed to resist all figuration. Two images from the 'terrible year' gradually extended their grip upon the memory: the martyrs of the war of 1870, and the spectacle of Paris ablaze. The situation changed in 1879, during the debates over an amnesty. At that point, however, discourse about the event and the representations of it was orchestrated within a wholly different context – the third Republic, unlike that of 1871.[49] The Commune thus continued to escape depiction – and such avoidance can also be read as one of the possible exit routes from a grave political crisis.[50]

The politicisation of French territory

These political struggles and imprecations should not obscure other, rather less imposing movements that took place. The fate of the other Communes is instructive in this respect. In Lyon and Marseille, the Communes were bloodily repressed (with 300 dead in the latter city), followed by a trial that sought to condemn the ringleaders. In locations where the movements did not last as long, such as Narbonne and Thiers,

48 Tillier, *La Commune de Paris.*

49 Laure Godineau, 'Retour d'exil. Les anciens communards au début de la Troisième République', PhD dissertation, Université Paris-I (2000).

50 Two different examples are given in Nicole Loraux, *La Cité divisée. L'oubli dans la mémoire d'Athènes* (Paris: Payot, 2005), and Éric Conan and Henry Rousso, *Vichy, un passé qui ne passe pas* (Paris: Fayard, 1994).

there were many acquittals, indeed sometimes sweeping ones.[51] This outcome was not the product of some abundance of goodwill. Rather, the juries wanted to ensure an immediate social peace. But there was more: in Thiers, the main leaders of the riot, Chomette, Chauffrias and Vedel, were elected to the town hall on 7 May. Of the twenty-seven councillors, seven were skilled workers and one a farmer – this working-class cohort representing a first since the days of the Second Republic. Finally, Chomette, who was also elected to the district council, was still on the town council in 1875, and the shoemaker Chauffrias was still on it in 1880.[52] Events therefore led to a reorganisation of the social composition of this body in Thiers. There was an even clearer such development in Algiers. Given the circumstances, no trial was held: Vuillermoz remained mayor. He even became an MP in the July 1871 by-elections, having run his campaign based on his role in the torment of 1870–71.[53] After resigning, he returned to the colonial capital in 1872 and regained his position at the bar and on the municipal council.[54] He died in 1877.

In other words, these individuals were able to turn the symbolic capital of their revolutionary engagement into political capital, in order to win election and then maintain their positions – despite the purge that was being enacted and the new government's intrusion into the electoral campaigns.[55] Here, we see the effects of what historians and political scientists have called the 'politicisation' of territory. This term, which has several meanings, refers to the imposition from above and the appropriation from below of new norms of political life. It is accompanied by the gradual establishment of a political space based on electoral

51 Judgment of the Puy-de-Dôme assize court of 27 August 1871. In Narbonne, the acquittal pronounced in November 1871 was followed by several convictions in absentia in March 1872. *Marc César, La Commune révolutionnaire de Narbonne (mars 1871)* (Sète: Éd. Singulières, 2008), p. 156.

52 (AD), Puy-de-Dôme, 8 BIB 294/2, *Album de Thiers*, 24 September 1871; 2O 430/4, Thiers town council. See also the report by the first president of the Riom court of appeal, Achille Moisson, 8 September 1871, in *L'Enquête parlementaire sur l'insurrection du 18 mars 1871* (Paris: Librairie législative Wittersheim, 1872).

53 ANOM, 12X37 and 12X42, Profession de foi du citoyen Vuillermoz.

54 ANOM, 12X290, Vuillermoz file.

55 The municipal authorities law of April 1871 allowed councils to elect the mayor, except in towns with more than 20,000 inhabitants. It was amended in 1874: the prefect could appoint whomever he wished. The government's interference in the 1871 election campaign was moderate. It increased after the period of restored 'moral order', and reached its peak during the elections that followed the crisis of May 1877.

competition and the formula 'one man, one vote', together with a redefinition of what is considered legitimate and illegitimate. This conversion of the revolutionary experience here appears as a trace of this phenomenon's roots dating back to the 1860s.[56] Indeed, despite the 'moral order' that had been established, these votes would soon become part of the bedrock on which the Republic would find support from 1875 onwards.

Yet the situation in Paris was, of course, exceptional. To the military manhunt was added a police one. The lists of individuals, kept in the archives of the Préfecture de Police, attest to the sheer scale of the searches mounted – fed also by the exchanging of denunciations within the individual neighbourhoods. There were many competing attempts to take matters in hand. On the authorities' side of things, the still-fresh traces of the struggle were whitewashed and, like forty-two other *départements*, the city remained under siege. This continued to be the case until 1876. The residents of Paris were still not allowed to elect their own mayor, and the city remained under the control of the two prefectures: those of the police and of the Seine *département*. As for law and order, the National Guard was abolished in August 1871, and the number of *gardiens de la paix* (neighbourhood policemen) was increased by 1,000 men. A project to militarise the police failed, however, reflecting the status quo characteristic of this period.[57] The situation in Paris had a similarly notable religious colouring. It was quickly decided to rebuild churches and the cross of the Pantheon. As elsewhere in France, processions were staged throughout the city in order to purify it of its excesses and impieties. More spectacularly, grand national funerals were organised for Monseigneur Darboy and the other executed hostages.[58] The erection of the Sacré-Cœur at the top of the Butte Montmartre, which had been planned before the events, took on the value of a symbol – of expiation for the crimes committed in Paris, of the establishment of religion, and of a return to order. There were also more varied forms of

56 See, for example, Michel Offerlé, 'Capacités politiques et politisations: faire voter et voter (XIXe–XXe siècle)' – (1), *Genèses* 67 (2007), pp. 131–49; and (2), *Genèses* 68 (2007), pp. 145–60; and Raymond Huard, *Le Suffrage universel en France (1848–1946)* (Paris: Aubier, 1991).

57 A rich perspective can be found in Chanet, *Vers l'armée nouvelle*.

58 Jacques-Olivier Boudon, *Monseigneur Darboy (1813–1871), archevêque de Paris entre Pie IX et Napoléon III* (Paris: Cerf, 2011).

reappropriation of the city, such as the tourism connected to the ruins.[59] But the phenomenon that most surprised observers was the rapid resumption of urban life, including the reopening of shops and the circulation of vehicles. Bicycles soon reappeared. In 1872, the proceeds from the octroi tax returned to the 1868 level. It seemed as if the modern city, with its flows and routines, showed a remarkable resilience after the shocks of the war and the civil war.[60]

The same thing happened politically: while the revolutionary movement was decapitated, the moderate left won the supplementary elections on 2 July. The election in 1873 of the republican Barodet, a lead player in Lyon's attempts at conciliation between Paris and Versailles, then led to the fall of Thiers. This realignment and resumption of power struggles can also be seen in the reconstruction of the buildings that had been destroyed in 1871. In August 1871, with Thiers's insistent backing, the rebuilding of the Hôtel de Ville was decreed. The new building was completed in 1882, inspired by the style of its predecessor. The Louvre was rebuilt, and the Vendôme Column re-erected, between 1873 and 1875, while the Palais de Justice was restored between 1872 and 1878. However, the Tuileries Palace, a symbol of France's monarchist past, could not withstand the republicans' arrival in power: it was razed to the ground in 1883. As for the Palais d'Orsay, due to a lack of funds its walls remained blackened for thirty years, before it was replaced by a railway station for the Exposition Universelle in 1900.

So, little by little, and indeed not without tensions, institutional, economic and urban routines, as well as modes of anticipation and expectation, were recomposed – even if they remained politically or socially divisive.[61] The situation seems to have returned to 'normal' – a term that took on full meaning, in the eyes of the actors involved, only after the major rupture experienced in the war, and then in the Commune.

---

59 Fournier, *Paris en ruines*.

60 Stéphane Rials, *De Trochu à Thiers (1870–1873)*, vol. XIV of *Nouvelle Histoire de Paris* (Paris: Hachette, 1985).

61 Reinhart Koselleck, *Futures Past: On the Semantics of Historical Time* (New York: Columbia University Press, 2004); Christophe Charle, *La Discordance des temps. Une brève histoire de la modernité* (Paris: Armand Colin, 2011).

Law and social norms: military tribunals

With this in mind, we can now turn back to the trials, which lasted some four years. Renowned figures (such as the delegate to the Sûreté Générale, Théophile Ferré, or the chief of the Commune's high command, Louis Rossel), individuals who were considered ringleaders, or fit the stereotype of the typical Communard, were severely punished: 93 were sentenced to death, 251 to forced labour, 1,169 to deportation to a fortified compound, 3,417 to simple deportation, 1,247 to life imprisonment, and 3,359 to jail terms – not to mention the 3,313 people who were convicted in absentia. Some of the rulings were obviously iniquitous, such as the sentencing to death of five alleged *pétroleuses* even though the charges were very thin (no evidence of possession of petroleum was provided). In the authorities' view, the city needed to be purged of its 'scum', and its webs of radicalism and revolution dismantled. These convictions left a mark on the history of French amnesty policies: a decade later, following lengthy debates, many of these convicts were amnestied (in two stages, in March 1879 and July 1880). However, sixty-six of them, including Blanqui, were subject to a legal innovation: if they were pardoned, they still retained their civic indignity. This idiosyncrasy, notes Anne Simonin, attests to the persistent impossibility under the Third Republic of establishing a clear consensus around the French revolutionary inheritance.[62]

That said, 2,445 cases ended in acquittal and 22,727 were dismissed, amounting to some 70 per cent of the total: these figures, say historians of these trials, indicate the effort made to respect the rule of law and to distinguish between those who had really participated in the Communard adventure and those who had not.[63] But there was no light-touch approach here, either. This work was constrained by the overcrowding of the sites where the accused were detained; and these decisions indicate that many people who were later declared innocent of

62 Anne Simonin, *Le Déshonneur dans la République. Une histoire de l'indignité (1791–1958)* (Paris: Grasset, 2008); Stéphane Gacon, *L'Amnistie. De la Commune à la guerre d'Algérie* (Paris: Seuil, 2002).

63 Jacques Rougerie, *Procès des communards* (Paris: Gallimard, 1978). See also the statistical review in Roger Gould, *Insurgent Identities: Class, Community and Protest in Paris from 1848 to the Commune* (Chicago: University of Chicago Press, 1995), pp. 224–5.

or alien to the deeds in question were arrested and held for several months without any specific charges, in terrible conditions.

However, these judgments probably also played a role in the defendants' return to social life, in the form of a rite of passage. During the hearings, they generally acknowledged the accusations levelled against the Commune, and claimed that they had not done anything, or paid lip service to the norms of the current society, in order to escape condemnation. 'I never did anything but follow my battalion', said one; 'I showed up . . . to ask for a job that would allow me to live decently', explained another.[64] In this way, these judgments also played their part in the symbolic reactivation of the 'normal' world.

The norms that were now restored were not only political or legal ones; they were social, too. In his study of 'insurgent identities', Roger Gould identifies two statistical biases in these judgments: individuals who fit the stereotype of the Communard, particularly the criminal figure, received harsher punishments. Conversely, those with wives and children received more lenient sentences. This indicates how important family values were to the victors. Other norms can be identified from targeted samples.

Foreigners, for example, were more likely to be killed during the Bloody Week.[65] Yet nationality seems to have been a less decisive factor in the courts – though it is difficult to be categorical, given the definitional uncertainties already noted.[66] The study of usurpations of office – the term can now be used – indicates the influence of social differentiation. Sentences were determined by many factors (the degree of coercion involved, the length of time in office, the activities carried out, and so on). But the gap between a defendant's social background and the status attached to the office clearly also played a role in the severity of the punishment. These correctional tribunals thus served to reassert social hierarchies and to restore the principles of selection that underpinned the allocation of public authority. Moreover, they thereby contributed to reconstituting the administrative boundaries that had

64 AVP, D2U6-13.

65 Robert Tombs, 'Les Versaillais et les étrangers', in Rougerie and Aprile, *La Commune et les étrangers*, pp. 34–42.

66 Foreigners accounted for 5 per cent of all those arrested, and 25 per cent of them were convicted – a figure comparable to the one for all defendants (the proportion of foreigners in the Parisian population was around 7 per cent in 1866).

been altered under the Commune: because they passed judgment from the 'real' administrative landscape, they could use judicial means to erase the redrawing of public functions that had taken place during the events themselves.

Even more instructive, finally, are the judgments against children and women. A study of the 1,050 women who appeared before the military tribunals reveals two rationales at work.[67] Women convicted of participating in the insurrection received harsher sentences. They were over-represented among the most heavily punished: 13 per cent were sentenced to death, 13 per cent to forced labour, and 13 per cent to deportation to a fortified enclosure, compared to 0.9 per cent, 2.3 per cent and 11 per cent, respectively, for men. This greater severity was apparent in the cases of Louise Michel, André Léo (on the run) and the so-called *pétroleuses*. The transgression of gender barriers, aggravated by the imaginary of 'monstrous' Communard women, provoked harsher sentencing. In other cases, however, the court was more lenient than with men for comparable actions. Captain Briot, tasked with the report on 'judicial operations concerning women', half-acknowledged this.[68] He also offered an explanation: the participation of women, he said, was owed above all to their ignorance and lack of moral sense (which he generally linked to prostitution). Others, more simply, 'were obeying the urge to shout and insult, which seems inherent in a certain kind of women's nature'. Nowhere was it suggested that women might possibly have had a political intent. Here we find the gender norms of the nineteenth century, in which women were supposed to be confined to maternal functions and the domestic sphere, and not considered capable of political action.[69] For Briot, these 'unfortunate women' could only have been 'led astray' by the Communard men. The judgment that the criminal court passed against Jeanne Bigeau, whom we met in the previous section, shows the concrete mechanisms at work.[70] There was no doubt

67 Quentin Deluermoz, 'Ambiguë criminalité: le traitement judiciaire des femmes de la Commune ou le retour à l'ordre sexuel et politique', in Frédéric Chauvaud and Gilles Malandain, eds, *Impossibles victimes, impossibles coupables* (Rennes: Presses universitaires de Rennes, 2009), pp. 133–47.

68 APP, DB 420

69 Michelle Perrot, 'Pouvoir des hommes, puissance des femmes? L'exemple du XIXe siècle', in *Les Femmes ou les silences de l'histoire* (Paris: Flammarion, 1998), pp. 213–26.

70 AVP, D3U6-2.

that she had participated in the Commune: she made cartridges during the insurrection, attended the clubs, and incited hatred against the government on several occasions. However, the case was dismissed. According to the indictment, her 'exaltation' could be attributed to the loss of her son during the 1870 war. This loss was real – but the argument denies the possibility that her action might have had any political significance, or that she could have been conscious of it: according to the prosecutor's reasoning, her actions were owed above all to the wounding of her status as a mother; in other words, to the alteration of her feminine nature. As we have seen, women struggled to assert themselves as actors during the Commune. The few openings they did manage to create were then denied before the Versailles courts. Paradoxically, they partly cooperated with this: most often, hauled before the judges, they too accepted these motives and their implicit definitions, always with the aim of avoiding conviction. The post-Commune period was thus a time in which gendered and social roles were reinstated.

The restored order was thus at once a political, legal, symbolic, familial, social, administrative and gendered order. This is not surprising: it represented the social order as it had been reconfigured and established throughout the nineteenth century. While it did not go uncontested, for those not involved in the Commune it constituted, in a sense, a minimal common reference point that could be mobilised in this moment – especially since the rest of the national territory had not seen a comparable revolutionary dynamic. We can understand why the majority of those who did not participate in the Commune felt relieved, or simply accepted this restoration of the 'normal' world. If some found this order threatening to natural hierarchies, and if others, on the contrary, criticised the inequalities it fostered, it was also a world in which they could again act. On the other hand, it is now easier to understand why, among those who were enthusiastic about the new 'partition of the sensible' (in Rancière's term) during the Commune, or about the possibilities they believed had been unleashed, this restoration could be experienced as a a terrible new blow of symbolic violence. Perhaps they had the impression that, in this stitching of wounds, they could see a certain re-establishment of society's deep 'imaginary institutions'? Louise Michel, better than anyone else, indicated how the scars nevertheless remained visible. She is, of course, an exceptional case. The woman whom Victor Hugo described as 'Viro Major' ('greater than a man') was one of the few who did not disown her actions before the courts. But her words speak volumes:

> Why should I defend myself? I have already told you, I refuse to do so. You are men who are going to judge me; . . . you are men and I am only a woman, and yet I look you straight in the eye. . . . What I demand of you, who claim to be a military tribunal, and who present yourselves as my judges . . . of you who are soldiers and who judge in front of everyone, is the camp of Satory, where our brothers have already fallen. I must be cut off from society; you have been told to do this. Well, the *commissaire* of the Republic is right.[71]

The fires, the massacre and the end of the Commune thus reveal, in turn, the content of the metropolitan social and political order of the 1860s–70s – as well as the space, at that moment, of its possible variations.

71 In Rougerie, *Procès des communards*, pp. 89–90.

10

The Commune, the New Global Spectre of Revolution

For reasons that the reader will now well understand, the echoes of the massacres and of the end of the Commune, and then their feedback effects, reverberated far beyond French soil. Germany and Great Britain – through military means in the case of the former and media coverage in the case of the latter – intervened in military reconstruction and subsequent efforts to restrain the massacre. It is therefore worth paying attention, in the chapters that follow, to this interplay of far-reaching echoes and counter-echoes which, even after the fact, continued to shape the development of the event both in France and beyond. Probably the most visible of these is the fabric of words that immediately came to describe this episode. This sometimes took on an almost knee-jerk and stereotypical quality. Referring, for example, to the problem of taxation in Bombay, a city described as 'ruined', the *Times of India* wryly commented on 3 June 1871:

> It would not do, like the Paris Commune, to set fire to the Town Hall, to batter down the unfinished Secretariat, or to blow up any of the new fountains or statues; that is, a way peculiar to Frenchmen when they desire to express their sentiments with becoming and particular emphasis, resembling very much the celebrated Chinese mode of obtaining roast pig by burning down a house every time they wanted that luxury.[1]

1 'Blighted Bombay', *Times of India*, 3 June 1871.

The aftermath of events – especially ones that have combined revolution, political transition and the end of a war – is often a moment of conflict over the proper labelling of what has just happened.[2] In the case of the aftermath of the Commune, the dominant tone was largely condemnatory. In France itself, the panorama described in Part I changed at the end of the civil war; expressions of support slowed, and a more shared reading increasingly developed.[3] Works on the international labour movement published in the 1970s clearly grasped this phenomenon when they spoke of a 'myth of the Commune'. They were then interested in the positive, working-class myth, and less in the more visible negative myth, which was thought to correspond to bourgeois elites or other elements of the societies studied.

And yet this latter myth – weighty, widespread, and less uniform and socially homogeneous than it might appear – is essential. The shared readings that it brought together – open for many uses, and sometimes related to potent social imaginaries – would indeed reframe understandings of the Parisian uprising. They therefore played a direct part in the processes of recomposition of the post-Commune period, whether shaping different actors' margins of manoeuvre or their possible freedom of expression. The international diplomatic reactions offer a first glimpse of this; but this reception is better perceived through the newspapers. Here, I use the same investigative method as in the earlier press analysis, taking the same precautions.[4] This should allow us to delve into some of the logics and effects of this transnational reconstruction of the Parisian episode.

---

2 Alban Bensa and Eric Fassin, 'Les sciences sociales face à l'événement', *Terrain* 38 (2002).

3 With regard to the French Revolution, this phenomenon is clearly identified in Jean-Clément Martin, *Révolution et contre-révolution en France de 1789 à 1995* (Rennes: Presses universitaires de Rennes, 1996).

4 On the European or Western reading of so-called distant events, see Olivier Cosson, *Préparer la Grande Guerre. L'armée française et la guerre russo-japonaise (1899–1914)* (Paris: Les Indes savantes, 2013); Hervé Mazurel, *Vertiges de la guerre. Byron, les philhellènes et le mirage grec* (Paris: Les Belles Lettres, 2013).

A Seemingly Unanimous Diplomatic Response

In diplomatic terms, the international reception of the event was clearly aligned with France's own. On 21 March, relating news of the uprising in Paris, Jules Favre had played down what was happening by referring to 'deplorable events' which 'it will not take long to put back in order'.[5] Three months later, the circulars of 26 May, 6 June and 23 June, sent to the four corners of the planet via France's embassies, adopted a quite different tone. The 6 June circular referred to 'the fearsome insurrection that the valour of our army has just defeated, [and which] has kept the whole world in such distress'.[6] Without doubt, between the two dates, Jules Favre had grown conscious of the importance of the Communard movement. But strategic choices were also essential: by June, the Commune and its supposed instigator, the IWMA, had to be made to appear as a threat to the 'civilised' nations of the world.

This appeal was heard, and sometimes even pre-empted, right from the beginning of the recapture of Paris. In Britain, Robert Peel made a statement in the House of Commons on 25 May in which he expressed his sympathy for France 'without reference to any form of government', in the face of such events 'without precedent in history'.[7] He called on the government to react. Maintaining the proper distance, Liberal prime minister Gladstone confirmed that 'there are no epithets that can in any degree give satisfaction to the feelings with which every man's heart must be oppressed'.[8] Still, nonetheless, wary that the defeated side might again raise its head, on 7 June the German chancellor, Bismarck, called for 'solidarity against socialist Europe'. A 13 July dispatch stated that Germany would support France 'like others', 'in the interest of the common peace and the general progress of

5 CAD, CP, England.

6 Circulars reproduced in Georges Bourgin, 'La lutte du gouvernement français contre la Première Internationale. Contribution à l'histoire de l'après-Commune', *International Review of Social History* 4 (1939), pp. 39–138.

7 Reproduced in *The Times*, 26 May 1871.

8 CAD, CP, Germany; Carole Witzig, 'Bismarck et la Commune: la réaction des monarchies conservatrices contre les mouvements républicains et socialistes (1870–1872) vue à travers les archives allemandes', *International Review of Social History* 17: 1 (1972), pp. 191–221.

European civilisation'.[9] For his part, the Austro-Hungarian emperor Franz Joseph, also a conservative, sent an address of sympathy to Thiers on 26 May, and congratulated him on the restoration of order. The Russian tsar did the same, while the Spanish king and government congratulated the French head of state 'for the energy with which he has saved France and Europe'.[10] In the Spanish parliament, the liberal interior minister Sagasta sharply condemned 'the acts that France mourns, of which humanity is ashamed and which history will record with indignation'.[11] The same public expression of regret was made in the Italian, Belgian and Greek parliaments, albeit in less vigorous terms. The United States was not to be outdone, either. Further south, on 12 June, the minister of the Argentine Confederation congratulated the head of the French government. Brazil's conservative government also lent its support. Although they were divided on the issue of the abolition of slavery, the Senate and the Chamber adopted an official joint resolution to express their 'horror at the anarchy that has succeeded in destroying the best part of the great capital of Paris and [to] hail the victory of the cause of civilisation and the principles of Christianity'.[12] More discreetly, the Turkish sultan acknowledged the improvement of the situation in Paris. Over in Asia, the sovereign of Siam sent a letter to Jules Favre on 28 May. The reply from the French foreign minister (the Siamese text has not itself been preserved) said that it would be impossible to 'express higher thoughts in nobler forms' – suggesting that the original missive had a laudatory tone.

Many public or official statements of support were voiced. The reasons for this were, obviously, various. In Siam, this stance sought to re-establish contact after the tensions of the previous months. In the Spanish and Brazilian cases, the responses were also directed against the domestic opposition, be it republican or liberal. Nor should we forget that entire countries and regions did not react, whether due to geographic distance, the fact that attention was directed elsewhere, or internal tensions (as in Colombia): in China, Favre and then Charles de Rémusat showed great caution. Nor was there any reference to the episode in the Japanese,

9 CAD, CP, Austria-Hungary, letter of 26 May 1871.
10 CAD, CP, Spain, letters dated 26 May 1871.
11 CAD, CP, Spain, 30 May 1871.
12 CAD, CP, Brazil, letter dated 2 July 1871.

Egyptian or Moroccan diplomatic correspondence (which only mentions the end of the Kabyle insurrection). But most striking is the sheer extent and apparent unanimity of the reactions.

In 1849–50, after the 'Springtime of Peoples', reactions were indeed more cautious, as the countries concerned followed divergent paths: some were crushed by the Reaction, others experienced renewed revolutionary upheavals, and still others remained divided by political struggles. In 1871, the limits of the event and its brevity favoured more convergent responses, especially since the fires offered grounds to denounce the insurgents' savagery while not going into too many details. Various ideals were called upon in order to justify these expressions of support. Sometimes this meant Christianity, patriotism or 'true freedom'. But the most recurrent term was 'civilisation' – occasionally 'European civilisation'. This notion, and its tumultuous relationship to barbarism, has been the subject of various studies.[13] It has permeated diplomatic language since the eighteenth century, and the phenomenon has continued to grow ever since.[14] In 1871, it appeared with remarkable homogeneity, as the lowest common denominator of diplomatic language on both European and intercontinental scales. The Paris revolt was generally described as an attack on this civilisation, which – as a matter of course – had to be defended.

Front-Page Headlines: 'French-Type' Fires and Massacres

This reading resonated with the media coverage of the event. There was a manifest connection with France, since French newspapers also set the tone for many publications abroad. Moreover, most of these foreign outlets' correspondents were now in Versailles, at a distance from the insurgent city. It is also possible here to broaden the horizons of our previous analysis of the reception of the Commune, since in this case there is a more extensive bibliography on its international echoes.

13 Antoine Lilti and Céline Spector, eds, *Penser l'Europe au XVIII siècle. Commerce, civilisation, Empire* (Oxford: Voltaire Foundation, 2014), pp. 139–66.

14 For one example, concerning prisoners of war, see Renaud Morieux, *The Society of Prisoners: Anglo-French Wars and Incarceration in the Eighteenth Century* (Oxford: Oxford University Press, 2019).

The fires, and to a lesser extent the massacres, occupied most British headlines. The same was true in Germany, even in the distant eastern province of Silesia, where, for example, the Oels daily newspaper *Lokomotive an der Oder* began a serial entitled 'The Tuileries and the Louvre' on 6 June 1871.[15] The event was followed intensely in the United States.[16] In Mexico, with the delay inherent in the circulation of news, the Catholic newspaper *La Época* raged indignantly on 13 July: 'So many perversities were committed in the insurrection that it would take a great deal of space to reproduce all that is reported by the French newspapers that have reached us.'[17] On the other side of the world, Australia's *Sydney Morning Herald* received the French news two months late via San Francisco, but not without interest: 'The friend of man willingly averts his eyes from the dreadful spectacle of the civil war in Paris.' On 26 July, a long editorial denouncing the Versaillais massacre was followed by an editorial on the fires, which hit higher lyrical notes: 'Imagine the darkened City, the deserted dwellings, traversed by figures gliding stealthily along, and infusing the deadly chemistry of destruction.' For this journalist, in that moment, Thiers appeared the best leader for getting France out of its morass.[18]

Admittedly, this back-and-forth of quotations does not tell us a great deal. It does suggest that newspapers were copying from each other, and also points to the range of horizons involved. We know from our count of Reuters telegrams that 54 per cent of words circulating on the British network were devoted to this event. And we should also recognise that this was just one among many circuits of information. As Map 3 shows, the circulation of news remained a truly global affair.

Perhaps we should now try to identify some of the discursive mechanisms at work. Three contrasting narratives of the Bloody Week (over the period 21–31 May) will help us here.

First, the content of the Reuters dispatches deserves our attention. They were the source of information for many outlets, and continued to provide the most neutral possible updates, in a tone that at least claimed to be objective: 'Outside Paris, 26 May, 3 p.m. The Versailles troops are

15 'Tuilerien und Louvre', *Lokomotive an der Oder*, 6–7 June 1871, at zefys.staatsbibliothek-berlin.de.

16 Philip Katz, *From Appomattox to Montmartre: Americans and the Paris Commune* (Cambridge, MA: Harvard University Press, 1998).

17 *La Época*, 7 July 1871.

18 *Sydney Morning Herald*, 26 July 1871.

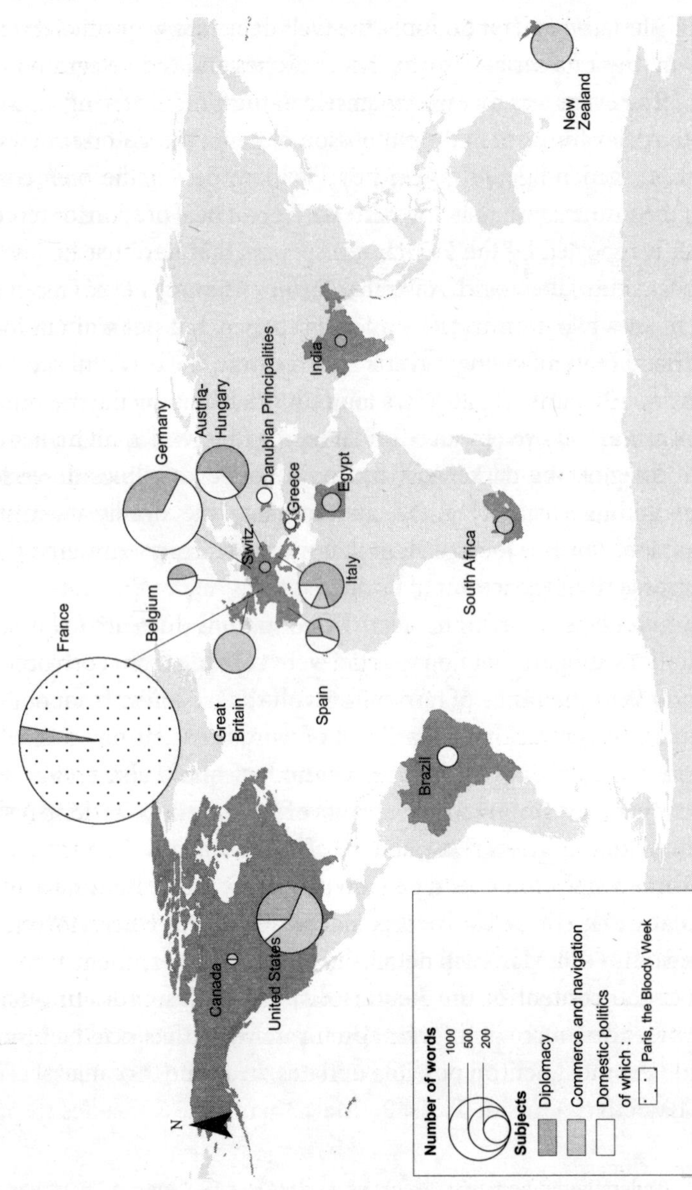

Map 3. The Bloody Week on the Reuters network

advancing from Pantin on the east. The insurgents are thus being attacked on three sides.' However, there was a notable shift. Caught up in the fighting, the *fédérés* no longer had a government or official publications of their own, and only the declarations and telegrams of the Versailles government were now in circulation. Also striking – and rarer in this type of reporting – is the use of the language of emotion and moral judgement. This was limited in scope (given the brevity of the texts), but no less notable for that: some battles were 'furious', and the flames 'terribly vivid'. On 29 May, one telegram stated that Paris's population was delighted to be finally freed from the 'yoke' of the Commune.[19] The reports thus increasingly endorsed the victor's point of view, which was disseminated far and wide.

Second, Britain's *Times* offers another glimpse into the rereadings of the Commune that were now underway. This conservative newspaper, one of the most widely reproduced and quoted in the world – indeed, a publication to which diplomatic correspondence paid great attention – could hardly be assumed to be among the French government's greatest sympathisers. At the beginning of June, it was one of the first to criticise Versailles's repressive practices. The situation in Paris was closely followed in several sections: articles by the French correspondent, Reuters telegrams, excerpts from French and foreign newspapers, editorials, and broader commentaries. The Bloody Week saw a noticeable shift in tone. On 22 May, the correspondent on the ground in France tried to make his way to the theatre of operations. He was delighted with the scene he was going to be able to offer the reader: 'In our time there has been no siege that could be seen so well as the present siege of Paris can be by the spectator on this side who knows where to select his ground.' The other articles detail the entry of government troops into Paris and the situation in the various neighbourhoods. Interestingly, some pieces even pointed to the absence of violence since the assassination of Lecomte and Thomas, apart from the 'outburst of madness of the last May'.[20]

19 *Reuters Telegraph Books*, 26, 29, 30 May 1871.

20 *The Times*, 23 May 1871, p. 9. Generals Claude Lecomte and Clément Thomas were killed by National Guardsmen on 18 March 1871, after government troops sent to seize the cannons of the Paris National Guard at Montmartre refused Lecomte's order to fire on the crowd. Both officers, seen as symbols of repression and betrayal, were captured and summarily executed – an event that marked the outbreak of the Paris Commune.

Yet there was a sharper change of tone with the first fires: '25 May, 7.45 PM. I have just returned from witnessing one of the saddest sights that has occurred in the world's history.' The editorial went on to say: 'The destruction of the Tuileries, the Louvre and the Hôtel de Ville will, perhaps, be branded in history as the most demonical deed of vandalism ever perpetrated.' The indignation was in the superlative case: 'The history of the world presents no such national tragedy. It began in vanity and weakness; it ends in crime, in horror, and in despair.'[21] In the following days, the description of the ruined buildings and the transformations they had undergone over time pointed to the scale of the tragedy: the journalists recalled the history of the Hôtel de Ville, built in the sixteenth century on the site of Étienne Marcel's *Maison aux Piliers*. They recalled the glory days of the Tuileries under the regency of Catherine de' Medici, and extolled the artistic richness of the Louvre's collections. Calling to mind the loss of structures and artworks that even the reconstruction of Paris could never replace allowed *The Times* to give its readers a feeling of the blow that the Commune had just dealt to history. The Communards had reached a new level of horror: they were barbarians who had reduced to ashes the slowly accumulated fruits of human brilliance. The Commune was now measured by the yardstick of the greatest historical tragedies, including those of ancient or biblical memory. This meant Moscow in 1812, of course, but

> the burning of Babylon, the fall of Jerusalem, the sack of Rome are the events to which we must revert to find a parallel for our own experience. And we shall look back in vain even across so many ages. Babylon, Jerusalem, Rome fell before foreign enemies, who wreaked upon them the vengeance of long-delayed victory; the pride of Paris has been brought to the ground by men whose avowed aim was to maintain above all things its supremacy.[22]

Other articles in *The Times* detailed what appear to have been typical narratives of the event, judging from the wider newspaper coverage of the period: the description of smoking ruins; the presence of women armed with petrol-filled containers, or pouring poison into wine; the

21 *The Times*, 25 May 1871.

22 *The Times*, 26 May 1871.

meticulous listing of the 'outlaws of all nations' among the members of the Commune's council and its Central Committee; the hunt for various personalities famed in Paris (Gustave Cluseret, Adolphe Assi, and so on). Such articles did not omit to mention the deaths caused by the Versaillais troops; they were even said to be 'very great in number'. But this was mentioned as neutral information, in the style of reporting on military developments. The bourgeois mob's revenge against the Parisian prisoners drew a more critical response: 'What difference, then, is there between the partisans of the Commune and those of the Government at Versailles?' Taken as characteristic of 'extremes' of which France alone was capable, these excesses on either side provided this daily with an opportunity to underline Britain's own superiority: if revolts existed in Britain, according to *The Times* they were tempered by the role of parliament, by the absence of a British 1789, by its leaders' more understanding attitude, and even by the sheer size of its Empire.[23] So, when *The Times* called for moderation in the repression in France, it did so less out of concern for the Communards than out of respect for the principles of the rule of law, of which appointed itsef the official champion as well as Britain's voice in the world.

It is equally instructive to read *L'Indépendance belge* alongside *The Times*. This Belgian daily had a well-established international reputation, and it had long taken an interest in French affairs. Moreover, it claimed to be progressive, and its local correspondent even called himself a republican.[24] This is our third narrative. Here again, the coverage of the French event was impressive: on 22 May, three-quarters of this daily were devoted to this news. The press's uniform tone should be seen in relative terms: *L'Indépendance belge* updated readers with articles from its correspondent on the ground and with editorials, but also via extracts from Reuters dispatches, of which the newspaper was a customer, as well as articles from *The Times* and other British and French dailies. At the beginning of the period, its articles were rather descriptive in character. They presented the way the Commune was organised, and predicted a rapid defeat for the *fédérés*. On 25 May, again, the tone changed: 'It's not just the gun they're wielding, but the flaming torch.

23 *The Times*, 29 May 1871. On British readings of France, see Fabrice Bensimon, *Les Britanniques face à la révolution française de 1848* (Paris: L'Harmattan, 2000).

24 *L'Indépendance belge*, 22 May 1871.

They want Paris to bear the indelible mark of their grip.' According to the 27 May issue, 'a barbarism unprecedented in the history of civilised peoples' was indeed taking place. The typical scenes were reported, with a few nuances: the description of the ruins was briefer, the image of the Versailles bourgeois ladies striking prisoners with their parasols more insistent, and the evocation of the women arsonists more sinister.

At the end of May, this progressive newspaper took a position that may at first sight seem surprising. While he was in Belgium, Victor Hugo had called on the Belgian government to take in Parisian refugees. The publication of his letter caused an outcry. His house was stoned on 27 and 28 May, and the writer was expelled from the country. *L'Indépendance belge* replied at length to the poet, whom, it declared, it held in great respect:

> We, too, have a right . . . and that is to express our reservations; the better to make heard, for our part, a protest against his characterisation of abominable acts, when he calls these political acts . . . We consider just, legitimate, unbreakable, this international law, drawn from the deepest part of the human conscience . . . But it is precisely because the right to asylum is sacred to us that we do not want to grant it to those who are clearly unworthy of it.[25]

This call for the restriction of the right of asylum did not prevent *L'Indépendance belge* from maintaining an editorial line on the left of the Belgian political spectrum. It was more concerned than its British counterpart about the death toll (estimated at between 10,000 and 20,000). It bewailed the sheer number of dead, closely monitoring Thiers's statements promising terrible reprisals with 'the law in his hand', expressing its hope that emergency laws would be avoided, and that the freedom of the press would not be overly regulated.[26]

So, different positions could be taken on the basis of the same elements and narratives. This same corpus also appears in the other newspapers consulted: in other words, the events presented in the previous chapter were filtered, selected and reread according to particular analytical lenses. We must now unearth them.

---

25 *L'Indépendance belge*, 28 May 1871.

26 *L'Indépendance belge*, 29 May 1871.

But first, some clarification is needed on this intriguing interplay between convergence and differentiation. To understand it properly, we must first keep in mind the extreme diversity of discourses on the Commune, taken as a whole. This was firstly a diversity of form: the flow of discourse always consists of a mixture of factual data, incendiary fragments, translations of official documents, and long analytical articles that tried to remain distanced. There was also a diversity of audiences: the discussion sometimes extended to a national scale, while sometimes, where the cultural divide was stronger, it remained restricted to urban elites. It also concerned the European space in the broad sense (including Russia) and the United States; then, more remotely, several Latin American countries, the Caribbean space, and the British dominions; and finally, European circles and ports in African and Asian spaces (whether colonial or otherwise). I have not found any trace of the local or colonised populations in these spaces taking up these discussions, although this area has not been sufficiently studied. Finally, there is a diversity of content: where they did draw interest, readings of the Commune remained marked by a multiplicity of voices and by political, social and cultural divides. As we have seen, these usages above all reflect the vernacular social and political issues within each country. To these, we should add the effects of varied censorship policies or temporal gaps – not to mention the fact that these receptions then found echoes in each other (for example, on the scale of the American continent). The scattering of perspectives was thus a constant reality, and cannot be overlooked.

But – as in the case of the publications just mentioned – a contraction of the ways of grasping the Commune is equally perceptible on this broader scale. It is apparent in the stereotyped visions, the received wisdom, the shared definitions, and the core ideas that can be found in many different locations. This ought not to surprise us. The media logics described in the first part continued to operate, while also being compressed by the shock of the Commune's end. Accordingly, news, dispatches, and excerpts from French and foreign newspapers ran through different channels of communication before being redistributed around certain information hubs (London, New York), then secondary ones (San Francisco): although widely circulated, the textual raw material itself remained rather meagre. Correspondents on the ground, moreover, were imbued with the increasingly hysterical atmosphere in Versailles. Lastly, the effects of mass-circulation production made themselves felt, heightened by the horror of the fires and the deaths: that is, the simplification of situations; the recourse to easily understandable plotlines; the repetition of generic ideas about revolution, violence and civilisation. Some journalists and commentators were well aware of this limitation. An exasperated reporter, John Russell Young, who had famously covered the US Civil War, noted: 'The newspapers do little more than scream, and you wade through column after column with much of the feeling of stumbling through a morass or a field of briers.'[27]

Perhaps, at this point, I should also mention some of the specific effects of these transcontinental and multifaceted interplays of circulations and re-uses. As studies on the connections between globalisation and literary serialisation in the nineteenth century have shown, the plurality of discourses and the repetition of discursive schemas go hand in hand: here, the singular and the multiple mutually reinforce one another.[28] This circulation of themes was moreover facilitated by the pre-existing, largely non-European audience of an entire strand of this nineteenth-century imaginary. Such is the case with the imaginary of revolution after the 'age of revolutions' (1775–1850), refracted by this transcontinental dimension into an infinite array of readings, which we also find here. The same is true of the romantic imaginary of the people, the Middle Ages, and the fascination for destructive passions. Without doubt, this mostly concerned the intellectual elites of the day; but it was also largely they who made their voice heard in these newspapers and books. The phenomenon perhaps appears even more clearly when it comes to the imaginary of the underworld, with its criminal organisations and threatening mobs.[29] Together, these various imaginaries trace a web of possible connections. They were, of

27 Quoted in Albert Boime and Olin Levi Warner, 'Olin Levi Warner's Defense of the Paris Commune', *Archives of American Art Journal* 29: 3–4 (1989), pp. 2–22, at p. 5.

28 See Matthieu Letourneux, 'La mondialisation à l'ère de la culture sérielle', *Romantisme* 163: 1 (2014), pp. 79–88.

29 Alain Vaillant, 'Pour une histoire globale du romantisme', in Vaillant, ed., *Dictionnaire du romantisme* (Paris, CNRS Éditions, 2012), pp. xiii–cix; Dominique Kalifa, *Les Bas-Fonds. Histoire d'un imaginaire* (Paris: Seuil, 2013). This is suggested by the multiple disseminations, translations and imitations that drew on the 'mysteries of Paris' as their source (from the 'mystery of London', to those of New York, of Rio de Janeiro, of Manila, and beyond).

course, adapted by those who transmitted them, each time tailoring them to the history, expectations and frameworks of understanding of the given places of reception.[30] In other words, in addition to the political debates, these perceptions of the Commune could resonate even in seemingly distant territories, while also acclimatising them to other ways of seeing. Conversely, the post-Commune period can be seen as a particular moment in this large-scale phenomenon of connecting pieces of imaginaries and received wisdom.

Revisiting the 'Myth' of the Commune

How, then, should we present the ingredients of this astonishing discursive forest? There is no shortage of a priori notions that can be drawn upon: 'public opinion', 'myth', 'the transnational social imaginary', and so on. For example, there was clearly a space of transnational media exchange, which makes us think of the idea of 'public opinion'. And yet, in each case, the various perspectives seem to have been turned back onto their given country of reception. Only the northern European press – especially the British – presented itself as a recognised supranational arbiter. Generally, however, the overall perimeter of their horizons seems too limited for this term to be appropriate. The widely used term 'myth' has the value of emphasising the work of fictional reconstruction that was in operation. It points to the anthropological scope of certain themes: the conspiracy, the fire, the woman stripped of her own true nature, or of the binary oppositions of good and evil, barbarism and civilisation, secrecy and transparency. Still, this notion is too rigid to account for the discursive dynamics observed, or for their evident historicity. The more flexible expression 'social imaginary', finally, seems more apt: it emphasises the creativity at work rather than the reiteration

30 In the French history of cultural transfers, *passeurs* (smugglers) are those who see to the passing of an idea, a form of knowledge, a literary form, or a set of representations from one cultural space to another. Often this is, in reality, a collective phenomenon and a chain of transmissions. These *passeurs* might be translators, authors, journalists, novelists, booksellers or scholars. During this process, they moreover tend to adapt these ideas or forms in order to make them comprehensible in the space where they are being received, and in the process introduce shifts of meaning.

of supposedly pre-given elements.[31] But it too presupposes a certain coherence in the webs of representations, which is far from evident in this case. We might more properly consider the back-and-forth between the texts: what emerges instead, then, are common schemes, around which clusters of themes gravitate, produced and used in different ways depending on place or need. I will present them in this form.

Violence vs. civilisation: the revolution and French tradition

One typical schema concerns the *violence* of the event – in terms of the violence of the Communards, of course, but also that of the victors. From May to September, the English-language press used the expression 'reign of terror' over and over again. It sometimes recounted anecdotes that would make its readers shudder: in Montmartre, according to one of the first American accounts of the event, by William P. Fetridge, the insurgents were said to have cut off the hands of twelve imprisoned soldiers before releasing them.[32] More often, however, the violence was evoked in general terms, as in this solemn statement from the Mexican newspaper *La Brújula*: 'The civil war that is now ruining this great nation will go down in history as one of the fiercest.'[33]

On this basis, different readings could become intertwined. The Bloody Week was rarely the result of a single set of circumstances, and its violence was generally linked to revolution as a phenomenon: the event was thus interpreted through the potent and already widespread imaginary of the Terror of 1793. Another reading – and they could also intersect – presented the Bloody Week as an explosion peculiar to the French and their hot-headed character. It could also be read as an incomprehensible outbreak of savagery in the heart of one of the cradles of civilisation. The mention of peoples deemed 'savages' – ancient barbarians, Indians, the Chinese, and so on – sometimes emphasised this character. Paris in flames finally allowed for long reflections on the fragile state of civilisation and the modern world. On 5 June, the correspondent for *L'Indépendance belge* deplored this 'unprecedented

31 Pierre Popovic, *Imaginaire social et folie littéraire. Le Second Empire de Paulin Gagne* (Montreal: Presses de l'université de Montréal, 2008).

32 William P. Fetridge, *The Rise and Fall of the Paris Commune in 1871* (New York: Harper, 1871).

33 *La Brújula*, 28 July 1871.

catastrophe that would never have been thought possible in the nineteenth century, which makes civilisation disappear and history regress.'[34]

The designated perpetrators of this debauchery of violence were, in general, supposedly well known. Together they made up a single list, which could be either roughly copied or discussed in fine detail: the drunkard, the criminal, the foreigner, the vagrant, the revolutionary, the prostitute.[35] The figure of the *pétroleuse* deserves particular attention, as it embodied this destructive violence and left a mark on people's minds. This was, as we know, a chimera: according to the most likely hypothesis, the figure found its 'real' substratum in the presence of women who fought on the barricades during the fires.[36] This account of women – sometimes hideous, sometimes falsely innocent – throwing petrol on Parisian buildings and setting off orgiastic fires, was nevertheless repeated in most countries, including the ones whose press we only briefly consulted. Their description takes the form of literary bravura pieces, or of the raw reporting which was thus endowed with an extra layer of realism: 'it is said that one *cantinière* caused the death of ten soldiers by putting poison in their wine . . . Women found throwing petroleum into houses have been shot on the spot.'[37] Especially striking are the graphic representations, which were particularly important in a nineteenth century strongly coloured by caricatures and other sensational images. Ugly, twisted, grimacing women took an unhealthy pleasure in lighting fires; while others, throwing themselves forth like modern furies, brought chaos and destruction through their folly. These images were then translated or reinterpreted; we are still lacking any systematic study of the circulations and appropriations of this theme, which is manifestly transnational in scope.[38] But what have been identified already are the foundations of this representation: they are based on the evocation of the famous *tricoteuses* of 1793, the Amazons of 1848 and, beyond that, on a more anthropological level, on the frequent association between women, unreason and destruction, deep-rooted in the

34 *L'Indépendance belge*, 5 June 1871.

35 Sometimes it was the worker – but the dominant tendency, as in France in the 1860s, was to distinguish between 'good' workers and 'bad'.

36 Edith Thomas, *Les Pétroleuses* (Paris: Gallimard, 1963).

37 *The Times*, 27 May.

38 Bertall's work is reproduced in British publications, for example.

imaginaries of the time.[39] It is almost possible to detect 'survivals' such as those identified by Aby Warburg and discussed in Chapter 8, above. To use Warburg's typology, we encounter the ancient figures of the 'woman in fury', the 'destructive mother', or the 'witch'.[40] This is not surprising, as a number of these ancient, biblical or medieval figures formed part of the cultural baggage of many publicists, men of letters and artists in the countries studied (for instance, the articles summon up Medea, Judith and the witches' Sabbath).[41] The *pétroleuse* thus offered, after the fact, an updated version of the monster in the Parisian chaos: a figure characterised by deviation from the norm, by the break with both the natural and social order, and by the call to return wisely to this order. The depth of this representation can explain the repetitive effect of these various images as well as their emotional force, even for the crudest among them. Subterranean resurgences were thus by no means confined to revolutionary times; for those who aligned themselves with the side of order and reason, they can also serve as an emotional and symbolic repellent against the supposed threat of dissolution and destruction. In this sense, these women embodied an absolute of otherness.

Figures of the other

The *pétroleuses* lead us to the other typical schema. In this case, the Commune stood as a figure of the other, which in turn allowed one to reaffirm one's own identity or civilisation. This particularly concerned the national dimension. The British perspective, as *The Times* suggested, is a notable case in point. In the United States, the *Nation* newspaper, close to the Republican Party, offers another example: in its words, the French 'care nothing about "checks and balances," about the independence

39 On the figure of the monster, see Anna Caiozzo and Anne-Emmanuelle Demartini, eds, *Monstre et imaginaire social* (Grane: Créaphis, 2008); Jean-Jacques Courtine, 'Le corps inhumain', in Alain Corbin, Jean-Jacques Courtine and Georges Vigarello, eds, *Histoire du corps, vol. I: De la Renaissance aux Lumières* (Paris: Seuil, 2005), pp. 373–86.

40 In Aby Warburg, *L'Atlas Mnemosyne* (Paris: L'Écarquillé, 2012).

41 Moreover, formulations of pathos are far from necessarily limited to the 'Western' space alone. See Aby Warburg, *Le Rituel du serpent. Récit d'un voyage en pays pueblo* (Paris: Macula, 2003).

Eugène Girard, lithograph, circa 1871,
Musée Carnavalet/Histoire de Paris, Paris.

of the judiciary, the freedom of the press, the protection of personal or local self-government . . . They care nothing even about a republican form of government, as Americans understand it.'[42] This practice of

42 In 'The Assembly and the Commune,' *Nation* 309 (1871). Quoted in Patrick C. Jamieson, 'Foreign Criticisms of the 1871 Paris Commune: The Role of British and American Newspapers and Periodicals,' *Intersections* 11: 1 (2010), pp. 100–15, at p. 105.

magnifying one's country in the distorting mirror of the Parisian drama may be called an instance of 'favourable comparisons'. They can be found in the German, Spanish, Italian and Mexican press – especially in non-socialist outlets: that is to say, the majority of them.

Canada offers an illustrative example. At the time, this recently declared British dominion (a status it gained in 1867) had not yet clarified its relations with the imperial power in London or with its American neighbour. According to a study by Alban Bargain-Villéger, the Commune had the entire press against it: 600,000 copies, regardless of language, region or political position.[43] The most systematic criticism concerned the attacks on the Church. The radical newspaper *Le Pays*, for example, denounced these 'red tyrants . . . who persecute priests and purport to forbid all religious worship'.[44] This is hardly surprising, given the importance of religious tolerance in Canadian history since the Quebec Act of 1774.[45] Yet this line of argument was not confined to Canada: it proved decisive in many countries, not only in the conservative camp. This was less visible in France itself, no doubt because of the weight of anticlericalism in the later history of the Third Republic. But this religious dimension is perhaps the only theme that extends beyond the geographical perimeter indicated earlier, also reaching as far as China. Back in Canada, the other consensual points of criticism concern the activity of women that we have just discussed, as well as opposition to socialism. A national comparison was easily made: 'While the unrestrained French populace slit each other's throats in the streets of Paris', rejoiced *Le Franc-Parleur*, 'we must be glad to see our intelligent workers flying the flag of the Faith, able to offer joy to the family and consolation to the unfortunate'.[46] Of course, there were differences: the French-speaking press seems to have been more worried about the evils of socialism than English-speaking outlets, which were both less perturbed and more detached.

43 Alban Bargain-Villéger, 'The Scarecrow on the Other Side of the Pond: The Paris Commune of 1871 in the Canadian Press', *Labour/Le Travail* 74 (Autumn 2014), pp. 179–98.

44 *Le Pays*, 13 May. Quoted in Bargain-Villéger, 'The Scarecrow on the Other Side of the Pond', p. 187.

45 For the first time in the British Empire, the Quebec Act preserved the status of Catholics in a predominantly Protestant country.

46 *Le Franc-Parleur*, 23 March. Quoted in Bargain-Villéger, 'The Scarecrow on the Other Side of the Pond', p. 192.

But there was a common note across the country. As in the US case discussed above, the French civil war appeared also as an event on the Canadian-national scale, and was surely not a negligible moment in the difficult process of determining Canada's own national identity.

In this sense, the Commune could of course be used, within the debates in different countries, to denigrate adversaries by association, casting them as dangerous figures embodying otherness. We have seen this in the case of the United States: the trend observed during the event was confirmed after May. In Spain, the conservative press revelled in the spectacle of Paris in flames, and turned this scene of horror against its republican and federalist opponents. The tone varied from country to country: in Germany and Russia, for example, it was more reactionary, perhaps because of press surveillance. In any case, even in the regions that expressed greater support for the Parisian revolt, the Commune generally ended up playing this role in the consolidation of self-identities. The spectrum was in fact broad, encompassing continental, regional, linguistic, social, political, religious and urban identities. But since the Commune was most often presented as cosmopolitan or specifically French, national identities – whatever form or content we give to this term – were particularly at stake. In this sense, the Parisian insurrection played a role, albeit a modest one, in the fixing and large-scale dissemination of the national reference point, which was likewise characteristic of the period.[47]

The communist plot: the IWMA in the dock

But the pattern that most structured reactions was the idea of the 'plot', and in particular the supposed plot led by the IWMA. In his circular of 6 June 1871, Jules Favre played on this: 'Alongside the parodistic Jacobins who had the pretension of establishing a political system, we must place the leaders of a now infamous society, which is called the INTERNATIONAL, and whose action was perhaps more powerful than

47 On national identity in the nineteenth century, see Anne-Marie Thiesse, *La Création des identités nationales. Europe (XVIIIe–XXe siècle)* (Paris: Seuil, 1999); Eric Hobsbawm, *Nations and Nationalism Since 1780* (Cambridge: Cambridge University Press, 1992), and *The Age of Capital, 1848–1875* (London: Weidenfeld & Nicolson, 1975); Pierre Singaravélou and Sylvain Venayre, eds, *Histoire du monde au XIXe siècle* (Paris: Fayard, 2017).

that of their accomplices, because it had a base of numbers, discipline and cosmopolitanism.' It is now clear that this denunciation was based on fiction: although the Paris members of the IWMA did play a definite role in the Council of the Commune and in the leadership of the National Guard, they nonetheless drew on other affiliations and identities. Moreover, the IWMA was never a secret society, and its General Council hesitated for some time before intervening, due to a lack of information but also out of caution. In no case, therefore, can the Commune be seen to be the emanation of the French branch of the IWMA. Thiers himself spoke of exaggeration in this regard during the parliamentary inquiry into the events of 18 March.[48]

But the collusion of images almost everywhere prevailed. 'The IWMA, which is today the whole world's concern, is confused with the Commune. So, what we say about the one applies to the other', remarked *El Monitor republicano*.[49] The confusion was even broader: the IWMA's General Council in London and Bakunin's International Alliance of Socialist Democracy, though at loggerheads, were often considered together.[50] The IWMA was also associated with Freemasonry and secret societies from the 1850s, such as the Marianne. The drawing of such connections was not always entirely baseless: the Freemasons did intervene in favour of the Commune, on 29 April. But making such links usually served to create analogies: for Paul de Saint-Victor, author of one of the most virulent pamphlets, the Commune was quite simply the 'Freemasonry of crime'.[51] In France, the period of active secret societies and political conspiracies had already come to an end by this point, but the imaginary

48 *L'Enquête parlementaire sur l'insurrection du 18 mars 1871* (Paris: Librairie législative Wittersheim, 1872).

49 'L'Internationale', *El Monitor republicano*, 28 July 1871.

50 The Alliance was sometimes called the 'Alliance for Socialist Democracy' and sometimes the 'International Alliance for Socialist Democracy'. It dissolved in 1868 to become part of the IWMA, but the International Brotherhood, a secret organisation, and Bakunin's networks persisted. They were sometimes called the 'Alliance' in this period, both by supporters and opponents; the term was then used to clarify the latent conflict within the IWMA in 1871, and even more so after the London Conference of September 1871. Understood in this way, they were indeed in conflict, and in any case it is a mistake to conflate the two.

51 Paul de Saint-Victor, *Barbares et bandits. La Prusse et la Commune* (Paris: Michel-Lévy, 1871), p. 249.

associated with them had not.[52] The functions of such an imaginary are well-known: the notion of the plot divides up the complexity of reality by designating a common enemy, and in turn calling for a unity against it (however temporary). This, moreover, makes it possible to 'excuse' the people after the fact, to render the event intelligible, and to make it easily shareable.[53]

The list of named plotters usually overlapped with the list of enemies already identified (the criminal, the foreigner, and so on), with the exception of women. But most often the plot was supposed to have been hatched by socialists or 'communists'. 'Die Roten' and 'the Reds' often appeared in headlines. These leaders then took on features that had already been used in 1793, 1830 and 1848: they were *partageux* (literally: advocates of redistribution) and thieves who deceived the people with fine-sounding words.[54] Using already hackneyed arguments, politicians and journalists insisted that these 'reds' had no respect for property and that, working in the name of an absolute equality, they threatened the income of the conscientious worker. This denunciation was accompanied by a whole labour of the recalibration of words, which notably concerned *liberté*: 'their liberty is robbery and murder, their equality is in vice, and their fraternity that of demons', as Canada's *New Westminster Mainland Guardian* summarised this idea.[55] This reassertion of what they called a 'true liberty' was, of course, opposed to the supposedly 'false' liberty of the democratic and social republic, which its promoters itself considered to be the only 'true' one because it was deemed really emancipatory. The struggle over the meaning of words, as identified by Michèle Riot-Sarcey, also played out on this broader scale.[56]

---

52 Jean-Noël Tardy, *L'Âge des ombres. Complots, conspirations et sociétés secrètes au XIXe siècle* (Paris: Les Belles Lettres, 2015).

53 Bronislaw Baczko, *Les Imaginaires sociaux. Mémoires et espoirs collectifs* (Paris: Payot, 1984); Pierre-André Taguieff, *La Foire aux Illuminés. Ésotérisme, théorie du complot, extrémisme* (Paris: Mille et une nuits, 2005).

54 *Partageux*: pejorative term for those who advocate the sharing of property and equal ownership. For instance, it was used by the 'Party of Order' in 1848 to whip up peasants' fear and their grievances against the young Republic.

55 *New Westminster Mainland Guardian*, 8 April. Quoted in Bargain-Villéger, 'The Scarecrow on the Other Side of the Pond', p. 187.

56 Michèle Riot-Sarcey, *Le Procès de la liberté. Une histoire souterraine du XIXe siècle en France* (Paris: La Découverte, 2016).

Here emerges an imaginary that must surely be described as bourgeois and liberal, in the sense that it was attached to respect for property, transparency, the moderation of impulses, the law, and political and economic freedoms. It encompassed a wide spectrum: even if discordant voices were expressed, this imaginary appeared in a great variety of forms in the monarchist and religious press, in liberal, republican and radical newspapers, and even sometimes in workers' and socialist outlets, which were anxious to distance themselves from the Commune (at least in this regard) as a show of their seriousness. In this moment, it was expressed as a lowest common denominator, operating across this large scale.

In so doing, these debates did in fact take up many elements from previous revolutions and counterrevolutions. But two features distinguished them. First, their consensual dimension. The great revolutions and insurrections that went before 1871 had given rise to more sharply divisive debates. This factor is probably linked here to the stronger social dimension of the Commune, as well as to the media effects mentioned above. The other particularity is the idea of the revolutionary movement having an organised and international character: this would suggest that, within these societies, there was an increased awareness of globalisation and a growing fear at what seemed to be new types of threats. Historians of the workers' movement have even noted, with some amusement, that this imaginary in fact pre-empted the more structured forms that these movements took on in the 1880s – and was certainly a factor, if an involuntary one, in encouraging that tendency.

A new figure: 'Dr Marx'

As we have seen, new international figures finally asserted themselves in this moment, in particular that of Karl Marx. The IWMA remained cautious at the beginning of the Commune. It took some time before Marx considered that, with the Commune, 'the [struggle] of the working class against the capitalist class and its state ha[d] entered upon a new phase with the struggle in paris [*sic*]', and even that a 'new point of departure of world-historic importance ha[d] been gained'.[57]

57 Marx to Kugelmann, 17 April 1871, cited in Gareth Stedman Jones, *Karl Marx: Greatness and Illusion* (London: Allen Lane, 2016), p. 505.

As early as April, it was decided to write an address in support of insurgent Paris, but the lack of precise information, the difficulty of the exercise, and Marx's illness delayed matters. Entitled *The Civil War in France*, the text presented to the General Council on 30 May – after the Bloody Week – was adopted unanimously by those present. Composed of four chapters, this address of some forty pages drew a vitriolic portrait of the Versailles government, of Thiers – a 'monstrous gnome' – and of the France of the Second Empire considered in political, social and economic terms. Then, after deploring the 'magnanimity' of the Parisian workers and the fact that the Communards had not seized the Banque de France, he offered a reasoned defence of the Paris Commune experiment, which he presented as 'the glorious harbinger of a new society'.[58]

The text was a rapid success. Three editions were published in two months (8,000 copies of the second edition were sold). The Spanish and Italian translations then gave it a second wind. Blocked by police surveillance, the French translation was made available in Belgium in 1872, but it did not circulate as widely.[59] In any case, it is significant for our purposes that the debate on the Commune, which was impossible in France, took place in English, both in Great Britain and the United States. The hateful discussions sparked by the text were followed by the interviews that Marx gave a few months after the events, notably to the *New York Herald*. The articles were then translated – for example, into French, in *Le Gaulois* of 22 August 1871.[60] Presented as 'Dr Marx', Marx once again explained the International's position:

> Much nonsense has been said and written about the grandiose projects for revolt hatched by the International. There is not a word of truth in this. The truth is that the International and the Commune functioned together for a certain period, because they were fighting

58 Karl Marx, *The Civil War in France*, at marxists.org.

59 The text had nonetheless become well known, indeed by perhaps unexpected means. It was translated as an incriminating document in Edmond Villetard, *Histoire de l'Internationale* (Paris: Garnier, 1872), which denounced the Commune as a plot by the International.

60 Maximilien Rubel, 'Deux interviews de Karl Marx sur la Commune', *Le Mouvement social* 38 (1962), pp. 7–27; Karl Marx, *Notebook on the Paris Commune (Press Excerpts and Notes)*, ed. Hal Draper (Berkeley, CA: Independent Socialist Press, 1971).

> the same enemy; but it is quite false to say that the leaders of the insurrection were acting under orders received from the Central Committee of the International in London.

Marx sought to reassert the International's policy – and to distance himself from the leaders of the insurrection. He indeed deplored their 'incapacity' (Bergeret had proved 'completely incapable', Assi was an 'idiot').

Marx's defensive claims had no bearing on the overall rereading of the event as just presented. Far from it: several passages of *The Civil War in France*, when deliberately reread in a biased way, could even strengthen the notion of a connection between the Commune and the IWMA, or the idea that it was intrinsically violent.[61] The Commune, on the other hand, also surely had its effects on Marx himself: it played a role in his thinking about the political form to be instituted in the future – not necessarily in the sense of a strong state, since he also discussed the Communard leaders' federalist ideals. Above all, it gave him a British, European and global renown, which perhaps also helped him to gain the upper hand over Bakunin within the International in this same moment.[62] 'The *Address* . . . is making the devil of a noise', he wryly commented in a letter of 18 June 1871, 'and I have the honour to be at this moment the best calumniated and the most menaced man of London. That really does one good after a tedious twenty years' idyll in my den.'[63] If the Commune could not be described as Marxist, it did bring international renown for Marx himself, whose analysis would later spill over into the interpretation of the event itself.

These were some of the fabrics of meaning and words that were stretched over the Commune after the fact, by non-revolutionaries and by those who called for reason, whose main themes clearly had widespread effects. With the conclusion of the events of 1871, initially scattered threads of well-worn talking points and assumptions fused together, in

61 Ibid., pp. 509–10.

62 Jonathan Sperber, *Karl Marx: a Nineteenth-Century Life* (London: Liveright, 2013), p. 302.

63 Marx to Kugelmann, 18 June 1871, *Marx/Engels Collected Works* (MECW), vol. 44 *(Correspondence 1870–1873)* (London: Lawrence & Wishart Electric Book, 2010), p. 158.

this way casting the Parisian experience as the new spectre of modern revolutionary deviance.

These clusters of representations would later be unpicked, to varying degrees in different regions and countries. But this overall depiction of the Commune persisted – and the rereading fed into the recomposition of power relations that followed the 'terrible year'. Many of its features, including its violence, but in particular the connection with the IWMA – later bolstered from a completely different perspective by the Marxist–Leninist view – would fix in place a certain long-enduring portrayal of the Commune. It would take historians almost a century to begin to pick apart these associations.

11

A Paradox? The Strengthening of the Liberal State

I have spoken of an imaginary of the Commune that cast it in the most monstrous terms. But its effects were not only at the level of media-political discourse. It also fuelled a series of reactions coming from other states, unfolding through the interplay of reverberations and feedback, as discussed earlier. This phenomenon affected the countries most concerned, whether they were nation-states or multinational empires, democratic republics or authoritarian monarchies. It also took on countless forms and had various impacts: it is difficult to identify categorically any uniform logic at work here, or to identify a general tendency.

Taken in combination, however, these reactions do seem to indicate a series of reorientations towards what we might call a 'tightening' of state practices. This involved a tightening of surveillance across states, a tightening of imperial rule by the European great powers, and a tightening of control within states themselves, consistent with new political forms that had taken shape over the previous decade or so. If we want to understand this turning of the screws, we also need to contextualise it within the broader reconfigurations of European and imperial society and politics over the 1860s and 1870s, and beyond. The form of state and the way of understanding the social world that were consolidated in reaction to the Commune were specific, and must be analysed as such. These considerations will lead us in turn to examine the Commune's status as an event and its effects – always a delicate task when dealing with a political event, revolutionary or otherwise.

International State Practices

The circulars issued by French foreign ministers Jules Favre and (from August 1871) Charles de Rémusat, like the responses from other governments, cannot in fact be reduced to any simple, stereotyped discourse. Right from the outbreak of the insurrection, Favre played on the Commune's ambiguous character, as both a municipal authority and a quasi-government, to help him assert the French nation-state's sovereignty in the international arena. Other considerations also took sharper form after May – especially the idea that the Commune expressed a possible revolutionary threat to all European states. Given the connections that were being made (however sincerely or instrumentally) between the Commune and the IWMA, this threat could easily appear both pressing and substantial. A further question arose concerning international law: while the French cabinet denied the existence of a rival authority in Paris, and the Commune itself remained undecided on the subject, observers across Europe had seen a revolutionary government operating in the French capital, and this over the course of several weeks. It is worth remembering that, in international law, the legal continuity of the state is held to persist independently of a change of regime – even if this implicitly requires that other powers recognise the new regime. Such was the case for the French Republic after 4 September 1870. By contrast, even the mere possibility of such recognition for the Commune was intolerable: this was a revolutionary movement that challenged the existing order of things, and in particular the social order – probably the most alarming element in the eyes of contemporary rulers. Might we discern here, in this treatment of the Commune, a precedent in international law, one that could subsequently be invoked against other revolutionary movements? What is certain, in any case, is that the existing states had to defend themselves against similar possibilities. This may also explain the unanimous response, at least on principle, even in countries which – judging by the diplomatic correspondence – felt less threatened by such movements: for instance, Italy and Austria-Hungary, where workers appeared to have much less social weight, or Great Britain, which felt strong enough to resist any such challenge.

These fears formed part of the backdrop to the repression now being put in place, which its proponents hoped to force through despite the existing national-level and legal constraints. This policy involved three particular points of focus. The first was extraditions. The French state was quick to begin making demands on countries where Communards had taken refuge. Even at the height of the Bloody Week, the French foreign minister proclaimed in a circular dated 26 May: 'I am hearing from all quarters the wish that the repression should be implacable.'[1] He added a few days later that the Communards were 'outside the limits of civilisation, beyond any right of refuge'.[2] Favre was responding to a classic problem in international relations, complicated by the recent glut of bilateral and multilateral treaties (which generally included extradition clauses). Two arguments were used to justify the extradition of Communards. The first was a tried-and-tested move: the Communards in exile were presented as common criminals, not political actors. The second was newer, and cited the IWMA's supposed involvement in the Commune as justification for a concerted response by states. For instance, one French government circular of 1872 proposed that 'international crime' – another legal innovation – should be considered grounds for extradition in international treaties.[3] The diplomatic contacts made from 1871 onwards were encouraging for the French government. Austria-Hungary, Russia, Denmark, Belgium and even Germany signalled their interest in such a response.[4] As early as June 1871, the Belgian foreign minister, the Baron d'Anethan, stated: 'an agreement among all governments on measures of vigilance and repression to be taken with regard to this dangerous association . . . is one of the most pressing needs of Europe's governments'.[5]

But when we look at specific cases, the situation turns out to have been rather more varied.[6] Great Britain quickly rejected any extraditions. After a brief debate, Gladstone pushed through this decision in

1 Jules Favre, 26 May 1871.

2 Paul K. Martinez, 'Communard Refugees in Great Britain', PhD dissertation, Sussex University (1981, never published), p. 19.

3 CAD, 2QO 84: 'L'Internationale et le droit pénal', Circular, 10 April 1872.

4 On Germany, see Carole Witzig, 'Bismarck et la Commune: la réaction des monarchies conservatrices contre les mouvements républicains et socialistes (1870–1872) vue à travers les archives allemandes', *International Review of Social History* 17: 1 (1972), pp. 191–221.

5 CAD, 2QO 84, 12 June 1871.

6 The analysis focuses once again on diplomatic correspondence and the relevant archives at the Archives Nationales.

the name of the Extradition Act, which had just been adopted, in 1870. This text, considered a model of liberal international law in the second half of the nineteenth century, specifically excluded political criminals from the extradition clauses of future bilateral treaties signed by Great Britain – be they foreigners, British citizens or even colonial subjects. While the British liberal and conservative press were at first hesitant about the decision, they eventually offered various expressions of support for it. It was argued that it was hard not to see a political dimension to these cases, from the actions of the Commune itself to the massacre of the Communards and the criminal proceedings they faced thereafter.[7] Belgium also rejected most extradition requests, citing more technical pretexts: the responses generally indicated that France's requests did not fulfil the criteria established in existing conventions, such as Articles 13 and 15 of the Convention of 29 April 1869.[8] Those same requests also met with equal resistance in Switzerland. In each case, these decisions were the product of intense national debates around the meaning of the right to asylum.

Spain, on the other hand, readily accepted the French requests. Despite appeals by republicans in parliament, Prime Minister Práxedes Sagasta and Foreign Minister Cristino Martos (from the centre-left) welcomed the 'repression led by Thiers'. They said that it did 'a service not only to Paris and France but to the cause of order and liberty in Europe and in the whole world'.[9] They, too, asked the French government to formulate its demands in accordance with existing treaties, to avoid opposition in the Cortes. But in Spain 'the insurgents [were] not considered as refugees but as guilty men'. The Portuguese authorities struck a similar attitude.[10]

Several other more geographically remote states also strongly backed the hunt for criminals. They did so either for their own domestic political reasons, out of a shared concern for the fight against socialism, or out

7 Martinez, 'Communard Refugees in Great Britain', On the Extradition Act and its effect on the treatment of the Communards, see Caroline Shaw, *Britannia's Embrace: Modern Humanitarianism and the Imperial Origins of Refugee Relief* (Oxford: Oxford University Press, 2015), pp. 147–76.

8 CAD, 2QO 91, 'Commune. Étrangers'. Other examples of these refusals are also presented.

9 CAD, CP, Spain.

10 AN, BB 30/1171, April 1872 letter.

of a desire to rebuild ties with France that had been weakened by the war of 1870. On 18 June 1871, the Sublime Porte reported that it had asked its agents in France to allow the police-checking of Ottoman ships. Its various provincial authorities were also invited to help French consulates root out insurrectionaries who had taken refuge in Turkey.[11] In Brazil, the French representative gave up insisting on extraditions, though the government there had seemed ready to grant them. In a fine example of the political use of geographical distance, he reported that Communards taking 'refuge down [in Brazil] is a way to get rid of this appalling rabble'. These various decisions did not always prove effective (exiles found refuge in countries that refused French requests, and few were actually extradited). But such breaches surely undermined the treaty system built up over previous decades.

At the same time, the policy of passport checks was stepped up, as a more direct means of preventing fugitives from leaving and entering. This policy was strengthened in all countries, with the exception once more of Great Britain. Border controls had previously been abandoned in the 1860s, as part of the liberalisation of trade and the movement of people. The Franco-Prussian War had prompted the reintroduction of this policy, after diplomatic discussions: it was decided that this would be a temporary measure, limited to the war period.[12] However, controls were maintained still after March 1871, in the wake of the Commune, and were sometimes even tightened: the United States reaffirmed this policy in April 1871, and in Belgium a decree of 5 May 1871 extended it to situations of civil war and revolution.[13] These decisions were also matched by a more cautious issuing of visas on either side of the border. This policy was not always effective, either. Fugitives often had false papers, as in the case of Eugène Razoua, who fled to Spain with a passport issued at the Spanish embassy in the name of Stephen Marques.[14] Technical issues also played their part: the long process of verifying documents jarred with the acceleration of transport and the new imperatives of keeping to timetables.[15] This, indeed, was the very reason why

11 CAD, CP, Brazil (letter of 2 July 1871), Turkey (letter of 28 June 1871).

12 Discussions in CAD, 2QO 58, 'passeports'. Circular of 30 July 1871.

13 NARA, RG 84; APP, BA 427.

14 AN, BB 30/488, extraditions, police report of 19 July 1871.

15 See Andreas Fahrmeir, 'Passports and the Status of Aliens', in Martin Geyer and Johannes Paulmann, eds, *The Mechanics of Internationalism: Culture, Society and Politics*

passport checks had been abandoned over the previous decade. 'This would be an ineffective measure and cause delays', the Dutch minister told Favre.[16] But the restoration of passport controls was not simply a return to the status quo ante. The policy of opening borders in the 1860s had in fact been accompanied by the rise of internal checks on individuals' national identity. These domestic controls were maintained when international border controls were reintroduced after 1870, so that the system now combined both levels.[17] The border-control regime was thus complemented by increased surveillance at the main points of passage and arrival within individual countries. Again in Belgium, the public security administrator had a circular issued to local administrations in May, which indicated that the formalities of passport checking had been re-established 'especially for the French', and that the police authorities had to ensure that the French who arrived after this date did indeed have passports. Lists were distributed to the authorities, identifying the individuals from France who were permitted to stay.[18] This other 'safety net' had its holes, too: but, taken together, these measures produced a period of greater control, in which nationality was taking on sharper definition. The year 1870–71 alone illustrates the general trend: the founding of the German Empire led to the creation of a new nationality, and the debates about the *optants* from Alsace-Lorraine (residents of this annexed territory, who had to leave in order to retain French nationality) forced special choices of national belonging. Further afield, the US Naturalization Act of July 1870 led to a convention between the United States and Great Britain at the start of the following year: it clarified the conditions under which naturalised citizens might lose their former nationality, formalising their choice of national allegiance. In this sense, this resumption of identity controls during and after the Commune (even though passport checks at borders were soon dropped) was part of a wider history of the practices for defining individual nationality

---

from the 1840s to the First World War (Oxford: Oxford University Press, 2001), pp. 93–119.

16 CAD, 2QO 84; 2QO 58.

17 On these shifts and this moment of rupture, see Fahrmeir, 'Passports and the Status of Aliens', as well as Andreas Fahrmeir, *Citizens and Aliens: Foreigners and the Law in Britain and the German States (1789–1870)* (New York: Berghahn, 2000).

18 APP, BA 472.

during this period. The lengthy checks required by countries of origin to obtain the return of their own 'nationals' arrested in Paris also point to this stepped-up effort to define who and what was 'national'.

Finally, new practices were introduced for police surveillance and institutional information exchange, directed primarily at exiled Communards and IWMA members. The repression of the International after May 1871 had several different variants: in France after the Dufaure Law (1872) or in Spain, it was direct and supported by specific legislation. In Germany, where the right of association was legally protected and could not be challenged, such an option was not possible. But police pressure, which could intervene in the intermediate space between law and deed, was here exerted with some effectiveness.[19] On an international scale, police officers in different countries were increasingly exchanging information on IWMA members or former Communards. This phenomenon is not always readily visible in the archives, since it generally assumed the form of international exchanges characteristic of the second half of the nineteenth century, relying on multilateral conventions and the sharing of information.[20] In matters of policing, it took the form of cooperation for specific political purposes, through either embassies or direct contacts between police officers.[21] Even allowing for these considerations, there was surely a notable intensification of exchanges. In general, agreements for information sharing and case-specific assistance were first enshrined at a ministerial level. According to the French consul in Vienna, the chancellor of the Austro-Hungarian Empire had, for instance, declared himself 'fully disposed to promote an exchange of information that would mutually facilitate the authorities' efforts'.[22] This exchange would then take concrete form, as evidenced by the archives of the

19 Paolo Napoli, *Naissance de la police moderne. Pouvoir, normes, société* (Paris: La Découverte, 2003).

20 It took the form of the international exchanges characteristic of the late nineteenth century, based on multilateral agreements and information sharing. See Madeleine Herren, 'Governmental Internationalism and the Beginning of a New World Order in the Late Nineteenth Century', in Geyer and Paulmann, eds, *Mechanics of Internationalism*, pp. 121–44.

21 Mathieu Deflem, *Policing World Society* (Oxford: Oxford University Press, 2002).

22 CAD, 2QO 84. There were also exchanges not including France. See Witzig, 'Bismarck et la Commune'.

surveillance operations carried out in three countries: Great Britain, Belgium (and through it, Germany) and Switzerland.[23] They reveal the circulation of both summary and detailed reports between police institutions, via embassies. They also show direct exchanges between police officers: in February 1872, a French and a British policeman sent a joint evaluation of the International's membership at the request of Britain's Home Office.[24] Finally, policemen were sent to follow the IWMA's efforts, with the agreement of the diplomatic authorities, and were sometimes put into contact with local agents. Despite the visible disappointment of the inspectors, who were bored at the meetings and also noted the difficulties of the exiles' and activists' lives, there was a noticeable tightening of the net of police surveillance. Their reports, which illustrated their concern to reproduce the words spoken and identify the individuals involved, also fed the production of a 'police knowledge', another of the tools of control wielded by states.[25] How can we get a sense of the real reach of these police measures? A comparison with the 1848 revolutions, which had operated on a completely different scale, is instructive here. After those events, despite an avowed distrust towards political policing, unofficial surveillance was carried out in Great Britain; a policing union of German states was also formed between 1851 and 1866.[26] By contrast, no such new creations can be found after 1871. Rather, the more circumscribed nature of the Commune as an event, and the memory of these precedents, may have helped reinforce existing surveillance practice. These two moments may thus be considered in combination: in this sense, they amount to a single sequence of post-revolutionary intensified state surveillance,

23 APP, BA 427 (Belgium), BA 428 (Great Britain), BA 431 (Switzerland).

24 APP, BA 428, 4 February 1872.

25 Michel Foucault, *Sécurité, territoire, population. Cours au Collège de France (1977–1978)* (Paris: Seuil, 2004). See also Vincent Denis, 'Les savoirs policiers en Europe', special issue of the *Revue d'histoire des sciences humaines* 19: 2 (2008).

26 On Great Britain see, in addition to Clive Emsley's work, Lindsay Clutterbuck, 'An Accident of History? The Evolution of Counter-Terrorism Methodology in the Metropolitan Police from 1829 to 1901', PhD thesis, University of Portsmouth (2002). On the German states, see Mathieu Deflem, 'International Policing in Nineteenth-Century Europe: The Police Union of German States (1851–1866)', *International Criminal Justice Review* 6: 1 (1996), pp. 36–57. For the Austro-Hungarian Empire, see Christos Aliprantis, 'The Origins of Transnational Political Policing in Europe, 1830–1870', PhD dissertation, University of Cambridge (2021).

parallel to the liberalisation of trade and the acceleration of migratory movements.

Thus, there was a tightening of international state practices, sometimes in a partial and temporary way, sometimes more enduring. Jules Favre and then Charles de Rémusat explained its principles on multiple occasions. 'What we want', De Rémusat explained to his German counterpart in 1872,

> is not so much a concert between governments as a set of simultaneous acts on the part of each of them. We agree with the objections that may be levelled against international arrangements that lead to a kind of mutual surveillance of states against each other. The liberal principles which the French government prides itself on professing would forbid it joining a league whose avowed purpose was an outright intervention in the future business of foreign countries. But on the other hand, we can hardly close our eyes.[27]

So, in keeping with the dominant principles of the 1860s and 1870s (state integrity and the possibility of circulation), the aim was to coordinate the policies of different states, and to step up exchanges in matters of surveillance so as to make them more effective.[28]

The Commune and Changes in National Political Divisions

These international policies came along with another phenomenon: the impact of the Commune within each country. The Paris insurrection tended to provoke a shift in political divisions, particularly in those countries where it had the strongest echoes or prompted the most heated debates. Schematically, we can say that a split appears to have opened up within liberal, republican and radical groups in reaction to the Commune. Many, faced with what they termed 'excesses', abandoned the revolutionary idea, or demoted it to a legacy of the past in order to

27 CAD, 2QO 84.

28 Renaud Morieux, 'La prison de l'exil. Les réfugiés de la Commune entre les polices françaises et anglaises (1871–1880)', in Marie-Claude Blanc-Chaléard et al., eds, *Police et migrants (France, 1667–1939)* (Rennes: Presses universitaires de Rennes, 2001), pp. 133–50.

engage more effectively in their countries' contemporary political development. Conversely, the more radical stepped up their defence of the revolutionary project of overthrowing the existing order, the better to secure the more immediate establishment of a society of true justice and equality. The tones and forms differed from country to country, and have made different kinds of mark on the historiography. We can begin by looking again at the cases examined above.

In the United States, the echoes of the Commune became more intense after the Bloody Week, both in commercial culture and in political debate. Despite the widely publicised support for the Commune – a subject to which we will return – the overall US reception was rather negative, even in the labour movement and among the ranks of Republicans and radical Democrats. During the great strike of 1877 there was frequent reference to the Commune – but in the sense of an example to be avoided. 'We are not followers of the Commune', said a trade-union leader in Cleveland in 1873, before embarking upon negotiations.[29] For historians Michel Cordillot and Philip Katz, the Commune corresponds more fundamentally to that moment in American history during Reconstruction, in which there was an observable split between the Republic and its revolutionary heritage.[30] That early part of the nineteenth century, in which a United States proud of its revolutionary past could support democratic and liberal causes abroad, was now over. While the particular fault-lines were different, a similar process could be observed in Spain: the Commune's Republican supporters in parliament – the likes of José María Orense or Emilio Castelar – kept a lower profile over the course of May. And when they opposed the torrent of indignation that swept the chamber, Soler and Pí y Margall declared that they supported the Commune 'while condemning its crimes'. These splits developed within the Republican Party, sometimes out of disgust, sometimes out of caution. The Republican Josep Clavé, who had been exiled for his political stances and who had been in Lyon and Marseille in 1870, declared that he no longer supported insurrectionary politics: he feared that the same thing would happen in

29 Quoted in Katz, *From Appomattox to Montmartre: Americans and the Paris Commune* (Cambridge, MA: Harvard University Press, 1998).

30 Michel Cordillot, *Utopistes et exilés du Nouveau monde: des Français aux Etats-Unis, de 1848 à la Commune* (Paris: Vendémiaire, 2013); Katz, *From Appomattox to Montmartre.*

Spain as in Paris.[31] As for those who have been called Republican workers and 'plebeians', we can see the same faltering. Some of them clearly distanced themselves from revolutionary politics.[32] But others, who considered their earlier struggles vindicated, drew closer to the Federal Republican Executive (FRE)–IWMA, which was becoming increasingly anarcho-syndicalist, and growing fast despite repression.

Romania offers yet another contrasting case in point: in mid-April, as the social dimension of the struggle in Paris became better known – and especially after the fires of the Bloody Week (an episode the government brazenly exploited) – liberals distanced themselves from the Commune. Some liberal outlets joined the conservative press in a moral crusade against savagery, violence and socialism. The fall of the Commune thus dealt a blow to the struggles that had arisen during the course of 1870; many liberals and progressives were now forced to change their approach, abandoning many of the hopes and oppositional practices that had developed after 1848.[33] According to Georges Haupt, this same process can be seen across Europe. The effects were less clear-cut in Mexico, as discussed below: the phenomenon seemed mainly to concern the countries of Europe and North America.

This was no doubt only the most visible aspect of more varied shifts in position. But many groups who then repudiated the Commune also stepped up their commitment to what they saw as the liberalisation or democratisation of institutions. Here, we might venture a hypothesis. Based on the work of William Novak, Stephen Sawyer and James Sparrow, we can ask whether the war and then the Commune did not in fact accentuate a broader tendency towards what they call a 'liberal state'.

31 Albert Garcia-Balañà, '1871 in Spain: Transnational and Local History in the Formation of the FRE-IWMA', in Fabrice Bensimon, Quentin Deluermoz and Jeanne Moisand, eds, *'Arise Ye Wretched of the Earth!': The First International in Global Perspective* (Leiden: Brill, 2018); José Álvarez Junco, *La Comuna en España* (Madrid: Siglo XXI, 1971); Carlos Serrano, 'L'Espagne, la Commune et l'Internationale', in Jacques Rougerie, ed., *1871. Jalons pour une Histoire de la Commune de Paris* (Paris: PUF, 1973), pp. 222–39; Clara E. Lida, 'La Comuna de París y sus repercusiones: el caso español', in Guillermo Palacios and Erika Pani, eds, *El poder y la sangre. Guerra, estado y nación en la década de 1860* (Mexico City: Colegio de México, 2014).

32 CAD, CP, Spain, September 1871. Some signed documents that their bosses had given to them, in which they promised to stand up against troublemakers.

33 Georges Haupt, 'La Roumanie', in Rougerie, ed., *1871. Jalons pour une histoire de la Commune de Paris.*

By this they mean a kind of state that responded both to the development of liberal frameworks of government, and to recurrent political crises (1848, the Civil War, the Commune). Such a state might draw on a constitution, regular electoral exercises, respect for political freedoms (and even decentralised forms of government), while at the same time being repressive and strong enough to withstand the periods of suspension brought about by civil wars, as well as more routine threats.[34] This in turn required further reorientations – within liberal circles, of course (themselves anything but uniform), as well as in conservative milieux, which also had to reckon with the transformative changes seen in recent decades. These shifts also varied from country to country. In Great Britain, some such change had already taken place, particularly after the Chartist upsurge of the 1830s–50s.[35] But in that country, too, 1871 saw a realignment that affected a range of forces, from republican circles to the trade unions – and even some of the British members of the General Council of the IWMA, who refused to support the Commune. The German case is also telling here. While the Reich responded to French calls for cooperation, it quickly proposed an alliance with Austria-Hungary and Russia, explicitly uniting these conservative and authoritarian monarchies against socialism. As Bismarck argued, the Commune merely highlighted the 'advantages of the monarchical constitution'.[36] Yet this should not obscure the realignments that also took place within existing political currents, including among liberals, which Bismarck himself identified.[37] Nor should we overlook, in parallel, the more general (moderate) tendency towards liberalisation that affected both of these authoritarian empires – a development increasingly well documented by historians.[38] The German case, finally, shows how this

34 See William Novak, James Sparrow and Stephen Sawyer, 'Toward a History of the Democratic State', *Tocqueville Review/La Revue Tocqueville* 33: 2 (2015); Stephen Sawyer, 'A Fiscal Revolution: Statecraft in France's Early Third Republic', *American Historical Review* 121: 4 (2016), pp. 1141–66.

35 See the final chapters of Malcolm Chase, *Chartism: A New History* (Manchester: Manchester University Press, 2007).

36 Bismarck to Wilhelm I, 4 April 1872, quoted in Witzig, 'Bismarck et la Commune', p. 210.

37 Ibid.: 'No attentive observer will have failed to note how strong and massive [since the Commune] has been and still is the conversion, in Germany, of red liberals into moderate liberals, of liberal convictions into conservative ones'.

38 The case of Austria-Hungary has been the subject of a growing body of

remoulding of the state's role also affected other fields, such as social protection. Conscious of the 'social problem' the Commune had highlighted, Bismarck indeed responded by setting up the first pension funds. 'After the terrible lesson of the events in Paris', the French ambassador to Germany noted, 'the statesmen and major industrialists understood the need to stimulate the zeal of the classes most directly under threat from socialist propaganda, and to arm the state against these tendencies.'[39]

These reactions were all distinctive, reflecting their national and local contexts. At the same time, they did point in a similar direction. It would be mistaken to focus only on the contradictions at play – for example, between tightened state power and the persistence of liberal-internationalist pressures. In reality, such arrangements had long been part of the way states operated. More generally, both liberal and authoritarian tendencies had characterised the sociopolitical dynamics of various countries since at least 1848.[40] This set of contradictory but convergent movements may thus, for want of a better term, be called a 'liberal order', even though the term risks giving a false impression of systemic coherence. This phenomenon concerned the 1860s–70s, and mainly the European and North American space. Never uniform, it revealed itself above all during particular events, or in reaction to specific problems. In this sense the Commune – through both the scandal it provoked and the unusually broad span of forces it rallied against itself – can be called a moment of the expression, articulation and further consolidation of this 'liberal order'.

Here, it may be useful to return to our analysis of developments in France itself. Thiers's attitude in the moment of the Bloody Week fitted well into this wider process. If anything, the correlation was even

---

scholarship. See Pieter Judson, *The Habsburg Empire: A New History* (Cambridge, MA: Harvard University Press, 2016); Natasha Wheatley, *The Temporal Life of States: Sovereignty, Legal Knowledge, and the Archive of Empire* (Princeton: Princeton University Press, 2023). This development is well known in the German case, and has produced much debate. See Thomas Kühne, 'Demokratisierung und Parlamentarisierung. Neue Forschungen zur politischen Entwicklungs-fähigkeit Deutschlands vor dem ersten Weltkrieg', *Geschichte und Gesellschaft* 31: 2 (2005), pp. 293–316.

39 CAD, CP, Germany.

40 On this dual trend, see Christopher Clark, 'After 1848: The European Revolution in Government', *Transactions of the Royal Historical Society*, sixth series, 22 (2012), pp. 171–97.

stronger in this case: as has already been underlined often enough by historians, the Commune in France broke apart the traditional association between the Republic and revolutionary practice.[41] Moreover, the state grew stronger while only partially respecting its own rule of law; the appeal for subscriptions to repay the German reparations, which met with a considerable popular response, confirmed the strengthened link between state and citizens; and the bid to restore the monarchy under Henri V partly failed precisely because liberal forms of government were maintained.[42] Finally, Thiers's 'Conservative Republic', which eventually prevailed, seems like a perfect illustration of these shifts – though in a particular, French variant. Seen in this light, what French historiography often found surprising appears more logical when seen in this international perspective. France, in its own way, belonged to this overall tendency.

Recompositions in the Colonial and Imperial Spaces

When we examine empires and the interplay of international influence, this hardening of state power is yet more apparent. Again, the war and the Commune ought to be considered in combination. France was hard hit, particularly in economic terms: the war cost 2.5 billion francs, added to which were 5 billion francs in reparations. However, in the medium term, agricultural and industrial growth were not severely affected. The war indemnities to Germany were paid back on time, and Paris quickly regained its place as the world's second-most-important financial hub.[43] Although weakened by the rise of newcomers such as Germany and the United States, France remained a great power, as its imperial domination makes clear. And while French influence did temporarily take a hit, in countries such as Persia or Morocco it was quickly re-established.[44] In

41 This point is a commonplace of the political historiography of the nineteenth century, highlighted by François Furet and Maurice Agulhon alike.

42 Nicolas Delalande, *Les Batailles de l'impôt. Consentement et résistances, de 1789 à nos jours* (Paris: Seuil, 2011).

43 Maurice Lévy-Leboyer and François Bourguignon, *L'Économie française au XIXe siècle. Analyse macro-*économique (Paris: Economica, 1985).

44 CAD, CP, Morocco, letter of 22 July 1871; CAD, CP, Persia, letter of 2 September 1871.

Siam and Haiti, 'gunboat diplomacy' soon reared its head once more. In the latter case, the arrival of the aptly named frigate *La Magicienne* suddenly eased the difficulties of recent months, and the authorities promised to fulfil their overdue debt payments.[45] The speed with which debts were repaid seems to have been especially crucial, as in the cases of Mexico, Peru and Turkey. Referring to the sultan's change of attitude, the French representative put it in a nutshell: 'A country that can summon up a victorious army of 100,000 men and 4 billions even in the aftermath of a disastrous war, has unquestionable vitality, and must surely be reckoned with.'[46] While competition between the powers (notably Britain and Germany) remained intense, inter-imperial cooperation also continued in certain parts of the world, particularly in China and Algeria, where the three vessels – the Spanish, British and Italian – remained all summer. The turmoil that had developed at the time of the Commune seemed quickly resolved.

The aftermath of 1871 was above all a time of mobilisation of the colonial territories – sometimes in well-established forms, sometimes in new ones. Such was the case when it came to deportations. In late 1871, noting the influx of prisoners in the forts and prisons, the US correspondent of the *Spirit of the Time*, George Wilke, who was also a director of the Lower California Company, made a rather odd proposal to the French government. He offered to take in as colonists a certain number of those sentenced to deportation, offering them agricultural concessions on the peninsula. The Viscount de Lorgeril, who presented the project to the National Assembly in January 1872, claimed that there they would find 'a happiness that they were seeking in their own quite peculiar way in France'.[47] The proposal was rejected, partly because exporting French prisoners as part of a foreign colonisation initiative did not seem legally watertight.[48] But the French government also made use of its own colonies: given the recent events, those sentenced to deportation were no longer sent to Algeria, but rather to New Caledonia. From 1867 onwards, in view of the appalling mortality rate in the Guiana prisons, the Pacific archipelago had indeed become the

45 CAD, CP, Haiti, letter dated 16 June 1871.

46 CAD, CP, Turkey, letter of 5 July 1871; CAD, CP, Peru, letter of 19 July 1871.

47 *Annales de l'Assemblée nationale*, 6 January 1872, p. 455.

48 Katz, *From Appomattox to Montmartre*, Chapter 6, 'The View from the 1870s'.

preferred destination for marginal populations, transported criminals and political deportees. A dual system of property had been established there, to the detriment of the Kanak populations, in order to facilitate what the islands' French governors called a policy of 'regeneration through work'.[49]

Between 1872 and 1876, there was a no-less-remarkable movement of people to this colony: this was a mass process bringing together both the Parisian Communards (4,500 individuals) and the Kabyle insurgents (120 individuals).[50] The law of 23 March 1872 relating to the insurgent Communards was in fact also used for the Kabyles judged at the Constantine court of assizes in 1873. This well illustrated the aforementioned circulation of repressive practices between the 'colonial laboratory' and the metropole. This surely allowed the authorities to suggest a certain proximity between the two types of 'barbarians', whether revolutionaries or *indigènes*, or both.[51]

But this policy also fitted into a broader change in the dynamics between the metropole and its colonies, with specific regard to penitentiary institutions. According to the historian Allyson Delnore, 1871 was a turning point in the reorganisation of the French prison system.[52] During the early nineteenth century, deportees and transported prisoners had been moved from one area of confinement to another, also including the metropole itself. This situation changed under the Second Empire. From the 1850s–60s, the metropolitan *bagnes* were closed. Deportation was now directed only towards certain colonial areas,

49 See Isabelle Merle, *Expériences coloniales. Nouvelle-Calédonie (1853–1920)* (Paris: Belin, 1995).

50 For the Communards, see Alice Bullard, *Exile to Paradise: Savagery and Civilization in Paris and the South Pacific (1790–1900)* (Stanford, CA: Stanford University Press, 2000). For the Kabyle insurgents, see Mélica Ouennoughi, *Algériens et Maghrébins en Nouvelle-Calédonie, de 1864 à nos jours* (Algiers: Casbah Éditions, 2008). They joined the insurgents of 1864.

51 A well-known phenomenon in the British Empire: Clare Anderson, 'Transnational Histories of Penal Transportation: Punishment, Labour and Governance in the British Imperial World (1788–1939)', *Australian Historical Studies* 47: 3 (2016), pp. 381–97. For the French Empire, see Sylvie Thénault, 'Une circulation transméditerranéenne forcée: l'internement d'Algériens en France au XIXe siècle', *Criminocorpus*, at journals.openedition.org, 2015.

52 Allyson Jaye Delnore, 'Empire by Example? Deportees in France and Algeria and the Remaking of a Modern Empire (1846–1854)', *French Politics, Culture and Society* 33: 1 (2015), pp. 33–54.

which also saw a kind of specialisation: French Guiana was now supposed to focus on colonial prisoners (African, Caribbean and Asian ones), and New Caledonia on those of European (and, it would seem, Algerian) descent.[53] This represented an overall reworking of the relationship between the metropole and the colonies, and between the colonies themselves: the former had to be preserved from the presence of 'barbarians', while the latter were meant to provide for their sorting and removal. Because of the simultaneity of the revolution and the Algerian colonial revolt – and even more so because of their repression – the Commune and the subsequent population transfers somehow confirmed this shift. This increased coordination between different spaces, with now more differentiated roles, thus pointed to France taking on a clearer imperial role.

Still, the most significant phenomenon was without doubt the tightening of metropolitan France's control over its main colony in 1871 and its aftermath. Algeria quickly regained its function as a reserve of land, which was meant to solve the political problems of the metropole. On 21 June 1871, the Assembly conceded 100,000 hectares of Algerian land 'free of charge' to people from Alsace-Lorraine who had opted for France – on condition that they undertook to go there and 'exploit the land thus granted to them'.[54] Above all, the French state reasserted its control over the colony. This also affected – as is sometimes forgotten – the insurgent republican colonists. The police *commissaire* of Algiers was quickly returned to his post, the municipal councils' headquarters were abolished, and many republican-led municipal councils were dissolved.[55] Opposition did arise, however: militia officers sent a resolution to Versailles, which also drew an interesting comparison between colonial contexts: 'We reject in advance the responsibility for any blood that may be shed, [which is instead on the hands of] those who, in defiance of the most sacred rights, would try to make Algeria into a Cayenne or a New

53 The insurgents of 1864 were sent here in 1867: Ouennoughi, *Algériens et Maghrébins en Nouvelle-Calédonie*, p. 55. Movements were more complex: the Guiana penal colony was not used between 1867 and 1885, at the time of the deportation policy. See Marc Renneville, 'Les bagnes coloniaux: de l'utopie au risque du non-lieu', *Criminocorpus*, at criminocorpus.revues.org, 2007.

54 Assemblée Nationale, 21 June 1871, in *Annales de l'Assemblée nationale* (1871), p. 551.

55 AN, F80/1682, Report 27 May, Prefect Hulot; and Report 7 September, Admiral De Gueydon.

Caledonia.' In any case, on 30 August 1871 the Chamber reaffirmed its constituent authority over Algeria, and the civil governor was placed in close contact with the metropolitan authorities. Admiral de Gueydon would remain in post until June 1873, before he was replaced by another military officer, General Chanzy. The ways in which control was reasserted over Algeria, and particularly this dependence on the metropolitan French authorities, were clearly linked to the upheavals caused by the republican colonists in 1870–71.

Of course, this reassertion of French state power primarily concerned the Arab populations. The victors – be they soldiers, metropolitans, colonists, republicans or Catholics – shared a common interpretation, even if it had various intentions behind it. On this reading, responsibility for the revolt lay with feudal chiefs; it was supported by dubious marabout brotherhoods, and based on the tribal structure. It was thus necessary to break these chains of the past and 'civilise' these barbaric masses. The scale of the war indemnities and confiscations has already been mentioned: this affected 500,000 hectares of land, the best of which was annexed to the Domaine, while the worst was bought back by the tribes. Charles-Robert Ageron thus evaluates the cost of the war at 70 per cent of the insurgent tribes' wealth – an unbearable strain on their resources.[56] Continuing an effort begun in previous years, albeit now moving away from the 'Arab kingdom' approach, the goal was clearly to destroy the tribal system. The Kabyle poet Si Mohand, whose father was executed and whose family property was seized in 1871, powerfully expressed the shock he felt. 'I had an incomparable garden with thick, vigorous shoots. May God protect its bounty . . . Now that a torrent has been directed at it, the landslide has swept away everything. There is no trace of it left.'[57]

This change was also reflected in the administration of the colony. The civil territory was extended, particularly under pressure from the colonists: after Chanzy's spell in office, it amounted to some 104,000 square kilometres. Full-fledged *communes* (local authorities) and mixed *communes*, henceforth considered a transitional stage, were developed. The presence of Muslim notables in positions of authority, or in

56 Charles-Robert Ageron, *Histoire de l'Algérie contemporaine (1830–1999)* (Paris: PUF, 1999 [1964]).

57 Si Mohand, *Les Isefra de Si Mohand* (Paris: La Découverte, 1987 [1969]).

deliberative bodies within the general or municipal councils, was drastically reduced – both numerically and in terms of their capacity to make decisions. The assimilation – integration of the colony into France proper – so desired by the republicans was now becoming a reality. As Annie Rey-Goldzeiguer notes, from this point onwards, Arab populations were more readily referred to as 'natives' (*indigènes*) than as 'Algerians'. Tellingly, the latter term began to be used to refer to French or European civil servants and colonists. Completing the developments already seen under the Second Empire, the colonisation of Algeria reached fresh heights.[58]

So there was a marked hardening of French state power. The year 1870–71 thus appears as one stage in the slow process of imperial transformation over the course of the nineteenth century.[59] Yet this remained a general tendency. In many colonies, these events had only a limited impact, and the situations varied: in Martinique, for instance, the main effect of the Southern insurrection was to further discredit the Békés. And the right to vote especially enabled republican elites of colour to strengthen their position within political institutions (in general councils, or in parliamentary deputations). This was clearly not the end of conflict or distrust – abstention rates remained very high – as the plantation system gradually gave way to sugar factories and the new forms of labour they required.[60] Moreover, no control was ever total. In Algeria, the religious structures of the early nineteenth century were shaken, but Sufi religious life changed only much later. While Kabyle village organisation was seriously undermined, it would long retain a certain autonomy.[61] Military and financial pressure also led to further revolts, such as

58 A good summary appears in James McDougall, *A History of Algeria* (Cambridge: Cambridge University Press, 2017).

59 The idea of a lull between a 'first colonial Empire' and a 'second colonial Empire' is now being called into question. See David Todd, 'A French Imperial Meridian (1814–1870)', *Past and Present* 210: 1 (2011), pp. 155–86.

60 On all of this, see Paul Butel, *Histoire des Antilles françaises (XVIIe–XXe siècle)* (Paris: Perrin, 2002); Silyane Larcher, *L'Autre Citoyen. L'idéal républicain et les Antilles après l'esclavage* (Paris: Armand Colin, 2014).

61 Alain Mahé, *Histoire de la Grande Kabylie (XIXe–XXe siècle). Anthropologie historique du lien social dans les communautés villageoises* (Saint-Denis: Bouchène, 2001). A good example of these effects on the social and religious spheres can be found in the micro-historical study by Karim Rahem, *Le Sillage de la tribu. Imaginaires politiques et histoire en Algérie (1843–1993)* (Paris: Riveneuve, 2008). See also Didier Guignard, *1871: l'Algérie sous séquestre: une coupe dans le corps social, XIXe–XXe siècle* (Paris: CNRS Éditions, 2023).

the one in 1879 in the Aurès region, which was quickly suppressed: colonial domination was always marked by this 'domination without hegemony', in which the metropolitan state's control of the territory is neither omnipresent nor omnipotent, but often discontinuous.[62] The Kanak insurrection of 1878, which encapsulated the main developments in this period, offers a good point of observation for all of these intersecting tensions. This revolt – which lasted from June to October 1878, caused several deaths and greatly worried the authorities – was the biggest of the twenty-five rebellions on the archipelago since 1853. It was a last-ditch reaction to the spoliation of the land, which had been accelerated by the installation of the penal colony, and was largely completed around 1876. With the exception of Louise Michel, who was passionate about Kanak culture and took the rebels' side, the Communard deportees took part in repressing the revolt (according to the penitentiary principles then in force, they had been allotted land upon their release). The repression was terrible: the military used an Algeria-style 'razzia' approach, again reflecting the circulation of practices across the imperial space. But the revolt also saw other famous scenes. In one of them, the chief Atai was put to death by his own warriors. The military, the authorities and the deportees saw in this famous moment a questioning of the chief by his men. In reality, as anthropologist Alban Bensa has shown, it corresponded to an ancient Kanak custom according to which the chief could ask to be put to death in order to settle potential disputes over his succession, thus allowing his men to leave the land: through his voluntary sacrifice, the chief affirmed his status as a warrior and made it possible to end the conflict. Although invisible to Europeans, this act of resistance has over several generations fed orally transmitted commemorative accounts, which play an essential role in Kanak sociopolitical relations.[63] Thus, the attack on local structures did not prevent the persistence or reinvention of existing perceptions of the world, forms of social organisation, feelings of injustice, and other political aspirations. Indisputably, colonial pressure had become more constant and more overwhelming; but it did not kill off the enduring multiplicity of vernacular histories.

62 Sylvie Thénault, 'L'État colonial', in Pierre Singaravélou, ed., *Les Empires coloniaux (XIXe–XXe siècle)* (Paris: Seuil, 2013), pp. 215–56.

63 On these issues, see Alban Bensa, 'Une parole kanak sur l'insurrection de 1878', in Alban Bensa (ed.), *Michel Millet, Carnets de campagne en Nouvelle-Calédonie* (Toulouse: Anacharsis, 2004), pp. 13–29.

Which 'Event'?

The three dynamics we have identified (international state practices, national political adjustments, imperial recompositions) each have complexities of their own, but all clearly converge. In a particular form, they brought together and redefined trends from the 1860s, which we can now explore more closely: a more formalised international law; a humanitarian discourse of promoting civilisation; the desire to maintain free trade; respect for the powers-that-be; practices of international cooperation; and the heightening of tendencies towards statehood, nationalisation, authoritarianism and liberalisation. All of these were adapted to both informal domination and the ongoing colonial enterprise. This is what I have called the 'liberal order' – here understood in an expanded form. In the language of the time, it was presented as a self-evident reality, and as the given order of things. Speaking of the choice of Austro-Hungarian representatives for exchanges with the Prussian government, in the fight against the International, the French ambassador in Vienna observed that 'these two [chosen] officials are jurists' because 'Andrassy wanted to avoid giving an impression that would give these talks a political character'.[64] A year earlier, with reference to the arrangement of an international meeting against the IWMA, Favre had likewise told the German foreign minister, 'We shall lose nothing in terms of political independence by meeting on the common ground of morality and economic science.'[65] In official language, these were not political acts at all, but neutral interventions obeying the laws of civilisation, based on justice, morality and science. Obviously, the Commune and its repression were not the primary cause of these transformations. They broke into tendencies that were already present or latent, reshaping them and helping to give them greater form and consistency. In this sense, it can be said that the Commune led to a strengthening of this liberal order.

Some clarification is needed on this score. When analysing a given event, historians are often tempted to make it the centre of all the transformations of the time. The events under examination here, however, must be placed within a broader global shift that took place from the

64 CAD, CP, Austria-Hungary, 15 June 1872.

65 CAD, CP, Germany, 15 July 1871.

1860s to the 1880s, accelerating after 1870. It is therefore necessary to specify the situated character of this post-Commune hardening, and its effects; these were indeed limited, in particular because of the multiple causes of change. It is worth making three kinds of consideration here. Firstly, we can point to certain transformations in this period where we do not see the Commune and its aftermath having any a priori, direct influence. For example, it does not seem that the Commune heralded the 1870s–80s movement of international groupings sometimes described as 'governmental internationalism', even if the IWMA did indeed inspire emulators among its opponents.[66] This trend is illustrated by the creation of the Universal Postal Union, or the decisions taken at the peace conference in The Hague in 1899.[67] A similar conclusion applies to colonisation: despite the hardening imperial control mentioned above, the reactions to the war and the Commune did not pre-empt the acceleration of the European imperial endeavour after 1880, particularly in Africa. Connections can always be forced, but these reactions surely do not foreshadow, too, the development of the protectionism that unfolded in response to the mounting economic crisis. Nor did the events of 1870–71 have any visible impact on the medium-term acceleration of trade, or on the vast Atlantic convergence of prices and wages, whose decisive turning point historians place between 1846 and 1854.[68] We should be wary of overly linear or teleological perspectives. Rather, the reactions to the Commune and this transformation appear circumscribed: they seem to correspond to the specific configuration of the 1850–1870s, which came into sharper view in this moment.

66 These emulators included the 'Black International', an organisation of conservative aristocrats set up in October 1870 and supported by the pope, which gained strength after the Commune. See Emiel Lamberts, ed., *The Black International/L'Internationale noire (1870–1878)* (Leuven: Leuven University Press, 2002).

67 Herren, 'Governmental Internationalism'. See also her *Internationale Organisationen seit 1865. Eine Globalgeschichte der internationalen Ordnung* (Darmstadt: WBG, 2009).

68 Kevin H. O'Rourke and Jeffrey G. Williamson, *Globalization and History: The Evolution of a Nineteenth-Century Atlantic Economy* (Cambridge, MA: MIT Press, 2001). Admittedly, these last two points have been discussed more recently. See David Todd, *A Velvet Empire: French Informal Imperialism in the Nineteenth Century* (Princeton: Princeton University Press, 2021). It would seem that the Commune and the reactions it provoked were among the factors in the broader transformation of French imperialism that took shape during the nineteenth century.

Similarly, the second point is that the shifts identified at the state, national and imperial levels can be reinterpreted from a more global perspective. As historians Charles Bright and Michael Geyer have shown, the 1840s–80s, and especially the 1850s–60s, were a time of intensified conflict across the planet.[69] While each case had its own specific traits, these conflicts had some similar outcomes. In Europe, the Italian wars of independence led to the formation of the unified Kingdom of Italy, and then a German empire was created in 1871. On the American continent, the US Civil War led to a stronger federal and democratic state, while at the same time accelerating the 'Indian Wars' that decimated the Sioux populations in the 1870s. Further south, the Paraguayan War of 1864 led to the destruction of the indigenous populations, and to heightened centralisation. In Chile and Mexico, during phases of 'regeneration', authoritarian regimes strengthened the role of the state, and put an end to the 'democratic moment' of the 1840s and 1860s.[70] In India, British colonial control was strengthened after the Sepoy revolt of 1857. Taking advantage of the weakening of the Ottoman Empire and the central Asian empires (notably the Chinese Empire), Russia began a process of Russification, while Japan embarked in 1868 on the industrialisation phase of the Meiji era. These wars do not have a global coherence akin to that identifiable at the end of the eighteenth century or in the twentieth century.[71] But nor were they unrelated: according to the authors cited above, the acceleration of transport and communications, and the improvement of armaments, placed these wars within the same framework of global interconnection. Taken together, these developments led, they argue, to a multiform acceleration of trends towards industrialisation, nationalisation and heightened state control. In this

69 Charles Bright and Michael Geyer, 'Global Violence and Nationalizing Wars in Eurasia and America: The Geopolitics of War in the Mid-Nineteenth Century', in Aram Yengoyan, ed., *Modes of Comparison* (Ann Arbor, MI: University of Michigan Press, 2006), pp. 226–71.

70 James Sanders, 'The Vanguard of the Atlantic World: Contesting Modernity in Nineteenth- Century Latin America', *Latin American Research Review* 46: 2 (2011), p. 122.

71 As observed in Kenneth Pomeranz and John McNeill, *The Cambridge World History, vol. VII: Production, Destruction and Connection (1750–Present)* (Cambridge: Cambridge University Press, 2015), 'Introduction', pp. 1–47. This is especially true given that in this period there were few wars between industrial societies, particularly in Europe, except for the Franco-Prussian conflict.

perspective, the observed hardening of the 'liberal order' was one such form – a situated expression of it, yet by no means a negligible one. What the reactions to the Commune do show, then, is one of the concrete sites of this broader mutation. They also give us a glimpse into the 'patterned mess' of which Michael Mann speaks in that period, in which nation-states and social classes are more or less temporary 'cages' in the process of naturalisation. The example of the Commune thus serves as a reminder that these vast mutations, which historians have sometimes presented in a cohesive manner for the purposes of narrative clarity, are in fact the result of multiple chains of causal relations.[72] Conversely, this widening of our gaze offers further confirmation of the hardening mentioned above.

The last consideration concerns the national scale. These broad perspectives – be they European, imperial or global – ought not to drown out the richness of individual national or regional circumstances by giving the impression that these overall trends prevailed in some automatic fashion. This is the well-known problem of scale-shifting in historical analysis: at certain moments, we are switching from one plane of reality to another, even if they are interconnected, much as in physics we switch between the quantum world and the Newtonian one. Within this broader framework, in France in 1871, it should indeed be remembered that political life – to stick to this level alone – was far from predetermined. Thiers was trying to establish his conservative republic. While more revolutionary forces seemed to be sidelined, and silence prevailed over the events in Paris, the republicans – moderate or otherwise – chose to safeguard this republican possibility. The majority of the National Assembly was still made up of monarchists or conservatives. Thus began the uncertain period known as the 'moral order', under the leadership of Marshal de Mac-Mahon, which was characterised by a return to order and religion, by an attempt to restore the monarchy, and

72 Immanuel Wallerstein has sometimes been criticised for this unilinearity, though his book on this period also expresses this transformation well: *The Modern World-System*, vol. IV: *Centrist Liberalism Triumphant (1789–1914)* (Berkeley, CA: University of California Press, 2011). Michael Mann leaves more room for contingency and unintentionally orientated processes: *The Sources of Social Power, vol. II: The Rise of Classes and Nation States (1760–1914)* (Cambridge: Cambridge University Press, 1993). On the value of this approach, see William H. Sewell Jr, 'Postscript: Macrohistory and Eventful Temporality', in Sewell, *Logics of History: Social Theory and Social Transformation* (Chicago: University of Chicago Press, 2005), pp. 113–23.

by an attempt to establish a strong executive. These efforts collapsed with the crisis of 16 May 1877, before the victory of the 'opportunist' republicans in 1879.[73] At this level of observation, the meaning given above to the term 'liberal' will seem too generic: liberalism here refers to groups of actors with variable contours.[74] What comes through, here, are struggles and capacities for action rooted in the frameworks of the nation-state and its modes of operation, which were just as crucial. The difficult part of the historian's job is to reconstruct such complex interconnections. This is a key problem of the global history of power: how to avoid the invocation of overly broad, overarching trends, and to restore the interplay of plural determinations at their proper levels.

This question in turn brings us back to a final one, which has loomed over our inquiry since the beginning of Part III: How, from this perspective, did the Commune come to count as an event? Certainly, we could speak of the temporal and political rupture it represented, or of its extraordinary media audience. But, according to the historian and sociologist William H. Sewell Jr, something can really be termed a historical event when what happens opens a sequence of occurrences leading to a 'transformation of structures'.[75] From this point of view, the Commune is a peculiar case. It certainly had an impact on workers' movements. But – and this is a frequent conclusion reached by studies of revolutionary phenomena – its most visible effect in the period under consideration came from these reactions and the associated strengthening of the state.[76] Its outcome thus proves ambiguous. On the one hand, the Commune tended to reorientate existing dynamics, leading to consolidation of a certain form of state on a relatively large scale: in this respect,

---

73 Arnaud-Dominique Houte, *Le Triomphe de la République (1871–1914)* (Paris: Seuil, 2014).

74 There is a truly vast bibliography on the variety of liberal positions. Among others, see Lucien Jaume, *L'Individu effacé ou le Paradoxe du libéralisme français* (Paris: Fayard, 1997).

75 William H. Sewell Jr, 'Trois temporalités: vers une sociologie événementielle', in Marc Bessin, Claire Bidart and Michel Grossetti, eds, *Bifurcations. Les sciences sociales face aux ruptures et à l'événement* (Paris: La Découverte, 2010); William H. Sewell Jr, 'Historical Events as Transformations of Structures: Inventing Revolution at the Bastille', in Sewell, *Logics of History*, pp. 225–70.

76 Theda Skocpol, *States and Social Revolutions: A Comparative Analysis of France, Russia and China* (Cambridge: Cambridge University Press, 1979).

it can be described as a global event. On the other hand, there remains the impression that the pre-existing social structure, to use Sewell's words, withstood this event rather well, unlike in 1789 or even 1848. From this perspective, the Commune belongs more to that class of events which are quickly absorbed by the existing structure, even if the situation that followed was not exactly the same. Both propositions are valid: at this point the Parisian insurrection can be defined as a quasi-event – one with significant effects, but which did not bring about a major rupture.

On another level, however, it did count as an event: namely on the symbolic level – or, in Sewell's terms, that of 'cultural transformations'. These two types of transformation go hand in hand, and there can be no change in the structure of social relations without a change in the imaginary associated with them. But, it would seem, the particularity of the Commune is that it corresponded to a cultural transformation within this same structure, with effects of its own. The previous chapter showed that, after 1871, a conceptual category called 'Commune' was created, which, enriched by certain of the changes described here, became a historical reality endowed with meanings, imaginaries and affects, in turn producing beliefs and actions. It then imposed itself indelibly – for some, as a terrible threat of disorder; for others, as a justification for struggles and promises of a new world.[77]

This calls for a final clarification. The hate-filled reactions to the ruins of the reconquered city cannot, on their own, account for the Commune's status. It is obviously also the fruit of all those who, from then on, would see Paris's martyrdom as a symbol of past, present and future struggles for the broadest possible emancipation of the oppressed. We must now turn to these lives – and afterlives – of the Commune.

77 On this creation of meaning through events, see W. H. Sewell Jr, 'Historical Events as Transformations of Structures'.

12

'The Body May Have Fallen, but the Idea Still Stands'

Shortly after the Bloody Week, a slogan began to gain traction, insisting that 'Le cadavre est à terre, mais l'idée est debout': 'The body may have fallen, but the idea still stands.' These words spoke, of course, to the crushing of the Communards' movement – but also to its defenders' desire to keep alive the flame that seemed to have been ignited.[1] The use of this slogan also points to the almost immediate spread, over the 1870s and 1880s, of echoes and recompositions of the Commune. They will be the focus of this final chapter.

Such an investigation could, once again, be vast in geographical scope. It also has peculiar content. The above-cited slogan itself tells us as much: for it consciously re-employed a phrase coined by Victor Hugo during his exile in Jersey under the Second Empire.[2] It thus places us right away within the sharp contraction of time already discussed. In other words, what concerns us here is the positive memory of the Commune, which presupposes a certain distance from the past, but more especially the uses of the Parisian event as a reference to the past (in the sense of an idea that is still alive) which were particularly notable

1 The expression was used in Prosper-Olivier Lissagaray, *Les Huit Journées de mai derrière les barricades* (Brussels: Bureau du 'Petit Journal', 1871); Pilotell, 'La Commune de Paris: le cadavre est à terre et l'idée est debout', caricature, 1871, parismuseescollections.paris.fr; *La Bataille*, 19 March 1885. See Julia Nicholls, *Revolutionary Thought after the Paris Commune (1871–1885)* (Cambridge: Cambridge University Press, 2019).

2 Victor Hugo, *La Voix de Guernesey* (Guernsey: Bichard, 1867).

in the period under examination.[3] We are therefore also looking at the way in which the Commune – its promises, or what it embodied – could on certain occasions burst into the present of the actors concerned, take on new meaning in their minds, and take root in this other terrain, possibly opening the way to other, later breakthroughs.

This perspective is somewhat out of step with the classical historiography of the workers' movement, which has explored this period extensively. It generally describes the post-Commune period as a transitional moment, symbolised by the crumbling of the IWMA, before this movement's renaissance in the 1880s and 1890s.[4] This later period saw renewed circulations of people and ideas, the formation of structured organisations (parties, trade unions, the Second International) and the development of more systematic currents of thought or ideology.[5] The memory of the Commune accompanied what is often called the 'modern' phase in the history of the workers' movement. In activist discourse and commemorative ritual, it became, along with other events such as the First of May, a common point of reference in resisting the bourgeois oppression of workers and of the dominated of the earth, notwithstanding other differences of perspective.[6]

---

3 On this notion of the idea, linked to that of the reference to the past, see Michèle Riot-Sarcey, *Le Procès de la liberté. Une histoire souterraine du XIXe siècle en France* (Paris: La Découverte, 2016), p. 302.

4 See Marcel Van der Linden, ed., *Workers of the World: Essays Toward a Global Labor History* (Leiden: Brill, 2008), p. 278. The period 1870–90, the third of the 'stages of development of working-class internationalism' is labelled here the 'transition'.

5 On the anarchist movement, see Benedict Anderson, *Under Three Flags: Anarchism and the Anti-Colonial Imagination* (London: Verso, 2016); Marcel Van der Linden and Jürgen Rojahn, eds, *The Formation of Labour Movements (1870–1914): An International Perspective*, vol. 1 (Leiden: Brill, 1990); Jean-Louis Robert, Friedhelm Boll and Antoine Prost, eds, *L'Invention des syndicalismes. Le syndicalisme en Europe occidentale à la fin du xixe siècle* (Paris: Publications de la Sorbonne, 1997). Other useful cues for reflection appear in Michel Cordillot, 'Archives et historiographie de l'AIT: un bilan et quelques éléments de réflexion', in Serge Wolikow, ed., *Une histoire en révolution? Du bon usage des archives, de Moscou et d'ailleurs* (Dijon: Éditions universitaires de Dijon, 1996), pp. 25–30.

Only in this moment did Marxism and anarchism take form: Eric Hobsbawm, *How to Change the World: Reflections on Marx and Marxism* (New Haven, CT: Yale University Press, 2011), pp. 176–99.

6 Philip Foner, *May Day: A Short History of the International Workers' Holiday (1886–1896)* (New York: International, 1986). On Britain, see Constance Bantman, *The French Anarchists in London (1880–1914)* (Liverpool: Liverpool University Press, 2013).

While not denying these processes of recomposition, this chapter paints a different picture, which is less monumental, more sensitive to discontinuities and ways of seeing, and attentive to collective movements as well as more distinctive readings. Grasping this diversity helps us to understand more clearly the evocative power that quickly attached to the word 'Commune'. This approach also makes it possible to address the various social and political movements that, from an early stage and in multiple forms, have challenged and reshaped the 'tightening' process described in the previous chapter. Since it is impossible to work through the whole vast corpus of existing studies, I will continue along the threads I have followed – the circulation of people and ideas, local impacts, and the situated uses and appropriations of the Commune – in order to grasp this other face of the revolutionary and radical current. In doing so, this examination will tie in with recent research on the 'global radicalism' of the 1860s to 1880s, in the sense of the study of radical positions (republicanism, mutualism, socialism, anarchism, Marxism, and so on). These also challenge the notion that this was simply a 'transitional moment', and places greater emphasis on the continuities, shifts and creativity at work during this period.[7] In its own way, the present investigation into the resurgences of the Commune contributes to the analysis of this vast movement of protest of the 1860s–1880s, which of course included, but was not limited to, the European workers' movement.

Republican and Working-Class Revolt, 1870–1880

The idea of a major setback for the forces of the working-class and republican (in the revolutionary sense) movement is surely no illusion. We see this in the French case: 93 people were sentenced to death, 4,500 deported and 1,250 sentenced to life imprisonment. The movement was decapitated, especially as the Dufaure Law of 1872 put an end to the IWMA's official existence. In addition, many Communards were forced

7 Ilham Khuri-Makdisi, *The Eastern Mediterranean and the Making of Global Radicalism (1860–1914)* (Berkeley, CA: University of California Press, 2013); Carl Levy, 'Anarchism, Internationalism and Nationalism in Europe (1860–1939)', *Australian Journal of Politics and History* 50: 3 (2004), pp. 330–42.

into exile, including the likes of Maxime Vuillaume, Jules Vallès, Victoire Tinayre and Eugène Pottier. Although it is difficult to count their exact number, the total is estimated at 6,000. For those who fled to Great Britain, Belgium, Switzerland, the United States and, to a lesser extent, Spain, Italy and South America, conditions were far from enviable. They sometimes struggled to integrate into social movements in their new homes – in Great Britain, for example, where the trade unions remained suspicious of the Commune.[8] In Switzerland and Belgium, where there were 800 and 1,700 exiles respectively, the ties established were rather stronger. But their activity was generally limited or not very effective, as the police officers responsible for monitoring them noted.[9] This does not mean that they fell silent. In 1871, Benoît Malon, a refugee in Switzerland who had become close to the (anarchist) Jura Federation, published his *La troisième défaite du prolétariat français* ('The Third Defeat of the French Proletariat'). He attempted to situate the Commune in the long history of revolutions, to identify its real import, and to draw up a critical assessment of its errors, the better to prepare for future struggles.[10] Five years later, Prosper-Olivier Lissagaray published his monumental *History of the Commune of 1871* from his exile in London, with the Belgian publisher Kistemaeckers.[11] It sought to offer a precise account of the facts, the organisations and the players involved, and to provide a coherent response to the Commune's critics, based on eyewitness accounts and the unearthing of a welter of evidence. In his second preface, in 1896, Lissagaray explained that his aim was to oppose those who would build 'false legends that are supposed to be revolutionary, as criminal as a cartographer who made misleading maps for tomorrow's

8 Laure Godineau, 'Retour d'exil. Les anciens communards au début de la Troisième République', PhD dissertation, Université Paris-I (2000). On the British case, see Laura Forster, 'Friends of the Commune: Trans-Channel Encounters and Collaboration (1871–1900)', PhD dissertation, King's College, London (2019).

9 Jacques Rougerie, *1871. Jalons pour une Histoire de la Commune de Paris* (Paris: PUF, 1973). The (rough) Swiss and Belgian figures are suggested in Marc Vuilleumier, 'Les exilés communards en Suisse', in Vuilleumier, *Histoire et combats. Mouvement ouvrier et socialisme en Suisse (1864–1960)* (Lausanne: Éditions d'En Bas, 2012 [2004]).

10 Benoît Malon, *La Troisième Défaite du prolétariat français* (Neuchâtel: G. Guillaume fils, 1871).

11 Prosper-Olivier Lissagaray, *Histoire de la Commune de 1871* (Bruxelles: Kistemaeckers, 1876) – transl. into English as *The History of the Paris Commune* (London: New Park Publications, 1976 [1886]).

fighters'.[12] Public demonstrations of support were also organised, such as those held in New York in July, and especially December 1871, when members of the IWMA organised a large demonstration, rallying 10,000 people in tribute to the martyrs of the Commune and the victims of the Cuban war. Members of German, Italian, US and South American political clubs, as well as Irish Fenians and feminists, including Victoria Woodhull, marched under a banner reading: 'Honor to the Martyrs of the Universal Republic'. References to the Commune were mixed in with ones to June 1848, the American Civil War and the Cuban struggle. While there was in fact a temporary increase in the number of IWMA sections on US soil, here, as in several other countries, the organisation fractured under the impact of both internal tensions and government pressure. It soon broke up, before disappearing outright in 1877.[13] For many social movements, the crushing of the Commune was a troubling sign, whether they identified with this event or sought to distance themselves from it.

This did not mean that at that moment the Commune had been suppressed from the collective consciousness, but its continuations took the form of tenuous or sometimes broken threads. Looking at the French case, Julia Nicholls, studying socialists' diaries and correspondence, has emphasised what a strong marker the Commune remained both for former Communards and the newer ranks of French revolutionaries.[14] Laure Godineau confirms that subsequent narrations of the event helped to keep its memory alive in a period that seemed to have become alien.[15]

---

12 Pierre-Olivier Lissagaray, 'Pour qu'on sache', Preface to Lissagaray, 'La semaine de l'incertitude', in his *Histoire de la Commune de 1871* (Paris: Dentu, 1896), p. 1.

13 Michel Cordillot, 'L'inexorable déclin', in Cordillot, *Utopistes et exilés du Nouveau monde: des Français aux Etats-Unis, de 1848 à la Commune* (Paris: Vendémiaire, 2013), pp. 294–334. For a detailed chronology by country, see Fabrice Bensimon, Quentin Deluermoz and Jeanne Moisand, eds, '*Arise Ye Wretched of the Earth!*': *The First International in Global Perspective* (Leiden: Brill, 2018).

14 Nicholls, *Revolutionary Thought After the Paris Commune.*

15 Laure Godineau, '"Elle n'est pas morte": quand dire c'est faire. Écrire et continuer la Commune de Paris dans les années 1880', in Quentin Deluermoz and Anthony Glinoer, eds, *L'Insurrection entre histoire et littérature (1789–1914)* (Paris: Publications de la Sorbonne, 2015), pp. 125–37. On the Commune's trajectories in France after 1880, see Madeleine Rebérioux, 'Le mur des Fédérés: rouge, "sang craché"', in Pierre Nora, ed., *Les Lieux de mémoire, vol. I: La République* (Paris: Gallimard, 1984), pp. 619–49; Éric Fournier, *'La Commune n'est pas morte'. Les usages du passé de 1871 à nos jours* (Paris: Libertalia, 2013).

Beyond this, the emergence of major socialist currents in Germany and Switzerland, before these were repressed, and the geographical redistribution of revolutionary movements towards the Mediterranean and South America, also point to a more complex onward path for the Commune as an 'idea'.

Situating the Paris Commune in History: Class Struggle or Spontaneous Upsurge of the Exploited?

First of all, the Commune and its resounding defeat were part of the ongoing debates on the conception and practice of revolution, as expressed in the activist press, correspondence, public statements and theoretical reflections. We have briefly looked at Marx's analysis of the Commune in his *The Civil War in France*, written in the heat of the moment. This was an uncompromising critique of the fallen Empire, a defence of the Commune-event, and a denunciation of 'the conspiracy of the ruling class to break down the revolution by a civil war'. It is now worth reading his interpretation more closely. As Gareth Stedman Jones points out, Marx's text combines a detailed description of the Commune's functioning, a sometimes abstract vision, a strong drive to put its evolving course in wider perspective and more personal views.[16] For example, for the British historian, Marx sometimes exaggerates the Communards' systematic determination to 'expropriate the expropriators'; similarly, judges and magistrates were in fact never appointed by popular election (even if the delegate for justice, Eugène Protot, did propose this). Nonetheless, Marx did offer a fine-grained analysis of the Commune – indeed, one whose thrust sometimes contradicts later, more stereotyped assumptions. It includes his famous criticism of the bourgeois state apparatus, according to which 'the working class cannot simply lay hold of the ready-made state machinery, and wield it for its own purposes'.[17] A few

16 Gareth Stedman Jones, *Karl Marx: Greatness and Illusion* (London: Allen Lane, 2016), pp. 494–510. See also Michel Cordillot, 'Karl Marx et la Commune', in M. Cordillot, ed., *La Commune de Paris. Les acteurs, l'évènement, les lieux* (Paris: Editions de l'Atelier, 2021), pp. 470–7.

17 Karl Marx, *The Civil War in France*, at marxists.org. This analysis is underlined by Lenin in his Chapter 3 of his *The State and Revolution* (London: Penguin Classics, 1983 [1917]).

pages later, the Commune is described as 'the positive form of [the] Republic', allowing for 'cheap government', which, moreover, 'breaks with the modern state power'. This 'working-class government' was then described, a few pages later, as 'the political form at last discovered under which to work out the economical emancipation of labour'.

This reading right away seemed to contradict the centralism hitherto defended by Marx. But, for him, the main issue was that this revolution *for* the people was being led for the first time, and to the fullest extent, *by* the people itself – and in particular by the workers. In his reading of the historical process, the Commune marked an essential moment, in that the working classes had become the protagonists of their own history. It is in this sense that we should understand Marx's claim that the 'great social measure of the Commune was its own working existence', and that 'its special measures could but betoken the tendency of a government of the people by the people'. He certainly had his criticisms, such as what he regarded as the Communards' excessive democratic scruples. At the same time, he was eagerly concerned to understand what was really happening. The famous analysis of the Commune as a 'thoroughly expansive political form', for example, corresponds fairly well to the specific characteristics of the 'movement' we have described. Marx's *The Civil War in France* is thus more complex and subtle than has sometimes been suggested afterwards. Published in multiple languages, though not without obstacles, it had a considerable influence on the reading of events – not to mention that, in the following years, analysis of the working class inspired by 'Marxist' positions (a label Marx himself rejected) gradually became more precise and influential.

Mikhail Bakunin's reading of the Commune was also essential, especially as the two men's interpretations soon clashed, including within the IWMA. After his unsuccessful efforts in Lyon and Marseille, from his new base in Locarno, Switzerland, the Russian anarchist soon concluded that Paris was a lost cause. But he believed that this was a partial realisation of the dream he had already conceived back in 1863 – an organised revolt of the Communes as the basis of a free and solidaristic society. The revolutionary expressed his positions rather less clearly than Marx did, for his analysis appeared in multiple overlapping texts. The first was an article published in August 1871 in *Il Gazzettino Rosa*. It responded to Mazzini's recurrent criticism of the Commune, which the Italian deemed an abnormal development of the Republic. Bakunin's piece was translated into French in a Belgian newspaper (18–19 August), then sent in a Spanish version to the IWMA organ in Barcelona. Another of his texts was a 110-page volume, *La Théologie politique de Mazzini et l'Internationale*, published in Neuchâtel in 1871, with a print run of one thousand copies. But the most famous and influential of his contributions was the preamble added to *L'Empire knouto-germanique et la révolution sociale* (Geneva, 1871) after the event. It was reprinted and published in 1878 by Élisée Reclus under the title *La Commune de Paris et la notion d'État* ('The Paris Commune and the Idea of the State'). Here, he famously described the Commune as an 'immense historical fact' and as 'a bold, clearly formulated negation of the State'. This expressed Bakunin's position in favour of the abolition of the state and the existing form of society, and for a revolution that would be social and not merely political. This Bakuninian reading, also taken up by some others, was likewise especially widely circulated after 1880: indeed, this was a posthumous success, following Bakunin's death in 1876.[18]

The debate between these two interpretations has been the subject of much comment. Historians and analysts have long noted the apparently paradoxical positions of the two revolutionaries: for the first, the defence of a form of federalism, and for the other, a partial rehabilitation of the Jacobins' actions that acknowledged their revolutionary virtues. Their positions gave rise to different analyses, and still today continue to fuel new interpretations of the two men's thought.[19]

---

18 On Bakunin, see Max Nettlau's work published at the end of the nineteenth century: *Michel Bakounine*, Œuvres *completes* (Paris: Stock, 1980). See also Michel Bakounine, *De la guerre à la Commune. Textes de 1870–1871*, ed. Fernand Rude (Paris: Anthropos, 1972); Arthur Lehning, 'Michel Bakounine. Théorie et pratique du fédéralisme anti-étatique en 1870–1871', in Jacques Rougerie, ed. 'Jalons pour une histoire de la Commune', in the aforementioned *International Review of Social History* dossier (vol. 17, 1972, parts I and II), pp. 455–77.

19 Jacques Rougerie, 'Les héritiers', in Rougerie, *Paris libre 1871* (Paris: Seuil, 2004 [1971]), pp. 264–70. Some commentators believe that Marx's position at the time of the Commune significantly enriches our understanding of his work, far beyond simple references to historical determinism or statist centralisation. See Daniel Bensaïd, 'Politiques de Marx', in Karl Marx and Friedrich Engels, *Inventer l'inconnu, Textes et correspondance autour de la Commune* (Paris: La Fabrique, 2008), pp. 11–106. The analysis of these texts is not a closed question: see, for example, the reflections of Miguel Abensour, *La Démocratie contre l'État. Marx et le moment machiavélien* (Paris: Éditions du Félin, 2012); and, on Bakunin, those of Jean-Christophe Angaut, 'Liberté et histoire chez Michel Bakounine', PhD dissertation, Université Nancy-2 (2005).

The Spanish case is interesting insofar as these conflicts of interpretation between Marxists and anarchists, which were then taking structured form, were particularly clear-cut in that country. For the Marxists, the Commune had failed for lack of a structured organisation:

> If the Paris Commune had known how or wanted to use the immense power that the revolution had placed in its hands, it is probable that the triumph of the universal proletariat would be a fact today. It can be said that the Commune died of an indigestion of Federation and liberty.[20]

Elsewhere, the Spanish Marxists criticised the Commune for having taken over the bourgeois state apparatus instead of replacing it with another one. On the contrary, for the anarchists, the Commune's real strength lay precisely in its anti-authoritarianism and spontaneity. As the anarchist González Morago wrote in a letter dated 6 July 1873:

> By giving the signal from a central point, the movement will take on that spontaneous character which is usually lacking in revolutions and which nothing can resist. If the major French cities had used this same method in 1871, the Commune would not have been defeated and the movement, spreading as if by enchantment to all the major centres, would have led to the triumph of the Social Revolution without any great effort.[21]

In this reading, the Parisian event proved the vitality of a revolutionary upsurge. It would seem, then, that this debate on the means of action and the strategies to follow was thus also a debate between different perceptions of historical change. In short, Marxists saw the Commune as part of a line of revolutions – as one stage from which lessons must be learned, the better to prepare for future struggles. Anarchists, on the other hand,

20 *La Emancipación*, 26 October 1871, cited in Joël Delhom, 'La Fédération espagnole de l'Internationale et la Commune de Paris (1871–1874)', in Jérôme Quaretti and Gilbert Larguier, eds, *La Commune de 1871. Utopie ou modernité*, conference proceedings (Perpignan, 28–30 March 1996) (Perpignan: Presses universitaires de Perpignan, 2000), pp. 161–76.

21 *La Emancipación*, 26 October 1871, cited in Joël Delhom, 'La Fédération espagnole de l'Internationale et la Commune de Paris (1871–1874)'.

saw the Commune as part of a constant struggle between the exploited and the exploiters, grounded in a more organic and germinal vision of revolution. From this perspective, the course of history is less predetermined, and revolution can occur at any moment. These contrasting conceptions were, moreover, far from uniform. For the anarchist geographer Élisée Reclus, for example, the revolutionary phenomenon was akin to a 'law of nature' that could not be resisted, but had to be brought into being. In his view, moreover, the driving forces of revolution were not confined to Europe alone: the social and libertarian (anarchist) revolution, he argued, would come from a multitude of diverse uprisings that would together make up what he called 'the socialist hydra'.[22] In this way, the Parisian event came to corroborate – as either a model or a counter-model – different conceptions of revolutionary time. These were alternative visions of history, distinct from, though not entirely alien to, the perception increasingly dominant at the time, that of *progress*. In this understanding, European societies were engaged in a process of economic, political and moral development, an uneven but undeniably real march of progress that was dragging in its wake territories deemed 'backward', whether or not they were under European domination.[23]

The exact crystallisation of these interpretations naturally varied across different national contexts. In imperial Germany, the reading of the event took on a particular colouring thanks to the importance of the Social Democratic Party (SPD) and figures such as Karl Liebknecht and August Bebel. After his timid defence of the Commune in the Reichstag in April 1871, Bebel gave a much firmer one on 25 May, with a fiery conclusion: 'The battle-cry of the Parisian proletariat "War to the palaces, peace to the huts, death to misery and idleness" will become the battle-cry of the entire European proletariat.'[24] The interpretation of the Commune in terms of class struggle and social revolution, in the Marxist

22 Nicholls, *Revolutionary Thought After the Paris Commune*, Chapter 2, 'Revolutions' (analyses drawn from articles for *Le Travailleur* between 1877 and 1878); and Élisée Reclus, *Histoire d'un ruisseau* (Paris: Hetzel, 1869), p. 7.

23 On this imposition of 'modern' time, see Reinhart Koselleck, *Le Futur passé. Contribution à la sémantique des temps historiques*; Francois Hartog, *Régimes d'historicité*; Christophe Charle, *La Discordance des temps* (discussed in chapter 7).

24 August Bebel, *Ausgewählte Reden und Schriften, vol. I: 1863 bis 1878. Bearbeitet von Rolf Dlubek und Ursula Herrmann unter Mitarbeit von Dieter Malik*, ed. Horst Barthel (Berlin: Dietz, 1978), p. 674; Jacques Droz, *Le Socialisme allemand de 1863 à 1918* (Paris: Centre de documentation universitaire, 1964).

sense, here appears more sharply. This reading was surely consolidated in parallel with the slow growth of Marxism and the class-struggle approach within the SPD after 1871, for which it also served as a catalyst.[25] It was probably also shaped by conjunctural conditions: in the aftermath of the Commune, the party of Ferdinand Lassalle tended to move closer to Wilhelm I's regime on questions of reform, while liberal organisations were more hesitant. At a time when Bismarck tried to stifle it, the SPD was compelled to assert its own outlook, in particular by taking up the defence of the Parisian event.[26] In any case, one may then ask whether these interpretations in terms of class struggle, which would endure for almost a century, may not have found here one of their strongest foundations, within what was then the most organised party and the most coherent socialist voice of the time.

Other countries followed different paths, depending on the internal political dynamics of the Left and organised labour. In Great Britain, for example, the dominant spirit in the immediate aftermath of the event stood in condemnation of the Commune, including within the trade unions. Only the radical positivists, such as Frederic Harrison, took to its defence, in the name of their critique of social inequalities – while rejecting what they perceived as its 'communism'. A decade later, the situation changed with the emergence of a new British socialist movement centred on organisations such as the Social-Democratic Federation and the Socialist League. They gave expression to a variety of anarchist, communist and socialist voices. More precisely, they combined the positivist heritage with a reading of Marx to cast the Commune as the greatest workers' revolt in history, and as the symbol of the bourgeoisie's betrayal of the toiling masses. The workers and the main representatives of the trade unions remained aloof. But in a later political moment, as

25 Jürgen Kocka, *Arbeiterleben und Arbeiterkultur. Die Entstehung einer sozialen Klasse* (Bonn: Dietz, 2015), pp. 406–7. On the consolidation of the concept of 'class' after 1870, see Thomas Welskopp, *Das Banner der Brüderlichkeit. Die deutsche Sozialdemokratie vom Vormärz bis zum Sozialistengesetz* (Bonn: Dietz Nachfolger, 2000). The Social-Democratic Workers' Party of Bebel and Liebknecht was known at the time as the SDAP. The SPD emerged in 1875 from the fusion with other currents, and in its early years adopted yet another name (Socialist Workers' Party). For clarity's sake (and because we are here interested in the overall dynamic), we use the generic name SPD for the whole post-1871 period.

26 Anne Deffarges, 'Bismarck part en guerre contre "l'ennemi intérieur": la social-démocratie', *Siècles* 31 (2010), pp. 81–93.

the alliance between Liberals and the working classes withered, a class-based reading of the Commune emerged here – one that would grow stronger in the decades that followed.[27]

Here it is worth mentioning what some social historians have called the 'myth of the Commune and the IWMA' – in this case, in its positive version: according to them, it was in this form that the Parisian event really took its place in the history of the workers' movement. While it did not have immediate social effects, it did contribute to the rise of a class consciousness and, by way of reaction, of more organised forms of struggle.[28] This process can be illuminated by E. P. Thompson's famous analysis: if the working class is not a 'thing', but a relationship – the fruit of conflictual relations between the ruling orders and the 'plebeians' – then we can say that the Commune was a moment in the formalisation of the idea of 'class', not only on a national but also on an international scale.[29] Through many of its echoes, it contributed to the crystallisation of the notion of the 'working class'. This is not to say that the groups of workers who identified with this term had suddenly become homogeneous: this additional category, or even the experience from a distance, added to the variety of experiences and horizons that already marked the world of labour. The Paris event was thus one of the ingredients in this complex story of dynamics acting both from above and below, and characterised by both clear structuring tendencies and an ongoing diversity of perceptions.

For this same reason, however, we cannot confine ourselves to this conclusion alone; it remains focused on the idea of a transitional moment, masking the diversity of other, different reappropriations. In the period of interest to us here, the Commune embodied the martyrdom of a cause whose contours were in fact rather more undefined. This event could also give rise to other rereadings, in which the terms 'class' and 'socialism', following in continuity with the 1860s, took on quite different meanings. Such readings can be found in these same

27 Geoff Eley, *Forging Democracy: The History of the Left in Europe (1850–2000)* (Oxford: Oxford University Press, 2002). On this particular subject, see Joshua Leifer, 'From "Cowardly Ruffians" to "The Greatest Heroes of History": The Paris Commune Revolt in Late 19th-Century British Political Culture, PhD dissertation, Princeton University (2016).

28 See the overview by Jeanne Gaillard, 'La Commune. Le mythe et le fait', *Annales. Économies, Sociétés, Civilisations* 28: 3 (1973), pp. 838–85.

29 E. P. Thompson, *The Making of the English Working Class* (London: Victor Gollancz, 1968 [1963]).

territories. For instance, in the German case, we can see them in the wave of support for the Commune expressed in Munich, Augsburg and elsewhere, by various groups. These could be workers, but were not necessarily so (for instance, in the case of democratic groupings who approved of the Commune). Or they came from sections of the IWMA, still animated by the language and organisational concerns of 1864. For example, at a congress of German weavers held shortly after the event, before joining the IWMA its members declared 'the need for all German factory workers to unite with each other and with their fellow brothers among other peoples in an internationality [*sic*]'.[30] The terms 'peoples' and 'internationality' were characteristic of this vocabulary.

There were many shifts in meaning. These also extended beyond Europe's borders, pursuing seemingly infinite journeys in constant recomposition. South America is a good field of observation in this respect. In Bolivia, where there was a strong republican and social movement, the impact of the Commune varied from one region to another: it was relatively insignificant in the west of the country, around the capital, La Paz. Artisans, who were often *mestizos*, concentrated their political fight on education, which was considered the best means of accessing the rights of citizenship. However, the Commune played a more important role in the Santa Cruz region, far from the country's economic and political centre, and particularly in the egalitarian movement headed by Andrés Ibañez, which took off after 1876. This region's greater social and ethnic homogeneity apparently made it easier to organise a common response to the growing development of liberal capitalism. Sometimes considered the first socialist movement in the Americas, this egalitarian cause brought together artisans, merchants and small property owners. It drew on ideas from the work of Proudhon and Lamennais, and thus on the example of the Paris Commune. Opposed to the big property owners, teachers, foreigners and immigrants, it spoke a language of federalism, municipal autonomy, and the equal distribution of land and wealth.[31] It

30 APP, BA 427.

31 Andrey Schelchkov, *La palabra 'socialismo' en Bolivia, siglo XIX* (La Paz: Vice Presidencia de la República/Centro de Investigaciones Sociales, 2016); Carlos Illades and Andrey Schelchkov, eds, *Mundos posibles. El primer socialismo en Europa y América Latina* (Mexico City: Colegio de México, 2014). I would like to thank the historian Esther Aillón Soria (Universidad Mayor de San Andrés La Paz-Bolivia) for her insights in this regard.

thereby pointed to the many possible ways of appropriating the Commune.

Of course, some of these appropriations could be more strongly associated with the presence of exiles – including, but not restricted to, figures who had taken part in the Paris Commune: Émile Dumas came to Argentina, Edmond Megy was welcomed in Panama, Jean-Baptiste Chardon in Haiti, and so on. But here, as elsewhere, this effect was not systematic: François de Bèze, who had been active in the Algiers Commune, continued his revolutionary activities in Chile, but was now confined to a narrow circle.[32]

Juárez's Mexico, which also took in Communards, illustrates a quite different path. As we have seen, Mexicans paid continued attention to the Parisian event. When news of the fires reached the country, Mexican liberals joined the conservatives in distancing themselves from the republican adventure in Paris: in their view, the Commune proved the lack of political maturity on the European continent. The workers', democratic, mutualist and, more recently, socialist movements – represented by associations such as La Social and the Gran Círculo de Obreros – took a slightly different view. An article already mentioned in *El Socialista*, dated 20 August 1871, delved into this problem. The young newspaper sought to explain the discrepancy between the 'innovations' proposed by the Commune (the separation of Church and State, and the tearing down of the nobility, the army and the propertied) and its catastrophic outcome. To do so, it resorted to the classic opposition between the honest worker and the criminal one: 'The world has been shaken to its core! The Commune has fallen, and with it many of the criminals, vermin and scoundrels of this many-faced Parisian society . . .' A distinction thus had to be made between these intolerable crimes and the principles they purported to represent, which were considered well suited to 'honest' workers in the Americas. The paper's attitude towards the

32 Marcelo Segall, 'En Amérique latine. Développement du mouvement ouvrier et proscription', in Rougerie, *1871. Jalons pour une histoire de la Commune de Paris*. Sergio Grez Toso is even more cautious: even if it is possible to identify the IWMA's ideas as having some influence after 1871, the Chilean workers' and popular movement was above all based on endogenous factors. Ideological elements arriving from Europe could combine with the latter, but they never amounted to an organised political force. See Sergio Grez Toso, 'Les Mouvements d'ouvriers et d'artisans en milieu urbain au Chili au XIXe siècle (1818–1890)', PhD dissertation, EHESS, Paris (1990), p. 491.

International was the same. On 10 September, it commented: 'It seems to us very timely to inform our readers of the rules of this useful association which so alarm the possessors of labour . . . *El Socialista* cannot help reproducing it, seeing as its programme is little different from that of the IWMA.'[33]

The Commune-idea then continued its journey, again caught between obscurity and resurgence. In June 1874, as in many other parts of the continent, a newspaper appeared entitled *La Comuna* and then *La Comuna mexicana*. It made explicit reference to the Paris Commune:[34] 'As long as there is a man or woman alive, the Commune will continue to exist, for great principles are immortal . . . The Commune is alive in France as in Mexico, in the United States as in Germany, in China or Arabia.'[35] The principle of different European and American 'modernities' remained at work: according to this newspaper, as the comparatist Bruno Bosteels explains, the idea of socialism could only become concrete by moving from Europe to the Americas. This was framed in terms of a contrast between, on the one hand, centuries of monarchical despotism in Europe, and, on the other, the vigour of the young Latin American republics, despite the threats looming over them. This reappropriation also proceeded through other channels, such as that of the Greek anarchist tailor Plotino Rhodakanaty. Influenced by the Hungarian experience of 1848, and having spent time in both Berlin and Paris, Rhodakanaty reached Mexico in 1861. There he thought he could see significant similarities between the ideas of Fourier and Proudhon and the Mexican peasants' ways of organising themselves. This major figure in the Mexican social movement later became a local conduit for these ideas. For his part, he believed that a Paris Commune could even take place in Mexico – a possibility he saw resurfacing during the great wave of strikes in the United States in 1877:

33 'La Internacional', *El Socialista*, 10 September 1871. This selection process was no isolated instance. We find it, for instance, in the writings of the Chilean intellectual Eduardo de la Barra, *Francisco Bilbao ante la sacristía: refutación de un folleto* (Santiago: Imprenta El Ferrocarril, 1872).

34 Bruno Bosteels, 'The Mexican Commune', in Shannon Brincat (ed.), *Communism in the Twenty-First Century; Whither Communism? The Challenges of the Past and the Present* (Santa Barbara, CA: Praeger, 2014), pp. 161–89.

35 *La Comuna*, 28 June 1874, cited in B. Bosteels, 'Mexican Commune'.

> In our view, according to the infallible law of analogy, the Commune was extinguished in Paris only in appearance, and . . . after germinating throughout Europe and crossing the ocean to the United States of America, it will not fail to visit us before long, like a migratory bird hovering above corrupt villages to purify them and devour the tyrants who infest them.[36]

These were bold interventions, expressing positions not necessarily shared by all workers or socialists; for example, Rhodakanaty was excluded from the Gran Círculo. But such interventions showed that the Commune had become an integral part of Mexican perceptions and Mexican history. The Parisian event took shape here as both a vehicle of international connections and a local reference point, coming to life on Mexico's own soil. It would later provide fuel for anarcho-syndicalism, socialism, agrarian communism and indigenous communalism.[37] It was as if, following seemingly unlikely circuits, there were simultaneous germinations of the communal idea, with unpredictable futures.

An Inspiration for Action: Strikes, Revolutions, Wars of Independence

But the Commune did not make its presence felt only in discussions about the definition and aims of revolutionary movements and revolts. Much as the various uprisings from 1789 to 1848 had inspired the Communards of 1871, the Commune itself became a point of reference for action. It was of a different texture: the Commune was thus that piece of the past which, combined with others, gave meaning to the moment of struggle, setting it within a wider cause, or even opening up the relationship with revolutionary time mentioned above. This often took the form of invocations of the Commune in the moment of

36 'La Comuna Americana', *El Combate*, August 1877 – cited in Bosteels, 'Mexican Commune', p. 171. On Rhodakanaty, see Carlos Illades, *Rhodakanaty y la formación del pensamiento socialista en* México (Barcelona: Anthropos/Universidad Autónoma Metropolitana Iztapalapa, 2002).

37 On the echoes in the early 1880s, see Clara E. Lida and Carlos Illades, 'El anarquismo europeo y sus primeras influencias en México después de la Comuna de París (1871–1881),' *Historia Mexicana* 51: 1 (2001), pp. 103–49.

struggle, without extensive discourse and yet full of polysemy – the kind of invocation that is often difficult to grasp in historical inquiry, and yet is essential to the analysis of insurrectionary phenomena.

The reference to the Commune was mobilised, for example, in the 'Cantonalist' revolt in Spain in summer 1873. In February 1873, the First Spanish Republic was established. It failed to resolve the economic and social crisis, or the political instability recently fuelled by the Carlist uprisings. Yet the creation of the Republic had itself spurred hopes, and with them a dynamic that the new regime proved unable to control. It moved to repress the agitation, and Cantonalist uprisings then broke out across Spain.[38] These sought to turn the principles of municipal democracy into a reality, driven by a particular republican and social impulse. The political fractures mentioned above were palpable: many federalist republicans (such as Presidents Pí y Margall and Emilio Castelar) now rejected insurrectionary action, falling into line with the conservatives and liberal monarchists. By contrast, intransigent federalist republicans and the revolutionary-socialist members of the Federación Regional Española (FRE) joined the terrain of struggle. Even in their cooperation, however, tensions were apparent, for these movements were themselves composed of many individuals responding to different logics of mobilisation.[39]

Closely followed in Spain at the time, the Commune in any case played a role in these movements. Refugee Communards were actively involved: the best known were Charles Alerini, a former member of the Marseille Commune, Paul Brousse, who had been convicted in Toulouse, and Camille Camet, a Communard *canut* from Lyon. The three founded a Comité de Propagande Révolutionnaire Socialiste de la France Méridionale ('Socialist Revolutionary Propaganda Committee of Southern France') in Barcelona in 1873. But this city did not itself join the Cantonalist movement. For that connection, we would have to

38 Compare Antonio Lopez Estudillo, *Republicanismo y anarquismo en Andalucía. Conflictividad social agraria y crisis finisecular (1868–1900)* (Cordoba: Ediciones de La Posada, 2001).

39 On Cartagena, see Jeanne Moisand, *Se fédérer ou mourir. Carthagène, 1873. Une commune espagnole et ses mondes* (Montreuil: Libertalia, 2022) – transl. into English as *A Spanish Commune: The Cartagena Canton and Its Worlds* (New York: Verso, 2025). What follows draws extensively on the analyses of this historian, who kindly gave me guidance.

look to other refugees, such as Fortuné Henry, an elected representative for Paris's 10th arrondissement and a member of the Commune's Subsistence Committee; Antonio de la Calle, a Spanish republican insurgent in 1869 who went on to become a company captain under the Paris Commune; and the famous Joseph Combatz, mentioned above. De la Calle and Combatz both took part in the Cartagena canton – the most significant in this moment. Yet this widespread reference to the Commune undoubtedly owed rather more to the rapid circulation of articles, pamphlets, translations of the Commune's declarations, and books: from summer 1871, Marx's *The Civil War in France* enjoyed massive distribution in Spain – quite unlike the rest of the continent. And republican newspapers bearing the name *Comuna* were not long in appearing.[40]

The historian Clara Lida long ago highlighted this role of the Commune in the Cantonalist movement in Spain. For her, the Commune, as an example and as a principle, breathed life into the Spanish federalist spirit and its chosen terrain of activity: the local canton.[41] The reference to the Commune surely did not operate in isolation. On the one hand, it resonated with the features of an insurrectionary movement based on forms of self-organisation and rooted in a tradition of discussing Proudhon's ideas. On the other, it took its place among a galaxy of other historical references, to which it certainly added a more social and international dimension. These included, notably, the Spanish Revolution of 1868, the insurrectionary liberalism of the 1800s, the French Revolution, and the *fueros* of the Middle Ages. Of course, as Jeanne Moisand points out, each canton had its own specific history, with its many conflicts and power struggles: the role of such a reference should not be overstated. But this presence was tangible, for instance in the formation of the 'committees of public safety' that governed most of the cantons, evoking both the Commune of 1793 and that of 1871. This very point invites us to ask whether, for the protagonists of the Cantonalist movement, the Commune was not at once a link with the past and – because it had been brutally interrupted – an anticipation, a

40 Ibid. See also Delhom, 'La Fédération espagnole de l'Internationale et la Commune de Paris'; A. López Estudillo, *Republicanismo y anarquismo en Andalucía.*

41 Delhom, 'La Federation espagnole de l'Internationale et la Commune de Paris'; Clara Lida, *Anarquismo y revolución en la España del XIX* (Madrid: Siglo XXI, 1972); Jose Alvarez Junco, *La Comuna en España.*

possible political form still to be pursued for the future.[42] At the same time, the spectres of revolution undoubtedly also haunted governmental and military practice: this was evident in the terrible repression that struck 'Red' Alcoy, a large town held for a few weeks by IWMA militants after a huge strike. The First Spanish Republic fell in January 1874, following a coup d'état, at the same time as the fall of the last canton, Cartagena. Francesco Serrano's authoritarian government was succeeded by the monarchy of Alfonso XII. Although it was more conservative, it remained a constitutional monarchy, as demonstrated in 1881 when the reins of government were handed over to liberals. The revolutionary dynamic, for its part, had suffered a major setback, but did not disappear outright. Many insurgents and anarchists from the FRE left Spain, when they could, for Latin America, among other destinations. They brought with them the experience of this Cantonalist movement, and part of this retranslated version of the Commune-idea, which then followed other paths.

In the Cuban case, the reference to the Parisian event was used in a different way: one that was at once somewhat out of step with others and at the heart of the military mobilisation. From 1868, the island witnessed a vast insurrectionary movement. In 1869 it culminated in the proclamation of the independent Cuban republic and the abolition of slavery. A long war against Spain ensued, and between 1868 and 1878 the metropole sent almost 180,000 men – the largest military contingent involved in a transatlantic war at any point in the nineteenth century.[43] The Cuban cause was soon taken up as the banner of the Universal Republic and the abolition of slavery. International volunteers came from the United States, Great Britain, Venezuela and the Dominican Republic to defend Cuba. From New York, Gustave Cluseret also promised, in 1869, to try to win over European opinion to this cause.

But while there was a certain synchrony with events in Paris, and a number of possible parallels can be drawn between them (the role of citizens' militias, the republican ideal, emancipation), no direct

42 In Gramscian terms, it plays the role of a 'future city' (*città futura*). See Riccardo Ciavolella and Armelle Choplin, 'Gramsci and the African *Città Futura*: Urban Subaltern Politics from the Margins of Nouakchott, Mauritania,' *Antipode* 49: 2 (2016), pp. 314–34.

43 On this and what follows, see Moisand, *Se fédérer ou mourir*.

reference to the Commune was made in Cuba in 1871 – at least according to the bibliography I have consulted. Unlike in the neighbouring countries, information probably circulated poorly because of the war and the subsequent shuttering of republican newspapers. Moreover, the actual conditions of the struggle (the mobilisation of often illiterate rural people, the confrontations between military officers and politicians, the impact of the racial question) may have made these similarities rather less obvious. Here, we again encounter the gaps and holes in the reception of the Commune.

The junction between the two events would come later, through peripheral points of contact, starting with the United States: the great demonstration in December 1871 organised by the IWMA was, it should be remembered, in honour of both the martyrs of the Commune and the victims of the Cuban war. Indeed, on US soil, Cuban exiles (at least 12,000 in number) and Communards (likely several hundred) could meet.[44] Still, these links were rather loose: the Cubans were divided into several camps, and many had settled in Florida. In New York, the only Spanish section of the IWMA was of little importance compared to the other German- and French-speaking ones.[45] Newspapers formed the second point of contact, via the ricochet effect I have already mentioned: the press, and the conservative press in particular, had been so keen to harp on about the misdeeds of the Communards – in turn associated with 'Cuban incendiaries' – that they unwittingly served as conduits for information about the Commune. Saturnino Martínez, a cigar maker and founder in 1867 of the workers' newspaper *La Aurora*, learned of the Paris event and the existence of the IWMA through this medium: in 1874 he defended the IWMA in an article, which led to his being deported to Spain.[46] The last point of contact, military and migratory,

44 Women and children included. See Michel Cordillot, *Utopistes et exilés du Nouveau monde: des Français aux Etats-Unis, de 1848 à la Commune* (Paris: Vendémiaire, 2013), p. 266.

45 Ibid.

46 Jeanne Moisand, 'Revolutions, Republics and IWMA in the Spanish Empire (around 1873)', in F. Bensimon, Q. Deluermoz and J. Moisand, eds, *'Arise Ye Wretched of the Earth!'*. See also Moisand, 'Les exilés de la "République universelle". Français et Espagnols en révolution (1868–1878)', in Delphine Diaz, Jeanne Moisand, Romy Sánchez and Juan Luis Simal, eds, *Exils entre les deux mondes. Migrations et espaces politiques atlantiques au XIXe siècle* (Mordelles: Les Perséides, 2015).

ran through that country: many penniless workers, and indeed convicts from 1873, joined the army in Spain in order to escape poverty or their prison sentences. From Spain, they were sent to fight the Cuban insurrection. Once there, however, some deserted to join the insurgents. Some were French, including even ex-Communard refugees in Spain. Charles-Philibert Peissot, for example, was a former soldier of the French Second Empire who had been disgusted by the Mexican expedition.[47] During the Paris Commune, he worked as a weapons engineer before taking refuge in Spain. The Spanish government then sent him to fight in Cuba, from where he joined General Vicente García, along with two of his comrades. According to the historiography of the Ten Years' War (1868–78), Peissot is said to have had some influence on the Santa Rita manifesto (1877), in whose call for a 'democratic and social republic' some historians have identified inspiration from the Commune. This claim should be treated with some caution, however, given that the manifesto was at the root of a split in the Cuban movement; Peissot's intervention may also have been used after the event to point the finger of blame at a foreigner.[48] No direct influence can be established. But it is more important and interesting to note – as Jeanne Moisand does – that the Commune here played less the role of a banner than that of a language capable of shaping insurgent vocabulary in a given context.

There were thus many kinds of layering of experiences and references that gave rise to unique trajectories. It is worth adding that in Cuba, too, after 1880, the Commune became a reference point for revolutionaries and certain progressives, albeit in an ambivalent form. The event was both a source of inspiration for a social republic and a reminder of the risks inherent in the revolutionary movement. José Martí, a key intellectual figure in the Cuban revolutionary movement and founder of the Partido Revolucionario Cubano (in 1892), who was also deported to Spain at the time of the Commune, took a similar stance. Indeed, on several occasions, Martí expressed a certain lack of

47 Victor Manuel Marrero Zaldivar, 'Sur les traces d'un communard de Paris', cited in Jean-Luc Laurent, 'Charles Peissot le révolutionnaire sans tombe de Cuba', jeanlucglaurent.over-blog.com, 2014.

48 See Raul Eduardo Chao, *Baraguá: Insurgents and Exiles in Cuba and New York During the Ten Year War on Independence (1868–1878)* (Washington, DC: Dupont Circle Editions, 2009), p. 331.

enthusiasm for the Commune, which he considered had also been an orgy of violence.[49]

I have paid particular attention here to Spain and Latin America, because they were chosen as the focus for this survey. But a study of Italy, already well signposted by the historiography, is likewise instructive. I have mentioned Mazzini's criticisms: for him, the Commune was proof of the deadly self-dissolution brought about by class war. Nevertheless, it did spur a major growth of the IWMA between 1871 and 1874. Although the figures must be treated with caution, by this date the organisation had 32,000 members, mainly among craftsmen (shoemakers, printers), day labourers and factory workers. The revolution in Paris also had an impact on the rising generation of Italian activists, embodied by figures born in the 1840s and 1850s such as Carlo Cafiero, Andrea Costa and Errico Malatesta. Finally, these changes saw the emergence of a strong current of libertarian socialism in Italy. This current stemmed from local dynamics (the federalist and atheist movements) and the presence of Bakunin, as well as the events in Paris. Moreover, in Italy, the Commune could just as well embody the cell of a future libertarian-socialist federation as echo the historical experiences of the peninsula's city-states.

This dynamic likewise accompanied the wave of strikes in Italy that began in the 1860s. It was followed by a few famous, albeit limited, insurrectionary attempts to mobilise the peasantry, such as those in central and southern Italy in 1874 and in Matese in 1877. In these cases, the instigators explicitly referred to the Commune and the Spanish Cantonalist rebellion, either as a point of comparison with their own contexts or as a spur to mobilisation (tellingly, the conference of federations, intended to launch the uprising of 1874, was held on 18 March).[50] While the state crackdown broke the movement, solid local pockets of

49 Carlos Ripoll, *José Martí, the United States, and the Marxist Interpretation of Cuban History* (New Brunswick, NJ: Transaction, 1984); Paul Estrade, *José Martí (1853–1895) ou les Fondements de la démocratie en Amérique latine* (Paris: Éditions caribéennes, 1987).

50 Nunzio Pernicone, *Italian Anarchism (1864–1892)* (Princeton, NJ: Princeton University Press, 1993), pp. 82–128; Luigi Parente, ed., *Movimenti sociali e lotte politiche nell'Italia liberale. Il moto anarchico del Matese* (Milan: Franco Angeli, 2001).

anarchism did endure; and for them, the Commune remained a landmark event.[51]

The combination of the Spanish and Italian cases also offers a further cue for reflection: When studying the reception of the Commune, should we not also consider what role local freedoms played in the political culture of the time? This great divide in European history, which has been rather sparsely studied, clearly mattered. Indeed, where such freedoms existed and were not in question, the echoes of the Commune seem to have taken root more strongly than in other areas where the central authorities had long resisted the assertion of local autonomy (Russia, Central Europe, and so on).

Yet the Italian aspect of this story did not end there, either: in the face of government reaction, from 1874 onwards some militants headed into exile around the Mediterranean, and particularly in Egypt – above all in the cities of Cairo and Alexandria. There they contributed to the development of distinctive anarchist currents. They joined radical circles that were already present, often composed of Greeks and Italians (Mazzinians) who had arrived through economic migration, or as refugees.[52] These circles were themselves sometimes tied to the local solidarity that was beginning to stir among the rural workers who had come to work in the Suez shipyards. The first union, the Workers' Brotherhood, was founded in 1872 by Greek workers. In 1876 these Italian exiles, who were in the minority, formed a branch of the IWMA in Alexandria: and in 1877 they founded the first anarchist newspaper, *Il Lavoratore* ('The Worker').[53] While the radical and socialist current in Egypt remained diverse, it took on a more consolidated form after 1880, adapting to changes in the world of work and in the colonial order. This takes us beyond the chronological limits I initially set; but the first explicit mention of the Commune we can find dates from 1889, in a poster published on the anniversary of 18 March:

51 Carl Levy, 'The Italians and the IWMA', in Bensimon, Deluermoz and Moisand, *'Arise Ye Wretched of the Earth!'*. See also Eva Civolani, *L'anarchismo dopo la Comune. I casi italiano e spagnolo* (Milan: Franco Angeli, 1981).

52 Beyond the references already cited, see C. A. Bayly and E. F. Biagini, eds, *Giuseppe Mazzini and the Globalization of Democratic Nationalism (1830–1920)* (Oxford: Oxford University Press, 2008).

53 On Italian militants in Egypt, see Leonardo Bettini, *Bibliografia dell'anarchismo, vol. II: Periodici e numeri unici anarchici in lingua italiana pubblicati all'estero (1872–1971)* (Florence: Crescita politica, 1976).

> Workers! It is now 18 long years since the founding of the Commune in Paris . . . The COMMUNE has taught us that everything that exists comes from THOSE WHO WORK and that misery and famine will reign supreme until the day when the PEOPLE are the absolute masters of their own labour.[54]

Finally, the first such reference in Arabic appeared a little later, in April 1894, in the famous *Al-Hilal*, a newspaper that specialised in presenting the socialist thought and thinkers of the day.[55] Perhaps earlier references did exist, but there is a dearth of studies identifying them.

Clearly, the threads of connection to the Commune are tenuous and multiple, and here we can only follow some of their paths. At the least, we can say that this was not a simple process of diffusion, fanning out from a single, Parisian centre. Rather, what we see is the polygenesis of a composite global figure of the Paris Commune between 1871 and 1880, building up around more or less substantial centres.

The Commune as a Critical Source for Reimagining the World

Other appropriations of the Commune are also worth examining, such as the artistic and poetic uses that built on its creative or subversive potential. Arthur Rimbaud, who took up the Communard cause, dedicated at least six poems to it. Indeed, he also had the Commune in mind when he wrote on 15 May 1871, in his 'letter from the seer' to his friend Paul Demeny, that 'the inventions of the unknown call for new forms'.[56]

54 Marilyn Booth and Anthony Gorman, *The Long 1890s in Egypt: Colonial Quiescence, Subterranean Resistance* (Edinburgh: Edinburgh University Press, 2014), p. 229 n 29.

55 James Gelvin and Nile Green, eds, *Global Muslims in the Age of Steam and Print* (Berkeley, CA: University of California Press, 2014); Anthony Gorman, '"Diverse in Race, Religion and Nationality . . . But United in Aspirations of Civil Progress": The Anarchist Movement in Egypt (1860–1940)', in Steven Hirsch and Lucien Van der Walt, eds, *Anarchism and Syndicalism in the Colonial and Postcolonial World (1870–1940): The Praxis of National Liberation, Internationalism, and Social Revolution* (Leiden: Brill, 2010), pp. 3–31.

56 'Lettre du voyant', correspondence with Paul Demeny, 15 May 1871 at essentiels.bnf.fr. See Kristin Ross, *The emergence of social space : Rimbaud and the Paris Commune* (Minneapolis: University of Minnesota Press, 1988); Steve Murphy, *Rimbaud et la Commune. Microlectures et perspectives* (Paris: Classiques Garnier, 2010).

But we shall also mention another mode of appropriation, in this case linked to practices of *détournement* even within the commercial life of industrial, liberal societies that were then at peace. The United States is a case in point. Here, the Commune resonated strongly within domestic political divisions. But it also found its way into the emerging media culture – a point I have not yet emphasised sufficiently. In New York in winter 1875, a static cyclorama – the 'largest ever seen in the United States' (120 metres long and 15 metres high), presented the *Siege of Paris and Assassination of the Archbishop of Paris at the Hands of the Commune of 1871*. Spectacular visual effects were used to immerse spectators in the scenes, the last of which was, unsurprisingly, one of the most striking. The Commune and the fires of Paris soon became a recurring theme in many major spectacles, advertised with flashy posters and huge panoramas designed to impress the viewer and stir their emotions. Building on studies on the culture of spectacle, the historian Michelle Coghlan recently showed how these stagings of the Paris Commune created both an entertaining image and, paradoxically, a bodily memory of the event, brought to life by the mobilisation of the senses.[57]

In fact, the proponents of American radical culture were quick to draw inspiration from these popular texts, shows and images in order to imagine new ways of immersing themselves in the Commune. A telling example is the organisation of 'festivals' on the anniversary of this event on 18 March. In 1879, in Chicago, one of the main centres of anarchism in the United States, the Socialist Labor Party prepared an Exposition building that could host some 40,000 people. It offered a full programme of speeches, songs, dances, plays and marches. The crowds created such a scrum that it was impossible to get through all the planned activities. The following year, in New York, the 'Strike for the Universal Commune!' festival, advertised on large posters, also featured concerts, banquets, balls and more. One of the distinctive features of these events was that they attracted such a wide variety of groups. These included the Société des Réfugiés de la Commune, the Socialistic Labor Party, the Freethinkers, the Women's Socialistic Society and the Arbeiter Liedertafel (Workers' Choir). There was also an assortment of nationalities, from French

57 Michelle Coghlan, *Sensational Internationalism: The Paris Commune and the Remapping of American Memory in the Long Nineteenth Century* (Edinburgh: Edinburgh University Press, 2016). The following analysis draws on Coghlan's study.

participants to Italians, Germans, Spaniards, Cubans, Venezuelans, and so on. These festivals expressed an international cause uniting women, workers and the oppressed, even as part of a US political culture that was in the process of becoming nationalised. The meaning of 'international' here is surely not the same as it is elsewhere, such as in the German SPD.

But another distinctive feature of these festivals was their very mode of functioning: through their shocking images, speeches, dances and marches, they mobilised both the body and the senses. We see here the appropriation of festive practices from commercial culture, repurposed for political ends. The Commune in this case took the form of a shared emotional and political resource, which made it possible to think of alternative paths beyond the present world and to fuel revolutionary desire in the United States. The over-mediatisation of the event, and its focus on the horrors of the Commune, could thus also produce its flip-side – another reception, which nonetheless preserved something of the effects of the culture of spectacle. This reception, in turn, could be refracted through mass culture, as shown by the way in which the generalist press reproduced the most resounding discourse: what the historian Coghlan calls a 'sensational internationalism'.

These practices and discourses suggest another use for the reference to the Commune: in such contexts, it could serve as a spur to an in-depth critique of the way the existing world was organised. Speaking of the negative reception of the Paris event in 1871, the famous anarchist feminist Lucy Parsons noted in an autobiographical text that it was the Commune 'that first directed my attention to the study of the social problems'.[58] We should doubtless be wary of reconstructed personal trajectories, especially when they serve after the fact to create a sense of coherence – the realisation of a personal fate. But such a memory also suggests the event's capacity to serve as an eye-opener – an oft-mentioned phenomenon. Much later, in 1914, Voltairine de Cleyre explained in an article: 'there are moments and occasions that reduce every man to direct, primitive feelings . . . For me, the commemoration of 18 March is one of those moments.'[59] Here a different appropriation of the Commune

58 Lucy Parsons, 'Honoring the Red Flag', *Chicago Daily Tribune*, 24 March 1889, cited in Coghlan, *Sensational Internationalism*, p. 96.

59 Voltairine de Cleyre, 'The Paris Commune', *Mother Earth*, March 1914, cited in Coghlan, *Sensational Internationalism*, p. 103.

appears, this time a feminist one. For these different authors, 'rediscovering' the Commune was then a way of accessing something essential, beyond the embodied forms of power, the divisions that organise social space, and perhaps even political battles that had sometimes become too routine. To think on the basis of this event was somehow useful for grasping the root of problems that were less visible because they were so hidden, or tacitly accepted. These might include the construction of gender difference, socioeconomic and racial inequalities, the principle of the organisation of the state, and the inertial force of 'everyday life'. In those contexts where the sociopolitical order is more regulated and incorporated – perhaps above all in a liberal democracy, where debate was possible – the reference to the Commune provided a way of thinking 'outside the box'. In this way, it became the tool of a radical critique, in the primary sense of a critique that gets to the root of a problem. This use is all the more important in that, while on the surface less immediately combative, it might represent a personal endeavour involving a large number of people, to widely varying degrees. In all these ways, the Commune cut across very different worlds, which could thus be linked together even as they remained unaware of each other's existence.

The 'Rhizomes' of Revolt

For all of these reasons, the re-actualisation of the figure of the Commune over the 1880s and 1890s cannot be reduced to a simple transitional moment, as if leading towards a clear and fixed redefinition of the event. Rather, the Commune immediately lent itself to a variety of uses. It followed winding paths, taking root in one situation, failing to do so in another. Sometimes it responded to significant power struggles, sometimes to more discrete echoes – though even the most insignificant could later prove to be the seeds of future genealogies, which were constantly reinvented retrospectively. These processes involved manifold situations, actors and forms. We have come across artisans, representatives of the urban bourgeoisie, intellectuals, factory workers, peasants, soldiers, and even formerly enslaved people.[60] The figure of the Commune appeared

60 On this diversity, see Marcel Van der Linden, 'Enjeux pour une histoire mondiale du travail', *Le Mouvement social* 241 (2014), pp. 3–29, in particular p. 25.

by turns as a locus of memory, a witness to solidarity, an emblem of the grievances of the times, a driving force for action, an operator of international connections, a political form to come, and a promise of possible futures.

Under these conditions, it is difficult to offer any coherent picture of the many ways in which this reference circulated. It is even more difficult to establish their impact, or to maintain the idea that they had a single source, even within Europe. The most obvious metaphor that comes to mind here is that of the rhizome: a subterranean plant formation that develops horizontally, polymorphically and multidirectionally. Gilles Deleuze and Félix Guattari described its characteristics and its relevance to the study of the social world: connections, multiplicity, and the absence of hierarchy between elements.[61] The development of the Commune-idea was rhizomatic.

As I have indicated, the study of the Commune can thus enrich not only the analysis of the transition period but also that of the 'global radicalism' of the 1860s.[62] These afterlives of the Parisian event illustrate the main characteristics of that radicalism, as identified by historians. They point to the idea of a growing synchronisation of struggles linked to the new modalities of globalisation – in the sense not of some coherent and organised coordination but of one made up of looser tangles of interrelations stemming from multiple sources. The Commune indeed became a point of reference shared by Chilean intellectuals and German weavers alike, in each instance following singular trajectories and giving it a specific content. In doing so, the study of these afterlives also supports the hypothesis that this synchronisation was not a post facto response to the acceleration of globalisation, but that these processes went hand in hand, starting from persistent areas of conflict. Finally, this examination suggests the geographical contours of the phenomenon, in a zone spanning Europe, the Atlantic and the Mediterranean. In this instance, the area seems to correspond more to imperial European migration patterns and the echoes of previous revolutions. It only imperfectly covers the

61 Gilles Deleuze and Félix Guattari, *Mille plateaux* (Paris: Éditions de Minuit, 1980). Constance Bantman speaks of 'informed internationalism'. Constance Bantman, 'Internationalism Without an International? Cross-Channel Anarchist Networks (1880–1914)', *Revue belge de philologie et d'histoire* 84: 4 (2006), pp. 961–81.

62 Ilham Khuri-Makdisi, *The Eastern Mediterranean and the Making of Global Radicalism (1860–1914)* (Berkeley, CA: University of California Press, 2013).

'clusters' of revolts of 1870–71 and the sphere of influence of French imperial power (for instance, the reference does not appear in Algeria or China). This is not to say that oppositions there had ceased, but rather that separations were becoming apparent between different spaces of revolt.

These considerations allow us to return, finally, to certain aspects of the history of the Commune after the Commune – and, in particular, after the Russian Revolution and the creation of the Soviet Union. Clearly, the post-1917 genealogical reconstruction recharged the Commune as a point of reference. It crucially enriched the geography of its uses by decisively adding Asian and then African spaces. The examination we have conducted, however, already shows why this communist rereading was able to have such a far-reaching effect: the Commune had a global impact as early as the 1870s – and had already fuelled, among other aspirations, a kind of transnational wave of socialist hope. This same analysis also explains why, in some places, the reappropriation of this reference, even if it came rather belatedly, seems to have been easy: it very often met with latent forms and an already local history that had altered its meaning. Finally, it sheds light on why, even at the moments of greatest orthodoxy, this reinterpretation was never able to prevail completely: for the Commune would continue to lend itself to the most varied rereadings and appropriations.[63]

63 This path corresponds to the transnational and imperial modes of dissemination of communist utopianism and internationalism after 1917. See Sabine Dullin and Brigitte Studer, 'Communisme + transnational. L'équation retrouvée de l'internationalisme (premier XXe siècle)', *Monde(s)* 10 (2016), pp. 9–32.

Conclusion to Part III: The Spectral and the Embodied

In our vigils of arms, we liked to talk about the struggles for freedom, and so, at the present time, in anticipation of a new germinal, we will talk about the days of the Commune, and the twenty-five years that seem almost a century, from the slaughter of '71 to the dawn that is breaking. Heroic times are beginning; crowds are gathering like swarms of bees in spring; bards are rising up singing the new epic, it is indeed the vigil of arms where the spectre of May will speak.

Louise Michel, *Memoirs*, 1898

Here we have the final element of our explanation: the ways and means of the post-1871 recomposition of the Commune, which partly erased the dissonance of the Parisian event and adjusted it to the general context of the 1870s. After the fact, the Commune became a moment when the notions of 'nation', 'international' and 'class' were fixed on a far-reaching scale, without detracting from the ever-changing multiplicity of political forms and social worlds.[1] In this other context, the Commune could well appear, albeit after the fact, as the 'dawn' of the revolutions to come, whether these were hoped for or dreaded.

This final part has dealt more specifically with social and political order. These orders, as noted in the Introduction, relate to political

1 Michael Mann, *The Sources of Social Power, vol. II: The Rise of Classes and Nation States (1760–1914)* (Cambridge: Cambridge University Press, 1993).

regimes, but likewise to power relations, social hierarchies, economic inequalities, technological environments, tacit and official norms, and cultural values. The study of the Commune and the post-Commune period adds a few useful indicators in this regard. It shows that, even when this order is relatively coherent on the scale of a city or a country, it is also bound up with long-distance chains of interdependence and reciprocal effect. Conversely, it also reminds us that the social order is embedded in routines, habits, levels of perception and the interplay of bodies.

These orders are, of course, fluid, socially variable, and deeply moulded by contradictory internal dynamics as well as by the criticisms and oppositions that constantly animate them. However, the Communard experience reminds us that these challenges and responses can operate at different levels, with a variety of effects, from the regulated forms of mediation to the undermining of more integrated social or cultural frameworks.

This study of the effects and legacies of the Commune thus raised the classic but always delicate question of how social orders change, or else persist over time. They evolve in a variety of ways, whether as a result of external pressures, internal political struggles, slow shifts in behaviour and perceptions, or long-range transformations in the economic, institutional and even environmental frameworks. Their whole history is made up of multidirectional processes. However, as we have seen, these orders are at the same time shaped by references to the past – spectres that can widen existing fault-lines, tear up previously shared interpretive schemas, and open up a sense of possibility when the time is right. It is hard to decide between the two visions, which seem opposed in every respect.

We should pause here to look more closely at two approaches to social worlds and action mentioned earlier. The first, more traditional but no less complex, is concerned with the processes of social transformation. It studies power relations, the meanings that naturalise or displace them, the more or less long-term dynamics that drive them, and the situated effects of individual actions. The second declares itself more sensitive to discontinuities, to modes of resistance and forms of subjectivation that can alter the perception of history; it unveils a different way of dealing with time. The first is based on the social sciences, such as anthropology and sociology, and strives for distance and objectivity. The second draws more on philosophy, art history and literature, and is open about its sympathies. Each has its own sense of what matters: while the first is concerned with great recomposed masses, the second focuses on detail, on subterranean but invisible movements and the emergence of meaning. Here there is no continuity, no causal relationship: this second approach forms a different history, at odds with the rules and conceptions of time and society of the first. Yet these two perspectives undoubtedly need to be considered in combination – by recognising this gap and its irreducibility. Indeed, this effort has proved necessary here in order to understand the disruptive force of the Commune, its effects, its limits and its aftermaths.

More generally, the analyses of the social, cultural and political history of the nineteenth and twentieth centuries would have everything to gain by incorporating this other possibility of history into our understanding, in the form of eruption or latency. This means grasping an evanescent and interstitial time linked to emotion and memory, which also underlies, but is not confined to, the social or democratic revolution.

Conclusion

Returning to the Commune-as-Event, II

I know the skies bursting into lightning, and the waterspouts,
And the surf, and the currents, I know the evening,
The dawn exalted as a crowd of doves,
And I have sometimes seen what man thought he saw.

Arthur Rimbaud, '*Le Bateau ivre*' (August 1871)

This Commune, or these Communes, have taken us on a journey. We have hardly unravelled all the threads of the brief but profoundly important event that took place in Paris, that global city of the second half of the nineteenth century. What we have gleaned, however, can begin to provide answers to some of the questions with which we began.

The 'Commune Moment' of the 1860s–70s

The answers to these questions are connected to the process of historical reinterpretation that first took place between the 1970s and the 1990s. This work showed that the Commune had to be freed from the overly rigid or excessively general theoretical frameworks in which it had long been embedded. To do so, the event's military and political contexts, the role of organisational and ideological conflicts, and the various definitions of the 'people' of Paris, all needed to be re-examined.

These reassessments put the Commune in a new light: the popular uprising in the French capital was a far-reaching movement, marked by powerful social and political antagonisms; the existence of a communal government, with its prominent figures and its significant measures, was itself remarkable. The first reaction of many Parisians, considered as a whole, was undoubtedly one of enthusiasm, astonishment and disorientation. These reactions fuelled the subsequent shifts in their attitudes, especially as old revolutionary memories resurfaced and the war with Versailles heightened the expression of a distinctive popular patriotism. The city itself was rife with tensions, with reactions ranging from open rejection of the communal government to efforts to repair intolerable injustices and to transform the existing social order. The tensions accelerated the process of redefining friends ('fédérés') and foes, as expressed in the pursuit and arrest of 'the proprietors', 'the Versaillais' and 'Prussian spies'. Finally, at the neighbourhood level, in some arrondissements, such as the 11th, in certain National Guard battalions, clubs and workshops, remarkable sociopolitical practices were enacted. These were rooted in the rich republican and socialist histories of the nineteenth century – and raise important questions about our own conception of democracy, social justice and equality. But the experiment was short-lived, and these achievements seemed limited. Quickly – well before the final massacre – the military difficulties became overwhelming. The landscape of the Commune that has emerged from these studies thus appears fragmented and plural, which helps explain why, as I noted in the Introduction, uncertainty pervades any general analysis of the phenomenon – especially once we have set aside more sweeping theoretical frameworks for grasping its significance.

Given this context, this study makes two main contributions that allow us better understand the Commune more clearly, and to reassess its importance. The first is the recovery of a bona fide 'Commune movement' – an expression I have adapted from historian Rémy Gossez's description of the revolutions of 1848 to describe a multiform, heterogeneous, concrete movement with a revolutionary character. This aspect of the event, and its political creativity, have perhaps received too little emphasis in earlier work.

Thinking about the Commune in these terms enables us to consider simultaneously both the complexity and the contradictions of the scenes that developed in the maelstrom of revolutionary Paris. It allows us, too, to achieve a better grasp of the lived experience of the Commune. The Commune took shape within a pre-existing fabric of popular and working-class sociability and solidarity, which also generated specific political visions (local democracy, a participatory vision of society, material demands and social struggles, and so on). Examining the everyday experience in which the Commune came into being – affecting its participants' relationship with time, the meaning of the words they used, their fears and passions – helps us to reach a better understanding of how some people came to perceive, in small ways, the advent of a republic that was concrete and immediate, a 'democratic and social republic' that took different forms in this unique political moment. This revolutionary experiment was distinctive: by comparison with previous revolutions, it redefined the 'people' more sharply as a socially rooted political collective, gave greater prominence to the figure of the worker, and articulated a clearer opposition to the imperial state, industrial capitalism and the 'monopolists.' To these, one might add a certain degree of messianism, an idealisation of urban autonomy, the impulse towards self-organisation, and a new confidence in science. These practices, words and visions of the future emerged here, waned there, then resurfaced – always adapted to the circumstances.[1] All of this produced a new historical category, destined to endure: the Commune.

In this sense, the Parisian event appears both to be rooted in nineteenth-century Europe and to escape from its confines. The Commune was obviously part of the era's political, industrial and social history, and it shared in the major shifts in ways of looking at the world already underway in the 1860s. Yet it also expressed other movements, produced other ripples, and articulated other anticipations of the future. While we should not overlook the uncertainties typical of such critical moments, it is clear that the Commune fits only imperfectly into the great linear narratives of the century (state expansion, or the prevailing notion of progress). It produced a distinctive temporality, a plurality of times that disrupts our usual readings of the course of history. It thus gives us a glimpse of another nineteenth century, or other nineteenth centuries, with richer rhythms and trajectories.

1 They took the form of what historian Sophie Wahnich has called 'utopias of broken lines', inseparable from conflicts or forms of indifference. Sophie Wahnich, 'Incertitude du temps révolutionnaire', *Socio* 2 (2013), pp. 119–38.

Seen in this light, the classic notion of the Commune as a short-lived experiment is also open to discussion. The Parisian revolt obviously seems like a brief affair of little consequence if we compare it – as the Communards themselves did – with previous revolutions, and especially the 'Great (French) Revolution', which spanned at least the decade, from 1789 to 1799. But if we place this movement alongside other insurrections of the century, or the Communes in the provinces – as contemporaries themselves did – then these three months, which generated a powerful albeit rough-hewn new political form, seem to have had considerable staying power. The abrupt ending of the event brought a sudden halt to these three months of invention. In other words, the vigour of the Commune was owed not only, as has sometimes been said, to its symbolic dimension: it also stems from the tension between this concrete, albeit indistinct, movement of social transformation and its violent ending. The event was thus characterised by a plurality of unrealised potentialities. In this sense, the Commune as revolution is perhaps above all a *historical expression of the possible*, which everyone can then reduce or magnify at will, or read as they see fit.[2] No doubt every event is susceptible in some measure to such varied readings. But the Commune's particular history and characteristics, the conditions under which it took shape, and its exposure to the gaze of all converge to make it into a unique case.

The second part of the answer concerns the transnational and global perspective. From as early as March 1871, the event assumed just such a dimension. The Commune was above all a Parisian event; however, it was part of a wider republican transition. Its provincial and colonial offshoots, rooted in other contexts, formed their own autonomous scenes. The Commune also found echoes in the Atlantic–Mediterranean recompositions of republican and socialist practices that were taking place from 1848 into 1880s – of which the IWMA was one of the vectors, though hardly the only one.[3] Lastly, the Parisian revolt shook an 'imperial society' that was already beginning to crack, weakened by a lost war

2 On this notion, see Quentin Deluermoz and Pierre Singaravélou, *A Past of Possibilities: A History of What Could Have Been* (New Haven, CT: Yale University Press, 2021).

3 This vast post-1848 trend clearly deserves further study. See Clément Thibaud, 'Pour une histoire polycentrique des républicanismes atlantiques (années 1770–années 1880)', *Revue d'histoire du XIXe siècle* 56 (2018), pp. 151–70.

and a difficult political transition.[4] This situation almost automatically generated reactions of opportunism, mistrust or support for the Commune in Europe, in the empires and beyond – from China to the American continent. The emergence of the Commune thus produced a vast constellation. One of the discoveries of this study concerns the Algerian case: shaped by the combination of a European war, a revolutionary movement and a colonial revolt, it demonstrates the ambivalences of nineteenth-century republican universalism, as well as the trans-imperial dynamics at play on the southern side of the Mediterranean. This history of the Commune, then, takes place in France as an imperial nation-state. Of course, research in international history today ought to be more focused on the 'Global South'.[5] But the work of global history, often centred on English-speaking imperial territories, would also benefit from integrating French imperial space.[6] Indeed, such territories carry with them other important themes, such as high culture, the Republic – and revolutions.

Without neglecting the fact that France was undoubtedly one of the main centres of power at the time, and a reference point for contemporary actors, this project has also sought to craft a less Eurocentric history of the country. The scope and significance of the Commune were indeed constructed partly outside Europe: through debates, appropriations and refusals that took root in these places and responded to other historicities. In this sense, the Commune's significance was generated both by the intensity of its own dynamic and, at the same time, by the processes of globalisation underway between the 1860s and 1880s – as well as by this multi-sited history. The tremendous diversity of meanings that the event could quickly assume is most apparent when we observe it on this scale. The Commune certainly did play a role, especially after the fact, in consolidating the notions of the 'working class' and of 'class struggle', and in reshaping the workers' movement after 1880. Readings produced

4 Christophe Charle, *La Crise des sociétés impériales (1900–1940): Allemagne, France, Grande-Bretagne. Essai d'histoire sociale compare* (Paris: Seuil, 2001).

5 Luke Clossey and Nicholas Guyatt, '*It's a Small World* after All: The Wider World in Historians' Peripheral Vision', *Perspectives on History* 51: 5 (May 2013), pp. 24–7.

6 For a reassessment, see David Todd, *A Velvet Empire: French Imperial Power and Economic Life in the Nineteenth Century* (Princeton, NJ: Princeton University Press, 2021).

outside France also make clearer its international character and its ability to internationalise the struggles that enlisted it. But the Commune also took part in frequent debates over republican federalism and decentralisation, which were very active in many countries during the 1860s. It likewise played a role in discussions of urban occupations, local autonomy and the associational practices of skilled workers. Such elements are not only to be found in countries in supposedly 'distant' contexts: a geographical detour helps us to find them also in European countries, where they have thus far drawn rather less attention from researchers.

Nevertheless, these considerations should not lead us to overlook the limited immediate impact of the Paris event and the apparent solidity of the 'organised disorder' referred to here as the 'liberal order', which in any case was far from uniform. These reactions against the Commune are also part of the overall construction of the event; they helped to make the revolutionary character of the episode clearer. This forms another, parallel aspect of the history of the Commune. Together, these elements make up what has been called in this book a 'Commune moment' during the 1860s and 1870s. The disjunction between these scenes, dynamics and roots ought not to be concealed. On the contrary, it is one of the keys to understanding both the multiple consequences of those seventy-two days of insurrection, their constant re-elaboration, and the initial difficulties in grasping them.

In the Eye of the Storm: Capturing the Critical, Revolutionary Event

Thus reconfigured, the Commune undoubtedly deserves to emerge from the solitude to which it has been consigned in recent years. Its irreducibility and singularity are evident – as this study reaffirms. But is this not the case with every landmark event? It would surely be more useful once again to make the Commune of 1871 into not just a model or illustration, but a true 'case study', which can be used to discuss crises, civil wars and revolutions – whether in history, the social sciences or other domains.[7]

7 On 'case thinking' in the social sciences, see Jean-Claude Passeron and Jacques Revel, eds, *Penser par cas* (Paris: Éditions de l'ÉHESS, 2005).

Because it was a relatively circumscribed event, and because it has already been the subject of a considerable amount of research, the study of the Commune – or of the Communes – is primarily of methodological interest. The configurational approach proposed here allowed us to combine several approaches that are commonly used today, and yet often kept separate. If we consider the study of the revolutions of the eighteenth and nineteenth centuries, the Russian revolution of 1917, the movements of May 1968, or more recent crises and revolutions, these might include: a transnational and local approach; analysis of the processes of dislocation; readings 'from below'; the interlocking logics of war, civil war and revolution; attention to the social positions of the actors; gender relations; consideration of revolutionary protagonism; emotions; the question of more or less long-term effects – and so on.[8]

The way in which these approaches have been articulated here obviously depends on the characteristics of 1871; these perspectives, of course, do not exhaust all possible ways of analysing the revolutionary phenomenon. But in this study it has been possible, for example, to extend the reflection on the causes of revolutions by cross-referencing both the conditions of possibility and the specific dynamics of the Commune, and by striving to reconstruct the proper articulation between internal causalities and the effects of transnational situations. It is worth further examining temporal depths and regimes of historicity, ideally for each of the locations we have examined. Finally, this study of

8 For example, in addition to the works already cited, for 1917, see Lyudmila Nivkova, 'The Russian Revolution from a Provincial Perspective', *Kritika* 16: 4 (2015), pp. 769–85; Etienne Forestier-Peyrat 'Retrouver le Caucase: histoire d'une diplomatie frontalière (1905–1938)', PhD dissertation, Sciences Po, Paris (2015). A general assessment is given in Sophie Coeuré and Sabine Dullin, '1917, un moment révolutionnaire', *Vingtième Siècle. Revue d'histoire* 135 (2017), pp. 2–17. For May 1968, see Boris Gobille, *Le mai 68 des écrivains. Crise politique et avant-garde littéraire* (Paris: CNRS éditions, 2018); Ludivine Bantigny, Boris Gobille and Eugenia Palieraki, eds, 'Les "années 68": circulations révolutionnaires', *Monde(s)* 11 (2017). On recent movements, see Amin Allal and Thomas Pierret, eds, *Devenir révolutionnaires. Au coeur des révoltes arabes* (Paris: Armand Colin, 2013); Mounia Bennani-Chraïbi and Olivier Fillieule, 'Pour une sociologie des situations révolutionnaires. Retour sur les révoltes arabes', *Revue française de science politique* 62: 5–6 (2012), pp. 767–96. On Syria, see Adam Baczko, Gilles Dorronsoro and Arthur Quesnay, *Syrie, anatomie d'une guerre civile* (Paris: CNRS éditions, 2016). On these different methodological shifts of the last few years, which represent what he called a 'new generation' in revolutionary studies, see Georges Lawson, *Anatomies of Revolutions* (Cambridge: Cambridge University Press, 2019).

the Commune invites us to consider more closely the way in which revolutions produce their own space-time, somehow creating worlds of their own (whether they last or not).

Other factors, more a matter of historical knowledge, are also worthy of mention. One of the initial questions I asked was how to situate the Commune within the history of revolutions, and in particular their global history.[9] This is the classic problem of historical periodisation. Many works speak of an 'age of revolutions' beginning in 1750 and sometimes ending in 1830, sometimes in 1848, but rarely at any point beyond that. Others deal with a twentieth century of revolutions that began with the global wave of 1917. The Russian, Turkish, Iranian, Mexican and Chinese revolutions of 1905–12 are generally forgotten. The Commune, for its part, is isolated. But are these temporal boundaries and divisions justified? A quick comparison between the sequence of the French Revolution and that of the Commune may offer an answer. The conditions of possibility proper to the 1750s are now well known: slow industrious and commercial 'revolutions', a process of reform 'from above' (in France, and in the Spanish and Portuguese empires), a surge of indigenous and anti-tax revolts, and the decisive role of the Seven Years' War (1756–63). The fiscal pressure generated by this military effort was one of the starting points of the American Revolution (1764–83). Along with other, smaller-scale uprisings, such as the Geneva revolt (1782) and the Patriot movement in the Dutch Republic (1780–87), the American Revolution contributed, from a distance, to the outbreak of the French Revolution – even if it was clearly also driven by its own national and local factors. Through the upheavals it provoked and the new concepts it foregrounded (citizenship, nation, the rights of man, and even 'Revolution' itself), the 'Great (French) Revolution' was a crucial moment in this global transformation. It led to or extended a series of insurrections in the Caribbean, particularly in Saint-Domingue (1791–1804). Through a complex interplay of circulations, its language spread across Europe and to the Latin American revolutions of the early nineteenth century – though they also had their own dynamics. The

9 To avoid repeating the bibliography cited, I will refer you to Manuel Covo, Quentin Deluermoz and Delphine Diaz, 'France, carrefour des révolutions. Genèses nationales et globales d'un espace-temps révolutionnaire', in Quentin Deluermoz, ed, *D'ici et d'ailleurs. Histoires globales de la France contemporaine* (Paris: La Découverte, 2021), pp. 91–136.

wars of the French Revolution and the Napoleonic regime then accentuated the effects of the revolutionary rupture in Europe, the Atlantic basin, and the rest of the world. These reverberations sometimes operated through rebound effects: these wars led, for example, to an acceleration of the British conquest of South Asian states. In the end, an immense upheaval took place, in which France was a pivotal actor but hardly the only one.

The revolutions of 1830, 1848, and the Commune did not have such significant structural effects on the rest of the world, as imperial and global histories have shown. But neither can the importance of these revolutions be overlooked. The 'Commune moment' confirmed and extended certain features of the first 'age of revolutions'. It reminds us of the role of inter-state and imperial wars in making the revolutionary moment possible (which had not been the case in 1848). For the protagonists of 1871, the context of conflict and civil war made the echoes of 1789 even easier to hear – just as it would later facilitate echoes between 1789–99, 1871 and 1917. Lastly, the resonances of the Commune were largely based on those already generated at the time of the French Revolution and its aftermath. Its impact is partly rooted in this background.

There were of course differences between the two revolutionary moments, which are also of considerable interest. The Commune in particular crystallised a vast array of revolts, challenges to authority, and demands characteristic of the post-1848 period. Following a trend that could be observed throughout the century, its expectations were also more visibly social. As for its lesser impact, as in the case of the French 1848, this may also reflect the fact that France was less of a financial, military and demographic power than it had been at the end of the eighteenth century – and that the fabric of technical, commercial, military and legal interrelations between states or regions had changed in the meantime.

Another difference lay in the geography of revolutionary spaces, which moved following the currents of imperial circulation: the Algiers 'Commune' had no precedent in 1848. And in 1870 the media treatment of the 'Free City' of Paris was specific. While it is not clear that this episode affected many new regions, the rise of the telegraph and the steamship accelerated and standardised knowledge of the facts. These new means of communication made it possible for the Commune to resonate in many locations at once – often without each being aware of the others, yet still linked together: the texture of the 'global' at the end of the nineteenth century was thus certainly not the same as it had been at the end of the eighteenth century.

Lastly, the Commune 'case' invites us to consider a polycentric and heterogeneous configuration of insurrection. It makes visible upheavals that were both connected and out of sync with each other, all the more so because the Commune was an unfinished movement that was liable to appropriation of very different kinds. The 'Commune moment' thus forcefully reminds us that the various revolutionary moments from the nineteenth to the twenty-first centuries have often emerged discontinuously, in the shadow of previous revolutions, while at the same time affecting other spaces, involving other groups, and opening new horizons. Describing them in this way offers a response to the question of chronological divisions: it would be hard to confine this history to a 'sequence' or 'age' of revolutions. From this perspective, it would be better to pay more attention to these interplays of echoes and appropriations, and to envision a much less simplistic and segmented unfolding of history from the seventeenth to the twentieth centuries. The moment of 1871 thus invites us to consider more carefully the question of time and temporal experience in this global history of revolutions, alongside the spatial dimension.

Seen in this light, this history of the Commune also extends the recent turns in imperial and global history of the nineteenth century – and takes note of the cautions that have been issued in recent years about it. Over the last ten years or so, the initial enthusiasm that had characterised this historiography has faded in the face of the political, economic, social and ecological crises generated partly by the deregulated globalisation of the 1990s.[10] Global historians have turned their attention to asymmetries and power relations, in contrast to approaches that were seen as disconnected from the realities on the ground because they focused solely on the movement of elites or goods. Historians brought in new populations: sailors, enslaved people, indentured labourers, missionaries, workers, soldiers, women, migrants, the excluded, and subalterns. The themes of this scholarship have opened up to include

10 Richard Drayton and David Motadel, 'Discussion: The Futures of Global History', *Journal of Global History* 13: 1 (2018), pp. 1–21.

resistance to globalisation, less mobile people, and borderlands and marginalised spaces. This reminds us that these vast transformations, far from being just a matter of ever greater integration, also produced new forms of exclusion and opposition. The study of revolutions (and not just the American and French Revolutions of the late eighteenth century) confirms that globalisation is also made up of divisions and struggles. In addition, this example of the Commune clearly illustrates the layering of different levels of regional integration at the end of the nineteenth century, and shows that global processes were plural, disjointed, and sometimes contradictory or in conflict. What emerges is a less smooth, richer global history, made up of power struggles, unevenness and varied dynamics.

In the end, more general problems of an almost anthropological nature, highlighted by this connected and comparative study of the Paris Commune, still remain. Such is the case of the 'family resemblances' that seem to link revolts distant in time and space. They raise the delicate but still topical question of the large-scale distribution of horizontal forms of power and practices of equality and, with it, the translatability of experiences among them.[11] Another issue concerns the distinction between so-called ordinary or routine situations and what are called situations of crisis and revolution: the former can persist in times of crisis, as shown by the (relative) durability of gender barriers during the Commune-event, and the latter can leave traces in the form of latent presences even where the social order appears to be very solid. These presences can resurface later, depending on the circumstances, adding extra energy and meaning to moments of action. This therefore represents more of a continuum than a sudden change of state between the two situations.

Spectres of the Commune, 1871–20

Ultimately, the history of the Commune traced here comes full circle: it affords us a better understanding of what animates the recent resurgences of the Commune idea, as mentioned in the Introduction.

In fact, if the Commune has become a site of memory, a bloc of other futures halted in its tracks, it also endures as a usable past – one that

11 Georges Balandier, *Anthropo-logiques* (Paris: PUF, 1974).

actors can summon in the heat of the moment; and that, as we have seen, is then capable of producing historical discontinuity. We find it in Russia in 1917, in Lenin's famous countdown hoping to exceed the seventy-two days of 1871, but also in the local-level movements of spring 1917, to the point that two peasant communes even took the names 'Paris Commune 1' and 'Paris Commune 2'.[12] This reference was used in the German Revolution of November 1918, in Berlin, and in the Bavarian council republic, to back up the workers' councils in their drive for self-government. It then gradually became a more general symbol of the struggle of the oppressed around the world, put to many different uses. It resurfaced in Shanghai in 1967, to justify the city's continued secession by pointing out the contradictions of the principles set out by Mao. It appeared in 1968, in Nantes (France) in particular, to mark the attempt at students' and workers' self-government.[13] When I began this study in 2013, as I said in the preface, the reference seemed finally to be in the process of fading away. This appeared to be linked to the post-Soviet political transition of 1989, to the weakened standing of France's centrality on the global scale, and probably also to the social transformation of Paris in the second half of the twentieth century (with the city centre increasingly dominated by the upper-middle classes).[14] It was not referred to by the Zapatista uprising, a movement which – despite differences in duration, organisational practices and general worldview – seemed similar.[15] Nor did it appear during the 'Arab Spring' of 2010–11. However, reference was made to the Commune when barricades were erected during the teachers' movement in Oaxaca in 2006, in order to unite people's energies and establish the legitimacy of the

12 Eric Aunoble, *'Le communisme tout de suite !' Le mouvement de communes en Ukraine soviétique 1919–1920* (Paris: Les Nuits Rouges, 2008).

13 Hongsheng Jiang, *La Commune de Shanghai et la Commune de Paris*, Preface by Alain Badiou (Paris: La Fabrique, 2014); Xavier Vigna, *L'insubordination ouvrière dans les années 68. Essai d'histoire politique des usines* (Rennes: Presses Universitaires de Rennes, 2007); Ludivine Bantigny, *1968. De grands soirs en petits matins* (Paris: Seuil, 2018).

14 See the maps showing the social composition of the French capital over the last two centuries in Jean-Luc Pinol and Maurice Garden, *Atlas des Parisiens. De la Révolution à nos jours* (Paris: Parigramme, 2009).

15 See Jérôme Baschet, *La rébellion zapatiste. Insurrection indienne et résistance planétaire* (Paris: Flammarion, 2005); June Nash, *Mayan Vision: The Quest for Autonomy in an Age of Globalization* (New York: Routledge, 2001).

movement 'from below'.[16] It has reappeared, in a less direct form, in the 'squares movements' of the last ten years, from Occupy Wall Street to Nuit Debout, this time implicitly associated with the idea of urban occupation, the local as opposed to the global, horizontal practices of deliberation, and reference to the 'commons'. It has resurfaced in feminist struggles, as in the project of some French ZADs (*zones à défendre*) to 'make a Commune' in occupied agricultural spaces.[17] Such uses have continued to re-emerge.

What does this spectre have to say to us today?

In an era that has been described as the 'Great regression', we face the continued development of neoliberalism, the visible increase in inequalities, new forms of technological control, the ultraconservative retreat into identitarianism, and the profound disruption of ecological balances.[18] Pessimists – or realists, depending on their perspective – will emphasise the fragility of these insurrectional sparks and the enduring strength of the established order. They will then call for more energy to be committed to liberal democracies, with their political freedoms, their space for debate, their devolution of power and their welfare state: democracies that are increasingly tired, perhaps, but still with us.

Others, whether more critical or more optimistic, will feel that the Commune makes visible the many forms of resistance by subalterns around the world. They will think that it reminds us of the plurality of possible forms of the political even in an era of globalised governance fuelled by the idea that 'there is no alternative'. They will consider that the Commune highlights the robustness of this long history of democratic insurgency, resistance to economic domination and the quest for alternatives. They will reckon that, even if these elements are sometimes buried, practices of reciprocity, social justice and the promise of full emancipation are also part of the history that has brought us this far.

---

16 Thanks to Alejandro de la Torre (Instituto Nacional de Antropologia e Historia, Mexico City) for these details.

17 ZAD, short for *zone à défendre*, refers to rural areas occupied by activists opposing large-scale infrastructure projects which they see as expensive and posing a threat to local populations and the environment. These zones are often self-managed and serve as both sites of resistance and experiments in alternative ways of living.

On the 'Gilets Jaunes' movement, which began after the French edition of this book was first published, see Ludivine Bantigny, 'Un passé ravivé. La Commune dans les engagements du présent', *Revue d'histoire du XIXe siècle* 63 (2021), pp. 97–111.

18 Heinrich Geiselberger, ed., *The Great Regression*, (Cambridge: Polity, 2017).

This more contemporary history of the Commune goes beyond the scope of this book. Its future meaning and form will be shaped by the women and men who seize on it at just the right moment, blending it with other sources of inspiration. Yet, whatever form it takes, the Commune will live on, carrying with it the ever-renewed hope of transforming the world in front of us.

Afterword
The Commune, Forever Renewed

This book was published on the eve of the 150th anniversary of the Paris Commune, in October 2020. It was caught up in the unexpected and intense outpouring of interest that marked this event, and has been the subject of discussion, exchange, debate and various readings. This public and critical reception provides an opportunity to revisit certain considerations a couple of years later.

Firstly, the approach adopted in this book was the product of an already extensive period of research.

My early studies had focused on social interactions in the urban context, and centred on the figure of the 'publicly visible' police officer. Looking through the prism of these interactions, this research explored power relations, the history of the state and institutions, social norms and the social imaginary, popular practices, and cultures of perception. Taking a medium-term anthropological perspective, and studying these topics from 'ground level', showed not only the existence of tensions and conflicts but also a profound change in the relationship to order in the Paris of the second half of the nineteenth century, sometimes grasped in some political discourse as a new and ambiguous form of 'urban civilisation'.[1]

I then turned my attention to a historian's concern par excellence – namely, time itself. For this, I especially focused on situations of

1 Quentin Deluermoz, *Policiers dans la ville. La construction d'un ordre public à Paris (1854–1914)* (Paris: Publications de la Sorbonne, 2012).

uncertainty: political crises, civil wars, insurrections and revolutions – all critical conjunctures with which the European nineteenth century is so richly textured. This choice made it possible to approach time in the sense of temporal dynamics, and thus to revisit the question of social and historical transformations. This approach involved examining long-term changes as well as rushes of acceleration, and the phenomena of inertia as well as surges, cycles and after-effects. The 'I' referred to here is in fact a 'we', given that these projects were carried out in collaboration with others.[2] But these situations – approached through investigations into the revolutions of 1848, the Commune, and civil wars from the seventeenth century to the present – were also an invitation to engage with time in another sense: that of temporal cultures. By this, I mean the kind of relation between past, present and future that prevails in a given society, not without discordance – a relation that became particularly salient in the era of the so-called 'modern regime of historicity'. Added to this is the way in which individuals experience the quality of time in those moments of crisis, as its texture changes. There also emerges the question of embodied habits, subjectivation, and the consciousness of acting in history.[3]

Although this work was relatively varied, my first research projects – whether regarding urban worlds, the connections between police and society, or indeed revolutionary moments or the nation-state – nonetheless seemed overly narrow. Implicitly, they remained part of a national (French) framework, which shaped their meaning and scope. A comparison of relations between uniformed policemen and the population in several European and colonial capitals in the nineteenth century – London, Paris, Berlin and Mumbai – made me aware of the real effects of what is known as 'methodological nationalism': taking the national framework as the natural setting for historical investigation. This is why I turned to connected and comparative approaches and, accordingly, to transnational, imperial, trans-imperial and global

2 For example, with Pierre Singaravélou, in *Pour une histoire des possibles. Analyses contrefactuelles et futurs non advenus* (Paris: Seuil – 'L'Univers historique' series, 2016, and 'Points Histoire' series, 2019), transl. as *A Past of Possibilities*.

3 With Boris Gobille, 'Protagonisme et crises politiques', *Politix. Revue des sciences sociales du politique* 112 (2015/4); with Ludivine Bantigny, 'Spécial: Historicités du XXe siècle. Coexistence et concurrence des temps', *Vingtième Siècle. Revue d'histoire* 117 (2013/1).

horizons.[4] There was nothing easy about this, because I was interested in the most recent versions of this approach: more demanding, more modest in their pretensions, sensitive to irregularities as well as to phenomena of exclusion. It proved necessary to break out of these implicit frameworks – the nation, the state, the arrow of time – not least given that they were themselves established precisely in that same historical moment. They were then entrenched on the basis of a singular vision of Europe's place in history, and of a truncated or warped knowledge of the rest of the world. In many respects, we are still heirs to these conceptions. However, the current vitality of research into non-European areas, whether in Africa, Asia, Oceania or the Americas, requires that we now take a completely different approach. Armed with this new knowledge, we need new ways of interpreting the changes and experiences of the European nineteenth century – the century of revolutions, science, nation-states, industrialisation, capitalism, colonisation, liberalism, socialism and conservatism.[5] A great deal of work, which can only be collective work, remains to be done.

At the same time, my past inquiries have continued to mobilise the same approach to so-called social and cultural history: one sensitive to the interdependencies and ways of seeing and feeling of the men and women of the past. As the Introduction to this book reminds us, this approach can be more accurately described as relational, interpretive and constructivist. This last term should not be misleading: the point is to emphasise that social worlds (and, with them, their non-human environments) are always the product of historical processes. But I do not mean to deny how deeply these worlds are internalised, consented to, and submitted to. On the contrary, this demands a combined study of the naturalising processes that make them so self-evident. This is where, for instance, a study of sensibilities – of affects and senses – comes into play: it is through them that we can best perceive both the

4 For the former, see Quentin Deluermoz, 'Capitales policières, État-nation et civilisation urbaine: Londres, Paris et Berlin au tournant du XIXe siècle', *Revue d'histoire moderne et contemporaine* 60–3 (2013/3), pp. 55–85. For the latter, see *Le Crépuscule des révolutions, 1848–1871* – 'France contemporaine' series, vol. 3, Paris: Seuil, 'Points Histoire' series, 2014); and Deluermoz, ed., *D'ici et d'ailleurs. Histoires globales de la France contemporaine* (Paris: La Découverte, 2021).

5 An example can be found in François-Xavier Fauvelle and Anne Lafont, eds, *L'Afrique et le Monde: Histoires renouées. De la Préhistoire au XXIe siècle* (Paris: La Découverte, 2022).

depth and the fragility of the ways in which the social world is embodied, as well as the movements that, over time, differentiate between a so-called 'them' and 'us'.[6]

Right from the outset, I have therefore been working on social orders in the age of nineteenth-century European 'modernity' and their contestation. This work explores what creates order in a society – what endures, what does not hold, and what changes. To do this, my investigation has focused on the key 'sites' of this historical transformation: the relationship between the individual and society, the city, the nation-state and revolutions. An extra-European and comparative perspective makes it possible, within this framework, to shake up the patterns of analysis produced at the time, and to improve our understanding of the powerful changes that then took place.

Here, the encounter with the Commune of 1871 takes on its full significance. This was an encounter in the strongest sense of the word, because it forced me to make adjustments, dig deeper, and move around in ways I could never have imagined. It soon became clear that trying to understand those seventy-two days would require a dizzying level of precision and perspective, calling for a certain kind of intellectual modesty.

Based on the knowledge produced by earlier research, and on interpretive debates that remained partially unresolved, this book's contributions can be summarised in three main points. The most visible is the global scope of the 'Commune' as an event. The waves made by the Commune are now clear, through the colonial extensions of the republican movement in Martinique and the Communard movement in Algiers; through the presence of transnational volunteers, the outpouring of external support, and the far-reaching media coverage; through the Commune's international military and geopolitical stakes; not to mention, lastly, through the rapid appropriation and mobilisation of the Commune during and after the event. In keeping with the spirit of the field of global history, the study has endeavoured to capture the plurality of viewpoints and dynamics, particularly outside France and then Europe. As far as resources allow, I have favoured a situated approach

6 With Hervé Mazurel, 'L'histoire des sensibilités: un territoire-limite?', *Critical Hermeneutics* 3: 1 (2019), pp. 125–70. See also the collective work we are doing with Thomas Dodman, Anouche Kunth, Hervé Mazurel and Clémentine Vidal-Naquet in the journal *Sensibilités. Histoire, critique & sciences sociales* (published by Anamosa).

– one that has sought, in the cases of the United States, Spain, Romania and China, to reconstruct the trajectories then underway in order to achieve a better understanding of the articulation between 'local' dynamics and the resonances of the Commune. What emerges is a more complex map than might be suggested from a 'diffusionist' approach, as if fanning out from the French centre to the supposed peripheries. This wider constellation instead brings out the real particularity of the Commune as an event. This was also, in a sense, a factor in events in Paris themselves – albeit not without certain discrepancies. If we consider the positive appropriations of the Commune, this reception elsewhere fuelled the *fédérés*' revolutionary energy and their certainty that they were acting for a universal cause, even if they were only partially aware of all these echoes (its US and Latin American reverberations, for example, were only faintly perceived). Conversely, while this reception accompanied the ups and downs of the 'Paris Republic', it was also characterised by an autonomy of its own. The idea of the Commune was, in this way, constantly broadened, while the Paris revolt quickly came to be seen as a large-scale connector between the various faces of the global radicalism of the 1870s. It is this shifting whole that I have called the 'Commune moment'. Needless to say, it did not span the entire planet: whole swathes of the global space, on the African and Asian continents in particular, were left unaffected. This resonance is clearly situated.

Another equally important dimension, albeit one rather less emphasised in the reviews of the book, concerns temporality. This is essential, since the later fate of the Commune is inseparable from the grand narratives of European modernity in which it was naturally placed after the event: liberal, Marxist, Marxist–Leninist, anarchist, republican, or otherwise. Jacques Rougerie had already broken this tether by setting the Commune within a more discontinuous history of nineteenth-century republicanisms and socialisms. In its central part, this study traces all the diverse dynamics in which the event was caught up, but also the ones that it itself generated. It is as if Fernand Braudel's famous temporal layers, set out in his *Mediterranean*, were compressed into a singular whole in the Communard adventure.[7] Far from the predefined

7 Fernand Braudel, *La Méditerranée et le monde méditerranéen à l'époque de Philippe II* (Paris: A. Colin, 1949) – transl. into English as *The Mediterranean and the Mediterranean World in the Age of Philip II* (Berkeley, CA: University of California Press, 1996). It is the temporal layers that are compressed, not the geographical one.

patterns that historians sometimes like to identify (such as nation-state formation or the rise of industrial capitalism), the Commune appears as a 'heterochrony' in its own time. This can be recognised as early as April 1871, in the mutual accusations of anachronism hurled at each other by the Parisian insurgents and the Versaillais. From this angle, the Commune allows us to take a critical distance from the 'grand narratives' of the nineteenth and twentieth centuries. But it also serves as a reminder, as against any overly linear reading of that century, of the existence of alternative experiences at the heart of European modernity, which may point to other horizons.[8]

The historical perception of the Communards themselves was also lacking – even though the expression 'the struggle of the future against the past' was one of their great leitmotifs. In insurgent Paris, the recent past of the Second Empire seemed already elderly; the vivid memory of past revolutions resurfaced, driving political commitment and opening up a horizon of possible radical transformation. Unlike the 'Springtime of Peoples' of 1848, this perception of the future was interestingly marked by both revolutionary messianism and the new confidence placed in science since the 1860s. This perception was made up of ebbs and flows, of real conflicts of time between insurgents and anti-Communards; it was also expressed in numerous projects, expectations and utopias – be they spontaneous or already well thought out. Yet it is hard to understand the meaning of words such as 'republic', 'emancipation', 'initiative' (a term frequently used by Communard women) – or even 'Commune' – if we do not consider this historical awareness.

Let us bring these first two points together: if we consider this dovetailing of perceptions and connections, the Commune appears as a 'revolutionary space-time'. As such, it cut through the web of power relations, socioeconomic arrangements and worldviews that were dominant at the time. It was also under this status, as an embodiment of another possible future, that the Commune would later be mobilised.

Here we get to the third element, the actors: the men and women of Thiers and Lyon, Algiers and Paris – and especially Paris, given the available sources and the intensity of the revolutionary experience there. The particularity of this study lies here in its microhistorical

8 For a discussion of the link between time and revolutions, see Enzo Traverso, *Revolution: An Intellectual History* (London/New York: Verso, 2021).

approach, conducted at the level of individuals, and on the scale of neighbourhood life: it spans everyone, from police *commissaires* to teachers, National Guards, canteen workers, caretakers, skilled workers, members of vigilance committees, city hall employees, and so on. Of course, the major measures adopted and the most famous figures are also taken into account, along with the groups, committees and organisations, and the political currents and conceptions currently becoming better known to historians (Blanquism, Proudhonism, Internationalism, and the like). Taken together, what emerges is an infinite variety of situations and an immense range of attitudes, from refusal of the Commune to commitment to its cause. On the one hand were dissent, flight, rejection and accommodation; on the other, mobilisation through mutual connections, neighbourhood and military solidarity, militant commitment, and ideological identification. There were also the hesitant, the indifferent, those who followed along for a day or two, and the fact that these attitudes changed from one week to the next. Having said that, this panorama also provides an insight into the Parisian factory of politics. Amid this maelstrom, in a city that was undergoing its second siege, a real collective movement was emerging to transform everyday political, social and economic relations. This movement was driven by the opposition between 'the people' and 'the enemy of the people'. It was dispersed, heterogeneous and multiform; it cannot be easily pigeonholed. This study nevertheless confirms the importance of issues such as the organisation of labour (as it was framed in the nineteenth century), the project of a 'democratic and social republic', and the place given to the principle of 'Association'. We also find, in many forms, the desire for self-organisation that this associationism fuelled: in other words, the desire to be 'one's own master'. As Jacques Rougerie put it, this meant 'self-administration, self-organisation' – and the historian also recalled the important role of 'local initiative' in most of the proposed reforms.[9] Also present is what Jean-Louis Robert later called the 'Communard polyphony', that singular harmony that brought together – not without some dissonance – the republican and patriotic National Guards and the

9 Jacques Rougerie, *Paris libre 1871* (Paris: Seuil, 2004 [1971]), p. ix. Further reflection on this theme can be found in Michèle Riot-Sarcey, *Le Procès de la liberté* (Paris: La Découverte, 2016), p. 248.

socialists' internationalist notes, the women fighting on the barricades, the democratic thinking in the workshops, the expression of a desire for emancipation, and the desire to be obeyed.[10] This was, in Robert's terms, the polyphony of a revolution wrangling with itself, just as it wrangles with us. This book, for its part, highlights the dynamics of the crisis itself: the creative aspect of the event that led to the Commune. It was, then, truly a process in motion – one that was then brutally interrupted in May 1871. Such a rupture made room for all subsequent readings, whether disappointed or enthusiastic, minimalist or maximalist, consensual or original. Given this material substance, the defeated Commune took on the features of a germ – what Castoriadis describes as an 'index of possibility'. This is why the Commune can be read as *an expression of the possible*, which continues to question our relationship with democracy, history, and the way the world is – or could be – organised.

This book does not, therefore, claim to offer an *exhaustive* understanding of the Commune (whoever could do that?). But these three aspects form a whole. The aim here is to contribute new knowledge, to open up new horizons, and, against reductionist readings, to make its own contribution to the work of broadening and interpreting the 'Commune-event' in general.

Numerous works have appeared since the initial publication of this book, particularly upon the 150th anniversary of the Commune. It has not been possible to incorporate most of them, although corrections and clarifications have been made to the present edition. These works can be divided into two broad categories. The first concerns the history of the Commune (or Communes) of 1871. Comprehensive surveys have been produced, either summarising the current state of research or offering new panoramas. Alongside the impressive work by Jean-Louis Robert, we could mention Carolyn Eichner's insightful overview, the collective volume edited by Laure Godineau and Marc César, and the extensive *Dictionnaire Maitron* edited by Michel Cordillot.[11] New research has

10 Jean-Louis Robert, *Nouvelle Histoire de la Commune de Paris* (Nancy: L'Arbre bleu, 2023). Jacques Rougerie's last book, *Eugène Varlin. Aux origines du mouvement ouvrier* (Paris: Éditions du Détour, 2019), also points to these tensions between thought and modes of political organisation.

11 Robert, *Nouvelle Histoire de la Commune*; Carolyn Eichner, *The Paris Commune: A Brief History* (New Brunswick: Rutgers University Press, 2022); Marc César and Laure

focused on specific figures and fields, such as Léo Frankel, or education.[12] Significant progress has also been made on the transnational dimension. We know more about the participation of Belgians thanks to the research of Loris Djebel, while historian Xenia Marinou has begun to publish in French parts of her important research on the role of Greeks in the event and its social resonance in Greece itself.[13] The British and Canadian echoes and receptions of the Commune are also better documented, and the historian Jeanne Moisand – in a book that aims to recall the importance of those revolutions 'erased' by the Parisian shadow that were the Spanish revolutions of 1873 – has tackled the uses of the Commune in the canton of Cartagena.[14] The 'living' memories of the Commune have not been forgotten either: historian Julia Nicholls has highlighted the richness of post-1871 socialist thought, while the strength of the twentieth-century echoes of this event, particularly in 1968, has been addressed in numerous works.[15] Microhistorical perspectives have continued to prove their value. Alexandre Frondizi's meticulous investigation of an 'ultraparisian' working-class neighbourhood, which includes the revolutions of 1848, has

---

Godineau, eds, *La Commune de 1871: une relecture* (Grane: Créaphis, 2019); Michel Cordillot, ed., *La Commune de Paris 1871. Les acteurs, l'événement, les lieux* (Paris: Éditions de l'Atelier, 2021). See also Roger Martelli, *Commune 1871. La révolution impromptu* (Paris: Arcanes17, 2021).

12 Julien Chuzeville, *Léo Frankel. Communard sans frontiers* (Montreuil: Libertalia, 2021); Jean-François Dupeyron, *À l'école de la Commune de Paris. L'histoire d'une autre école* (Dijon: Éditions Raison et Passions, 2020).

13 Loris Djebel, '*L'union fait la force!* Des solidarités belges dans la Commune de Paris (1870-1871)', master 2 dissertation, Université de Strasbourg (2022); Xenia Marinou, 'La Grèce dans la guerre franco-prussienne: les multiples facettes du mouvement de volontaires grecs', in Nicolas Bourguinat, Alexandre Dupont and Gilles Vogt, eds, *La Guerre de 1870. Conflit européen, Conflit global* (Montrouge: Éditions du Bourg, 2020), pp. 169–82. See also Mark Lause's *Soldiers of the Revolution: The Franco-Prussian War and the Paris Commune* (London: Verso, 2022), which sheds new light on international volunteers in the 1870–71 war and the Paris Commune.

14 Laura C. Forster, *The Paris Commune in Britain: Radicals, Refugees, and Revolutionaries after 1871* (Oxford: Oxford University Press, 2025); Alban Bargain-Villéger, 'Un repoussoir idéal: la Commune de Paris de 1871 et le projet national-libéral canadien', *Revue d'histoire du* XIXe *siècle* 63: 2 (2021), pp. 141–4; Jeanne Moisand, *Se fédérer ou mourir La commune de Carthagène et ses mondes, 1873* (Paris: EHESS, 2024) – transl. into English as *A Spanish Commune: The Cartagena Canton and Its Worlds* (New York: Verso, 2025).

15 See Ludivine Bantigny, 'Un passé ravivé. La Commune dans les engagements du présent', *Revue d'histoire du XIXe siècle* 63: 2 (2021), pp. 97–111, and *La Commune au présent. Une correspondance par-delà le temps* (Paris: La Découverte, 2021).

challenged the classic idea of the Commune as a post-Haussmanian re-conquest of Paris from its margins.[16] Étienne Hudon has brought to light the long-, mid- and short-term implications of the famous decree on night work for bakers, as well as the less-well-known but essential decree on the municipalisation of employment.[17] Finally, Chloé Leprince has provided new insights into the Union of Women for the Defence of Paris and Care of the Wounded. Beyond the compelling figures of Élisabeth Dmitrieff and Louise Michel, there were many modes of female participation, ranging from the reorganisation of women's work to the politicisation of traditionally gendered care and educational roles.[18] Through these actions, these women were also blurring, along different avenues, the established barriers of politics. The question of gender relations in the Commune, and comparisons with other revolutions, are undoubtedly among the most promising avenues of research. So, the history of the Commune is again on the move, even if the questions of Versaillais society or the sociological study of the soldiers responsible for the May 1871 massacre are drawing rather less interest.[19]

The second category of works focuses more on the contemporary history of a broader class of phenomena, and on what might be called the 'Commune' idea or form.[20] A recent work by Bruno Bosteels, for example, looks at the long-lasting echoes of the Commune in Mexico over the nineteenth and twentieth centuries.[21] Others analyse the links – either direct or by way of comparison – between the event of 1871 and various contemporary struggles, battles or experiences: the Zapatistas in Chiapas, the French ZADs ('zones to be defended'), the movement

16 Alexandre Frondizi, *Le Grand Paris du XIXe siècle* (Paris: Payot, forthcoming). 'Ultraparisian' is an adjective coined by the author.

17 Étienne Hudon, 'La boulangerie parisienne en révolution: une micro-histoire de la Commune de 1871', master 2 dissertation, Université Paris Cité (2022).

18 Chloé Leprince, 'Une organisation sérieuse de citoyennes au travail pour la révolution: Approcher par en bas rapports de genre et engagement féminin dans la Commune de Paris', master 2 dissertation, ENS/EHESS (2022).

19 Laure Godineau offers this latter line of inquiry in her animated film produced together with Joris Clerté, *La Boîte noire* (Doncvoilà Productions/Lardux Films/Origine Films, 2020).

20 For an example of the transition between the two, see Robert St Clair and Seth Whidden, eds, 'La Commune n'est pas morte', *Nineteenth-Century French Studies* 49: 3–4 (Spring–Summer 2021). On the 'Commune Form', see Kristin Ross, *The Commune Form: The Transformation of Everyday Life* (London/New York: Verso, 2024).

21 Bruno Bosteels, *La Comuna mexicana* (Mexico City: Akal, 2021).

around the Kurdistan Workers' Party and the Rojava 'Commune' – not forgetting the emancipation movements in Chile and Colombia.[22] Several of these studies point to an intense south–south discussion on the fight for greater democracy and equality, in which reference to the Paris Commune sometimes plays a notable role.[23] In a similar vein, studies in philosophy and political sociology are developing reflections on the Commune as a fresh way of thinking about Marxism in the age of neoliberalism, based in particular on the approaches advanced by Miguel Abensour and Daniel Bensaïd.[24] Some also draw on the Commune in order to help refine the many possible kinds of project for a more expansive democracy. Political scientists, for example, have compared the experience of 1871 with Murray Bookchin's communalism and the libertarian municipalism of the 1960s–2000s.[25] Others are using it to refine the constitution of 'democratic repertoires' that are richer than one might imagine, incorporating radical democracy, communalism or confederalism.[26] Such thought also seeks to make sense of a set of localised and less enduring scenes and struggles, which demonstrate a common desire to reappropriate power from below and to experiment with more egalitarian social forms. Characteristic of these various projects, one international, interdisciplinary effort sets out to think about the 'global Commune form' – in other words, looking back at the event in Paris 'from the point of view of today's global

22 See, for example, Collectif, *La Commune du Rojava, L'alternative kurde à l'État-nation* (Paris: Syllepse, 2017).

23 See the discussions at the conference 'From the Commune to Communalism? The Paris Commune and Its Meaning for Democratic Theory and Practice', ed. Gaard Kets, Laura Roth, Mathijs van der Sande and Nijmegen (May 2022).

24 Miguel Abensour, *Democracy Against the State: Marx and the Machiavellian Moment*, transl. Max Blechman and Martin Breaugh (Cambridge: Polity, 2011). Original French edition: *La démocratie contre l'État: Marx et le moment machiavélien* (Paris: Le Félin, 2004). See also Daniel Bensaïd, Éloge de la politique profane (Paris: Albin Michel, 2008).

25 Marion Carrel, Paula Cossart, Guillaume Gourgues, Pierre-André Juven and Julien Talpin, eds, 'Vives les communes! Des ronds-points au municipalisme', *Mouvements* 101 (2020); Paula Cossart, 'Le communalisme naît-il de la Commune?', *Revue d'histoire du XIXe siècle* 63: 2 (2021), pp. 75–96. See also the research-in-progress by Sixtine van Outryve, 'Theory and Practice of Direct Democracy: The Commune as the Locus of Self-Government' (UC Louvain).

26 Gaard Kets and Mathijs van der Sande, eds, *Communalism as a Democratic Repertoire: From the Paris Commune to the Present* (New York: Routledge, 2025).

society' and examining 'the relevance of the political potential of the Commune'. It takes care, too, to avoid simplistically asserting its replicability across time and space.[27] In a slightly different way, the Paris event has also been a focus of the growing discussion on the 'commons', here more linked with environmental concerns, in a variety of formats.[28] Whether within informed intellectual and activist circles or more spontaneous expressions of grievance and conflict, the Commune still seems to make sense today in the struggles to overcome capitalism and state or supra-state governance; it expresses a more general desire for revolt, democracy and justice.

These two lines of approach – the Commune of 1871 and the Commune form – seem quite different, but there is a fragile thread between them. Some of the discussions in this book offer clues as to how to link them together: avenues that would obviously need to be explored in greater depth, but which can be briefly illustrated here.

The first would be a project in its own right: an overall history of the resurgence and living memories of the Commune after 1880. Since this constitutes an immense field of inquiry, only a few key points can be outlined here. While the resonance of the Commune is not, as this book shows, owed solely to its later appropriation by the USSR, the year 1917 and its aftermath clearly marked a turning point both for thinking about the Commune and for the broader history of revolutions. With the creation of the Soviet order, the Commune came to be seen as a positive model – or even as one to be surpassed – as a form of 'dictatorship of the proletariat' and a foundational moment of the expected world revolution. From there, knowledge of the Commune spread on an unprecedented scale, within the Soviet zone of influence, and particularly towards Asia and Africa. However, this did not prevent more diverse and richer uses of the reference to the Commune. It was taken up by the Spartakists during the German Revolution of 1918–19, and found a place in the anticolonial movements of the 1930s, as demonstrated by the Vietnamese Communists' visits to the Mur des

27 Irene Peano, Camilla De Ambroggi, Alioscia Castronovo, Niccolò Cuppini Carla Hung and Itandehui Reyes-Díaz, 'Planetary Commune: The Commune as an Expansive Political Form, a Digital and Transnational Project', at planetarycommune.org.

28 Christian Laval, Pierre Sauvêtre and Ferhat Taylan, eds, *L'alternative du commun* (Paris: Hermann, 2019).

Fédérés. A second important moment in the spread of this reference took place during the Maoist era in China. While historical references to France initially seemed far removed from the experience of the People's Republic of China, the most classic Marxist–Leninist version of the Commune was revived for propaganda purposes with the 'Great Leap Forward' (1958), and then the Cultural Revolution (1966–69). This version then circulated through new channels: those of Maoist ideas themselves, whose sheer reach is better known to us.[29] Here again, this reference was adopted in a variety of ways, some of them in opposition to the pressure coming from the Communist authorities. In Shanghai, in February 1967, a student and worker revolt took the name of 'Commune'. A similar revival took place in Prague in 1968, albeit along different lines. These movements continued to work themselves out in a complex interplay of appropriations and counter-echoes – all the way to France in 1968, of course, particularly, though not solely, in the 'Nantes Commune'.[30]

How should we understand these revivals of the Commune? There are without doubt strategic uses of this event, and routinised ways of drawing upon it. But we also need to consider the added meaning and international dimension that the reference to the Commune brings with it, while at the same time being part of ongoing local dynamics that, in each case, add a new layer of meaning. This repetition produces differences, and vice versa.[31] This book has discussed the survivals of the Commune (in the art historian Aby Warburg sense): and this theme can be reused here to consider both this almost anachronistic 'core' of meaning, and the diversity of these appropriations and redefinitions. Two further elements can be added to the discussion developed in this book. First, the analysis of the 'reference to the past', inspired by the work of Michèle Riot-Sarcey, should be complemented by a 'reference to elsewhere' – that is, uses made in other places or regions of the world

29 Maurice J. Meisner, 'The French Revolution and Chinese Socialism', in Joseph Klaits and Michael H. Haltzel, eds, *The Global Ramifications of the French Revolution* (Cambridge: Cambridge University Press, 1994), pp. 177–94; Julia Lovell, *Maoism: A Global History* (New York: Knopf, 2019).

30 Hongsheng Jiang, *La Commune de Shanghai et la Commune de Paris* (Paris: La Fabrique, 2014); Xavier Vigna, *L'Insubordination ouvrière dans les années 68. Essai d'histoire politique des usines* (Rennes: Presses universitaires de Rennes, 2007).

31 See Gilles Deleuze, *Difference and Repetition*, transl. Paul Patton (New York: Columbia University Press, 1994).

– which produces a similar effect of discontinuity and expansiveness.[32] Second, as Laurent Jeanpierre argues in an analysis of the echoes of the Commune in the Gilets Jaunes movement, attention to these survivals must also account for what Warburg called *pathosformeln* – that is, 'an intensity of experiences from the past, including the most distant'. We must therefore (but with what sources?) add the emotional charge that the shared reference to the Commune can stir in the given moment.[33] Lastly, the study of this layering of meanings needs to take into account the unpredictable dynamics of each episode – the attempt at the insurrection, the 'Great' revolution, the creation of an alternative space, social revolt, debate, and so on – and, indeed, to consider the contradictions between these contrasting redefinitions. Understood in this way, the Commune appears to us, in the early twenty-first century, overloaded with meanings. Far from being limited to those seventy-two days in Paris, or to the history of France alone, it proves, through these different revivals, to be a major historical phenomenon of the nineteenth to twenty-first centuries, and one that ought to be analysed as such.

So how can we understand the Commune's way of crossing times and spaces? This is a major question, especially for historians, as it has to do not only with memory, but with the translatability of experiences itself.[34] A Latin American example, on which I was able to shed some light after discussions with Argentinian colleagues, will help us to achieve a better understanding.[35] As we have seen, the Paris Commune

32 This idea, like many of the analyses that follow, owes a great deal to the 'Nineteenth-Century Revolutions and the Social Sciences' seminar that I have been organising for several years, together with Caroline Fayolle and Boris Gobille. I would like to thank them for these crucial exchanges.

33 Laurent Jeanpierre, 'Commune de Paris et Commune des ronds-points', *Cahiers d'histoire. Revue d'histoire critique* 148 (2021), pp. 109–22.

34 See Riccardo Ciavolella's remarks in 'L'exercice de la comparaison: penser l'expérience du commun depuis la Commune de Paris (1871)', with Quentin Deluermoz, Claire Judde de la Rivière, Riccardo Ciavollela and Guillaume Mazeau, Collège de France, 13 June 2017.

35 Thanks to Gabriel Entin and Jorge Meyers for their invitation to discuss these ideas at the study day 'Una polisemia exacerbada: el concepto "comunidad" entre el republicanismo y la revolución social en la era de los conceptos que se bifurcan: Europa-América Latina, 1810–1890', University of the Republic, Montevideo, 9–10 December 2021. The texts have been published in Gabriel Entin and Jorge Myers, eds, *Itinerarios de un metaconcepto. La comunidad en el siglo* xix *latinoamericano* (Madrid: UAM Ediciones, 2024), pp. 385–408. I would also like to thank Clément Thibaud, who also provided invaluable insights into these issues.

had its echoes in several countries around the region. But to understand it properly, we need to dig deeper into its history. Between the 1850s and 1870s, several Latin American states experienced a 'democratic moment'.[36] This was not unconnected with 1848, since the Springtime of Peoples had far-reaching echoes on this continent, both in terms of organisational methods (clubs, associations) and slogans (the right to work, political freedoms).[37] But its echoes also correspond to a rather older historical process. The historian Hilda Sabato has shown that a federalist republicanism existed in several countries between 1840 and 1870, complete with clubs, citizens' militias, rejection of the state, mass rallies, and demands for autonomy.[38] Added to this were the many debates on municipal freedoms and working-class associationism, which seem quite comparable to what we have observed in Paris. In other words, the Commune seemed to carry within it a drive that extended beyond the French or even European context, and made sense far beyond that continent alone. Let us go a step further: the historian Clément Thibaud has long emphasised the need to consider a Latin American historicity of political modernity that does not simply reproduce those generally observed for Europe or the United States.[39] Such considerations are especially relevant here, for more than one reason. First, this Latin American modernity had its characteristic vocabulary: the term *comuneros*, which is widely used in the northern regions of Latin America, was part of the vast social, political and conceptual upheaval of the eighteenth and nineteenth centuries. Second, it had its specific practices: the Communard idea of a 'Republic of Paris' – half government, half city hall – may seem incongruous in French history, but it corresponds fairly well to the forms of 'municipal republics' organised in the 1810s. In eighteenth-century Colombia and Venezuela, the republic was linked to the idea

36 James Sanders, *Contentious Republicans, Popular Politics, Race, and Class in 19th Century Colombia* (Durham, NC: Duke University Press, 2004); Carlos Forment, *Democracy in Latin America, 1760–1900* (Chicago: University of Chicago Press, 2003).

37 Cristian Gazmuri, *El '1848' chileno: Igualitarios, reformistas, radicales, masones y bomberos* (Santiago: University of Santiago Press, 1999).

38 Hilda Sabato, *Republics of the New World: The Revolutionary Political Experiment in Nineteenth-Century Latin America* (Princeton, NJ: Princeton University Press, 2018).

39 Clément Thibaud, *Libérer le nouveau monde. La fondation des premières républiques hispaniques. Colombia and Venezuela (1780–1820)* (Bécherel: Les Perséides, 2017).

of the community – in other words, the 'people' – without this contradicting religion or the monarchy, which could encompass these other notions. This allowed for the 'old' to be preserved even within the 'new'. According to Thibaud, the *comuneros* movements of the late eighteenth century did not herald a future revolution, but expressed a 'political culture rooted in popular culture' that might, in a later context, take on clearer meaning. With the fall of the Spanish monarchy in 1808, the municipalities indeed became the foundations of political legitimacy. They could defend the monarchy against republican exclusivism, but they could also make possible 'a republicanism founded on the sovereignty of communities'.[40] These municipalities were also seen in a positive light by indigenous communities anxious to regain their lost functions of self-government. The connection between commune, municipality and republic was here structured around these complex associations. Beneath the surface, these forms of continuity played an essential role: in 1871, there was a specifically Latin American historicity to the notions of commune and republic. In other words: at that moment the Paris Commune brought with it an international dimension, a definition of socialist struggles, and an insertion into industrial and nation-state frameworks that echoed broader transformations underway in the region (the emergence of the 'modern' state, the rise of political parties, the development of the army, the capitalist economy). At the same time, however, there was a genuinely localised appropriation of part of its political project. Federalist republicans, socialists, workers' associations and other supporters thus had good reason to say that the Commune was better suited to 'American soil'.

This still does not explain why the Commune makes sense in such different contexts. Shared structural phenomena of the century, such as growing economic interdependence and the rise of new forms of state and control, undoubtedly play a role, as do certain situational homologies (revolutions, urban uprisings). But that alone is not enough to explain this recurrence. Perhaps we need to look deeper.

Several works appearing since the first publication of this book have confirmed and clarified one of the historical-anthropological hypotheses explored at its core – starting from Jacques Rougerie's initial

40 Ibid., p. 228.

question about the 'first degree of democracy'.[41] Various points are now well established in the anthropology of egalitarianism: what are called 'stateless', 'egalitarian' societies can no longer be read, romantically, as original 'reservoirs' of 'primitive egalitarianism', since such societies were in fact never free of hierarchies and forms of exclusion (particularly in terms of age and gender). Rather, constant tensions between hierarchy and equality may be observed in each form of human organisation, in an infinite range of possible situations. And, in their capacity to make political arrangements for themselves, humans have often, it is true, expressed the desire for equality and, more broadly, sought forms of autonomy and democratic practices (understood here as the exercise of egalitarian power in assemblies, and by extension the rejection of all vertical and hierarchical forms). This would seemingly corroborate the argument that the Commune was a moment when this potential was realised in its own time. However, the authors of a recent special issue in the anthropology journal *L'Homme* offer an important corrective that avoids over-simplistic genealogies.[42] When it comes to understanding so-called 'stateless' societies, which they prefer to describe as societies 'that seem to obey a logic other than hierarchy', we should move away from the binary of equality/hierarchy. This pairing, they argue, refers to societies that have established principles of equivalence and comparison (societies with a measure of standardisation, meaning a specific form of state, common standards and exchanges). These authors tell us that if we want to steer clear of a rereading that corresponds to modern and retrospective European criteria, we need to identify other characteristics of these societies: autonomy, mutuality and incommensurability. This important insight is a reminder that the Commune set out a political project of democracy and equality in a hierarchical, unequal and interconnected world.

It should be noted, however, that these other characteristics were also present under the Commune. For example, while 'mutuality' refers to a relational integration of autonomous individuals – and in this vein

41 For example, David Graeber and David Wengrow, *The Dawn of Everything: A New History of Humanity* (London: Allen Lane, 2021).

42 Natalia Buitron and Hans Steinmüller, 'Les fins de l'égalitarisme', *L'Homme*, 2020. See also the review by Judith Scheele, 'Égalité et égalitarisme en anthropologie: Quête des origines ou quête des possibles?', at laviedesidees.fr, 2021. I would like to thank Judith Scheele for our discussions on this subject.

presupposes a specific socialisation and learning process – such an ambition can be seen in the Communards' educational projects examined by the philosopher Jean-François Dupeyron.[43] Perhaps certain persistences can still be observed.

Such observations raise the question of whether the Commune, conversely, may have seen an undermining of the processes of equivalence and classification typically associated with the establishment of a 'modern' form of state and market logic. Keeping in mind that we are exploring only one of the potentials at work in 1871 (including also the possibilities of institutionalisation and a stronger government at city hall), it may be useful here to apply a kind of reversal of perspectives, such as has long been advocated by many anthropologists, and thereby apply a non-Western perspective to European history. Drawing on the Amazonian experience, the Brazilian anthropologist Eduardo Viveiros de Castro, for example, invites us to consider what he terms a 'politics of multiplicities', understood as an 'omnipresent virtual functioning of society-against-the-state' that is not external but internal. This produces singularity and multiplicity, and resists all classification. This reversal of perspective is not intended here to be systematic, but serves as a support to analysis. In this regard, this perspective can help to improve our understanding of the Commune, and in particular of one of its features that has been taken for granted from the outset, and never questioned: its so-called draft-like character, and the impossibility of cataloguing it.

Seen in this light, neither of these elements should be seen as weaknesses, but rather as defining features: a 'politics of multiplicities' could be found at work beneath the Commune, even in the archives (based, for example, on a study of the fluid occupation of public posts). That is not to say that this dimension is out of time: it corresponds quite well to some traits of the democratic and social republic of the second half of the nineteenth century, or rather to certain extensions of its principles – for instance, 'being one's own master'. Politically, this helps to explain, in 1871, both the army's inability to impose obedience and the Commune's capacity to attract people and grow. We can thus refine the formulation: the hypothesis that the Commune was a moment in which this potential was realised – at the heart of industrial, national and state modernity, and to which it then gave both an outline of form and a

43 Dupeyron, *À l'école de la Commune de Paris.*

name – finds corroboration. Its particular resonance also stemmed from the fact that it took place in the second-largest imperial power at the time, in a highly important symbolic capital, and was the subject of intense transcontinental media attention. Then follow the reappropriations and reinterpretations, and with them the many shifts in meaning. Here we have a better understanding of what this 'germ' of potential, or rather part of it, may have consisted of.[44]

All this brings me once again to my final point – namely, the continuing relevance of the Commune today. In France, in the early 2000s, the 'living' memory of the Commune had seemed to be waning – a development that was still apparent upon the 140th anniversary in 2011. The idea among researchers was that, with the fall of the communist regimes, the end of grand narratives, and the supposed disappearance of the great ideologies (since the most liberal ones were doing so well), the Paris Commune seemed to have lost its burning intensity. However, over the past ten years, references to the Commune have heated up again. This highly international reference point does not have exactly the same texture as it did in previous periods. While debates go on and there are surely constant overlaps, today references to the Commune point less – compared to the 1930s–70s period – to the workers' movement, class struggle or urban revolt. Still linked to a radical critique of (growing) inequalities, it now fuels, more than before, greater reflection and struggle around direct democracy, bottom-up popular sovereignty, gender equality, and the creation of alternative political and economic territories capable of fostering more respectful ways of relating to 'nature'. Lastly, we can more closely examine this shift in meaning, which is itself hardly trivial. Clearly, it is owed to a change in the focuses of political attention. But there may be another, deeper explanation in play. In the 1880s and 1890s, European societies – and also some outside this continent – underwent an anthropological transformation in terms of their institutions and politics, with the rise of organisations, parties, trade unions, nation-states, large factories, long-distance relations, and the strengthening of group belonging. This period, explains the historian Yves Cohen, can be defined by the figure of the 'leader'. The critique of

44 Further details can be found in Quentin Deluermoz, 'Epílogo. La Comuna de París, una perspectiva arqueológica y comparada (Europa–América Latina, siglos xix–xxi), in Entin and Myers, *Itinerarios de un metaconcepto*, pp. 385–408.

the Commune for having lacked firmness, and with it a more structured organisation and ideology, made sense in this context. Since the 1980s, however, these twentieth-century institutional forms have been crumbling, as shown for example by the rise in electoral abstentionism and the loss of confidence in political parties and trade unions, among many other indicators. Thus, it is no accident that the reference to the Commune was revived by many of the 'leaderless movements' of the 2000s.[45] This makes sense in the context of the growing demand for more horizontal power relations and more direct and visible economic links. Also important is the Commune's apparent capacity to connect different heterotopias and experiences 'from below' across the world, particularly in the Global South. This explains why these resurgences of the Commune are so relevant today. They are one expression, among many others, of the profound transformation of power relations that we are currently experiencing. Interestingly, this context is also resurrecting old debates, since with it returns the question of the value of institutionalising and structuring these social and political movements so that they can be an effective force for change.

It is not in the nature of an afterword to dig further into the details. But these considerations may help us to understand these less-than-direct links between the Paris Commune in 1871 and the Commune as an idea and form across history. As I write these lines, such observations may seem a little underwhelming. From the pandemic to economic crises, the climate catastrophe and the war in Ukraine, the situation is becoming ever darker; the great regression mentioned in the first edition has become even worse, and around the world the defenders of inequality, bureaucratic logics, nationalistic impulses, and racist and authoritarian tendencies are on the rise. This all serves as a reminder that the twentieth century was declared dead-and-buried just a little too quickly. Emancipation movements such as Black Lives Matter, the Chilean

45 These remarks draw heavily on the work of Yves Cohen. For an analysis of the late nineteenth century, see Yves Cohen, *Le Siècle des chefs. Une histoire transnationale du commandement et de l'autorité (1890–1940)* (Paris: Éditions Amsterdam, 2013). On leaderless movements, see Yves Cohen and Marco Santana, 'Du Brésil au monde et retour: mouvements sociaux localisés et en résonance', *Brésil(s)* 7 (2015), pp. 103–22. See also Nabila Abbas and Yves Sintomer, 'Les trois imaginaires contemporains du tirage au sort en politique: démocratie délibérative, démocratie antipolitique et démocratie radicale', in *Raisons politiques*, 2021/2, pp. 33–54.

constitutional movement and the Iranian women's uprising, as well as attempts to inject a little content back into tired liberal democracies, may not seem to count for much compared to the sheer force of these processes. Yet this history of the Communes shows that localised events can reflect deeper movements that make sense on a large scale, that our already-exhausted words can mask richer and reinvented meanings, that history never heads in just one direction. And that utopia, struggle and hope are surely better than resignation.[46]

Paris, November 2022

This afterword is dedicated to Dominique Kalifa (1957–2020), Jacques Rougerie (1932–2022) and John Merriman (1946–2022).

46 I wish to thank Jessica Edwards, Anne Légier and Nathan Perl-Rosenthal for their assistance in proofreading the translation of the present edition.

Index of Names

Ageron, Charles-Robert, 347
Agulhon, Maurice, 8, 142, 343n41
Alexander II, 95
Allix, Jules, 182, 217
Alfonso XII, 374
Appert, General, 40
Arendt, Hannah, 12
Arnaud, Antoine, 161
Arnould, Arthur, 216
Artières, Philippe, 178
Assi, Adolphe, 135, 217, 313, 328
Atai, 349

Bargain-Villéger, Alban, 322
Barodet, Désiré, 298
Bayly, Christopher, 25
Bebel, August, 50, 365, 366n25
Ben Choucha, 76
Benjamin, Walter, 17, 88, 225
Bensa, Alban, 349
Benton, Lauren, 81
Bergeret, Jules, 44, 278, 328
Bernstein, Samuel, 89
Berthet, Louis, 162
Beslay, Charles, 124, 136, 139, 171, 231, 238
Bèze, François de, 369
Bigeau, Jeanne, 220, 301
Bismarck, Otto von, 26, 306, 341–2, 366
Blanc, Louis, 168
Blanchecotte, Malvina, 206, 209, 235, 237, 278
Blanqui, Auguste, 210, 217, 299
Bonaparte, Louis-Napoleon, 154
Bonaparte, Pierre-Napoleon, 115
Bourbons, 100
Bourguignon, Alexis, 213
Bowen, Henry, 98
Bright, Charles, 352
Briot, Captain, 301
Brocher, Victorine, 194–5, 202, 209, 220
Brousse, Paul, 372
Brun (known as 'Pelade'), 158

Brunel, Paul Antoine, 43
Burstin, Haïm, 214–15, 220, 243

Cabet, Étienne, 248
Cafiero, Carlo, 377
Camet, Camille, 372
Carol I (Karl of Hohenzollern), 104
Caron, Jean-Claude, 277, 277n2
Castoriadis, Cornelius, 266, 268, 410
Challemel-Lacour, Paul-Armand, 161
Champenoys, Pierre, 204
Chanzy, General, 348
Chardon, Jean-Baptiste, 369
Chaudey, Gustave, 217
Chauffrias, François, 157, 296
Chauvet, Pierre, 176
Chépié, 160
Chomette, Jean-Jacques, 157, 162, 296
Chong-Ho, 68–9
Cipriani, Amilcare, 39
Claretie, Jules, 294
Clastres, Pierre, 263
Clavé, Josep, 339
Cleyre, Voltairine de, 381
Clinchant, General, 282
Cluseret, Gustave, 38, 43–4, 45, 96, 189, 190–1, 217, 313, 374
Codé, Cléo, 140–1
Coghlan, Michelle, 380
Combatz, Joseph Lucien, 43, 373
Confucius, 69
Conway, Moncure D., 89–90
Cordillot, Michel, 218, 339, 410
Costa, Andrea, 377
Cottereau, Alain, 251
Courbet, Gustave, ix, 96, 111, 113, 117
Coussat, Démophile, 181
Crémieux, Adolphe, 73, 75, 148
Crestin, 161
Cuza, Alexander, 104
Czarnowski, Roman, 44

Dabot, Henri, 210, 212
Darboy, Archbishop, 217, 276, 297
Découflé, André, 7
Delaire, 185
Deleuze, Gilles, 383
Denis, Pierre, 129–30, 196
Deschamp, Marcel, 31
Descimon, Robert, 178
Descola, Philippe, 263
Desplats, Charles, 211, 234
Deyi, Zhang, 23–4, 68
Di Cornetto, Malato, 42
Didi-Huberman, Georges, 1, 258
Dobry, Michel, 17, 147, 214
Douris ('La Grande'), 158
Du Bouzet, Charles, 74, 147, 148, 151
Duby, Georges, 262
Dumas, Alexandre (*fils*), 294
Dumas, Émile, 369
Dupont, Pierre, 269
Dupront, Alphonse, 262
Durrieu, Baron, 74, 144
Duval, Émile-Victor, 43, 187, 222

Eccarius, Johann Georg, 46
Elias, Norbert, 21, 285
Elloy, Pierre, 187–8
Ermakoff, Ivan, 166
Esquiros, Alphonse, 33, 64

Eudes, Émile François, 43–4
Evans-Pritchard, E., 263

Fabre, Marius, 175
Fairbank, John, 71
Fanelli, Giuseppe, 101
Fariola, Octave, 101
Favre, Jules, 54, 56, 58–9, 61, 69, 72, 117, 168–9, 198, 306–8, 323, 331–2, 335, 338, 350
Favy, Étienne, 44
Ferdinand, Franz, 95
Ferré, Théophile, 181, 299
Fetridge, Wiliam Pembroke, 318
Flaubert, Gustave, 1
Flores (Lieutenant Colonel), 30
Flourens, Gustave, 39, 222, 278
Foa, Jérémie, 211
Force, Frédéric, 203
Fourier, Charles, 248, 370
Fournier, Éric, 277, 279
Franclieu, le Marquis de, 111
Frankel, Léo, 40n50, 45, 126, 199, 411
Frapolli, Luigi, 30
Fresneau, Armand, 292
Fureix, Emmanuel, 209
Furet, François, 8, 343n41

Galliffet, General, 282
Gambetta, Léon, 27, 29, 53, 54, 147, 247
Garcia-Balañà, Albert, 101–2
Garcin, Captain, 282
Garibaldi, Giuseppe, 28–30, 31, 35–7, 38, 39, 42, 127, 160, 161n65
Garibaldi, Menotti, 30
Garibaldi, Ricciotti, 30, 34
Gautier, Théophile, 293
Gautret, 180
Geyer, Michael, 352
Ginzburg, Carlo, 20n46
Girardin, Émile de, 63
Gladstone, William Ewart, 306, 332
Gobille, Boris, 163
Godelier, Maurice, 19n44, 266
Godineau, Laure, 360
Gossez, Rémi, 249, 390
Gould, Roger, 7, 214, 300
Graeber, David, 265
Grant, Ulysses S., 98
Grévy, Jules, 169
Gribaudi, Maurizio, 249
Grill, Charles, 43
Grotius, Hugo, 54
Grousset, Paschal, 111, 113–16, 117–18, 125, 216, 236
Guattari, Félix, 383
Gueydon, Louis Henri de, 73–4, 76–7, 142, 150–3, 150n35, 288, 347
Gysin, Brion, 272

Hachi, idir, 78
El-Haddad, Sheikh, 76, 80, 286
Harrison, Frederic, 366
Haupt, Georges, 340
Haussmann, Georges Eugène, 88, 207, 245
Hénon, Jacques-Louis, 160, 162
Henry, Fortuné, 372–3
Honneth, Axel, 12
Hugo, Victor, 229, 294, 302–3, 314, 356

Ibañez, Andrés, 368

Johannard, Jules-Paul, 45, 115
Jourdan, Maxime, 122, 146n22
Jourde, François, 3

Katz, Philippe, 97–8, 339
Koskenniemi, Martti, 57

Lafont, Claude, 176
Lalande, 180
Lamartine, Alphonse de, 206
Lamennais, Félicité Robert de, 368
Lautrec, Pelet de, 141
Lavigne, Antoine, 44
Leach, Edmund, 263
Lebeau, Émile, 119
Leblanc, Albert, 162
Lecomte, Claude, 311
Lefebvre, Henri, 7
Lefort, Claude, 12
Lefrançais, Gustave, 124, 155
Léger, Ferré, 269
Lehideux, Émile, 234
Lejeune, Xavier-Édouard, 210–11, 221–2, 251, 279
Lelièvre, 208
Le Mel, Nathalie, 200
Lenin, Vladimir Ilyich, 5n4, 400
Léo, André, 301
Lepileur, Alexandre, 202
Leroux, Pierre, 196
Lesourd, 179
Lida, Clara, 373
Lidsky, Paul, 293, 294
Liebknecht, Karl, 365, 366n25
Lincoln, Abraham, 94–5
Lisbon, Maxime, 43
Lissagaray, Prosper-Olivier, 359
Longuet, Charles, 119, 130
Lorgeril, Hippolyte-Louis de, 344
Lostau, Baldomero, 101
Lubert, 186
Lubin, Léopold, 141–2
Lumina, Sophie (known as 'Surprise'), 140, 143

Mac-Adaras, Dyer, 31
Maintenon, Augier de, 141
Malatesta, Errico, 377
Malon, Benoît, 168n76, 170, 197, 359
Manet, Édouard, 295
Mann, Michael, 353
Marble, Manton, 99
Margall, Pí y, 102, 339, 372
Marques, Stephen, 334
Martí, José, 376
Martinez, Saturnino, 375
Martos, Cristino, 333
Marx, Karl, 46–7, 49, 99, 254, 326–8, 361–2, 363n19, 366, 373
Massard, Désiré, 175
Matuszewicz, Ludomir, 43
Mayne Reid, Thomas, 115
Mazzini, Giuseppe, 108, 362–3, 377
Megy, Edmond, 369
Meillet, Léo, 115, 117
Melotte, Colonel, 40
Mendès, Catulle, 294
Michel, Louise, vii–viii, 194, 301, 302, 349, 385, 412
Michelet, Jules, 109
Michot, François, 221
Millaud, Polydore, 84
Millière, Jean-Baptiste, 170
Moisand, Jeanne, 373, 376, 411
El Mokrani, Mohammed, 79
Morago, González, 364

Mourat, 140
Le Moussu, Benjamin, 227, 230
al-Muqrani, Bou Mezrag, 76, 78

Napoleon I, 211
Napoleon III, 27, 61, 66, 72, 74n56, 98, 107, 145, 245
Negri, Toni, 12
Nero, 277
Nicholls, Julia, 360
Nikoladze, Niko, 132
No Zowai, Chen, 70
Noir, Victor, 115
Norodom, 61
Novak, Wiliam, 340

Okolowicz, Auguste, 39, 45
Orsini, Felice, 74
Osterhammel, Jürgen, 25
Oudet, 186

Paradis, Charles, 177
Parisel, Louis-François, 192, 277
Parsons, Lucy, 381
Pascal, Blaise, 135
Pecqueur, Constantin, 129
Peel, Robert, 306
Peissot, Charles-Philibert, 376
Penhoat, Admiral, 35, 37
Philipps, Wendell, 99
Picard, Ernest, 149
Pistre, Inspector, 179
Plaskowski, Alexis, 41, 45
Poniatowski, Prince, 41
Pottier, Eugène, 359
Protot, Eugène, 359
Proudhon, Pierre-Joseph, 196, 368, 370

Le Quillec, Robert, 1

Razoua, Eugène, 334
Reclus, Élisée, 267n65, 363, 365
Rémusat, Charles de, 307, 331, 338
Rieder, Doctor, 182–3, 192
Rigault, Raoul, 3, 175, 181–2, 186n41, 216–17, 218
Rimbaud, Arthur, 294, 379, 389
Riot-Sarcey, Michèle, 234, 325, 415
Robert, Jean-Louis, 42
Robespierre, Maximilien, 196
Roczinski, Stanislas, 44
Rogowski, Maximilien, 37
Ross, Kristin, 12
Rossel, Louis, 43, 190, 299
Roth, François, 29
Rougerie, Jacques, 5n4, 6, 9–10, 18, 48, 128, 179, 249, 263, 407, 409, 418–19
Rozalowski, Vladimir, 44–5
Russell, William Howard, 87

Sagasta, Práxedes Mateo, 100, 102, 307, 333
Saint-Joanis, Guillaume (known as Lancelot), 156
Saint-Simon, Claude-Henri de Rouvroy, 248
Saint-Victor, Paul de, 324
Samejima, Taka Nabou, 62
Sand, George, 145, 294
Sanders, James, 109
Sawyer, Steven, 340
Schaffer, Mrs, 117
Schamyl, Iman, 121
Scott, James, 263
Senisse, Martial, 219–20

Serrano, Francesco, 374
Sewell, William H. Jr, 17, 354–5
Simonin, Anne, 299
Soler, 339
Sparrow, James, 340
Spinoy, Adolphe, 43
Sponsan, Charles, 203–4
Stedman Jones, Gareth, 361
Stevenson, Robert Louis, 115
Suquet, 'called the Zouave', 157–8

Telgard, Louis, 140, 143
Testart, Alain, 264
Theisz, Albert, 179, 183–4, 217
Thénault, Sylvie, 74
Thévenot, Nicolas, 43
Thiers, Adolphe, 2, 54, 96, 108, 113–14, 154, 167, 235, 290–1, 296, 298, 307, 309, 314, 324, 327, 333, 342–3, 353
Thomas (known as Clément-Thomas, Jacques Léonard), 311n20
Thompson, E. P., 257, 367
Tillier, Bertrand, 277, 295
Tilly, Charles, 241
Tinayre, Victoire, 359
Tolain, 46, 170n82
Tombs, Robert, 9, 43n58, 281, 283–4
Traugott, Mark, 215, 241
Treillard, Camille, 176
Tridon, Gustave, 116
Tseng-Kuo-Fan, 67, 70

Vaillant, Édouard, 48
Valat, Rémy, 42
Valentin, Edmond, 161
Vallès, Jules, ix, 3, 121, 359
Varlin, Eugène, 3, 38, 48, 96, 168n76, 217–19
Vattel, Emmerich de, 54
Vedel, Jacques, 155, 156, 296
Verlaine, Paul, 294
Vermersch, Eugène, 121, 130
Vésinier, Pierre, 119, 130
Veuillot, Louis, 293
Vogt, Gilles, 32
Vuillaume, Maxime, 359
Vuillermoz, Romuald, 145, 147–8, 149, 150, 296

Wahnich, Sophie, 391n1
Walton, Alfred, 46
Warburg, Aby, 258, 320, 415–16
Warlin-Esterhazy, 146
Warnier, Auguste, 74, 146, 150
Washburne, Elihu, 118
Weber, Max, 12
Wernicki, Alexander, 44
Wilhelm I, 64
Wilhelm II, 366
Williams, George D., 87
Winder, Gordon, 91, 94
Woodhull, Victoria, 99, 360
Wroblewski, Walery, 40n50, 44

Young, John Russell, 316

Zamoyski, Count, 41
Zedong, Mao, 400
Zola, Émile, 294

Index of Places

Ain-Guettar, 75
Alexandria, 30, 378
Algiers, 64, 72, 74–6, 82, 95, 120, 140, 144–53, 296, 346, 369, 397, 406, 408
Algeria, 30, 33, 38, 42, 42n57, 59, 72–82, 120–1, 134, 142, 145–53, 286–9, 344, 346–9, 384, 393
Alsace-Lorraine, 2, 49, 58, 120, 335, 346
Alsace-Moselle, 57
Argentina, 56, 60, 86, 369
Asia, 60, 91, 119, 133, 267, 307, 352
Australia, 91, 120, 133
Austria-Hungary, 56, 120, 331, 332, 341
Al-Azhar Mosque, 80

Basel, 47
Balkans, 103
Barcelona, 28, 50, 100, 101, 363, 372
Bastille, the, 2, 236
Beijing, 66–8, 69
Belgium, 40, 46, 119, 120, 314, 327, 332, 333, 334, 335, 336, 359
Belleville, 2, 219, 246
Berlin, 50, 86, 370, 400, 404
Bogotá, 90
Bône, 145
Bordeaux, 2, 33, 37, 53, 68, 167
Bordj Bou Arreridj, 76
Bou Taleb, 77
Bouches-du-Rhône, 28, 33
Bougie, 76
Bourges, 31
Brazil, 28, 30, 86, 307, 334
Brunswick, 49
Brussels, 50, 117
Bucharest, 103, 105

Cambodia, 61
Canada, 91, 120, 322–3
Caprera, 28
Caracas, 62
Cartagena, 33, 373–4, 411

Cayenne, 346
Chagny, 35
Chalon, 35
Chile, 30, 56, 86, 106, 352, 369, 413
China, 1, 24, 64, 65, 66, 69, 71–2, 79, 80, 85, 307, 322, 344, 370, 384, 393, 407, 415
City, the (London), 60
Cochinchina, 61, 66
Cologne, 63, 119
Colombia, 90, 106, 116, 307, 413
Constantine, 29, 72, 74, 76, 145, 146, 151, 152, 345
Constantinople, 31, 33, 64
Corsica, 29, 33, 114
Crete, 39, 43
Creusot, Le, 3, 34, 37, 139, 153
Crimea, 39, 42, 56, 72, 87, 104
Croix-Rousse (Lyon), 159–63
Cuba, 100, 121, 133, 142, 360, 374–6

Dijon, 36, 77
Dresden, 50, 160

Egypt, 31, 33, 63–4, 378
Elberfeld, 50
Ecuador, 117
Europe, 65, 67, 86–7, 95, 103, 109, 111, 113, 118–23, 127, 227, 238, 250, 266, 273, 306–7, 331, 333, 340, 352, 365, 370, 391

Florence, 50, 256

Geneva, 47, 50, 54–5, 114, 162, 363, 396
Germany, 1, 5, 20, 27, 59, 61, 84, 94, 105, 120, 123, 282, 304, 306, 309, 323, 332, 336–7, 342, 343–4, 361, 365, 370
Great Britain, 20, 31, 46, 50, 56–7, 58, 59–60, 62, 66, 83, 85, 89, 91, 94, 119, 120, 152, 304, 306, 311–13, 327, 331, 332–7, 341, 344, 359, 366, 374
Greece, 6, 122, 264, 411
Guillotière (Lyon), 159, 160–3

Haiti, 61, 62n31, 143, 343, 369
Hamburg, 50, 105
Hanover, 50
Hautes-Bruyères, 38, 190, 191
Havana, 86, 107
Havre, Le, 32, 33
Hôtel de Ville de Paris, 2–3, 4, 45, 107, 111, 123, 124, 125, 126, 128, 130, 155, 161, 162, 167, 171–3, 174, 189, 193, 194, 195, 197, 204–5, 207, 208–10, 211, 219, 222, 224, 234, 241, 260, 277–8, 280, 298, 312
Hungary, 5
Hyde Park (London), 49

India, 79, 91, 120, 133, 142, 263, 352
Ireland, 31, 38, 123, 360
Italy, 28–30, 31, 42, 46, 56, 72, 85, 120, 123, 148, 152, 331, 352, 359, 377

Jamaica, 86, 143
Japan, 62–3, 68–9, 86, 120–1, 352
Jerusalem, 64, 312

Kabyle, 75n63, 77–81

Latin America, 5, 6, 56, 60, 89, 91, 109, 120, 315, 370, 374, 377, 416–18
Lausanne, 47
Leipzig, 50
London, 28, 39, 46, 49, 58, 60, 62, 85–6, 87, 91, 95, 128, 129–30, 160, 252, 315, 316n29, 322, 324, 328, 359, 404
Lyon, 3, 20, 37, 38, 39, 44, 48, 77, 95, 128, 139, 140, 155, 157, 158, 159–63, 170, 201, 286, 295, 298, 339, 363, 373, 408

Madrid, 30, 86
Maghreb, 79
Maisons-Alfort, 39
Malta, 33
Marseille, 3, 28, 29, 33, 37, 38, 64, 68, 77, 82, 95, 128, 139, 145, 153, 286, 295, 339, 362, 372
Martinique, 20, 133, 140–4, 145, 164, 165, 348, 406
Mecca, 79
Médéah, 155
Medjana, 976, 79
Medina, 79
Mediterranean, 31, 33, 60, 64, 128, 287, 361, 379, 383, 392, 393
Mexico, viii, 42, 60, 72, 90, 97, 105–10, 309, 340, 344, 352, 369–71, 412
Middle East, 79
Mitidja, 76
Modena, 30
Moldavia, 104
Montevideo, 30
Montmartre (Paris), viii, 2, 192, 211, 275, 297, 318
Montsouris, Parc (Paris), 275
Moulins, 77

Nantes, 33, 400, 415
Narbonne, 153, 295
New Caledonia, 344–6
New Orleans, 107
New York, 50, 86, 90, 315, 360, 374, 375, 380
Nice, 28
Notre-Dame de Paris, 211
Notre-Dame-des-Victoire (Paris), 66, 223, 227, 228

Oakland, viii
Oaxaca, viii, 400
Odéon, 208
Oran, 29, 72, 74, 145, 147, 149, 150, 155

Palermo, 122
Palestro, 76, 286
Paraguay, 263, 352
Pennsylvania, 50
Peru, 56, 60, 90, 344
Philippeville, 145, 146
Poland, 30, 41, 44–5, 46, 103, 123, 127
Pondicherry, 133
Porte de Saint-Cloud, 276
Portugal, 56, 333, 396
Prussia, 2–3, 9, 26–7, 32, 46, 49, 54, 56–7, 98, 104, 161, 169, 240

Reichshoffen, battle of, 72

Reichstag, 50, 365
République, Place de la, viii
Réunion Island, 66
Rio de Janeiro, 30, 316n29
Rojava, viii, 412
Romania, 32, 103–4, 340
Rome, 28, 42, 227, 271, 312
Rouen, 48
Ruhr, the, 64
Russia, 56, 58, 89, 121, 123, 160, 315, 323, 332, 341, 352, 378, 400

Sacré-Cœur, 297
Sahara, 76
Saint-Cyr, 38
Saint-Domingue, 171, 396
Sainte-Geneviève (the Panthéon, Paris), 224
Sainte-Lucia, 143
Sainte-Pélagie, 115
San Francisco Hall, 97
Savoy, 43
Schleswig, 22
Sebastopol, siege of, 87
Senegal, 65
Sétif, 76
Shanghai, 65, 400
Sicily, 22
Sierra de Ronda, 43
Sinaloa, region of, 107
Sinskin, 120
Souk-Ahras, 75
South Africa, 91, 133
Spain, viii, 1, 20, 32, 46, 56, 97, 100–3, 120–1, 148, 152, 323, 333, 334, 336, 339, 359, 372–7, 407
St Petersburg, 44, 86, 95
Suez Canal, 63, 378
Switzerland, 31, 46, 130, 160, 333, 337, 359, 361, 362
Syria, viii

Thiers, 20, 140, 153–8, 157, 158, 295
Thuringia, 57
Tientsin, 24, 66–70
Toulouse, 3, 33, 77, 372
Tours, 29, 32–3, 53, 73, 147
Trapani, 42
Tuileries (Paris), 211, 277, 278–9, 298, 308, 312
Tunisia, 31, 74
Turkey, 31, 60, 90, 123, 344
Tyrol, 43

United Provinces (Dutch Republic), 130, 396
United States, viii, 1, 7, 20, 30, 38, 46, 56, 59, 66, 83, 85, 86, 89–90, 91, 94, 97–100, 107, 113, 120, 130, 307, 309, 315, 320, 323, 327, 334, 335, 339, 343, 359, 370, 374, 375, 380–1, 407, 417
Uruguay, 28, 30, 89

Vaise (Lyon), 159
Vanves, 40
Vendôme Column (Paris), 122, 171, 211, 298
Venezuela, 62, 374, 381, 417
Veracruz, 107
Versailles, 2–3, 9, 41, 68, 77, 88, 96, 111–12, 114, 120, 134, 136, 156, 162, 167–9, 176–7, 183, 198, 210, 217, 222, 225, 227, 235–6, 246, 270, 272–3, 282, 290–1, 292, 293, 298, 302, 308–10, 313, 316, 327, 346, 390

Vienna, 30, 31, 58, 336, 350
Vierzon, 39
Vosges, 29, 30–1, 34–6, 37, 44–5

Wallachia, 104
Washington, 55, 94
Wissembourg, battle of, 72
Woerth, battle of, 72